THE COMPLETE CIVIL WAR
JOURNAL AND SELECTED
LETTERS OF
THOMAS WENTWORTH HIGGINSON

# THE COMPLETE
# Civil War Journal
## AND
# Selected Letters
## OF
# Thomas Wentworth Higginson

EDITED BY

*Christopher Looby*

THE UNIVERSITY OF CHICAGO PRESS
*Chicago and London*

Christopher Looby is associate professor of English at the University of
Pennsylvania, and author of *Voicing America: Language, Literary Form, and
the Origins of the United States*, published by the University of Chicago
Press.

The University of Chicago Press, Chicago 60637
The University of Chicago Press, Ltd., London
© 2000 by The University of Chicago
All rights reserved. Published 2000
09 08 07 06 05 04 03 02 01 00   1 2 3 4 5
ISBN: 0-226-33330-2 (cloth)

Library of Congress Cataloging-in-Publication Data
Higginson, Thomas Wentworth, 1823–1911.
    The complete Civil War journal and selected letters of Thomas
    Wentworth Higginson / edited by Christopher Looby.
        p.    cm.
    Includes index.
    ISBN 0-226-33330-2 (cloth : alk. paper)
    1. Higginson, Thomas Wentworth, 1823–1911 Diaries.
    2. Higginson, Thomas Wentworth, 1823–1911 Correspondence.
    3. United States. Army. Colored Infantry Regiment, 33rd
    (1864–1866)   4. United States—History—Civil War,
    1861–1865—Participation, Afro-American.   5. United States—
    History—Civil War, 1861–1865 Personal narratives.   6. United
    States— History — Civil War, 1861–1865—Regimental histories.
    7. United States—Race relations   8. Soldiers—United States
    Diaries.   9. Soldiers—United States Correspondence.
    I. Looby, Christopher.   II. Title.
    E492.94 33rd H53   2000
    973.7′415′092
    [B]—DC21                                          99-31436
                                                          CIP

♾ The paper used in this publication meets the minimum requirements
of the American National Standard for Information Sciences–
Permanence of Paper for Printed Library Materials,
ANSI Z39.48-1992.

*For Joseph Dimuro*

# Contents

CONTENTS

CONTENTS

# CONTENTS

CONTENTS

CONTENTS

CONTENTS

# CONTENTS

*Illustrations follow p. 204*

# Acknowledgments

I am grateful for the assistance and encouragement of friends and colleagues at the University of Chicago and the University of Pennsylvania. A National Endowment for the Humanities Travel to Collections Award (FE-27680-93), summer 1993, funded an initial visit to the Houghton Library, Harvard University, to examine Higginson's Civil War journal and letters; and a Joan Nordell Fellowship, Houghton Library, Harvard University, August 1994, enabled me to transcribe and begin editing this volume. I am grateful to the Houghton Library and its staff for their assistance, and for permission to publish these texts; and I wish also to thank Christopher Hallowell and other descendants of Higginson for their kind permission to publish. Thanks as well to Susan Gillman and the other (anonymous) reader for the University of Chicago Press. At the Press, Alan Thomas, Randolph Petilos, Julie Needler, Mike Brehm, Carol Saller, and Erin Hogan have been exceedingly helpful and attentive, and they have my deep appreciation.

# *Introduction*

A LITERARY COLONEL

Camp-life was a wonderfully strange sensation . . .
Thomas Wentworth Higginson, *Army Life in a Black Regiment*[1]
War feels to me an oblique place . . .
Emily Dickinson to Thomas Wentworth Higginson,[2]

## WRITING

In the middle of a blustery night, March 29, 1864, as Colonel Thomas
Wentworth Higginson's period of service with the 1st South Carolina Volunteers was drawing to a close, and as he was dwelling in his thoughts on
the meaning of the remarkable and strange experience this military undertaking had been for him, he got up and began to write in a notebook he
kept handy. He was, no doubt, also thinking of the future literary use he
would make of his recollections. "The furious wind—kept me awake in
the night & this introduction shaped itself in my mind so strongly, it was irresistible, at last, to rise & write. The dawn was growing gray apparently
but I did not look at my watch & wrote by candlelight till my orderly came
in before reveillé at 6—then turned in again and slept an hour or two."
This "introduction" to an anticipated published account began as follows:

> I desire to record, as simply as I may, the beginnings of a momentous
> military experiment, whose ultimate results were the reorganization of
> the whole American army & the remoulding of the relations of two races
> on this continent. Having apparently accomplished my share in the prac-
> tical solution of the problem, there remains the pleasant duty of record-

1. *Army Life in a Black Regiment* (1870; New York: Norton, 1984), 30. Hereafter cited
parenthetically as (*AL* [page]).
2. *Letters of Emily Dickinson*, ed. Thomas H. Johnson and Theodora Ward, 3 vols.
(Cambridge, Massachusetts: The Belknap Press of Harvard University Press, 1965),
2:423.

ing it. I can only hope that the importance of the subject may save me from that egotism which makes great things seem little & little things seem less in the narrating. For I certainly feel that if ever a man had a task put into his hands which was at the same time important in its issues and congenial in its performance, I was that fortunate man.[3]

Higginson would, indeed, eventually write and publish a memoir of his experience, *Army Life in a Black Regiment* (1870), a book that drew extensively upon the diary he kept during the 17 months he commanded his black regiment. *Army Life* contains, in fact, long excerpts from the diary (somewhat reworked editorially), for, as Higginson wrote therein, "There is nothing like a diary for freshness" (*AL* 30), and he wished the book to convey as honest and direct an impression of his military experience as possible.

> Perhaps diaries are thought to be tedious; but I would rather read a page of one, whatever the events described, than any more deliberate narrative,—it gives glimpses so much more real and vivid. (*AL* 122)

This aspiration to an immediacy of sensation, to an uninterrupted transmission of his embodied experience into the written and printed word, was certainly one of the governing motives of Higginson's writing. This ambition is perhaps most aptly emblematized in the very first entry of the diary itself, where Higginson, en route to South Carolina, and watching as he shakily covers a page with script, notes that "the steamboat thrills through my handwriting, as you perceive." This direct address to "you" in the text also characterizes the diary generally: unlike other diarists who address only themselves, the diary itself, or perhaps a fictive other, Higginson addressed a small group of familiar readers to whom he sent the diary in installments, as if it were a circular newsletter. Higginson, at the end of his military service, recognized his act of writing to take place in a brooding scene of nighttime reverie and compulsive retrospection. This insight is characteristic of the man; often in the course of his sojourn in the South he confessed to feeling as though the whole experience were a dream, and his diary exhibits patterns of free association and uninhibited expression that seem to tap deeply into his unconscious mind. For this reason the diary is, among other things, a peculiarly uncensored record of the cultural unconscious of Civil War America: its revelations about the deep struc-

3. Thomas Wentworth Higginson, "Scattered notes about T. W. H.'s colored troops, 1864," Houghton Library, Harvard University, MS Am 784 {928}, 2–3. Some of the language in this passage was used at the very beginning of TWH's "Leaves from an Officer's Journal, I," *Atlantic Monthly* 14 (November 1864), 521–29; it was not thereafter included in *Army Life in a Black Regiment,* although most of this magazine article was.

ture of Higginson's (and others') fundamental assumptions about such aspects of social identity as race, gender, ethnicity and class, as well as about such other compellingly mysterious phenomena as (in the famous words of Ralph Waldo Emerson, one of Higginson's most important intellectual and spiritual mentors), "language, sleep, madness, dreams, beasts, sex"[4] etc., are of intensely absorbing interest. I will sketch out some questions and make some observations on these areas of inquiry, and their connections with each other, but it will be well to stay, for a moment, with the question of writing itself.

Shortly before his army life began, Higginson testified, in another notebook (his "Field Book," in which he made observations of nature), to the utterly crucial importance—almost the organic necessity—the activity of writing had for him:

> The bee to the flower, the kingfisher to the lake, the statesman to the cabinet, the artist to his pencils, but my instincts guide me to words. The atmosphere for my words must not be a library, but the fresh air. To enjoy life & to write a few perfect sentences, & then to die is all I ask. It is not for power I seek this, nor even for the relief of self-expression,—but let me feel that I have achieved beauty & I am content. I do not care to impress any one else, but to seek my own aim: I do not care to win immortality, but to say something so well that it makes the thought of immortal fame unimportant. This is my instinct & here or elsewhere it will be gratified— no matter which. Other powers wh. I hv. in me, as the active & administrative,—I can as easily sacrifice for this as the bird strips her bosom to soften the nest for the young she has never seen.[5]

Higginson wrote these words sometime in the autumn of 1861, when war was in the air and he was caught between his desire to participate actively in the coming military struggle and the countervailing personal obligations that deterred him—chiefly his duty to care for his invalid wife. Almost as if according to the Emersonian doctrine of compensation, he turned to his nature studies and to writing as substitute undertakings, and tried to convince himself that he didn't mind collecting water lilies instead of fighting rebels. But it is this same imperative sense of writing as a compelling "instinct," experienced almost as a commanding physiological urge, and invested with an aesthete's selfless devotion to an ideal of "beauty," that Higginson a year later brought to the keeping of his wartime diary.

4. Ralph Waldo Emerson, *Nature* (1836), in *Essays and Lectures* (New York: The Library of America, 1983), 7.

5. Thomas Wentworth Higginson, Field Book 1860–1862, Houghton Library, Harvard University, MS Am 1162.4, p. 85 [after August 30, 1861].

There are probably few if any military diaries that are as studiously *aesthetic* in their concerns as Higginson's: it is as if he engaged in the "active & administrative" duties of an army commander in large part, if not primarily, in order to find the material out of which he would be able to "write a few perfect sentences." One of the regular complaints he makes during his term of military service is that so much of his time is taken up by routine, practical writing: sending and answering letters, issuing orders, requisitioning supplies, submitting reports, and so forth. The leaders of other companies (white companies, he avers) are better supplied with secretaries who take the burden of ordinary writing tasks off their commanders' hands; thus, in Higginson's view, one of the sacrifices he makes as commander of an understaffed black regiment is that he must personally perform more of the "vexatious writing" his official position demands.[6] But it is remarkable that he managed nevertheless to write as much as he did in the more exalted mode of his diary, and in his often equally beautiful and fascinating letters from the same period.

Writing about his military endeavors was a natural extension of his prior aesthetic and natural-scientific efforts, since in fact the 1st South Carolina Volunteers had as one of its most important missions a symbolic or expressive one: these ex-slaves were meant to display, before the skeptical eyes of the national white public, a model of perfect military valor—and thus persuade the world that black men were the fighting equals of white men. This improvised script of symbolic actions necessarily included some real battlefield encounters, but it also far exceeded the regiment's war mission. Higginson was always a bit self-conscious about the fact that he and his men had made a relatively minor contribution to the combat effort of the Union Army. In the "Scattered Notes" where Higginson inscribed brief memoranda of topics to take up more fully in writing later, he noted resentfully at one point, "Rosecrans sd. that all our battles were bushwhacking."[7] Higginson, on the contrary, was proud of his company's courageous service in the face of danger when they were exposed to it; but he knew that their real mission was one of propaganda, of successfully meeting the "glare of publicity" to which all the slightest undertakings of this "most daring of innovations" were subjected (*AL* 30). Their chief mission was the blazoning forth to the world of what he would describe understatedly as "the equal military availability of the colored race." The lived rhetorical mission of the troops—their mission of publicity—thus

6. To Mary Channing Higginson, May 9, 1863. Further references to Higginson's letters to his wife will be given parenthetically, using the abbreviation MCH.

7. "Scattered Notes," n.p.

meshed nicely with Higginson's instinct to write about them, extending their symbolic achievements.

If the very undertaking of the black regiment and Higginson's writing about it are parallel acts, his diary and the letters he was writing at the same time are, it must also be said, circumstantially contiguous documents forming a complex intertextual whole: he wrote them at the same time, for the same audience (wife, mother, and sisters), and frequently the journal and letters cross-reference each other explicitly. Much would therefore be lost if they were not read together. He wrote his diary in fairly regular installments, on large loose sheets of paper, usually folded in half crosswise to make a four-page missive which he most often filled up and then promptly sent in the mail to his wife, Mary Channing Higginson. She in turn was expected to pass each installment of the diary on to Higginson's mother Louisa Storrow Higginson, and it is clear that others—chiefly women—in Mary's and Louisa's households formed part of the audience Higginson was quite consciously addressing. Higginson's sisters Louisa and Anna, living with their mother, and various friends, relatives, and hired companions and servants who lived at various times with his wife, all were assumed to be readers of the diary as it was received. Thus it was a family audience, but one that also included some unrelated and less familiar, if intimately associated, readers.

The personal letters he wrote simultaneously—most of them to his wife and his mother—sometimes supplement or overlap the content of the diary, and are frequently indistinguishable from it not only in the kind of content but also in style, tone, mode of address, and so on. And while it is evident that the diary was conceived by Higginson as a continuous, if intermittent, composition, the letters have a more occasional quality— more personal gossip, for instance, both about happenings in the army and happenings among family and friends at home, and more everyday details about such matters as money, housing, and personal illness.[8] They all form together a more or less coherent composition that completes Higginson's contemporaneous account of the experience. These writings ob-

8. TWH's wide and numerous circle of family and friends has made it difficult always to identify the persons to whom he refers (some of them only by first or last name or cryptic abbreviation) in his diary and letters. Members of his family often shared names—Stephen Higginson (his brother) and Stephen Perkins (his cousin), Storrow Higginson (his nephew) and Samuel Mary Appleton Storrow (an uncle), Martha LeBaron, Martha his older half-sister, and a "Cousin Martha"—which frustrates efforts to determine the identity of someone he refers to only as "Stephen" or "Storrow" or "Martha." When an identification or a good guess has been possible, I have provided it; quite often, however, I have left such indeterminate references unfootnoted.

viously do not displace *Army Life in a Black Regiment,* which is deservedly a classic. But they provide a fuller and sometimes more candid glimpse of Higginson in this passage of his interesting life, and thus they supplement, amplify, and complicate the account he composed for publication.

During the periods of Higginson's several military expeditions, in particular, as well as during his furlough in the late summer of 1863, the letters help to provide narrative continuity, since the immediate press of business and the interruption of normal routines prevented Higginson from sending regular installments of the diary during those intervals. There is a notably long hiatus in the diary between July 7 and August 22, 1863 (the time of Higginson's expedition up the Edisto River, his concussion injury from a close call with a rifle ball, and his subsequent furlough), and the diary entries grow significantly more intermittent in late January / early February, 1863 (period of the St. Mary's River expedition), and early March, 1863 (beginning of the occupation of Jacksonville, Florida). The letters do not merely help fill in these narrative gaps, however; because they address a somewhat more individualized audience, they have a measurably more private feeling to them, and Higginson is often more blunt in his personal observations in the letters and more confessional in his self-reflections. Conversely, in the diary he is addressing if not a very large public, at least a small collective audience—one that he knows may include unforeseen readers, and he is also very deliberately accumulating material with an eye toward future published writing.

In October 1864, shortly after Higginson returned home from the war and rejoined his wife, (who had during his absence relocated their residence from Worcester, Massachusetts to Newport, Rhode Island), Higginson copied passages from Henry David Thoreau's diary, which had come to his hand, into his "Field Book." He noted with amazement its "resemblance" to his own nature diary, and recognized also that Thoreau "used this material for his printed works exactly as I do."[9] That is to say, Higginson had drawn on his own "Field Book" for the series of natural history essays he wrote in the years immediately before the war, making some initial revisions in pencil in the diary itself and then copying the revised passages (with further revisions) into his essays as he composed them. It seems fair to assume, therefore, that when Higginson wrote in his war diary, he did so with the intention already formed of drawing on it later for publication, and this framework of conscious anticipation distinguishes it constitutively from the letters it otherwise so closely resembles. Although he says, "I hope it will never be my lot to write military memoirs" (Journal,

9. Field Book, {201}.

May 2, 1863), he soon thereafter makes a conscious effort to refurbish his authorial skills: "Let me see, if I have not forgotten all my literary arts, whether I cannot coin my Captains into sentences" (Journal, May 17, 1863), and proceeds with a copy-book exercise in the composing of "characters." Referring, in a letter to his mother, to his sister Anna's copying of the diary, he comments, "I am so glad she is making one, because I am not going to write anything for print, now, & this will be my only memorial of this most interesting experience."[10] To his wife, somewhat later, "I never feel the smallest desire to write anything for print here & have not written a word with that intention since I left home; it seems a sort of profaning this experience & mixing incompatible lives. Hereafter . . . I may grind it into paint" (To MCH, May 16, 1863). While it is certainly true that he did not *simultaneously* enact this experience and write about it for publication, the frequency with which the question of publishing arose in his mind during his military service testifies to the pre-formation of a literary motive; the eagerness with which, toward the end of his service, he anticipated returning to "the literary trade" (To MCH, April 4, 1864), and the alacrity with which he began to publish writing about his military career also sustain this judgment. His first essay was published in September 1864, a few short months after leaving his company, and even before he had formally resigned his commission; and the first chapters of what would become *Army Life* appeared in *The Atlantic Monthly* with regularity in October, November, and December 1864, and January 1865.[11]

## READING

It can sometimes seem, when reading Higginson's journal and letters, as if nothing could happen to him without it suggesting a literary analogy. These documents are so replete with literary reference, quotation, and allusion as to make it unmistakably the writing of a "literary colonel," as he called himself therein with some self-deprecation. Perhaps it would be more accurate to say that Higginson could only undertake this military command because the patterns of behavior, modes of consciousness, and ideals of heroism he had internalized from his literary education made the

---

10. To Louisa Storrow Higginson, December 22, 1862. Further references to Higginson's letters to his mother will be given parenthetically, using the abbreviation LSH.

11. "Regular and Volunteer Officers," *Atlantic Monthly* 14 (September 1864), 348–57; "A Night in the Water," *Atlantic Monthly* 14 (October 1864), 393–99; "Leaves from an Officer's Journal, I," *Atlantic Monthly* 14 (November 1864), 521–29; "Leaves from an Officer's Journal, II," *Atlantic Monthly* 14 (December 1864), 740–48; "Leaves from an Officer's Journal, III," *Atlantic Monthly* 15 (January 1865), 65–73.

command of the 1st South Carolina Volunteers seem like a pre-scripted literary adventure.

On the steamboat carrying him from New York to South Carolina to undertake his command, a "little orphan girl" brings to his mind Cosette from Victor Hugo's *Les Miserables* ( Journal, Nov. 23, 1862). The experience of floating on the flood tide into Beaufort reminds him of when "Captain Stedman floated into lovely Surinam" ( Journal, Nov. 24, 1862). In recounting a skirmish his men had with rebels outside Jacksonville, Florida, he tells how when they crouched in the long grass and then rose suddenly in concert they appeared to him "like Roderick Dhu's men" in Walter Scott's *The Lady of the Lake* ( Journal, Mar. 28, 1863). Wandering about his camp at night listening to the soldiers around their campfires leads him to link himself to "Haroun Alraschid wandering through his streets in disguise," possibly alluding to Tennyson's poem as well as to the *Arabian Nights*. "I seem like Rajah Brooke in Borneo," he writes (in a letter that also contains allusions to Shakespeare and Whittier), comparing himself to a literarily celebrated philanthropist-colonizer (To LSH, Dec. 10, 1862). "I feel like Hosea Biglow's militia officer," he writes upon acquiring a "magnificent" coat that will grandly signify his official status, citing his friend James Russell Lowell's dialect satire of Mexican War-era jingoism, *The Biglow Papers* (To MCH, Jan. 14, 1863). Upon his return from furlough to a woebegone camp he credits his inexplicable high spirits to "the Mark Tapley element in me," adducing the ever-cheerful character in Charles Dickens' *Martin Chuzzlewit* (To LSH, Aug. 23, 1863). Gazing across the river from the Union-held island where he is encamped to the Rebel-controlled mainland and discerning evidences of human habitation, he quotes Tennyson's sentimental ode to a deceased male friend: "So near & yet so far" (To LSH, Jan. 6, 1863). A heart-stopping turn of events in a court-martial proceeding is immediately suggestive of incidents from popular sensation fiction of the time, as he says in a letter to his mother: "It was such a thing as happens in novels & the scene was worthy of Miss Braddon" (To LSH, Nov. 26, 1863). Not one to waste a good literary allusion, he uses it also in a letter to his wife: "we had a scene worthy of Miss Braddon" (To MCH, Nov. 26, 1863).

A great many of Higginson's literary references are to what might loosely be categorized as literature of chivalric romance. Sir Walter Scott's novels of border warfare were among Higginson's favorites; Charles Kingsley's historical romance *Westward Ho!*, set in Elizabethan times, of valorous combat against the Spanish Armada mixed with romantic rivalry also comes into play ( Journal, Feb. 4, 1863). Other literary references in this category include Emerson's account of Napoleon as a representative of modern military genius (Journal, May 7, 1863) and Thomas Hughes' representation of ideal young English Christian manliness in *Tom Brown's Schooldays* (To LSH, Oct. 26, 1862); similarly, Higginson's repeated assimilation of Colonel Augustus B. Sprague, his former commander in a white Massachusetts regiment, and his military "beau ideal," to Prince Rupert. Even such small dictional details as Higginson's preference for the word "damsel" in referring to women with whom he comes into contact indicate that, not unlike a certain celebrated knight errant whose poor brain was stuffed with the detritus of inherited chivalric literature, Higginson was thinking and acting from within a conception of military endeavor deeply informed by textual models. Fortunately, he seems to have been largely aware of this tendency, and aware too of its possible comic appearance. He asks himself and his readers at one point, "Did I write of the Battle of the Clothes Lines?," and tells of a scouting party that from a distance mistook some clothes drying on a fence for a rebel encampment of 22 tents (Journal, Mar. 28, 1863). The distinctly Cervantine cast of this anecdote—recalling as it does Don Quixote's mistaking windmills for battling giants, and his many other misperceptions—as much as concedes on Higginson's part that his penchant for dressing his experiences in the fancy garb of romantic adventure is an inclination of which he must be wary.

Many of Higginson's references are to contemporary literature, even the most recent magazine fiction and newspaper articles; evidently he was reading widely and voraciously in camp, despite the press of business, his ill health, and other factors that might have slowed him down. Perhaps most interesting was his reading of Civil War stories and poems, texts that reflected back to him the experiences he was having (some of them in uncanny ways, one must infer—like Louisa May Alcott's story of a nurse's relationship to a "contraband" in her story "The Brothers," of which more in a moment). Even odder still must have been the memoirs and other narratives that were published even as the war was continuing: thus as he enacted his own war script in anticipation of later reworking it for literary purposes, he also was reading contemporary literary renditions of the war experiences of others (one of them even concerning his own regiment—Luther Goodyear Bingham's *The Young Quartermaster* [1863]). Near the start of this undertaking Higginson made a point of having sent to him back issues of *The Atlantic Monthly* containing a series of essays he had published in recent years on notable slave revolts, what he called his "Insurrection Papers": it is as if he wanted to study his past writings to help make sure his present endeavors, slated for future literary redaction, would provide material he could later turn into equally good copy.

The literary field, to borrow Pierre Bourdieu's phrase,[12] that was present to Higginson's mind and eye as he conducted his military career can be broken down, for brevity's sake, into some rough categories. This will give a sense of the broad and heterogeneous textual universe that impinged upon him as he undertook his military role—a textual universe that largely provided the terms of understanding that he used to frame his record of that undertaking. There are Higginson's own past writings, to which he adverts frequently; also the slave songs and spirituals that he hears with fascinated ears in camp and, in fact, records assiduously for future anthologization (along with Civil War marching songs and patriotic ditties); there is the fictional and nonfictional literature of slavery, including antislavery and proslavery fiction, memoirs like Fanny Kemble's and travel accounts like Frederick Law Olmsted's; the writings of his New England contemporaries, chiefly the Transcendentalists and what would later be called the genteel writers like James Russell Lowell, Oliver Wendell Holmes, Theodore Winthrop and George W. Curtis; notably, many of the popular women writers of the time, now quite inaccurately (for the most part) called sentimentalists, some of them his friends and protégés like Harriet Prescott, Charlotte Hawes, Gail Hamilton (Mary Abigail Dodge), Rose Terry (later Cooke), Lydia Maria Child, Louisa May Alcott; classics of ancient and world literature, such as the Bible, Homer, Dante, Socrates, Seneca; American regional and dialect writing, such works as Seba Smith's *Life and Writings of Major Jack Downing*, which came to his mind periodically apropos of the wild dialogic mixture of tongues and accents Higginson heard every day in camp; the works of European Romantic authors such as Byron, Carlyle, and Goethe, but especially Jean Paul Richter, whose *Titan* (trans. 1862) Higginson referred to as "my only book," one he professed to read over and over so deeply did it speak to his present experiences; English poets (Robert and Elizabeth Barrett Browning, Jean Ingelow, William Shakespeare) and English novelists and essayists (Daniel Defoe, William Makepeace Thackeray, Jonathan Swift, Elizabeth Gaskell, Harriet Martineau, Charlotte Brontë, Charles Lamb); contemporary periodicals, highbrow and lowbrow, like *Frank Leslie's Magazine* and *Illustrated Newspaper*, the New York *Tribune*, London *Spectator*, Boston *Journal*, the local Beaufort *Free South*, as well, of course, as *The Atlantic Monthly*, to which he made sure to subscribe so as to receive it promptly; and narratives of exploration and discovery or colonial mission, like Sir John Franklin's two *Narratives* of Arctic exploration and the

12. Pierre Bourdieu, *The Field of Cultural Production: Essays on Art and Literature*, ed. Randal Johnson (New York: Columbia University Press, 1993), 46–47, 162–64, and passim.

previously mentioned Sir James Brooke's *Narrative of Events in Borneo and Celebes*.

One last addition should be made to this rough inventory of the contents of Higginson's literary field: as a nonprofessional soldier, and also as a commander deeply invested in the aesthetic production of military spectacle, he relied upon—and, indeed, seems to have been enchanted by—Silas Casey's *Infantry Tactics*, George Brinton McClellan's *Regulations and Instructions* and *Manual of Bayonet Exercises*, plus the *Regulations for the Army of the United States, 1861*, and other works outlining military protocol and practice. Higginson was notoriously one who commanded strictly by the book, a fanatical stickler for rules, regulations, and red tape, and if we think of his consulting the whole range of his previous reading with only somewhat less obeisance than that with which he consulted the official manuals of military order we will catch some of the essential character of the man's style of military action.

## WARRING

After an initial abortive effort to join the war effort in November 1861, and his compensatory return to natural history, Higginson determined the following summer to enlist in the army despite Mary's reliance on him. In his "Field Book" he wrote, "I have not mentioned it to Mary, & may not have strength to carry it through, but it seems to me that if I do not, I shall forfeit my self respect & be a broken man for the remainder of my days. I have sacrificed the public duty to this domestic one as long as I can bear."[13] Two days later he told Mary of his decision, and promptly undertook to raise a company of men, which succeeded readily. "Never in all my life has anything gone so easily as these military plans, & never hv. I been so perfectly free fr. schemes or selfishness." Higginson experienced this sensation of successful accomplishment with an exultant rush:

> I see at every moment that all the currents of my life converge in this direction & that my time is absolutely come. All qualities I need seem ready & as I never found it so easy to exclude ambition or selfhood, so I am repaid by finding all easy before me. I seem to myself to have risen above ambition. What I could write, I hv. written & should I never write anything more, no matter.[14]

Although he would be abruptly diverted in a few months from the 51st Massachusetts, his first (white) regiment, by a surprise invitation from

13. Field Book, {188}.
14. Field Book, {189}.

Gen. Rufus Saxton to serve as Colonel in the 1st South Carolina Volunteers, a regiment made up of refugee freedmen, the latter undertaking was, if anything, a more perfect convergence of all the previous currents of his life. Nevertheless, he accepted this suddenly offered commission only reluctantly, not wanting to undertake it if the American government and military establishment were not wholeheartedly in support of the arming of black men. As he wrote retrospectively in his "Scattered Notes,"

> I had in my profession of literary man, made their wars & insurrections a special study, & in my profession of Abolitionist had tested well their quality. In one of the most perilous positions of my life a fugitive slave had stepped in before me and intercepted the danger; I had no more misgivings of the race then than the nation has now. The doubt was of a different nature. Had the time come for the experiment? Was it to be tried in earnest? Had Saxton the purpose & the power to make his offer avail anything? or was it to end in some abortion, a mere chimera of missionary & military enterprise combined, each paralyzing the other? This was the point of infinite anxiety. I was enlisted for the war, and I intended to get to it; whether in the society of white or black men was to me a secondary consideration. Given a fair opportunity to organize & drill a regiment of freed slaves, and it seemed the culmination of the training of a life. But to assist in the formation of a mere plantation guard, or a Sunday school in regimentals was by no means the entertainment to which I wished to be invited.[15]

Feeling reassured that he would indeed be supported in his aim of making this a model military regiment, he accepted the offer. A brief biographical excursus is perhaps called for here.[16] A consecutive account of Higgin-

15. "Scattered Notes," 5–7.
16. Several fine biographies of Higginson have been written, and they have all been drawn upon for the present account. See Tilden J. Edelstein, *Strange Enthusiasm: A Life of Thomas Wentworth Higginson* (New Haven: Yale University Press, 1968); Mary Thacher Higginson, *Thomas Wentworth Higginson: The Story of His Life* (Boston: Houghton Mifflin Company, 1914); Howard N. Meyer, *Colonel of the Black Regiment: The Life of Thomas Wentworth Higginson* (New York: W. W. Norton & Company, 1967); Anna Mary Wells, *Dear Preceptor: The Life and Times of Thomas Wentworth Higginson* (Boston: Houghton Mifflin Company, 1963). See also Mary Thacher Higginson, ed., *Letters and Journals of Thomas Wentworth Higginson 1846–1906* (Boston: Houghton Mifflin Company, 1921). Higginson also published several autobiographical reminiscences, in addition to *Army Life*. See especially *Cheerful Yesterdays* (1898) and *Part of a Man's Life* (1905). I have also drawn freely, throughout this Introduction, on two previously published articles of my own, "'As Thoroughly Black as the Most Faithful Philanthropist Could Desire': Erotics of Race in Higginson's *Army Life in a Black Regiment*," in *Race and the Subject of Masculinities*, ed. Harry Stecopoulos and Michael Uebel (Durham, NC: Duke University Press, 1997), 71–115,

son's life in relation to various historical contexts may be found in the Chronology at the end of the present volume; it covers his entire life but is particularly detailed (for the sake of providing a straightforward reference) in the sections that cover his military experiences (1862–1864). Here it will be well to summarize the previous "currents of [his] life" that "converge[d]" so beautifully in this military undertaking.

Higginson usually receives only a footnote in American literary history, for he is remembered today mostly for his dubious role as Emily Dickinson's "preceptor."[17] He deserves to be better known, however, and for other reasons, for he was a politically engaged intellectual and artist at the forefront of radical antislavery, labor and feminist causes.[18] Born in 1823 into a formerly wealthy New England Brahmin family descended from first-generation Puritans, Higginson entered Harvard in 1837, just after Emerson delivered his famous and controversial address on "The American Scholar" to the Phi Beta Kappa Society. Higginson imbibed the rich blend of idealist metaphysics, spiritual perfectionism, and social reformism that constituted Transcendentalism from, among others, his freshman Greek tutor, the poet Jones Very; he also studied French with Henry Wadsworth Longfellow. Upon graduation he first became a tutor in a suburban school, then private tutor to three children of a widowed cousin whose somewhat advanced ideas of social reform began Higginson's moral and political radicalization. The next few years saw him immersed in philosophy and romantic literature as a non-

---

and "Flowers of Manhood: Race, Sex and Floriculture from Thomas Wentworth Higginson to Robert Mapplethorpe," *Criticism* 37, 1 (Winter 1995) 109–56.

17. Despite his contemporary high reputation and his central institutional role as editor and journalist, Higginson is mentioned in a recent authoritative survey of New England literary culture almost without exception only in conjunction with Dickinson, and unfortunately he receives similarly short shrift in most literary histories. See Lawrence Buell, *New England Literary Culture: From Revolution through Renaissance* (Cambridge: Cambridge University Press, 1986). On Higginson's role in Dickinson's life see Cynthia Griffin Woolf, *Emily Dickinson* (1986; Reading, Massachusetts: Addison-Wesley, 1988), esp. 249–59; see also Barton Levi St. Armand, *Emily Dickinson and Her Culture: The Soul's Society* (Cambridge: Cambridge University Press, 1984), 181–217, and idem, "Fine Fitnesses: Dickinson, Higginson, and Literary Luminism," *Prospects* 14 (1989), 141–73.

18. Higginson turned after the war decisively from antislavery to feminist reform causes, and suffered a different sort of personal stigma as a result; William Dean Howells in a letter to Charles Dudley Warner in 1874 referred derisively to Higginson (who had in 1872–1873 been an associate editor of the *Woman's Journal*, a publication supporting the principles of the American Woman Suffrage Association, and with whom Howells had long had an edgy relationship) as "Lady Wentworth Higginson." See William Dean Howells, *Selected Letters*, Vol. 2, *1873–1881*, ed. George Arms, Christoph K. Lohmann, and Jerry Herron (Boston: Twayne Publishers, 1979), 54.

matriculating scholar at Harvard, and gradually drifting toward social reform purposes like temperance, female suffrage, and, especially, abolitionism. Entering Divinity School in 1844, he left it in despair the next year, but returned in 1846 with renewed hope that writing, preaching, and social action could be integrated in a productive and satisfying career. He was forced to resign from the first pulpit he occupied after ordination, in Newburyport, Massachusetts, having offended members of his congregation with his ardent abolitionism and his undisguised Free Soil political work.

Continuing to speak, write, and campaign for Free Soil politics following his resignation from Newburyport in 1849, he accepted the pulpit of a Free Church in Worcester, Massachusetts in 1852 after much pleading from the congregation; having married his cousin Mary Channing (who had influenced his turn toward radicalism) soon after his ordination, he also supported her in what soon became a career of chronic invalidism. Mary did not disguise her lack of desire for children, and her preference, combined with her husband's solicitousness of her delicate health, probably led them to conduct their marriage relatively chastely. At the same time, Higginson was given to intense romantic friendships with other men, relationships that approached the limits of what were then socially acceptable forms of same-sex attachment. This is to say that Higginson's relationship to the normative institution of heterosexual marriage, like his relationship to many social conventions, was not an entirely untroubled or complacent one.[19]

19. Higginson's second wife observes in her biography that the letters (from which she prints excerpts) between her husband and his college friend, the South Carolinian William Henry Hurlbut, were "more like those between man and woman than between two men." See Mary Thacher Higginson, *Thomas Wentworth Higginson: The Story of his Life* (Boston: Houghton Mifflin Company, 1914), 125. In a letter to his mother in 1848 Higginson said Hurlbut was "like some fascinating girl," and he frequently praised Hurlbut's appearance: "a true Southerner, the best sort—slender, graceful, dark, with raven eyes and hair," "so handsome in his dark beauty that he seemed like a picturesque oriental." See Edelstein, qtd. 81, 64, 313. Referring to Hurlbut, Higginson observed, "I never loved but one male friend with passion—and for him my love had no bounds—all that my natural fastidiousness and cautious reserve kept from others I poured on him; to say that I would have died for him was nothing." Qtd. Mary Thacher Higginson, 126. Robert K. Martin discusses Hurlbut's fascination for the novelist Theodore Winthrop, who fictionalized him in *Cecil Dreeme* (as Higginson also did in his only novel *Malbone*), in the context of nineteenth-century ideas of romantic friendship. See Robert K. Martin, "Knights-Errant and Gothic Seducers: The Representation of Male Friendship in Mid-Nineteenth-Century America," in *Hidden from History: Reclaiming the Gay and Lesbian Past*, ed. Martin Duberman, Martha Vicinus, and George Chauncey, Jr. (1989; New York: Meridian, 1990), 179–80. For more on male romantic friendship in nineteenth-century Amer-

Higginson had, of course, been deeply dismayed by the terms of the Compromise of 1850 and by the Fugitive Slave Act in particular, and he was therefore prepared to undertake prompt action when, in 1854, the fugitive slave Anthony Burns was seized in Boston at the behest of his pretended owner, Col. Charles T. Suttle of Alexandria, Virginia. While a public meeting of antislavery activists was being held in Faneuil Hall and police attention was fixed on that crowd, Higginson bought handaxes and led an assault on the Court House to free Burns forcibly. The attempt failed, however, and Higginson suffered injury from a court house guard's cutlass, while another guard was killed by a bullet. But Higginson's militancy only increased following this failed rescue. 1856 found him in Kansas promoting free-soil emigration in the attempt to forestall that territory's emergence as another slave state. In 1858 he was involved as one of the so-called Secret Six who backed John Brown's plan for inciting violent slave insurrection in the South. When the Harper's Ferry raid failed miserably, Higginson was the only one of the six backers to admit and even proclaim his assistance to Brown's effort, resolved to face the consequences of his participation in the illegal scheme rather than flee or disclaim responsibility.

In 1860, in order to prepare himself for what he expected to be the coming conflict, Higginson began the serious study of military science, and formed a series of drill clubs, as well as taking fencing lessons and frequenting the gymnasium. Around this time, he also contributed numerous essays to *The Atlantic Monthly*, many of them treating the related subjects of male health, bodily fitness, and military heroism.[20] Throughout these essays Higginson worried that American men had become dangerously feminized and had suffered physical decay as a result of their overcivilization; he looked to athletics and war as welcome opportunities for collective masculine reinvigoration. He also habitually linked the question of masculine depletion to racial comparisons: he worried that "we pale faces" lacked the courage naturally possessed by "Africans,"[21] and he claimed that athletic exercise would restore to the oversophisticated white

ica see John W. Crowley, "Howells, Stoddard, and Male Homosocial Attachment in Victorian America," in *The Making of Masculinities: The New Men's Studies*, ed. Harry Brod (Boston: Allen & Unwin, 1987), 301–24.

20. "Saints, and Their Bodies," *Atlantic Monthly* 1 (March 1858), 852–895; "Physical Courage," *Atlantic Monthly* 2 (November 1858), 728–37; "A Letter to a Dyspeptic," *Atlantic Monthly* 3 (April 1859), 465–74, and its sequel, "The Murder of the Innocents: A Second Epistle to Dolorosus," *Atlantic Monthly* 4 (September 1859), 345–56; "Barbarism and Civilization," *Atlantic Monthly* 7 (January 1861), 51–61; "Gymnastics," *Atlantic Monthly* 7 (March 1861), 283–302; "The Ordeal by Battle," *Atlantic Monthly* 8 (July 1861), 88–95.

21. "Physical Courage," 732.

man "a little of the zest of savage life" possessed also by the "South-Sea Islander" and the "Indian."[22]

The racial envy characterizing Higginson's discourse of the male body and character links it to another series of essays he published in the *Atlantic* at the same time concerning the history of slave insurrections.[23] Higginson here made disparaging comparisons between, for instance, the "effeminate, ignorant, indolent white community" and the "infinitely more hardy and energetic" black population in Jamaica,[24] and he was plainly fascinated by the Scotsman John Gabriel Stedman's love affair and marriage with the slave girl Joanna whom he met when sent as an officer of the Scots Brigade of the Dutch Army to restore rebel maroons to slavery. Higginson noted that one result of Stedman's erotic encounter with the colonized Other was that he found upon his return to Europe that white people's "complexions were like the color of foul linen . . . when compared to the sparkling eyes, ivory teeth, shining skin, and remarkable cleanliness" of the blacks he had left behind.[25] Stedman's eroticization and aestheticization of the racial Other, to which Higginson responded in a lively manner, and the invidious racial distinctions he made between black manhood and white, as well as the general anxiety he felt about masculine vigor and the interest he took in male bodily condition and appearance, were all densely compacted in his immediately subsequent military adventures.

22. "Gymnastics," 285.

23. "The Maroons of Jamaica," *Atlantic Monthly* 5 (February 1860), 213–222; "The Maroons of Surinam," *Atlantic Monthly* 5 (May 1860), 549–557; "Denmark Vesey," *Atlantic Monthly* 7 (June 1861), 728–744; "Nat Turner's Insurrection," *Atlantic Monthly* 8 (August 1861), 173–187; "Gabriel's Defeat," *Atlantic Monthly* 10 (September 1862), 337–345. Higginson collected these essays in *Travellers and Outlaws* (Boston 1889).

24. "The Maroons of Jamaica," 214.

25. "The Maroons of Surinam," 557. Stedman was a frequent reference point for Higginson during his army life. As he approached the Sea Islands he wrote in his diary, "The shores were soft, though low & as we steamed up to Beaufort on the flood tide this morning, it seemed almost as fair as the canal between whose banks Captain Stedman floated into lovely Surinam" (November 24, 1862). Quoting this passage in *Army Life* Higginson edited it slightly (*AL* 33). Mary Louise Pratt discusses Stedman's transracial love affair as "a romantic transformation of a particular form of colonial sexual exploitation" in a section of her aptly titled chapter on "Eros and Abolition," *Imperial Eyes: Travel Writing and Transculturation* (London and New York: Routledge, 1992), 95. Compare Higginson in a June 26, 1863, letter to his mother: "All white soldiers *look* dirty, whether they are or not, from the sunburn & the beard, whereas my men's complexions are the best possible to hide it; a shiny black skin always looks clean. . . . Then the artistic effect of the line of white officers against the sombre & steady background is very good. Any artist would prefer to hv. his soldiers black."

## NATURES

Another current of his previous life that flowed into his military endeavors was less obviously of immediate relevance, but proved to have an important bearing on Higginson's attitudes. This is his interest in the outdoors, his amateur efforts in natural science, and his belletristic nature writings.[26] These essays, as already noted, were produced out of the notes he kept in his "Field Book," and it is there that one sees the origin of his habit of anthropomorphizing natural phenomena. "Much of my enjoyment of nature seems to come fr. the fact that all animals & even plants are more *human* to me than they appear to most people. When I come suddenly on a beautiful flower in a lonely place it is like meeting with a rare person there, & I never forget the association."[27] It was common in Victorian culture to assimilate people (especially women) and flowers—hence the fashion for naming women after floral species (Violet, Daisy, etc.)—but when Higginson does so the simile seems more deeply invested than a mere sentimental cliché. Charlotte Forten (later Grimké), Higginson's friend and a reformer who came to the Sea Islands to teach contraband slaves, was "that quadroon rose," while Annie, the infant daughter of the company quartermaster, First Lieutenant G. M. Chamberlin, whom Higginson celebrated for the length of a chapter in *Army Life* as "The Baby of the Regiment," was to him "a flower in the midst of the war" (*AL* 180). Higginson's organic metaphors for military undertakings are numerous. When he lamented the "continuous stream of visitors, military and civil," who "watched with microscopic scrutiny" all the regiment's endeavors, he expressed his frustration and impatience thusly: "I felt sometimes as if we were a plant trying to take root, but constantly pulled up to see if we were growing" (*AL* 30). In his diary on July 7, 1863, at a moment of relative inactivity, Higginson rapidly modulated between several analogies that linked his literary, floral, and more general vegetative interests:

> Still I enjoy it here. I like to perfect details always and fuss over my camp as I used to do over a vase of flowers or an Atlantic article. A camp is a sort of landscape gardening or model farm. There is always some small improvement to be made.

26. "Water-Lilies," *Atlantic Monthly* 2 (September 1858), 465–73; "April Days," *Atlantic Monthly* 7 (April 1861), 385–94; "My Out-Door Study," *Atlantic Monthly* 8 (September 1861), 302–309; "Snow," *Atlantic Monthly* 9 (February 1862), 188–201; "The Life of Birds," *Atlantic Monthly* 10 (September 1862), 368–76; "The Procession of the Flowers," *Atlantic Monthly* 10 (December 1862), 649–57. These essays appeared, with others, in collected form as *Out-Door Papers* (Boston: for Ticknor and Fields, by Welch, Bigelow, and Company, 1863), while Higginson was in the army.

27. "Field Book," 59 (July 2, 1861).

Literary practice and floral metaphor are conjoined also when Higginson refers to the colorful snippets of exotic discourse he culls from the conversations he hears among his men as "Dusky Flowers of Speech" (April 1, 1863). Such a reference at once dignifies these men's speech—since a long classical tradition had characterized eloquent speech as "flowers of rhetoric"—but also seems almost to categorize the men as botanical species. The insistence with which Higginson links the two—black men and exotic flowers—tends to elide the differences between them in favor of what appear to him to be their striking similarities: their colorful beauty and their exoticism.

In another, especially densely-impacted diary entry, Higginson's botanical metaphor reflects some of his ambivalence with respect to the violence and suffering attendant upon a military project:

CAMP SHAW. FEBRUARY 11. 1864.

> On the 4th inst. I found the bloodroot in bloom; there is a quantity of it just outside our camp lines. Last year also I found it early in February; two war winters rolling over its head & just the same white creature here as in Massachusetts. It symbolizes military life, though, whose forms & pageants are all innocent enough to look at,—baby watches dress parade every day—till some morning unearths the ensanguined root of it all. Well, if Nature has room for the bloodroot, I suppose it has room for us.

The bloodroot, *Sanguinaria canadensis*, also called red poccoon (from Algonquin *pocoon*), a woodland plant native to eastern North America, has a single pale flower standing erect upon a fleshy rootstock that yields red juice and can be used to make a red dye.[28] There is little mystery, probably, about its extraordinarily evocative metaphoric use in this context. It is "the same white creature here [South Carolina] as in Massachusetts," according to Higginson, the adduced floral likeness figuring a complex recognition of the white racial sameness of Northern and Southern enemies. The war's end was widely assumed to be imminent in 1864 after the interminable and bloody conflict had exhausted the opposed sides for not only the two winters Higginson had so far endured in camp but for one previous winter as well. The reappearance of the bloodroot each spring, despite the massive destruction wrought by the war, places the martial violence (as Higginson's metaphor has it) in a context of ineluctable natural cycles, and

28. A picture of the bloodroot can be found in William A. Ewing, *Flora Photographica: Masterpieces of Flower Photography from 1835 to the Present* (New York: Simon and Schuster, 1991), plate 23.

thereby carries a note of hope for the future restoration of peace. But this natural harbinger of reconciliation, this white flower, has its own buried ambiguity, growing as it does upon a bloody root—as if to signify that peace and war are not immutably opposed but mutually and organically co-implicated, peace and beauty dependent upon war and periodic destruction, bloody war being "the root of it all."

If the bloodroot symbolizes the fundamental natural co-implication of war and peace in a cosmic or natural-cyclical perspective, it also represents, in a more mundane sphere, the coalescence of the aesthetic and the violent in the martial arts of war. Higginson, always fond of military display, and believing that black soldiers were instinctively better at marching and drilling than white soldiers, as well as that their blackness made a superior "soldierly appearance" (To LSH, June 26, 1863), takes the visible flower of the bloodroot as a signifier of the attractive "forms and pageants" of military activity: banners and flags, spit and polish, ceremonial drilling and so forth. These "innocent" aesthetic forms conceal, however, even as they emerge from, the real or "root" activity of wounding flesh and spilling blood. The "dress parade" is, as it were, a deceptive metonym for this destruction, "the ensanguined root of it all." James Branch Cabell's scathing report that Higginson had culminated his Florida campaign (which involved robbing and burning of farms and torching Jacksonville) with "a poetic touch, cull[ing] for his lapel a white tea-rosebud, to be a memento of Jacksonville, which he left on fire," also captures (with a hostile inflection) this sense of dissonant signification.[29]

All throughout his military adventures, but with increasing febrility toward the end (when he was exhausted and sick, and looking to nature—to climatic influences, bathing, and homeopathic remedies—for restoration), Higginson's passionate investments and ambivalences with respect to his military endeavors came to be projected onto the natural world. In one of the last diary entries, dated April 11, 1864, he wrote:

The woods are beautiful now, I rode yesterday into a great tangled swamp, set with large trees & more vine than trees, interlacing all the gnarled live oak boughs & the pines that counterfeit the writhed shapes of live oaks, with a thousand intertwisted sets of cordage, just beginning to put greenness on; the level floor spread with new ferns & the stiff fan-shaped leaves of the Spanish thorn or Yucca spicata, while the distant openings were blocked with masses of wild plum bushes, a mass of emerald. Everywhere through these woods run lines of trench & dyke, ancient

29. [James] Branch Cabell and A. J. Hanna, *The St. Johns: A Parade of Diversities* (New York: Farrar & Rinehart, 1943), 209–210.

plantation landmarks, soon looking venerable as does everything where vegetation is so swift & rank: & there is even this early a sort of steaming fervor of vegetable vitality that pervades the atmosphere.

One is tempted to read all kinds of analogies into this passage. Where once the black men had depended on their white officers (like vines upon the trees they cling to), now the blacks outnumber and outperform the whites (more vine than trees); yet the swamp forest is such a tangled mass of interdependence that priorities and hierarchies of dependence can hardly be sorted out. Moreover, one natural species can imitate another ("the pines that counterfeit the writhed shapes of live oaks"), so that the identity of species (or races) is not easily maintained. The evidences of human habitation—the alterations to the natural landscape that the slaveholding economy had wrought ("lines of trench & dyke, ancient plantation landmarks")—are now succumbing to the inexorable forces of nature, the pattern of tangled interlacing that nature aggressively authorizes and reauthorizes ("beginning to put greenness on").

## IDENTITIES

Almost immediately upon leaving South Carolina and returning to his interrupted literary career, Higginson published in the *Atlantic* an essay on "Regular and Volunteer Officers" that examined some aspects of the social dynamics peculiar to the military, and recognized the transformations of those dynamics that the Civil War had produced. The essay begins:

> It is pleasant to see how much the present war has done towards effacing the traditional jealousy between regular officers and volunteers. The two classes have been so thoroughly intermingled, on staff duties and in the field,—so many regular officers now hold in the volunteer service a rank higher than their permanent standing,—the whole previous military experience of most regulars was so trifling, compared with that which they and the volunteers have now shared in common,—and so many young men have lately been appointed to commissions, in both branches, not only without a West Point education, but with almost none at all,—that it really cannot be said that there is much feeling of conscious separation left.[30]

Although Higginson's immediate reference is specifically to the social distinctions peculiar to the military—the distinction between professional

30. Thomas Wentworth Higginson, "Regular and Volunteer Officers," *Atlantic Monthly* 14 (September 1864), 348.

soldiers and volunteers enlisted for a term during the present conflict—it is clear that these particular distinctions are connected to other, extramilitary social categories (level of education, for instance), and that Higginson is actually thinking also of the ways in which the war had dislocated the received system of social distinctions at large in American culture. Remember the nighttime writing discussed at the beginning of this introduction, where Higginson averred that the successful military employment of black troops had initiated "the remoulding of the relations of two races on this continent." His own military experience was such as to bring these disruptions boldly into relief: he goes on, later in this essay, to discuss some of the ways in which the strongly socially-marked racial difference between white and black played into (and sometimes cut against) the routines and practices of military order. The most general point to make here is that, as a rule, the army functions by effacing individualities, reducing soldiers to indistinguishable component parts of a fighting machine; the violent efficiency of the army grows in proportion to the *esprit de corps* of the troops, the submergence of individual agency into the disciplined mass—the reduction of a multitude of men's bodies to one body, the collective body of the obedient army under the single command of its leader. One anecdote Higginson relates illustrates this fantasy of collective embodiment comically: in the midst of the excitement produced by the threat of an attempted rebel invasion of the Sea Islands, when the regiment had to be up and ready to move at a moment's notice, "nobody committed the mistake once made by an excited soldier of our Qrmaster's former regiment, who was found during an alarm endeavoring to put his own boots on another man's feet" (Journal, March 16, 1864).

This fundamental effacement of personal difference in the interest of military unity obviously was at odds with the general culture of a nation devoted, North and South, to maintaining crisply differentiated racial identities. Higginson delighted to observe the way military experience confused and even dissolved racial distinctions, and throughout his diary and letters he recounts incidents and anecdotes in which such dissolution is manifested. In the regiments of the U.S. Colored Troops, to Higginson's disappointment, officers were drawn exclusively from the ranks of white men, and so the command hierarchy of the army perpetuated racial subordination; and one can see repeatedly that this conservation of racial difference by aligning it with distinctions of military rank had the unfortunate effect of retaining in the military context some of the habits of domination and deference that pertained to the social order of the plantation. Nowhere is this more poignantly and unsettlingly evident than when, on November 24, 1862, Higginson records in his diary his first encounter with one of his soldiers, a man who had been wounded in a recent expedition. "Did you think that was more than you bargained for?" Higginson asked him. "Dat's just *what I meant for Massa*," the man replied. Does Higginson even notice that the man called him "Massa"? Did the man, facing his new and untested commander, calculatingly offer him a traditional deferential salutation, not sure whether it was expected or required? Was this one of the soldiers who, as Higginson sometimes relates, had not yet fully internalized the fact of his new status as a free man? Perhaps this new fact would not have been very plainly evident anyway, since the strict discipline and elaborate hierarchy of the army so resembled the structures of command and obedience familiar to a black from his former condition of enslavement. When Higginson blithely writes of this encounter, "Very good for my first exchange of remark with my men, was it not?," are we to understand that, as a volunteer officer suddenly catapulted into a new situation and a higher rank, he is grateful to have evidence that his soldiers will readily respect his authority? The incident is almost opaque in its rich inscrutability, and as is often the case, the degree of Higginson's consciousness of its implications is somewhat uncertain.

The disorientations of gender identity in Higginson's army are almost as numerous as the dislocations of race—and gender proves to be intimately connected to race in various insistent ways. The present edition contains a letter dating from Higginson's service with his original white regiment, the Massachusetts 51st, in which he describes for his mother an all-male ball held at Camp Wool outside Worcester. This extraordinary letter (To LSH, October 13, 1862) rewards close reading, for it describes the weekly performance of gender masquerade in the all-male confines of camp: some of the "younger & more delicate" soldiers take the part of women, and these "ladies are distinguishable by a handkerchief tied to the arm." One young lieutenant is "swept away by the charms of the prettiest of the Sergeants, named Fairweather," and leads "her" in a waltz; here a conventionally subordinated gender difference is evoked by congruent distinctions of rank—one cannot imagine a lieutenant being wooed by a sergeant, his military subordinate—and perhaps of age, as well as distinctions of physical type and evaluations of physical beauty. But while, in Higginson's account, the men in the absence of women simulate cross-gendered ceremonial sociality (and heterosexual partnering), they also seem to prefer to suspend distinctions of gender and indulge in vigorously athletic same-gendered dancing that is described in language that vibrates with the same "pent up physical energy" it ascribes to the dancing men: "they dance like Maenads or Bacchanals, their whole bodies dance, in the pauses between the figures they throb & tremble all over." Some of the

same fascination Higginson feels in gazing on this scene of all-male ecstasy is apparent also in his repeated fond gazing upon the black soldiers as
they participate in the traditional African-American ritual known as the
"shout." From the diary, December 3, 1862:

> From a neighboring camp fire comes one of those strange concerts half
> powwow, half prayer meeting . . . men singing at the top of their voices—
> often the John Brown war song, but oftener these incomprehensible Ne-
> gro Methodist, meaningless, monotonous, endless chants, with obscure
> syllables recurring constantly & slight variations interwoven, all accom-
> panied with a regular drumming of the feet & clapping of the hands, like
> castanets; then the excitement spreads, outside the enclosure men begin
> to quiver & dance, others join, a circle forms, winding monotonously
> round some one in the centre—some heel & toe tumultuously, others
> merely tremble & stagger on, others stoop & rise, others whirl, others ca-
> per sidewise, all keep steadily circling like dervishes, outsiders applaud es-
> pecial strokes of skill, my approach only enlivens the scene, the circle
> enlarges, louder grows the singing about Jesus & Heaven, & the ceaseless
> drumming & clapping go steadily on. At last seems to come a snap and the
> spell breaks amid general sighs & laughter. And this not rarely but night
> after night—

I will return below to the theme of the body, to Higginson's deep interest in
the physical realities of embodied fleshly existence, of which passages like
this one are exemplary; his interest in the human body and embodied experience is obviously related to his literary ambition of communicating in
words the immediacy of his lived experience. This embodied experience,
however, is believed by Higginson and by most members of his society and
culture to be the ground of personal identity: race, gender, and other social identities are presumed to be essentially tied to physical features of
persons (skin color and so forth). Thus the gender-switching that Higginson described in the letter quoted above both took advantage of given
physical characteristics of people (e.g., the youth and beauty of Sergeant
Fairweather) but also needed imaginatively to transform or disguise such
features.

There was a remarkably frequent incidence of gender transvestism in
the army camp. Some of the noteworthy occurrences include the rumor
in Jacksonville that "a white man in woman's clothes has been seen going
into a certain house—undoubtedly a spy" (Journal, March 16, 1863). The
cross-dressing spy turns out, however, to be merely a Catholic priest. During a Christmas party at General Saxton's headquarters the general and
his wife exhibit remarkable success in "interchanging characters," she ap-

pearing "as a Lilliputian officer" and he "as a strongminded wife," who in the performance was gallantly caught up in the ostensible military man's protective arms (Journal, December 28, 1863). In a fragmentary letter of March 20, 1864, Higginson describes how the Adjutant, First Lieutenant Dewhurst, came into his parlor one night "with a handsome young officer in new uniform—really very handsome—who turned out after a while to be Mrs. Dewhurst." At around the same time he notes briefly in his diary the occurrence of "a dance in the parlor" with "one officer acting as lady" (March 16, 1864).

These incidents of actual transvestism find rhetorical counterpart in a peculiarity of the speech patterns of his soldiers that interested Higginson: their inversion (measured by the standard of white English usage) of gendered pronouns. An anxious soldier with a sick wife and another who was about to be married both refer to their female partners as "he," as Dr. Rogers apparently noted (Journal, New Year's Eve, 1862); a soldier professes to Higginson his affection for the woman he is to marry, saying "I lub he"—"Meanwhile *he* stands by, an unattractive female, impenetrably black, in an old pink muslin dress, torn white gloves, & a bonnet beyond the wildest dreams of Irish girl & descended through generations of tawdry mistresses" (Journal, June 27, 1863). This last anecdote illustrates how when gender assignments get confused, other categories seem to mutate also: racial blackness seems here, as it often does, to suggest Irishness to Higginson, and the comically elegant dress of the bride suggests a failed attempt at the dignity proper to a higher social class. Higginson admits that the grammatical conventions of the blacks begin to influence his own speech: "I get so accustomed to hearing the use of he & his for she & hers that I insensibly fall into it myself" (Journal, May 25, 1863). Higginson's sharp memory for the sight of a "little boy with no rag of clothing except the basque waist of a lady's dress, wrong side before, with long whalebones perceptible"(Journal, March 13, 1864—the backside-forward manner of wearing the garment echoing the gender inversion); the description of Captain James Rogers "revelling in his men as a girl in her paper dolls" (Journal, May 17, 1863); the observation that "the strongest men in my regiment have arms which would make the fortune of an English belle, in all but color, round & satiny, without a trace of hair" (Journal, June 27, 1863); and Higginson's self-representation of his leisurely tour of neighboring plantations while recuperating from illness as "staying about as ladies do, without any particular object" (To LSH, October 26, 1863)—all these suggestions of gender fluctuation sort oddly with Higginson's regular insistence for himself on qualities of character and behavior conventionally assigned as masculine (strength, vigor, courage) and his perpetual insistence that what he was doing in the army was, essentially, making his black soldiers into men.

If gender assignments were—in actuality or in imagination—loosening up in the army camp, racial assignments were doing much the same thing. Higginson had long been acutely aware of the conceptual meaninglessness and empirical inadequacy of binary racial categories (black and white) given the high incidence of interracial sexual relations in the South in particular, and the visible prevalence of persons of mixed racial ancestry (in the vocabulary of the time, mulattos, quadroons, octoroons, etc.). The Civil War must be understood to have everything to do with the wish on the part of Southern political leaders and ideologues to credit binary racial difference, in the face of increasingly plain countervailing experience, as the basis and justification for the institution of slavery; few who opposed slavery had as fine a sense as Higginson of how vacant such arguments were in their very premises. This is not to say that Higginson doesn't recognize and credit such racial differences at all: at many moments he depends upon them quite explicitly, and he is possessed of some fairly silly (if potentially quite harmful) ideas about the character of blacks, Irish, and other racial and ethnic groups. But he is acutely aware of the manifold social and historical processes that are progressively undermining such generalizations. For one thing, he frequently encounters individuals whose identities are bafflingly hybridized: "Among Montgomery's recruits there is one handsome Mulatto with an Irish name & unexceptionable brogue, with scarcely a trace of Negro in it. I have not learned his history" (Journal, February 28, 1863). One can infer a plausible history for this man—of mixed racial ancestry ("Mulatto"), he may very well have been his master's offspring, promoted to a house slave, who acquired the Irish-inflected English his father/master spoke. This anecdote follows in the diary upon a reference to a Belgian drum major who "has been in a dozen armies" and whose "talk is a mixture of all tongues."

Just as Higginson professes to be unwittingly acquiring the grammatical habits of his soldiers, he claims at various times to be altering his racial identity. Very soon after coming to South Carolina and finding himself suddenly in the racial minority, he notes that at dress parade he is overwhelmingly outnumbered and perceptually surrounded by black men, and only when the relatively few white officers step forward at the close of the exercise is he "reminded that my own face is not black as a coal" (Journal, November 28, 1862). Jokingly he pretends that the rebel pickets across the river have unwittingly mistaken the race of Dr. Rogers when they yell out an inquiry about a white horse the previous regiment's surgeon had up for sale: "Little they knew that our surgeon's complexion was black (for we commonly speak of ourselves as colored officers)—and that of his horse sorrel" (Journal, April 6, 1863).

## BODIES, PERFORMANCES

In commenting on Higginson's attitude about and execution of writing, I discussed how he aimed to impart to his text the quality of sensory immediacy; and that his longstanding interest in male health and bodily fitness fed into his military experience. In reading his Civil War diary and letters it pays to attend closely to his constant interest in embodiment and sensation, for it is in this register that he sometimes makes his keenest observations. In part, this interest reflects the reform culture of his time, with its attention to temperance, new physical therapies, the seemingly chronic debilitation of men and women, the health and hygiene of the lower classes, and so forth. But it also reflects Higginson's aforementioned engagement with the questions of racial and gender identity, and the fungibility of identities: early in his military sojourn, for instance, Higginson records in his diary his observation that the soldiers "love passionately three things beside spiritual incantations—namely sugar, home & tobacco"(Journal, Dec. 2, 1862). The craving for sugar he attributes to black men engages his thoughts: "As for sugar, no white man can drink coffee after they have sweetened it—perhaps I could, I never tried it—& perhaps this sympathy of sweetness is the real bond between us." A certain taste for or tolerance of the saccharine seems, at first, to mark a racial boundary, for white men could not stand coffee as sweet as black men make it. But then Higginson, in the next sentence, entertains the possibility that he, of all white men, might be able to drink coffee sweetened according to black men's preference, although he avers that he has not yet tried the experiment. But this speculative identification with black men's taste for sweetness mutates, in the next sentence again, into a "sympathy of sweetness" that underwrites the "real bond" between this particular white man and black men in general. Higginson is using the word "sympathy" here quite carefully. Adam Smith, in his *Theory of Moral Sentiments*, had definitively described sympathy as the power of the imagination to conceive what another person is feeling bodily. "By the imagination we place ourselves in his situation . . . we enter as it were into his body, and become in some measure the same person with him, and thence form some idea of his sensations."[31] The moral idea of sympathetic identification with the

---

31. Adam Smith, *The Theory of Moral Sentiments*, ed. D. D. Raphael and A. L. Macfie (1790; Indianapolis: Liberty Fund, 1984), 9.

experiences and sufferings of others was a key presupposition of the various progressive reform movements of the late eighteenth and early nineteenth centuries, including abolitionism. Thus Higginson is enacting here, in textbook fashion, the essential moral moment of the antislavery cause—he is identifying with black men's pleasures, as he elsewhere does with their pains. While he is certainly not without the condescension that often accompanies pity or compassion for others' suffering, his willingness to identify with black men has the additional dimension of an exultant, ecstatic willingness to transfuse their sensory delights as well.

Despite what I have characterized as the widespread insistence in Higginson's society on marking and maintaining the boundary between different races characterized by different physical features, there is plenty of literary evidence that this same culture had a taste for identity-switching as well. Perhaps these two impulses—identity-maintenance and identity-transformation—are not as contradictory as they appear at first glance. Perhaps the actual fragility of identity boundaries is what motivates people to labor to reinforce them; perhaps the coercive lie of identity is what prompts people to struggle to evade or undercut it. Examples abound, but here are a few noteworthy ones. J. Hector St. John de Crèvecoeur, himself an Anglophilic Frenchman who embraced the idea of America only to find himself imprisoned and deported as a Loyalist during the Revolution, wrote in his *Letters from an American Farmer* (1782) of the opportunities for self-transformation offered by America; that book famously ends with its narrator, Farmer James, despairing of the social upheaval brought by the Revolution, as he resolves to move with his family to live among the Indians.[32] Deborah Sampson was so carried away with patriotic fervor that she concealed her sex and enlisted in the army during the American Revolution; her story was later told by Herman Mann.[33] Lucy Brewer's tale of cross-dressed military service in the War of 1812, *The Female Marine*, went through numerous editions in the following years.[34] Mary Jemison, unlike most other tellers of Indian captivity tales, chose to remain among the Indians with whom she had quite happily lived for many years; the *Narrative of the Life of Mrs. Mary Jemison* (1824), as related orally to James E. Seaver, detailed her cultural assimilation and her eventual metamorphosis into

32. J. Hector St. John de Crèvecoeur, *Letters from an American Farmer and Sketches of 18th-Century America*, ed. Albert E. Stone (New York: Penguin, 1981).

33. Herman Mann, *The Female Review: or, Memoirs of an American Young Lady* (Dedham, Massachusetts: Printed by Nathaniel and Benjamin Heaton for the Author, 1797).

34. *The Female Marine and Related Works: Narratives of Cross-Dressing and Urban Vice in America's Early Republic*, ed. Daniel A. Cohen (Amherst: University of Massachusetts Press, 1997).

hybrid identity as "the white woman of the Genesee."[35] Frederick Douglass's classic *Narrative* (1845) is structured, as the author frames it, around the transformation of a slave into a man.[36] The theme of identity-transformation abounds in American literature and is promoted in the many narratives of economic self-improvement (from Benjamin Franklin onward), spiritual regeneration, racial passing and geographical removal.[37] Popular drama and stage performance in America also promoted this theme. Blackface minstrelsy, which has been called the first form of mass entertainment in the United States, was widely popular: it featured white actors and singers impersonating the appearance, speech, music and habits of black people.[38] Higginson's writings may be added to this archive of narratives of identity-shifting, and he corroborates that archive's overarching claim that the performance of identity is itself constitutive of identity.

The last, and possibly most important, way in which the following texts can be profitably read is to understand them as suffused with a sense of performance. By that I mean several related things. There is the sense of performance as something accomplished, completed, carried through: despite the fact that the war was not over when Higginson left his regiment, and the vast undertaking of "the remoulding of the relations of two races on this continent" was, sadly, far from complete, there is a definite sense from him that the most immediate practical purpose of his enlistment had been carried out successfully. Black men were under arms, they had proven their mettle, and the deep-seated racial prejudice that held them unsuited for this privilege and duty of citizenship was, if not destroyed, then at least permanently unsettled. But in the course of performing this task there were numerous everyday performances that were carried out, and, indeed, the army camp as Higginson describes it was a veritable theater of performances small and large. Soon after arriving at Camp Saxton he records, "I have entered on command and am trying to play Col. Sprague as well as may be" (Journal, Nov. 24, 1862). This sense of playing a role, of learning a new role, is characteristic of Higginson's re-

35. James E. Seaver, *A Narrative of the Life of Mrs. Mary Jemison* (1824; Syracuse: Syracuse University Press, 1990).

36. Frederick Douglass, *Narrative of the Life of Frederick Douglass, an American Slave*, ed. Houston Baker (1845; New York: Penguin, 1982).

37. See the essays in *Passing and the Fictions of Identity*, ed. Elaine K. Ginsberg (Durham, North Carolina: Duke University Press, 1996).

38. See Eric Lott, *Love and Theft: Blackface Minstrelsy and the American Working Class* (New York: Oxford University Press, 1993) and W. T. Lhamon, Jr., *Raising Cain: Blackface Performance from Jim Crow to Hip Hop* (Cambridge: Harvard University Press, 1998).

lationship to his military career. That he should frame this role as an attempt to "play Col. Sprague," his commander when he was previously a Captain in the 51st Massachusetts, tells us how deeply his sense of role-playing or performance was a matter of the inheritance and reinhabitation of pre-existing scripted parts.

Recall, as I mentioned above, that Higginson repeatedly compared his model of military virtue, Col. Augustus B. Sprague, to Prince Rupert, whom Higginson had written about in one of his *Atlantic Monthly* stories, "A Charge with Prince Rupert." What charmed Higginson about Prince Rupert, a Cavalier leader, was largely his military theatricality: he was handsome, beautifully coiffed, dashingly arrayed in cloak and white-plumed hat, and so forth. He enacted daring bravado and authoritative command so plausibly that it became a reality. This helps explain what otherwise might seem Higginson's curious and perhaps excessive attachment to appearances, his fascination with forms of military ceremony (parading, drill, speechmaking, etc.), with the cleanliness and clothing of his troops, with their physical beauty and the aesthetics of blackness, with the careful fulfillment of military punctilio. It also helps explain his devoted observation of the everyday dramatics of the camp: his diary and letters offer countless vignettes of small happenstance encounters between persons, as well as the musical and verbal performances of the soldiers and their officers, the games of charades played by officers and their wives on holiday occasions, and the instances of cross-dressing and racial masquerade discussed above.

We see that soon after undertaking to "play Col. Sprague" Higginson takes note of the dark blackness of the first soldiers he marched, and the "red legs" these men wore (Journal, Nov. 24, 1862). He liked their darkness of skin, and has much to say about its superior virtue for the making of visual spectacle; he hated the red pants, and soon got them dark blue trousers instead. Higginson's devout interest in appearances, the most superficial determinations of identity, is matched by his equally intense exploration of the deepest psychic grounds of identity. He can equally appreciate the dramatic oral performance of a man's narrative of escape from slavery and the account given within that narrative of the nuances of calculated performances of false identity. He thus records, with obvious delight, the story he overheard one night (during one his frequent evening rambles around the camp) told by "one old Uncle, Cato by name," who was telling it to a rapt circle of thirty or forty other men around a fire. The story was about Cato's escape from slavery, and the various dramatic subterfuges he employed to elude capture. In describing Cato's telling of the story, Higginson compares him to "Harriet Tubman & such wonderful

slave comedians" ("comedian" here simply means actor or stage performer, although Higginson is certainly attentive to the comic element in
any performance) whose lectures he had heard, and to Harriet Beecher
Stowe's redaction of such performances (she had undoubtedly, like Higginson, been in the audience at such talks) in her novel *Uncle Tom's Cabin*.
Cato "described his efforts after food & shelter on the way; acting out
everything as he described it." Cato warily approaches "de man," a presumably suspicious southerner, and asks, "very humble," for food; the
man will not give food except in exchange for money or for the hatchet
Cato carries. So persuasive is Cato's sly performance of abjection and deference, so convinced is "de man" that Cato is a harmless old slave who
knows his proper place, that the man stupidly warns him to be careful of
"de Yankee Pickets" who are nearby—presumably just the protectors
Cato is looking for! "Den I say *Good Lord, Mas'r, am dey?*"—the exquisite inflection of which Higginson glosses by adding parenthetically, "words
cannot express the unutterable dissimulation with which these accents of
terror were uttered" (Journal, Nov. 27, 1862).

Here Higginson notes the strategic deceit which can prompt a black
man to call a white man "Mas'r," but he never quite connects this to those
moments when he himself is addressed as "Massa" by his soldiers. At all
times Higginson is an acute reporter of the everyday dramatics of the
camp, but only sometimes is he a trustworthy interpreter of such exchanges. For even as he records for posterity these wonderful exchanges,
he feels compelled to frame them with comparisons to prior dramatic performances he has witnessed. Cato's "acting out," having been compared
to the speeches of Tubman and other orators, and to Stowe's fictional slave
speakers, is also compared to the temperance lectures of the famous reformed drunkard John Bartholomew Gough further, his succession of
crafty deceptions is likened to those in a Molière play, and then to the
"wiles of an ancient Ulysses," while the collective performance of the
gathered men is called "a more than Shaksperian comedy," an enactment
"that made the Ethiopean minstrelsy of the stage appear no caricature,"
in which each participant is a "Sambo" (Journal, Nov. 27, 1862). This odd
assortment of analogues, ranging from classical epic to modern reform
novel, from working-class popular blackface theater to elevated literary
drama, perhaps expresses Higginson's ongoing difficulty in integrating his
present experience with past models: hence his constant registration of it
as "strange," dreamlike and compelling but mysterious and excessive as
well. That is, he often seems to know that he's missing a clue somewhere,
even as the quality of his absorbed attention is utterly remarkable, and it is
to this fineness of attention that we owe these remarkable documents.

The story of black troops in the Civil War has been ably told by a number of very accomplished historians, therefore there is no need for me to reiterate it here.[39] Higginson's war diary and his contemporaneous letters certainly add to the historical record of this subject, but their chief claims on a reader's interest must be found elsewhere. They are the product of a unique and compelling act of writing: they fulfill Higginson's literary ambition in composing them, providing their initial readers and now others with "real and vivid" access to the mission he undertook and the experience he underwent. And they take us inside the mind and heart of a man struggling morally and physically to do his part to right one of the most egregious wrongs of human history. He "was that fortunate man" who found an opportunity to put his powerful literary education to work in the service of important social action—a "literary colonel" paying back literature for the fund of wisdom and inspiration it had provided him.

39. Noah Andre Trudeau, *Like Men of War: Black Troops in the Civil War, 1862–1865* (Boston: Little, Brown and Company, 1998), provides a detailed, battle-by-battle account of the more than 175,000 black troops who served in the Union Army. The standard histories include Dudley Taylor Cornish, *The Sable Arm: Black Troops in the Union Army, 1861–1865* (1956; Lawrence, Kansas: University Press of Kansas, 1987); Joseph T. Glatthaar, *Forged in Battle: The Civil War Alliance of Black Soldiers and White Officers* (New York: The Free Press, 1990); James M. McPherson, *The Negro's Civil War: How American Blacks Felt and Acted During the War for the Union* (1965; New York: Ballantine Books, 1991); Benjamin Quarles, *The Negro in the Civil War* (1953; New York: Da Capo, 1989); Howard C. Westwood, *Black Troops, White Commanders, and Freedmen During the Civil War* (Carbondale: Southern Illinois University Press, 1992); George Washington Williams, *A History of the Negro Troops in the War of the Rebellion, 1861–1865* (New York: Harper & Brothers, 1888); Joseph T. Wilson, *The Black Phalanx: African American Soldiers in the War of Independence, the War of 1812, and the Civil War* (1887; New York: Da Capo Press, 1994). See also "The Black Military Experience, 1861–1867," in Ira Berlin, Barbara J. Fields, Steven F. Miller, Joseph P. Reidy and Leslie S. Rowland, *Slaves No More: Three Essays on Emancipation and the Civil War* (New York: Cambridge University Press, 1992), 187–233. Several informative documentary collections are also available: Edwin S. Redkey, ed., *A Grand Army of Black Men: Letters from African-American Soldiers in the Union Army, 1861–1865* (Cambridge: Cambridge University Press, 1992); Ira Berlin, Joseph P. Reidy, and Leslie S. Rowland, eds., *Freedom: A Documentary History of Emancipation, 1861–1867*, Series 2, *The Black Military Experience* (Cambridge: Cambridge University Press, 1982).

# Note on the Texts

This edition of the Civil War journal and letters of Thomas Wentworth Higginson presents "diplomatic" or "noncritical" transcriptions of the documents in question; they are reproduced essentially without editorial emendation so as to preserve as fully as possible the substance and texture of the writing. This has seemed the appropriate editorial practice for at least two reasons: first, as textual scholar G. Thomas Tanselle has argued, historical documents like these are "best served, as a general rule, by editions that attempt to present the texts exactly as they appear in the surviving documents, thus stressing the evidentiary value of those documents;[1] second, the reason for publishing Higginson's diary and letters is, in part, their immediacy and freshness as an on-the-spot record of unique and compelling events and experiences. These qualities are best preserved by reproducing the somewhat unpolished form of the texts as the writer first

1. G. Thomas Tanselle, *A Rationale of Textual Criticism* (Philadelphia: University of Pennsylvania Press, 1989), 63–64. See also idem, "Recent Editorial Discussion and the Central Questions of Editing 1974–79," in *Textual Criticism Since Greg: A Chronicle 1950–1985* (Charlottesville: University Press of Virginia, 1987), 65–107, esp. 103; idem, "Texts of Documents and Texts of Works," in *Textual Criticism and Scholarly Editing* (Charlottesville: University Press of Virginia, 1990), 3–23. Incidentally, this choice of editorial practice also best serves the admonitions of Jerome J. McGann, who argues that because "authors, their works, and their texts [are] not isolate phenomena," but rather "human products with the broadest cultural interests and relationships," it behooves editors to reckon with "the social dimension which surrounds the process of literary production." This requires editors to consider more flexibly how to preserve that sociality (and historicity) in a published edition. *A Critique of Modern Textual Criticism* (Charlottesville: University Press of Virginia, 1992), 118, 121, 113. The unexpectedly cooperative nature of the production of this text—its fortunate transcription by Anna Higginson—as well as the rhetorically constitutive character of this text as a communication written by Higginson to an immediate female audience of family members, and in some measure as part of a dialogic correspondence with them—means that to preserve the accidental textual features of the documents is to preserve valuable traces of this occasional, historically situated, dialogical quality.

created them. Written under the pressure of events at some times and under conditions of considerable leisure at others; written on board steamboats, in hospitals, in camp, or elsewhere, the texture of the prose varies considerably according to circumstances, and this is an important dimension of its value as historical document and as act of writing. The experience of reading it would be distorted irremediably if modified editorially. Higginson's spelling is occasionally uncertain or archaic and often inconsistent, and there are grammatical and stylistic irregularities that he would certainly never have allowed into print himself. These features do not materially interfere with reading and understanding him and so are best left untouched; there are, however, a few general exceptions. Underlined words have been rendered, according to convention, in italics, although underlined superscripts have been rendered in roman type. In addition, Higginson used parentheses and square brackets interchangeably; these have all been rendered as parentheses here for the purpose of distinguishing them from occasional bracketed editorial emendations.

The Higginson journal is preserved in two forms in the Houghton Library at Harvard University. Large parts of the latter sections of the journal survive in Higginson's original autograph manuscripts (Houghton Library, MS Am 784 [858–870, 910–927]). These parts, together with what may be presumed to be the entire remainder of the journal, are also preserved in a copy made by Higginson's sister Anna in four small bound notebooks (Houghton Library, MS Am 784 [20–23]). Evidently Higginson mailed off installments of the journal as he wrote them, sending them to his wife Mary Channing Higginson, who was expected to pass them on to his mother Louisa Storrow Higginson, with whom his sister Anna resided; Anna then made her copy. The purpose of sending off periodic installments was most probably for safekeeping, so that the journal was not in its entirety exposed to the possible accidents of war.

The copy-text for this edition of the journal is, therefore, chosen from among available texts in the interest of capturing the writing as nearly as possible in the form in which Higginson produced it: the autograph manuscripts, on a series of loose sheets, serve as copy-text for those parts of the journal where these original manuscripts survive (i.e., by dates, June 27, 1863-April 25, 1864); and the copy made by Anna Higginson serves as copy-text for the rest of the journal (i.e., November 22, 1862–June 16, 1863). In addition, the journal entries for four dates—November 6, 1863, March 17 and 28, 1864, and April 9, 1864—though falling within the chronological span of time for which Higginson's autograph manuscripts are extant, nevertheless do not appear to survive in that form, and so the copy-text for these entries is also Anna Higginson's copy.

Comparison of parts of Anna Higginson's notebook copy with the autograph manuscripts they duplicate shows that Anna herself made, in effect, a very good "diplomatic" or "noncritical" copy. Apart from a small number of misreadings or slips of the pen on her part, she was a faithful and accurate copyist. So we can be confident that, despite the hybrid nature of the copy-text this edition must resort to, the journal survives intact, more or less complete, in a relatively good and consistent state of textual accuracy. Higginson's handwriting as well as Anna's are only rarely illegible. In the few places where Higginson's penmanship was inscrutable, I have referred to Anna's copy to help with deciphering it (she, as a practiced reader of his handwriting, is a reliable witness). I have not sought to provide in this edition an elaborate textual apparatus itemizing such textual cruxes; the small number of scholars who might be interested in such details can readily consult the original documents. Where I simply cannot read the words, and Anna's transcription provides no help, I have left a blank within square brackets. In several places, installments of the journal were either delayed in the mail (notoriously unreliable in wartime) or held by Mary rather than sent on in a timely fashion, and so reached Anna (and were copied by her) out of consecutive order. I have restored these to their proper chronological place, and noted the fact in footnotes.

The copy-texts for the letters are, without exception, Higginson's autograph manuscripts (Houghton Library, MS Am 784 [718, 727–729, 752, 754–854, 871–890). As the disposition of Higginson's handwriting on the page is often somewhat irregular, especially when he sends off a quick note on the eve of departure on an expedition or otherwise writes under pressure of time, the reproduction of the letters in print involves a certain inevitable regularization. But I have not systematically regularized salutations, datelines, or other features of the letters. As with the journal's text, where I have been unable to decipher a word I have left a blank within square brackets. In a few places some letters have been mutilated, either by accidental tearing or by deliberate excision of some lines; it may be inferred in the latter case that these lines contained information or reflections that possessors of the manuscripts at some time wished to suppress. In these few cases I indicate this with a footnote. The headings above the individual letters, quotations taken from the texts themselves, are added editorially.

The war journal and war letters, being composed for Higginson's own purposes and as family communications, unsurprisingly contain many shorthand references and allusions that would have been have easily decipherable by their addressees; this has called for rather extensive annotation, so as to identify named persons and events, clarify literary and other cultural allusions, and so forth. It has not proved possible to identify all such allusions and references; friends and neighbors, as well as relatives, are often referred to by first name only, and while it has been possible to infer the identity in some cases, other such references remain obscure. If a proper name or other reference is not footnoted here it is because I have been unable to determine with any certainty who or what is in question; but these instances are relatively few and mostly trivial. A chronology of Higginson's life, covering its entire span but with greater detail provided for the period of his Civil War service, is appended to this edition so as to provide a larger and more general context for the sequences of events covered in the text.

# THE
# *War Journal*
## OF
# *Thomas Wentworth Higginson*

———"Black faces in the Camp,
Where moved those peerless brows & eyes of old!"
Browning's 'Luria.'[1]

STEAMER COSMOPOLITAN
SATURDAY MORNING NOV 24 (I.E., 22)[2] 1862

We are just opposite Cape Hatteras which should be the stormiest part of
our trip & is the calmest, though the steamboat thrills through my handwriting, as you perceive. We have sails as well as steam & are going at a
tremendous rate. Opposite is a low white line of shore which has a broken
line of woods behind it, suggestive of dim tropic lands, though the breeze
has as yet nothing tropical. Just now we have passed a steamer ashore too
far off to distinguish her real needs, a mute appeal which our Captain totally disregarded.

I reached New York early Thursday morning, breakfasted at the Astor[3]
& went to the U.S. Quartermaster to ask about the steamer. He at once &
totally refused me passage. The steamer was more than full already and it
was doubtful if there was even room in the next one—besides—he did
not know if Gen Saxton's[4] pass was sufficient—another official said Dr

1. Robert Browning, *Luria* (1846), is a tragedy in blank verse concerning a black Moor
who is hired to serve as military commander of the Florentine forces in a fifteenth-
century war against the Pisans, thereby displacing the native Florentine commander. As
Luria and his friend Husain (also a Moor) enter in Act II, Domizia, a noble Florentine
lady, says, "He comes—his friend—black faces in the camp / Where moved those peerless brows and eyes of old." *The Complete Works of Robert Browning*, Vol. IV, ed. Roma
A. King, Jr., et al. (Athens, Ohio: Ohio University Press, 1973), 296. In a December
22, 1862, letter to his mother TWH writes, "Tell Louisa her lines fr. Luria were thrilling &
fascinating; I cannot recall them. I shld. like them written in the beginning of my journal, Anna's copy." Above this epigraph in Anna's copy of the journal (Houghton Library,
Harvard University, MS Am 784 [20], serving as copy-text here) is written: "These copies
of T. W. Higginson's War Journal were made by his sister. / *Vol. 1st.*" Below the epigraph
is inscribed: "Copy of a journal written by / T W Higginson."
2. TWH seems to have mistaken the date here, since his very next entry is dated November 23.
3. The Astor House, an elegant and fashionable hotel in New York City.
4. Brigadier General Rufus Saxton (1824–1908), who recruited TWH for service in
the black 1st South Carolina Volunteers; a Massachusetts native, moderately antislavery
in his sentiments, he held various commands and titles during the Civil War, serving at

Lyng was the only person who had any real power over these steamers, that he filled them up with his teachers & superintendents, black white & grey and officers & soldiers had to wait &c &c. So off I went in the rain to the steamboat itself, hoping to meet this omnipotent cousin thinking that between church and state I might get through. I found the boat full of passengers & their friends & asked the Captain if he could take me. "Every birth full" ["]Can't I go in the *forecastle*"? He looked at me with surprise. "I can give you a mattrass on the cabin floor"—so I put this offer in writing, made him sign it, and posted back in the rain to the Quartermaster; who groaned when he saw the paper and then wrote me a pass himself. I had just time to hurry to the Astor, & get my small luggage, before the ostensible time of sailing of the boat—but it didn't really sail till night.

I like the floor arrangement, which I share with some dozen others, very well except that I have to go to bed at 8 to secure the mattrass & rise at 6 to make room for breakfast. However two out of the three probable nights have passed & we expect to arrive tomorrow aft (Sunday) making just 3 days—I have not been sea sick, though somewhat uncomfortable all yesterday, which withal was cold & rainy—today is better.

There are some 40 cabin passengers, half ladies—beside as many more soldiers in steerage. Part are officers, part teachers and superintendants of plantations. It is evident already that there is no love lost between these elements—the officers call the Lyng apostles *Gideonites* or *Gideon's band* or more familiarly *Gids*,[5]—charge them with sectarianism, hypocrisy, money-making &c; while the *Gids* call the officers pro slavery, heartless towards the slaves &c. Yet one of the most zealous anti *Gids* on board is a queer Mrs Hale[6] of Boston, one of Theo. Parker's[7] people, who has kept a school for colored children in Boston for 20 yrs & now superintends a

this time as military governor of the coastal islands off South Carolina and Georgia. TWH wrote admiringly about Saxton in "Civil War," chapter 8 of *Cheerful Yesterdays* (Boston: Houghton, Mifflin and Company, 1898), 235–70; "Intensely Human," chapter 6 of *Part of a Man's Life* (Boston: Houghton, Mifflin and Company, 1905), 114–38; and "A Massachusetts General, Rufus Saxton," chapter 13 of *Carlyle's Laugh and Other Surprises* (Boston: Houghton Mifflin Company, 1909), 173–82.

5. Derisive nicknames fastened by soldiers upon a militant group of zealous abolitionists who went to the Sea Islands of South Carolina to participate in the Port Royal Experiment, an effort to educate and otherwise prepare ex-slaves for freedom.

6. Mrs. Elizabeth B. Hale, one of the first band of missionaries to Port Royal.

7. Theodore Parker, a radical preacher and leading abolitionist, with TWH a backer of the 1859 effort by John Brown in Harper's Ferry, West Virginia, to foment slave rebellion. TWH's biographical sketch, "Theodore Parker," was published in the *Atlantic Monthly* 6 (October 1860), 449–57.

hospital at Beaufort. She says the leading Gids are Baptists & Methodists, and very narrow & it is not because of their anti Slavery views that they are disliked. My Gen. Saxton sustains these missionaries & Gen Brannan,[8] Mitchel's[9] successor, hates them and the negroes alike. It seems that Gen Saxton has no direct control over the army here—but he & Hunter[10] agree very well, and if Hunter returns as is expected, he is *over* this objectionable Brannan.

These represent the parties between whom I have to navigate—but so far I only hear the negro regiment well spoken of though Brannan, they say, hates even that. Recruits are constantly coming in for it from the main land, & the white line officers[11] are so far good—There has been a general belief, they all say, that the negroes will not fight—let them show that they will and the soldiers will respect them.

There is a very pleasing young Harvard graduate, named Kemp, from Boston, going out to be a superintendant—he is a friend of Storrow's[12]—also several army surgeons who are pleasant men and a Mr Judd[13] who is one of the principal superintendants, & has given me much information about affairs at Beaufort. My regiment is in camp about 4 miles from Beaufort and in good condition in all respects. It seems a good deal as if I were on my way to Fayal[14] again.

8. Brigadier General John Milton Brannan (1819–1892), previously stationed at Key West, Florida, had led the assault on Confederate gun emplacements on the St. John's River in Florida.

9. Brigadier General Ormsby MacKnight Mitchel (1809–1862), briefly served as commander of the Department of the South; he contracted yellow fever and died in Beaufort, South Carolina on October 30, 1862, within a few weeks of his appointment.

10. Major General David Hunter (1802–1866), who commanded the Department of the South, and abolished slavery in the Department on May 9, 1862; President Lincoln repudiated the order on the grounds that Hunter had exceeded his authority. He first enlisted black troops early in 1862, but disbanded them when he failed to secure authority to muster them into the service of the United States. Soon afterwards he was authorized to raise a black regiment, the 1st South Carolina Volunteers.

11. Line officers, as TWH explains below (November 27, 1862) are the captains and lieutenants, the class of officers who are in direct command of combat units.

12. Samuel Storrow Higginson, TWH's favorite nephew, son of his older brother Stephen; a Harvard graduate who served as Chaplain of the 9th Regiment U.S. Colored Infantry, a Massachusetts black regiment.

13. H. G. Judd, a Gideonite; General Superintendent on Port Royal Island, South Carolina.

14. Fayal, also spelled Faial, is an island of the central Azores in the northern Atlantic. TWH visited it in 1855, and published an account of his visit, "Fayal and the Portugese," *Atlantic Monthly* 6 (November 1860), 526–44.

SUNDAY MORNING NOV 23[D]
OFF CAPE FEAR. 120 MILES FR CHARLESTON
173 " " HILTON HEAD

The loveliest of Sunday mornings—with just breeze enough to keep our sails full. We shall reach Beaufort tomorrow morning. It is amusing to see how the stiffness disappears from people after being a few days at sea, how they cease to mount guard against each other, and find out who is who; which are the important officials, which the Herald reporter,[15] which the Rev[d] Dr Peck,[16] which the distressed widow & the eligible young lady & so on. Especially the transition is marked with officers who at first can only locate each other by the shoulder straps, & the second lieutenant is deferential to the unknown Major until the Major turns out a greater goose than even the Lieutenant.

As I approach the mysterious land I am more & more impressed with my good fortune in having this novel & uncertain career open before me when I thought everything definitely arranged. My dear mother was wrong in regretting that I exchanged the certain for the uncertain. Every thing I hear of this new opportunity the more attractive it becomes. My lot in the 51st regiment[17] was too smooth; I already had the best company in what was regarded as the best of the 9 months regiments;[18] three first class officers above me took off all difficult responsibility; it was becoming mere play. Either of my lieutenants could take my work & carry it on well. Here is, on the contrary, a position of great importance; as many persons have said, the first man who organizes & commands a successful black regiment will perform the most important service in the history of the War; & this undertaking will be more easy to me than to almost any one, perhaps, because it falls so remarkably into the line of all my previous preparations. To say that I would rather do it than any thing else in the world is to say little; it is such a masterpiece of felicitous opportunity that all casualties of life or death appear trivial in connexion with it. It would seem too good to become real, but for the similar good fortune which has marked all my entrance on military life and indeed all my life heretofore.

15. The New York *Herald*.

16. George B. Peck, member of the first company of volunteers of the Port Royal Mission.

17. The 51st Massachusetts Volunteers, a white regiment TWH had helped to raise in Worcester, Massachusetts, from which he resigned to accept his commission with the 1st South Carolina Volunteers.

18. Volunteers in both the Union and Confederate armies enlisted for various shorter or longer terms; Massachusetts in 1862 was offering nine month enlistments.

Now there is a pretty group; the ladies are singing hymns & three or four soldiers with them; three or four grim fellows in the foreground join in the chorus, while they wash their faces in the deck buckets; a squad of younger soldiers lean their heads above from the hurricane deck, & listen; a little orphan girl, the pet of all the passengers stands eagerly listening, with bare head, black eyes & brown cheeks, a little Cosette;[19] over head a white gull hovers with black tipped wings, & the innumerable waves toss their white heads around.

I have certainly escaped one duty which would have been painful, by coming thus, alone; to see all my nice boys sea sick in the miserable quarters allotted necessarily to troops on transports would have been very uncomfortable, even with the favorable weather we have had; while such scenes as those which the recent regiments experienced in Boston harbor would have been simply horrible. I can judge of that from the little I have seen in the same line. So you see I have improved my lot in some respects.

Now the soldier boys are in ecstacies at a school of porpoises & run lumbering from one side the deck to the other to watch them. They are much like porpoises themselves, young Maine recruits, tumbling about the deck in noisy play till they almost roll overboard; & still the sweet singing goes on, and brown little Cosette listens & the gulls hover & the white waves sparkle over blue depths for we are nearing the Gulf Stream.

The superintendant told me a Miss Helen Windsor[20] of Boston, a girl of 23 who must be a remarkable person, undertook the Eustis estate in addition to one she already managed; and with the most perfect success. No trouble about discipline & she without any male assistant has managed the cotton planting & carried on a school on each estate, ever since.

RIVER OPPOSITE BEAUFORT
MONDAY. NOV 24 10 A M

Yesterday afternoon we steamed over a summer sea, the deck level as a parlor floor, no sail in sight, nor land, till at last one light house (Cape Romaine) & then a line of trees & two distant vessels and nothing more. The sunset, a great bubble of light, submerged in a vast line of rosy suffusion; it

19. Cosette is a street urchin character in Victor Hugo, *Les Miserables (The Wretched): A Novel*, 5 vols., trans. Charles E. Wilbour (New York: Carleton, 1862).

20. Ellen H. ("Nelly") Winsor, member of the original band of Gideonites, who had almost been debarred from participation on account of her extreme youth; she married Josiah Fairfield, a neighboring superintendent, on May 7, 1863.

grew dark, after tea all were on deck, the ladies sang hymns, the moon set, a moon but two days old, a curved pencil of light, reclining backward on a radiant spot which rose from the ocean to meet it; it sank slowly & the last tip wavered and went down like the mast of a vessel of the skies. Toward morning the boat stopped & when I rose before six

> The watch lights filtered on the land
> The ship lights on the sea[21]

Hilton Head lay on one side & the naval vessels on the other; all that was raw & bare in the low buildings of the new settlement softened into picturesqueness by the early light. Stars were still overhead, gulls wheeled and shrieked & above us the broad lagoon rippled towards Beaufort.

The shores were low & wooded, like any New England shore—there were a few men of war & twenty schooners with a few steamers—one the famous "Planter" which Robert Small the slave presented to the nation.[22] The shores were soft, though low & as we steamed up to Beaufort on the flood tide this morning, it seemed almost as fair as the canal between whose banks Captain Stedman floated into lovely Surinam.[23] The air was cool as at home yet all the trees were green, glimpses of stiff tropical vegetation showed along the banks, with great clumps of some pale flowering shrub. Then appeared on a picturesque point an old plantation with decaying avenues and house & little church amid the woods, like Virginia; & behind a broad encampment of white tents—and *there* said my companion is your regiment of Maroons.[24]—

21. John Greenleaf Whittier, "At Port Royal.—1861.,"*Atlantic Monthly* 9 (February 1862), 244: "The tent-lights glimmer on the land, / The ship-lights on the sea."

22. Robert Smalls (1839–1915), a slave from Charleston, South Carolina, who had been hired out by his master as a pilot, skillfully ran this Confederate ship through the harbor fortifications and delivered it to the Union blockading fleet on May 13, 1862.

23. John Gabriel Stedman, *Narrative of a Five Years' Expedition Against the Revolted Negroes of Surinam*, ed. Richard Price and Sally Price (1796; Baltimore: The Johns Hopkins University Press, 1988), records the experiences of this Scotsman who inherited his father's commission in the Scots Brigade of the Dutch Army and was sent in that capacity to Surinam in 1773 to restore to slavery the escaped slaves who were terrorizing plantation owners. On February 2, 1773, he recorded that "the fleet entered the beautiful River *Surinam* . . . Here the Air was perfumed with the most odoriferous Smell in Nature by the many Lemons, Oranges, Shaddocks &c with which this country abounds" (p. 38). TWH had written about Stedman in "The Maroons of Surinam," *Atlantic Monthly* 5 (1860), 549–57.

24. "Maroon" was originally a term for one of the black persons who lived in the mountains and forests of Dutch Guiana (Suriname) and the West Indies, forming isolated societies in remote locations. From French *marron*, "runaway black slave," in turn from American Spanish *cimarrón*, "runaway slave."

10 P.M. *CAMP SAXTON—*
*QUARTERS OF 1ST REGT S.C. VOLUNTEERS—*

I have entered on command and am trying to play Col. Sprague[25] as well as may be. Spent morning with Gen. Saxton who is quite absorbed in this regiment & gave up all else for me—He gives me Carte blanche—I am to send for Dr Rogers & James.[26] The line officers I like much, young & not highly educated but thoroughly manly & very ready to meet me as I wish. My adjutant is a Boston Fraternity[27] man and heard me in my Crumble lecture say *Come* & is delighted to have me, as they all are. Gen. S. had many applications for the place but left it to me. The Lieut. Col. & Major[28] I like least as military men. I am to live in a tent when I can get one. Meanwhile in a forlorn plantation house. Soon after my arrival this morning, in marched a company of my men, to be mustered in—all black as coals as Margaret[29] predicted, not a mulatto among them, but marching well with their red legs[30] which are the only peculiarity of their uniform, as distinct from the ordinary. Gen. Saxton talked to them a little—so did I & they know what they are doing, I assure you. Being introduced to one who has been wounded in the late (second expedition)[31] I said "Did you

25. Col. Augustus B. Sprague, TWH's former commanding officer in the 51st Massachusetts Volunteers.

26. Seth Rogers, a hydropath who practiced in Worcester, Massachusetts, was TWH's good friend and choice to be surgeon of the 1st South Carolina Volunteers. Some of Rogers' letters from the period of his service with TWH have been published as "A Surgeon's War Letters," *Proceedings of the Massachusetts Historical Society* 43 (1909–10), 337–98. Captain James S. Rogers, his nephew, served with the 51st Massachusetts and then followed TWH to the 1st South Carolina.

27. First Lieutenant George W. Dewhurst was the adjutant; he was evidently a member of Theodore Parker's Free Church in Boston. The adjutant is a staff officer who assists the commanding officer with administrative affairs.

28. Lieut. Col. Liberty Billings; Major John D. Strong.

29. Margaret Fuller ("Greta") Channing, TWH's niece (daughter of his wife Mary's brother Ellery). Margaret was by this time practically an adopted daughter, having lived in her uncle's household for many years as a result of the poverty and domestic trouble of her parents; in 1853 her mother Ellen (Fuller) Channing, sister of Margaret Fuller (after whom her eldest daughter had been named), came with her other three children to TWH's household. See also January 19, 1863, below, for a more complete version of Margaret's saying.

30. Union troops wore a variety of uniforms, some regiments with red pants, which TWH detested; below (February 15, 1863) he happily notes their replacement by the dark blue trousers he favored.

31. Prior to TWH's arrival, the 1st South Carolina had proved themselves as combat troops by conducting raids along the Georgia and Florida coasts, November 3–10, 1862.

think that was more than you bargained for"? "Dat's just *what I meant for Massa*" says he. Very good for my first exchange of remark with my men, was it not?

It was certainly odd to go about among five hundred men, and not a white face—to see them go through all their cooking & talking & joking (this was after dress parade[32]) just as if they were white. They look so much alike at first too. I saw their 2nd dress parade, almost as good as our 2nd at Worcester & the precision of *time* with which they slapped down their hands after saluting, was astonishing, so in marching. Our camp is by a beautiful river where I can bathe & row or rather be rowed up to the city to-morrow.

With this letter—farewell—

CAMP SAXTON
NEAR BEAUFORT S.C.
NOV 27. 1862

Thanksgiving Day; and it is the first moment I have had for writing, during these three days, which have installed me into a new mode of life so thoroughly that they seem three years. Scarcely pausing in N.Y. or Beaufort, there seems but one step from the Camp at Worcester to this one, & that step over leagues of waves.

It is a holiday wherever Gen. Saxton's proclamation[33] reaches; the chilly sunshine & the pale blue river seem like New England but nothing else. The air is full of noisy drumming & of gunshots, for the prize shooting is the great celebration of the day and the drumming is chronic. My young barbarians are all at play. I look out from the broken windows of this forlorn plantation house through avenues of great live oaks, with their hard shining leaves, like the petisporum hedges we used to see in Fayal, & their branches drooped with an universal drapery of soft long moss, like fringe trees struck with grayness. Below, the sandy soil, scantly covered with grass, bristles with sharp palmettos & aloes & here & there a magnolia—all the vegetation shining & nothing soft or delicate in its texture. Numerous plantation buildings totter around, all slovenly and unattractive, & all the interspaces are filled with all manner of wrecks &

32. Dress parade is a daily ceremony in which a regiment assembles on the parade ground in the order of battle (i.e., as the troops would be disposed for combat), forming a line for inspection; reports are collected from companies, orders are issued, and so forth.

33. Saxton issued a Thanksgiving Proclamation declaring November 27, 1862, to be a general holiday in celebration of military victories and the freedom of slaves in the Port Royal region.

refuse, pigs, fowls, dogs & omnipresent Ethiopean[34] infancy. All this is the universal Southern panorama; but five minutes walk beyond the hovels & the live oaks brings one to something so un-Southern that the whole Southern coast at this moment trembles to think of it—the camp of my South Carolina Volunteers.

One adapts oneself so readily—or I do—to new surroundings, that already the wonderful novelty is passing or past. Each day, at Dress Parade, I stand with the befitting folding of the arms before a regimental line of faces so black that I can hardly tell whether they stand steadily or not. Every black hand moves in ready cadence as I vociferate "Battalion! Shoulder arms!" and it is not till the line of white officers comes forward as parade is dismissed, that I am reminded that my own face is not black as a coal.

During the first few days of remoulding & tightening reins for a regiment, the Colonel must deal almost entirely with the officers, & I have had scarcely any chance as yet for personal intercourse with my Maroons. Thus far they appear to me in bulk, so many consumers of rations, wearers of uniforms, holders of muskets. But I am already getting the whole machine well into my hands & am deciphering the individuals. There is more variety than one would suppose even in the different companies as wholes. Some are chiefly made up of men who have been for months under drill, in the Hunter brigade & have been in battle. There is a difference even in the color of the companies. When the whites left this region they took all the house servants & mixed bloods with them; so that the blacks of this region are very black. But the men brought from Fernandina (Florida),[35] the other day, are much lighter in complexion & decidedly more intelligent—so that the promptness with which they are acquiring the drill is quite astounding.

It needs but a few days to show the absurdity of doubting the equal military availability of these people, as compared with whites. There is quite as much average comprehension of the need of the thing, as much courage I doubt not, as much previous knowledge of the gun, & there is a readiness of ear & of imitation which for purposes of drill counterbalances any defect of mental training. They have little to sacrifice, are better fed, housed & clothed than ever before & have fewer vices such as lead to

34. "Ethiopean" here does not refer specifically to the country in northeast Africa, but more loosely to all African descendants, and connotatively to popular literary stereotypes; see below (under this same date) TWH's reference to "the Ethiopean minstrelsy of the stage."

35. On their periodic raids along the coast, one of the objectives of the 1st South Carolina was to recruit soldiers from among the slaves and refugees they encountered.

insubordination. At the same time I think, as I always did, that the sort of paradisaical innocence attributed to them by their first teachers were founded on very imperfect observation. They are not truthful, honest or chaste. Why should they be? but they are simple, docile and affectionate. The same men who have stood a fire in open field with perfect coolness, have blubbered in the most irresistibly ludicrous manner on being transferred from one company in the regiment to another.

In learning the elements of drill they are quite as apt as whites, learn to "double & undouble"[36] with less trouble, more rarely mistake their left for their right, & are more grave and sedate in drill. The extremes of jollity & sobriety being greater with them, they are less liable to be intermingled; these companies need less rebuking than my former one, which was the strictest in the regiment; but the moment they are dismissed from drill every tongue is loosed & every ivory tooth visible. This morning I wandered round among different companies target shooting and the enthusiasm was contagious. The shouts of "Ki! ole man" over some steady old turkey shooter who brought his gun down for a single instant's aim, and then hit the mark—& then when some unwary youth fired his piece into the ground at half cock, such infinite guffawing & delight, such rollings over in the grass, such dances of ecstacy, that made the Ethiopean minstrelsy of the stage[37] appear no caricature.

*Evening.* Better than this was a scene I saw tonight. Strolling outside in the cool moonlight, I was attracted by a brilliant light beneath the trees & approached it. A circle of thirty or forty soldiers sat round a fire of logs, to whom one old Uncle, Cato by name was narrating an interminable story to the insatiable delight of his auditors—and after I came up he still continued not displeased with an added listener. It was a narrative of his adventures in escaping from his master to the Union vessels; & even I who

36. "Double quick step" is a particular accelerated pace for marching, and drilling sometimes involved ordering the troops to quicken their pace from the "direct step," which was a pace of 28 inches at a rate of 90 steps per minute, to the double quick step, 33 inches in length at a rate of 165 to 180 steps per minute. TWH appears (see January 25, 1864, below) to have relied upon Silas Casey, *Infantry Tactics, for the Instruction, Exercise, and Manoeuvres of the Soldier, a Company, Line of Skirmishers, Batallion, Brigade, or Corps d'Armée*, 3 vols. (New York: D. Van Nostrand, 1862), the most commonly used manual of tactics in the Civil War, where these rates are given at 1:30, 32.

37. Blackface minstrelsy (white performers impersonating black persons, using burnt cork to darken their complexions, and exploiting such popular racial stereotypes as Jim Crow) was an immensely popular form of stage entertainment in antebellum America; TWH frequently adduces these popular representations of blacks as a point of reference during his military life.

have heard Harriet Tubman[38] & such wonderful slave comedians narrate their adventures, never heard anything comparable to it. The brightest things in Uncle Tom[39] are a far off imitation. He described his efforts after food & shelter on the way; acting out everything as he described it.

"Den I go up to de man, very humble & say would he please gib ole man a mouthful?

["]He say, he must hab the valeration ob half a dollar. Den I go away, Den he say, gib him de hatchet I had!

["]Den I say (with infinite comic seriousness) I mus hab dat hatchet to defend myself *from de dogs*" (Immense applause, & a sympathetic auditor says chuckling "Dat was your *arms*, ole man," which exploded the house again.)

["]Den he say, de Yankee pickets was near by & I must be very careful.

["]Den I say *Good Lord, Mas'r, am dey?*["] (words cannot express the unutterable dissimulation with which these accents of terror were uttered).[40] And so on. Then he described the efforts he made to enter the house by night & get some food, how a dog flew at him, how the whole household black & white rose & chaced him, how he scrambled over a high fence &c—all in a style of which Gough[41] alone among speakers can give any impression, so thoroughly was every word dramatized—Then his getting down to the river & trying to decide whether the vessels were "de Yankee boats." "Den I see guns aboard & I feel sure ob it." "Den it pop in my head, *Seceshky*[42] *hab guns too*—" Then he described sleeping in the bushes till morning. "Den I open my bundle & take my ole white shirt & tie um on ole pole and wave um, & ebry time de wind blow, I tremble all over & drop down in de bushes"—because the Secessionists were on shore & he might be seen from that side first. And so on, with a succession of tricks beyond

38. Harriet Tubman escaped from slavery in 1849 and became an abolitionist and the leading conductor on the Underground Railroad; she came later to the Sea Islands and worked as a nurse and scout for the Union army. Anna Higginson appears to have mistranscribed "Tubman" as "Tutman," and it has been corrected.

39. Harriet Beecher Stowe, *Uncle Tom's Cabin; or, Life Among the Lowly* (Boston: J. P. Jewett, 1852), an immensely popular, passionately abolitionist novel (frequently adapted to the stage in the years immediately following its publication), was often credited with influencing public sentiment decidedly against slavery.

40. There is an amply documented tradition among American slaves of "puttin' on ol' massa," i.e., conforming to a behavioral stereotype of African-Americans treasured by racist whites (here, blacks as frightened and gullible) in order to deceive them.

41. John Bartholomew Gough (1817–1886) was a noted temperance lecturer, famous for his dramatic and emotional speaking style.

42. Secessionists (i.e., Confederates).

Moliere,[43] of acts of caution, foresight, patient cunning such as seemed incredible to hear, while they were yet listened to with perfect comprehension & infinite gusto by every listener. And all this to a circle of Maroons, with the brilliant fire lighting up their red trousers & gleaming from their shiny black faces—eyes and teeth all white with glee in the tumult of enjoyment. Overhead the weighty limbs of a great live oak with the weird moss swaying in the smoke, & the high moon gleaming faintly through.

If you could realize the hopeless impenetrable stupidity in the daylight faces of most of these very men; the solid mask behind which Nature has concealed all this wealth of mother wit. This very narrator is one whom you would point to as he hoed lazily in a cotton field, as one the light of whose brain had gone out; and it seems like coming by night upon some conclave of black beetles & finding them engaged in a more than Shaksperian comedy. This is their university; every young Sambo,[44] as he turned over the sweet potatoes or peanuts which were roasting in the ashes, listened in reverence to these wiles of the ancient Ulysses & educated himself for the same. Thus wonderfully does Nature vindicate itself under all conditions—oppression simply crushed the upper faculties of the head & crowds every thing into the perceptive organs. Probably if I get into the enemy's country, I should be only too glad to put myself as a child into the hands of Ole Man Cato.

I think the men have enjoyed the day greatly, this morning each company shot for small prizes given by their Captains; & this P.M. the three best in each company competed for three prizes of $3 $2 & $1 offered to the three best in the regiment by the field officers. Then they had a thanksgiving Dinner—how could you ever guess what a dinner? The oranges cost a cent apiece & the Cattle were Secesh & presented by Gen. Saxton.

After the afternoon's shooting, instead of dress parade we had out an empty box & the Lieut. Col. & I made little speeches to the men, rousing them pretty thoroughly for the first time since I have been here—for I do not propose to make many speeches. I think they are coming to understand me sufficiently.

Now as to our officers. The line officers (Capts & Lieuts) are without exception good, earnest, well meaning young fellows, who understand what they have attempted & mean to do it. Half of them were in the Hunter Brigade; they are from Maine & Pa regiments chiefly & well drilled,

43. Molière was the pseudonym of Jean-Baptiste Poquelin, a French comic playwright of the seventeenth century, whose dramas often involve complex dissimulations.

44. Sambo was a stereotypical character from the blackface minstrel stage, a caricatured simple-minded plantation Negro (conventionally counterposed to another stereotype, Tambo, the urban black dandy).

though not up to the Sprague standard; so that the mere fact of what I have learned in a first class Mass^tts regiment gives me an advantage over these men: & I have been able to tighten up the reins a good deal in these few days, while forming very pleasant relations with them. We live in a queer way lodging & boarding about in squads in these different houses & rooms. I happened to squat at once upon the Lt. Col. & adjutant who occupy a small 2^d story room, where I spread my blanket on the floor. & in the same way I stumbled on taking my meals with the adjutant. To my amazement we live in clover—William takes care of our food, William the quiet & the good looking, the pattern of house servants, William the noiseless, the observing, the discriminating, who knows every thing that can be got & how to cook it—so that we have corn bread, rice, sweet potatoes milk & hominy in unfailing abundance; the river affords occasionally fried fish & oysters; the plantation no meat but pork, unfortunately; in all else we are well bestead; every [thing] is clean and orderly.

It is cold; last night it froze hard at the camp, but when I said this to William this morning he replied "Cold, Mas' ? dis is warm. In the winter you'll see the snow that deep on dese yere trees" meaning I suppose that it will hang in wreaths on the long moss, which will look weird enough. Still I send you some wall-flowers & the latest rose & I have seen three butterflies all new to me. The sun is bright at noon but it is cold & damp every night & our walls are thin & windows broken. I have valued Mrs Brown's[45] sleeping boots very much.

My adjutant is a young Bostonian named Dewhurst, a very quiet pleasant fellow, who is soon to send for a wife to come out here and marry him. He is a thorough business man & therefore perfectly reliable as adjutant; my quartermaster[46] who is the other main stay is also perfection. My Lieut. Col. is a large, soft, amiable man, with long curly black hair & blue spectacles, thoroughly well meaning, & unmilitary to the last degree. My Major has been here little, but seems still less military & less amiable. In all matters of drill & discipline they will probably be altogether useless, but they may have some usefulness among the men. But these being my only green officers I can do very well while my own life & health are secure, for there is nothing to call me away from the camp for an hour, so far as I can now see. I have now no horse, & no need of one till, we begin battalion drill & can get nothing better than some aged hack.

45. TWH refers in various letters to a Mrs. Brown as a neighbor and friend of his mother in Brattleboro, Vermont.

46. Captain Charles T. Trowbridge. The quartermaster is responsible for the food, clothing, and equipment of the troops.

My own Thanksgiving dinner took place in the Quartermaster's room, borrowed by a lieutenant, my host.

Bill of fare     Stewed Chicken
                       Roast Beef (a great rarity)
                       White Potatoes.
                       Sweet Potatoes. (here as white as the others, but insipid)
                       Rice (exquisitely cooked as always here)
                       Bread Pudding (good)
                       Dried Apple Pie (dubious)
                       Pumpkin Pie (an immense success)

You need feel no anxiety lest we should not have enough to eat, only that the meat is predominantly pork and the water poor.

I believe among our good things I have not mentioned Gen. Saxton. That a man of such simple New England good sense and earnestness should have survived West Point and an army career seems simply amazing. His zeal for these poor people is so inexhaustible that I only fear his doing more for us than the War Dept. will sustain. Still if Gen^l. Hunter comes I think all is safe. but Gen. Saxton certainly needs holding back rather than urging in our behalf & it has already come to that between him and me. His confidence in me seems perfectly unbounded, so that I feel embarassed in asking, lest he should give more than he ought: & he has already after 4 days acquaintance expressed his hope soon to see me at the head of a brigade of these troops. I hope he does not overlook means in his zeal for ends—yet he has managed everything admirably so far, & if some signal reverse does not happen, must perform a leading part in Affairs. He is exceedingly opposed by Gen. Brannan now in command at Hilton Head & I believe that even some of Gen. Hunter's staff are not his friends. He lives in a great deserted mansion at Beaufort in the simplest way.—a shortish compact man, with a mild absorbed face, with short curling black hair & beard; on horseback he looks a perfect hussar, as he is, being a splendid rider; but a very different style from my courtly Prince Rupert Sprague.[47] A mail goes tomorrow & here my journal ends for tonight. This is the 2^nd instalment.

47. Here TWH amalgamates his former commander in the Massachusetts 51st, Augustus B. Sprague, and the Prince Rupert he wrote about in "A Charge with Prince Rupert," *Atlantic Monthly* 3 (June 1859), 725–37. This was a story set in the English Civil War, wherein Prince Rupert is called "the one formidable military leader on the royal side" (pp. 730–31), praised as the "darling of fortune and war, with his beautiful and thoughtful face of twenty-three, stern and bronzed already, yet beardless and dimpled, his dark and passionate eyes, his long love-locks drooping over costly embroidery, his graceful scarlet cloak, his white-plumed hat, and his tall and stately form" (p. 726)—in

HEADQUARTERS 1ST REG. S.C.V.
CAMP SAXTON BEAUFORT
DEC 1. 1862

How absurd is the impression about these Southern blacks, growing out of a state of slavery, that they are sluggish or inefficient in labor. Last night after a pretty hard day's labor (tents & guns being just issued) an order came from Beaufort that we should be ready in the evening to unload a steamboat's cargo of boards, some of those captured by our men, & now assigned for their use. I felt a little suspicious that they might grumble at the night work, but the steamer arrived by seven & it was bright moonlight when we set them at work. Never have I beheld such a jolly scene of labor. Lugging these wet & heavy boards over a bridge of boats ashore, then across the slimy beach at low tide, then up a steep bank, & all in one great uproar of merriment for two hours. Running the greater part of the time, chattering all the time, snatching the boards from each other's hands as if they were some treasure begrudged, getting up eager rivalries between different sets, pouring great choruses of ridicule on the heads of all who shirked, they made the whole spectacle so entertaining that I staid out in the moonlight for the whole two hours merely as a spectator—and all this without any urging on our part, or any promised treat, but simply as the most spontaneous & jubilant method of doing the thing. The steamboat captain said they unloaded faster than any white gang would have done; and they felt it so little that when, later in the night, I reproached one whom I found sitting up by a camp fire cooking a surreptitious opossum— telling him he ought to be in bed after his hard work, I was answered ["]O no, Cunnel dat no work at all, Cunnel; dat only jess enough to *stretch we*"

Yesterday was the first soft & relaxing Southern day, with a haze like ours in May. Gen. Saxton has lent me a house & I had a ride through the plantation to a strange old fort of which there are two here, like those in St Augustine built by a French explorer about the time of the Pilgrims & older therefore than any remains in New England, even the Higginson house at Guildford, Conn.[48] They are built of a curious combination of

---

short, a dashing Cavalier whose combination of martial character, adventurous daring, and romantic beauty enchanted TWH. Under January 12, 1863, below, TWH avows that Sprague was "the only man who ever enabled me to understand what Prince Rupert might have been."

48. The Whitfield-Higginson house, an "old stone mansion" in which TWH's ancestor Rev. John Higginson married the daughter of Rev. Henry Whitfield, whose assistant pastor he was. See Thomas Wentworth Higginson, *Life and Times of Stephen Higginson* (Boston: Houghton, Mifflin and Company, 1907), 11 (illus. facing 10).

oyster shells & cement, called Lupia & are still hard & square, save where waterworn. One is before this house & a mere low redoubt; the other, two miles off is a high square house, bored with holes for musquetry & the walls still firm; though a cannon-ball would probably crush them.

There is no more monotonous riding than over these sandy hills, now dry with winter & covered with great glossy ravens, & through the tangled woods of live oak, with the omnipresent moss (Tillandria). Nothing can be finer in its way than the groves on this plantation, but one would soon weary of it while a New England thicket, with its infinite variety of blossom & vine, is inexhaustible. William our attendant speaks with contempt of the cultivation of this famous plantation—"No yam, Sa; no white potato, no *brimstone*" which is the startling name given to the *yellow* sweet potato such as we have at the North, but which is superseded here by a smaller & more insipid white one. After reaching home I bathed in the river; the day was lovely but the water very cold.

A boat load of holiday negroes crossed the river & as the women in gay colours with head-kerchiefs, were carried ashore in the men's arms, I was reminded of similar scenes in Fayal, while the continuous sing song talk might as well have been Portuguese as English. I am constantly struck with this resemblance; a peasantry is a peasantry I suppose, black or white, slave or free; it has certain characteristics. Those dirty irregular negro houses & their surroundings are much like the Fayalese; though there is not here that beautiful whiteness of clothing, & the people are more degraded. This was considered an especially severe plantation & there is a tree which was used as a whipping post, so that the marks of the lashes are still to be seen. This is thought to account for an inferiority of the slaves on this plantation; the bright ones are all from elsewhere. The house servants were very generally removed by the planters, leaving only the blacker & duller field hands.

Today has been as soft & relaxing as yesterday—uncomfortably so & tonight is a summer moonlight. It is as marked as our New England transitions and makes thick clothing very uncomfortable—yet I suppose in a few days we shall need it all.

I believe I have not yet named the probable drawbacks to the success of this regiment, if any. We are exposed to no direct annoyance from the white regiments, being out of their way & we have as yet no discomforts or privations which we do not share with them. I do not see as yet the slightest obstacle in the nature of the blacks to making them good soldiers, but rather the contrary. They take readily to drill & do not object to discipline; they are not especially dull or inattentive, & they fully understand the importance of the contest & their part in it. They show no jealousy or suspicion towards their officers.

There is one serious drawback & one only. Were this a wholly fresh experiment, I doubt not the regiment would have been full to overflowing ere this. That objection is the failure of the Govt to support the Hunter regiment[49] & the consequent fact that there are men here who have remained 8 months without pay. These men, though the best soldiers in the regiment, are therefore the least hopeful of success; it is natural that they should grow weary of pledges unfulfilled—& if they are homesick for their families the temptation is strong to run away; or if they remain, their influence hardly goes to the production of enlistments. Now if Gen. Saxton can possibly secure the payment of the regiment, even for the month they have been in camp, all this distrust would vanish, and the recruits would at once flow in, I doubt not. But while the plantation laborers are promptly paid & the Government laborers at Hilton Head, these soldiers are constantly twitted by their friends & families with working for nothing. Then there is an impression among their families, fostered I think by the white soldiers, that these black regiments are to be put in front, & especially exposed & all that sort of silly talk, the object of the soldiers being to prevent our being employed on regular service at all. All these considerations they feel precisely as white men would, no less, no more, and they are inevitably influenced by them.

But Gen. Saxton has thus far accomplished all he has promised—for instance our full supply of arms & tents have just arrived—& this gives me faith that his project of borrowing money from the cotton fund to pay these troops a month's wages may be also successful. This would undoubtedly [be] the one thing needed for filling up our ranks. Then all are expecting an advance of our lines, before a great while, which will bring many more slaves under our protection who will doubtless go to fill up this Brigade.

I should explain that the Cotton Fund is the balance due the Govt from sales of cotton, after payment of the laborers, & it is under Gen. Saxton's control. We gain a few recruits daily, & I doubt not shall be full in time, whether the men are paid off or not, but nothing could make a difference so great.

I shall mail this without waiting, as we do not always know when steamers come & go.

49. See note 10 above. Despite being ordered to disband his nascent black regiment, Hunter kept two companies together, under Captains Trowbridge and Goddard, first on St. Helena Island, South Carolina, and then on St. Simon's Island, Georgia, where they chased Confederate guerillas, remaining there until Gen. Saxton was authorized to raise a black regiment, of which they then became a part. These are presumably the soldiers who have been waiting eight months for pay.

Dec 2nd First letters last night. How the first mail bridges the interval & makes communication seem possible. Mr Bowditch's[50] munificent offer of a house too, takes a great trouble and expense from me, as houses are here difficult to obtain.

Today Gen. Saxton has returned fr Fernandina (Florida) with 76 recruits, & every Captain was eager for them. The Fernandina men being much brighter than those hereabouts & this makes 600.

## DEC 3. 1862

What a life is this I lead! It is a dark, mild drizzling evening, 7 o'clock & as the foggy air breeds sandflies, so it calls out melodies & strange antics from this mysterious race of God's grown up children. All over the camp the lights glimmer from the tents & as I sit at my desk in the open door way there come mingling sounds of stir & glee—boys laugh & shout, a feeble flute stirs in some tent, not an officer's—a drum throbs far away in another—wild plovers cry over us, day & night.—and from a neighboring camp fire comes one of those strange concerts half powwow, half prayer meeting, of which Eliza Dodge's "negro spirituals" & Olmstead's descriptions[51] give each but a part. These fires are often enclosed in a sort of little booth made neatly of palm leaves & covered in at top, a native African hut in short; this at such times is crammed with men singing at the top of their voices—often the John Brown war song,[52] but oftener these incomprehensible Negro Methodist, meaningless, monotonous, endless chants, with obscure syllables recurring constantly & slight variations interwoven,

50. Henry Ingersoll Bowditch, a prominent member of the General Committee of the Educational Commission, supporters of the Port Royal Experiment. In his December 10, 1862, and April 10, 1863, letters to his wife, TWH mentions Bowditch's pecuniary benefactions.

51. Frederick Law Olmsted was later best known as the landscape architect of New York City's Central Park and other urban oases, but he had earlier published a number of journalistic works recounting his travels in the antebellum plantation South: *A Journey in the Seaboard Slave States in the Years 1853–54, with Remarks on Their Economy* (New York: G. P. Putnam's Sons, 1856); *A Journey Through Texas; or, a Saddle-Trip on the Southwestern Frontier* (New York: Dix, Edwards & Co., 1857); *A Journey in the Back Country 1853–1854* (New York: Mason Brothers, 1861). A compilation from the three appeared as *The Cotton Kingdom: A Traveller's Observations on Cotton and Slavery in the American Slave States*, 2 vols. (New York: Mason Brothers, 1861), which has been republished in a one-volume edition of the same title, ed. Arthur M. Schlesinger (New York: Knopf, 1953).

52. "John Brown's Body," an anonymous composition first published in 1861, the tune of which became the basis for Julia Ward Howe's "Battle Hymn of the Republic" (1862).

all accompanied with a regular drumming of the feet & clapping of the hands, like castanets; then the excitement spreads, outside the enclosure men begin to quiver & dance, others join, a circle forms, winding monotonously round some one in the centre—some heel & toe tumultuously, others merely tremble & stagger on, others stoop & rise, others whirl, others caper sidewise, all keep steadily circling like dervishes, outsiders applaud especial strokes of skill, my approach only enlivens the scene, the circle enlarges, louder grows the singing about Jesus & Heaven, & the ceaseless drumming & clapping go steadily on. At last seems to come a snap and the spell breaks amid general sighs & laughter. And this not rarely & occasionally but night after night—while in other parts of the camp exhortations & prayers are going on as profusely.

A simple & loveable people, whose graces seem to come by nature and whose vices by training. Yet some of the best superintendants confirm the early tales of innocence & Dr Zachos[53] told me last night that on his plantation, a sequestered one they had absolutely no vices. Nor have these people yet shown any; during this week we have had no man intoxicated, & but one small quarrel, & there is scarcely any swearing. Take the (Progressive Friends) & put them in red breeches, & I think they would fill a guard house better than this regiment. If a camp regulation is violated, it is always through forgetfulness. They love passionately three things beside spiritual incantations—namely sugar, home & tobacco. Their love for the last is the chief reason why they long to be paid off; they speak of their last quid as if it were some deceased relative, too early lost & to be mourned forever. As for sugar, no white man can drink coffee after they have sweetened it— perhaps I could, I never tried it—& perhaps this sympathy of sweetness is the real bond between us.

I have no doubt that the pride which military life creates, afforded one reason why the plantation vices diminish here. For instance these men make admirable *guards* at night & allow nobody to pass them. It is far harder to pass in or out of this camp in the evening than in that of the 51st Mass. & that *conniving* in this respect which marked some companies there, is here unknown, or at least escapes notice. Nor are they lazy, either about work or drill: in all respects they seem better material for soldiers than I had ventured to hope.

The Fernandina company is I think the finest looking company I ever saw, decidedly superior to mine in the 51st. They range finely in size, have remarkable grace & beauty of figure, & march splendidly. All visitors are astonished at them; yet they have only been drilled a fortnight & part only

53. Professor John C. Zachos, one of the original band of Gideonites.

two days. The companies recruited hereabouts are far below them both in physique & intelligence—& even the black Fernandina men share the superiority.

In one of the companies here there is a superb looking woman as laundress wife of one of the men.[54] She is jet black, with good features, & a figure & gait which are queenly, that erectness of head which comes from burdens. A black Fayalese; and she has an eye for costume & wears a shapely dark blue sack & a string of beads, while most of the black women here are utterly repulsive in aspect & attire.

One can easily see how men must degenerate into vices, living as planters on these solitary estates. Life must be so inconceivably monotonous where even Nature is—these endless sandy levels & melancholy woods—no inhabitants nearer than Beaufort & no road but the one leading thither—Men's lives must strike down through this sand into a subsoil of sensuality—

Dec 4—Give these people their tongues, their feet, & their leisure & they are happy. Every twilight the air is full of talking, singing, clapping of hands in unison & often of speeches. One of their favorite songs is very plaintive,

> C'ant stay behind, O Sinner
> C'ant stay behind
> C'ant stay behind O sinner
> C'ant stay behind

Then comes a burden which at first I called the Romandar, because I could not make out the words & it is very impressive—it is Room Enough—

> Room enough, Room enough
> Room enough, in de heaven for de sojer
> C'ant stay behind[55]

It always excites them more to have us look on, but they sing these at all seasons. I have heard this song droning on at XI.P.M. & tracing it into the recesses of a cook tent, have found an old fellow coiled away among the

54. Perhaps Susie King Taylor (b. 1846), who was married to one of the soldiers, Edward King, and who later published a memoir, *Reminiscences of My Life in Camp with the 33d U.S. Colored Troops, late 1st S.C. Volunteers* (Boston: The author, 1902), with a preface by TWH. He mentions Taylor by name below, April 21, 1864, and also describes her there as "jet black."

55. In chapter 9, "Negro Spirituals," in *Army Life* (pp. 189–90), the refrain is given as "Room in dar" rather than "Room enough," which makes better phonological sense of TWH's mistake in calling it "the Romandar."

pots & provisions, chanting away with his "C'ant stay behind sinner" till I
made him leave his hymn behind.

This evening after working themselves up to the highest pitch, they suddenly all rushed off, got a barrel & mounted a man upon it who said "Gib
anudder song, boys, & I'se gib you a speech"—& after some hesitancy & mutual shouts of "Rise de music, somebody" & ["]stand up for Jesus, brudder"
rather irreverently put in by the juveniles, they got into the John Brown song
which is a great favorite, with one verse I have never heard elsewhere—

> We'll beat Beauregard[56] on de clare battle field"—

Then came the speech, & then seven other speeches on different barrels
by different men, all being tugged affectionately toward the pedestal & set
on end by their fellow soldiers. Every speech was good, without
exception—with the queerest oddities of phrase & pronunciation, there
was an invariable enthusiasm & power of expression, & a perfect understanding of the points at issue, which made them perfectly thrilling. They
made those slaves in "Among the Pines"[57] seem ordinary men. The most
eloquent perhaps was *Prince Lambkin* just arrived from Fernandina a man
who had expected all this war ever since Fremont's[58] time, whom he knew
all about. He described most impressively the secret anxiety of the slaves
to know about the election of Pres. Lincoln, & their all refusing to work on
March 4th.[59] He had finally the most impressive sentence about the American flag I ever heard. "Our mas'rs dey hab lib under de flag, dey got dere

56. Pierre Gustave Toutant Beauregard (1818–1893), Confederate General in command of Carolina and Georgia coastal defenses, stationed at Charleston; he commanded the bombardment of Fort Sumter on April 12, 1861, forcing the Union
surrender, and later fought in other theaters of the war.

57. James R. Gilmore [pseud. Edmund Kirke], *Among the Pines: or, The South in Seces-
sion-Time* (New York: J. R. Gilmore, 1862). Gilmore describes himself, in this account of a
Northerner visiting friends in South Carolina immediately following secession, as an
"anti-Abolitionist and Southern-sympathizer" (p. 57), but also as a confirmed opponent
of slavery who hopes that "the direful upheaving, which is now felt throughout the
Union, is the earthquake that will bury it forever (p. 27). The book uses traditional dialect
humor to depict the varieties of "darkies" encountered, some of whom are decidedly
eloquent, intelligent, and determined to seek their own freedom.

58. Major General John Charles Frémont (1813–1890), prominent antislavery Republican (his party's Presidential candidate in 1856), briefly Union commander of the
Western Department at St. Louis in 1861, where, on August 30, he issued a proclamation
emancipating Missouri's slave population (which President Lincoln revoked, at the same
time relieving Frémont of his command). TWH refers in a letter of March 4, 1864, to a
book written by the general's wife, Jessie Benton Frémont, *The Story of the Guard: A Chronicle of the War* (Boston: Ticknor and Fields, 1862).

59. The date of Abraham Lincoln's first inauguration.

wealth under it, & ebry ting beautiful for dere chil'en & under it dey hab *grind us into money* & *put us in dere pocket*; & dat minute dey tink dat ole flag mean freedom for us dey pull it down & run up de rag ob dere own; but we'll nebber desert it boys, nebber, we hab lib under it for 1862 years (!!!) & we'll die for it now"! This is a poor reminiscence in prose, but I wished for a phonographer[60] in my pocket. This was the tone of all; & mingled in were queer Methodist phrases & set expressions & almost every speaker had some hit at the short rations which have recently prevailed for a few days. & some very sensible satire on the soldiers who grumbled over them—these reproofs are always bringing down the house. At last they hoisted up little old Simon Grier, one of our crack shots, (the greatest fool in the regiment) whispered his captain to me, but old Simon made a very pithy speech, short as himself; & then they all broke up. They evidently enjoyed the officers' presence, but made no effort to call them out & I am very sure that no eight among the officers could have spoken on the spur of the moment with such easy eloquence and such telling effect.

## December 5 — Camp Saxton[61]

"Dwelling in tents, with Abraham, Isaac & Jacob."[62] A moving life, tented at night, this I have tasted before the luxurious wood-fires of the Maine forests,[63] & upon the lonely prairies of Kansas,[64] but a stationary tent life, going to housekeeping under canvass, I have never had before, though in our barrack life at Camp Wool,[65] I often wished for it—

60. The phonographer was an early sound-recording device that picked up sound vibrations by means of a membrane and recorded them by means of a point that traced them on a cylinder.

61. In the copy of TWH's journal made by Anna, the words "(this was accidentally delayed)" appear here; the following December 5 entry is transcribed after the December 9 entry, apparently having taken longer to arrive in the mail; hence the parenthetical note, added no doubt by Anna herself. I have relocated the December 5 entry to its proper chronological place.

62. "Dwell[ing] in tents" appears in Genesis 4:20, 9:27 and 25:27.

63. TWH had written of a hiking trip in Maine in "Going to Mt. Katahdin," *Putnam's Monthly Magazine* 8 (September 1856), 242–56.

64. Following passage of the Kansas-Nebraska Act in 1856, which left it to those territories to choose whether to admit slavery or not and to adopt state constitutions accordingly, TWH had supported the effort to send antislavery settlers to Kansas to swell the population in anticipation of such a choice. As agent of the Massachusetts Kansas Emigrant Aid Society, he travelled to Kansas twice in 1856, investigating the state of affairs and bringing arms and ammunition; it may have been in Kansas that he first met John Brown.

65. Camp Wool, outside of Worcester, Massachusetts, location of the 51st Massachusetts, TWH's former regiment.

My tent here is nearly as large as my room there, for it is double, made of two placed end to end, office & bedroom, each 9 ft. square & seperated by a fly of canvass; this being raised behold a long room with a pillar in the middle. There is a good board floor & a mock board all round, increasing the height, & excluding dampness & cold more effectually. The furniture of the office is a good secretary, secesh by origin, a clumsy wooden settee from the old negro church, (now used for commissary stores) & one stool—this last is composed of a cane seat which I found under the plantation house, two legs of a broken bedstead & two more of the native oak, all put together by a black sergeant. Bedroom furniture, a couch made of gun boxes covered with condemned blankets,—another church settee, 2 pails, tin cup & basin (we prize any tin or wooden ware as savages prize iron)—& a valise.

I don't see that anything more is needed, save another chair & perhaps something for a washstand higher than a settee—

Today it rains hard & the wind quivers through the closed tent & makes one feel at sea. All the talk of the camp outside is fused into one cheerful & meaningless hum, pierced constantly by the wail of the hovering curlews. Sometimes a face, black or white, peers through the canvass door with some message. As the light penetrates, though the rain cannot, it conveys a feeling of charmed security, as if an invisible boundary checked the pattering drops & held the morning wind.

The front office I share with my unexceptionable adjutant; in the inner apartment I reign supreme; bounded in a nut shell, with no bad dreams— In all pleasant weather the front fly of the tent is wide open, & men pass & repass, a chattering panorama. I constantly think of Emerson's Saadi "As thou sittest at thy door, on the desert's yellow floor"[66]—for these bare sand plains, gray above are yellow when upturned anywhere, & unlike all other sands, are as fertile as any land in the world when cultivated, though there is scarce a grass blade in the camp.

Three times a day we go to our meals (at 7, 12 & $5\frac{1}{2}$) the officers boarding in different messes; the adjutant & I still adhere to William & Hetty, who set our table in their one room, near a great wood fire. There are we forever supplied with pork & white sweet potatoes & hominy & rice & cornbread & milk—mysterious griddle cakes of corn & pumpkin, preserve made of pumpkin chips & other fanciful products of Ethiop art. Mr G B Emerson[67] promised the superintendants who come out here "all the luxuries of home"; & we certainly have much apparent if little real variety. Once

66. Ralph Waldo Emerson, "Saadi," in *Poems* (Boston: James Munroe & Company, 1847), 205. "While thou sittest at thy door / On the desert's yellow floor."

67. George B. Emerson, longtime member of the General Committee of the Educational Commission, sponsors of the Port Royal Experiment.

William produced with some palpitation something fricasseed which he boldly termed chicken, it was very small & seemed in some undeveloped condition of ante-natal toughness—after the meal he frankly avowed it for squirrel. Oysters we have too, occasionally, & at such times abundant, & sometimes little fried fish. Reports of wild ducks, but nobody to shoot them, as yet. Today we have some nice corned beef, a rare luxury. Fresh meat & good water are the desiderata; the latter I rarely imbibe; it is sulphurous as slavery, but so far I can always get milk.

In describing the tent I omitted to describe the camp stove, not yet set. A singular structure—all funnel, no bottom.[68] A funnel ending in a tunnel which is simply clapped down in a box of sand & there you are. A slide in one side admits your fire & gives draft. In such an edifice I dwell & such an one is being upreared beside me by the adjutant who proposes to bring hither his bride, who, if she be as capable and intelligent as she looks in photograph, will grace it very well.

## DEC 7

Every night a "shout" (as they call these singings & dancings) goes on somewhere in the camp.

"Raise something sperritual" is the cry.

> *The Gospel Ship*
> De gospel ship is sailing
> Hosann—san
> O Jesus is de Captain
> Hosann—san
> De angels are de sailors
> Hosann—san
> O is your bundle ready?
> Hosann—san
> O hab you got your ticket
> Hosann—san[69]

The chorus is given with unspeakable unction.
But nothing equals my picturesque Romandar as I at first called it, which is almost always sounding in the evening air.

> "O my mudder is gone, my mudder is gone
> My mudder is gone to Heaven my Lord

68. See the gallery for TWH's sketch, as copied by Anna Higginson.
69. The third version of "The Ship of Zion," in *Army Life* (p. 206).

I can't stay behind
There's room enough &c
2. O my fader is gone &c
3. O my teacher is gone &c
4. O the angels are gone &c
5 O I'se been on de road, I'se been on de road
I'se been on de road to de Heaven, my Lord
I c'ant stay behind
Room enough, room enough
Room enough in de heaven for de souls
I c'ant stay behind—"[70]

(Every man who comes within reach, oldest & youngest, is wriggling & shuffling, as if by an irresistible necessity. & even those who affect the sarcastic, glancing round at us, are drawn into it ere long.)

### DEC 8

Today a squad of men were brought in from Georgetown S.C. Such forlorn looking recruits, lame halt & blind & not clearly understanding why they were brought here or what they are expected to do. I felt like a slave driver as I partitioned them about to eager captains, each anxious to make up his number, even if the material were unattractive. So different from our fine Florida fellows. So prompt & ready to go to war. Next week we expect 100 more of those & then another hundred will complete the regiment to its minimum 830.

I hear tonight of two steamers arriving at Hilton Head & hope most ardently for Dr Rogers—it is probably too soon to look for James, unless the 51st was greatly delayed at Worcester & then his pass would have gone to Newbern N.C. & so missed him, I fear.—Probably the steamer will bring a mail also—quite delightful, as I have heard but once from home, & I am quite ready for further advices.

Dec 9. No mail by the steamers, only it turns out that the Banks expedition[71] is not to come here, & this remains a subordinate station. Perhaps

70. See above, note 55.

71. Major General Nathaniel Prentiss Banks (1816–1894), former Republican governor of Massachusetts, named to command the Department of the Gulf on November 8, 1862, was charged to open the Mississippi River, which was under Confederate control; he assumed command in New Orleans, Louisiana on December 16, and the next year led his troops on a successful expedition to reestablish Union control of the Mississippi by assaulting the Confederate garrison at Port Hudson, Louisiana.

this is quite as well for the 1st South Carolina, as this leaves Gen Saxton free to employ us as he will, if he can only get steam boats. & there are plenty of things to be done hereabouts, which the white regiments now here are not likely to interfere with.

## Dec 11. 1862

Haroun Alraschid wandering through his streets in disguise,[72] scarcely came upon a greater variety of groups than I in my evening strolls among my own camp fires.

Beside some, the men are cleaning their guns or rehearsing their drills, beside others smoking in silence their very scanty supply of the beloved tobacco, beside others telling stories & shouting with laughter over the broadest mimicry in which the officers are not always spared I suspect. Always somewhere the everlasting "shout" is going on, with its mixture of piety & polka & its castanet-like clapping of hands. Then there are quieter prayer meetings, with ardent & often touching invocations; & slower psalms, deaconed out from memory, by the leader two lines at a time, in a wailing chant. Elsewhere there are conversaziones round fires with a woman as the centre, her Nubian[73] face, earrings, bead necklace & white teeth, all resplendent in the lustrous firelight. Sometimes the woman is spelling slow, monosyllables out of a primer, a process which always commands all ears. Elsewhere it is some solitary old cook, some aged Uncle Tiff[74] with enormous spectacles, who is perusing a hymn book by the light of a pine splinter, in his deserted cooking booth of palmetto leaves. By another fire there is an actual dance, red legged soldiers doing right & left & "now lead de lady over", to the music of a quite artistic fiddle which may have played, ere now, for Barnwells &

72. Haroun Alraschid figures in a number of the tales of the Arabian Nights; in one his insomnia leads him to don merchant's garb, sail down the Tigris River, and seek amusing new sights and sounds. See *The Book of the Thousand Nights and a Night*, ed. and trans. Richard F. Burton (The Burton Club, n.d.), 9:188–207. One of TWH's favorite writers published a poem featuring Haroun Alraschid: Alfred Lord Tennyson, "Recollections of the Arabian Nights," *The Poems of Tennyson*, 3 vols., ed. Christopher Ricks (Berkeley: University of California Press, 1987), 1:225–31.

73. Nubia was an ancient kingdom in the Nile River Valley of southern Egypt and northern Sudan; "Nubian" became a byword for dignified African beauty, especially applied to women.

74. Uncle Tiff was a character in Harriet Beecher Stowe's second antislavery novel, *Dred: A Tale of the Great Dismal Swamp* (Boston: Phillips, Sampson, 1856). He shared certain characteristics with the title character of *Uncle Tom's Cabin*, namely extraordinary Christian benevolence.

Hugers.[75] And lastly there is some stump orator perched on his barrel, pouring out his mingling of liberty & Methodism in quaint eloquence—tonight for the first time I have heard an harangue in a different strain, quite serious, skeptical & defiant, and appealing to them in a sort of French materialistic spirit, & boasting of personal experience of battles. "You d'ont know nothing about it boys, you tink you's brave enough, now you tink if you stand dare in de open field,—here you & dar de secesh? You's got to hab de right ting inside of you, you must get it '*served* in you, like dese yer sour plums dey 'serve (preserve) in de barrel; you's got to *harden it down inside ob you* or it's notting"—He rather satirized the Methodists, said "when a man got de sperrit o' de Lord in him, it weakens him out, c'ant hoe de corn",—had a good deal of broad common sense in his speech—& presently some others began praying vociferously close by, as if to drown this free thinker, & at last he said in conclusion "I mean to fight de war through; & die a good sojer wid de last kick—dat's *my* prayer,["] & jumped off the barrel. It was quite curious to me to observe this reverse side of the temperament, the devotional preponderates so enormously & the greatest scamps kneel & groan at their prayer meetings with such entire zest.

Their love of the spelling book is perfectly inexhaustible, & they stumble on by themselves, or aiding each other, with the most pathetic patience. The Chaplain is getting up a schoolhouse, where he will teach them as he gets opportunity.

Tonight is milder than usual, after a sultry day—& the night grasshoppers are chirping in the grove; Roses still bloom but I like the climate as little as any I have ever known; the nights & days are so unlike—Hitherto we have had almost constant sunshine, with one hard storm for a day.

Dec. 13. I must send this scrap as it is, for there may be a mail—all well till today—Lovely spring day.


DEC 14


## PASSAGES FROM NEGRO PRAYERS

"Let me to lib dat when I die I shall *heb manners*, dat I shall know what to say when I see my heavenly Lord"

"Let me lib wid de musket in one hand and de Bible in de oder—dat if I die at de muzzle of de musket, die in de water, die in de land, I may know I hab de blessed Jesus in my hand, and hab no fear."

75. Prominent plantation owners in South Carolina. TWH later visits the Barnwell plantation; see below, April 12, 1863.

["]I hab leff my wife in de land ob bondage, my little ones dey say ebry night, where is my fader? But when I die, when de bressed morning rises, when I shall stand in de glory, wid one foot on de water & one foot on de land, den, O Lord, I shall see my wife & my little chil'en once more."

These are passages from one of the most thrilling & impassioned prayers to which I ever listened, offered beside one of the camp fires last night. The same person was the hero of a singular little contretemps at a funeral in the afternoon. It was our first funeral—The man had died in the hospital at Beaufort & we had a picturesque place marked out by the river, near the old church & a little nameless cemetery used by centuries of slaves—We had a regular military funeral, the coffin draped with the American flag, the company marching behind, and guns fired after the services at the grave; During these services we had singing, the Chaplain deaconing out the hymn as usual. This ended, he announced his text. "This poor man cried & the Lord heard him & delivered him out of all his trouble." Instantly, to our great amazement, the cracked voice of the cho- rister was uplifted, intoning the text as if it were the first verse of a hymn. So calmly was it done, so imperturbable all the black countenances that I began to half believe that it was meant by the chaplain for a hymn, though I could imagine no prospective rhyme for *trouble* unless *debbil*, a favorite theological word with them. But the Chaplain, peacefully awaiting, gently repeated his text after the chant, & quite to my relief old Sandy omitted his recitative & let the discourse proceed.

They know a good deal of Scripture phrases & history, but in the most chaotic state & most of the great events of the past they straightly credit to Moses. One of my captains last Sunday at Beaufort heard an exhorter say "Paul may plant & *May Parish* water, but it w'ont do at all,"—in which the sainted Apollos would hardly have recognized himself.[76] Just now one of the soldiers came to me to say that he was going to be married to a girl in Beaufort & would I lend him $1.75 to buy some things? I thought that mat- rimony on such moderate terms ought by all means to be encouraged, and so responded to the appeal.—

## Dec 16. 1862.

Today a young recruit was sent out here, who had belonged to a certain Col Semmes or Sammys[77] of Florida. Two white companions walked him out,

76. Perhaps the garbled quotation is 1 Corinthians 3:6, "I have planted, Apollos wa- tered; but God gave the increase."
77. Sammis, who appears soon below.

who seemed rather inferior retainers of the Colonel—and I could do no less than ask them to dine. Being refugees they had some experiences to tell,—one was English born; the other Floridian, a dark sallow Southerner, well bred enough. The Colonel was a man of wealth who had lost all, they said; & after they had gone, he appeared. I repeated my hospitality & after a while he quietly let out "Yes, that white friend of whom you speak is a boy raised on one of my plantations, he has travelled with me to the North and passed for white, & always keeps away from the negroes." Certainly I never should have suspected it. Perhaps he may have been his own son. There are two men in the regiment who would pass for white, one a little elderly man who drums. I have often seen children & young women as fair, among fugitive slaves, Alice Green for instance. But it touched me much more to see this man who had spent half a life in this darkened estate & for whom it seemed too late to be anything but a "nigger"—This word by the way is almost as common with them as with us—they have meekly accepted it. "Want to go out to de nigger houses, sa," is the universal impulse of sociability, wishing to cross the lines & lounge at the plantation buildings. "He needn't try to come de white man ober me" was the protest of a soldier against his corporal the other day—& last Sunday I scolded them for this want of self respect. On the other hand there is really nothing of that sort of upstart conceit one sometimes sees among the free negroes of the North; I thought freedom and regimentals would have produced it. They seem the world's perpetual children, docile & gay & loveable, in the midst of this war for freedom upon which they have intelligently entered. Last night there was the greatest noise in camp I had ever heard & I feared a riot—Going out I found the most tumultuous sham fight in pitch darkness, two companies playing like boys, beating tin cups for drums. When they saw me they would come & say beseechingly "Cunnel, you hab no objection to we playing, sa," which of course I had not, but soon they all subsided & scattered merrily. Afterwards I found that some officer had told them I thought there was too much noise, so that I felt a mild self reproach when one said "Cunnel, wish you had let we play little longer, sa." Still I was not sorry, for these sham fights between companies would lead to real ones among white soldiers, & there is a latent jealousy here between the Florida & South Carolina men, about which I feel some anxiety.

The officers are more patient & kind with them than I should expect, as drilling always tries the temper, & the officers are mostly young; but they are aided by a hearty faith in them; I have never yet heard a doubt expressed as to their superiority to white troops in aptitude to drill & discipline. One of the best Captains said to me today "I have this afternoon taught my men (wad.) in 9 times, & they can now do it better than my former company in the engineers' did it in three months." Our best lieutenant, Stockdale[78] an Englishman, taught his company the whole of the "Skirmishers drill"[79] yesterday, in one lesson of two hours; that is I myself saw them go through all the main movements in that time, which it took me a series of lessons to teach my company in the 51st, though. I have not yet found any one who has made me feel myself his inferior as a drill master. Per contra in those parts of drill which require a ready comprehension of principles—as doing a thing first by the right flank & then by the left—they certainly do not equal my former company—or I suppose any well educated body of men.

The habit of carrying things on their heads commonly gives erectness, even to those who are physically disabled. I have seen a woman with a brimming water pail on her head—or perhaps a cup, saucer & spoon—stop, turn round, fling something, light a pipe & go through many movements undisturbed. It is odd to see a well dressed girl on Sunday stride along smoking a pipe—the passion for tobacco of our soldiers is absorbing, & I have most piteous appeals addressed to me for it, or to make some arrangements by which they can buy it on credit—Their imploring "Cunnel, we can't *lib* widout it, sa," goes to my heart & I can't hold out against it much longer, spite of all counterblasts,[80] think of that!

## Dec. 19

It is a piece of my accustomed good luck to have fallen on such a pleasant simple, capable, companionable fellow as my Adjutant. With the aristocratic name of George Dewhurst, he is a young Boston bookkeeper, one of Theo. Parker's Fraternity,[81] with a wholesome antecedent faith in his

78. First Lieutenant William Stockdale, formerly of the 8th Maine; resigned May 2, 1863.

79. George Brinton McClellan, *Regulations and Instructions for the Field Service of the U.S. Cavalry in Time of War, To Which is Added, the Basis of Instruction for the U.S. Cavalry, from the Authorized Tactics; Including the Formation of Regiments and Squadrons, the Duties and Posts of Officers, Lessons in the Training and Use of the Horse; Illustrated by Numerous Diagrams, with the Signals and Calls Now in Use. Also, Instructions for Officers and Non-Commissioned Officers on Outpost and Patrol Duty, With a Drill for the Use of Cavalry as Skirmishers, Mounted and Dismounted* (Philadelphia: J. B. Lippincott & Co., 1862). The "Skirmish Drill for Mounted Troops" is at pp. 197–216.

80. TWH wrote an article against tobacco entitled "A New Counterblast," *Atlantic Monthly* 8 (December 1861), 696–705. "The use of tobacco must . . . be held to mark a rather coarse and childish epoch in our civilization, if nothing worse," he wrote (p. 700). "Counterblast" was, as the article's epigraph notes, borrowed from King James's *A Counterblaste to Tobacco* (London, 1604).

81. Theodore Parker's congregation in Boston, a so-called Free Church, was the model after which TWH's Worcester congregation had been patterned; it was imbued with radical sentiments of all kinds, especially antislavery.

Colonel. The Adjutant is practically almost a Secretary to the Colonel, and as we two board together and write in the same tent, it is a very risky relation. Dewhurst's prospective wife is a pretty, well educated, spirited girl who sets types in a Boston printing office, & is coming out here very soon, to rough it with him! Writing to ask him about buying table linen, he writes her back that as our table linen consists of two N.Y. Tribunes & a Leslie's Pictorial,[82] it is hardly necessary to invest largely. As for napkins he has supplied me ever since I came & it was to match his silver fork & spoon that I sent for my iron ones. He writes to his intended profusely, & stops every now & then to write a note to some business friend, for some added article of convenience which he is always buying from N.Y. in contrast to my Spartan simplicity. I told him I had no doubt he must get them terribly mixed up. "Beloved Hattie; please forward ten pounds of brass headed nails per next Steamer." "Friend Jones; I am anxiously awaiting your invoice, one lock of auburn hair & your precious self following." He takes it all imperturbably. He had her photograph in an apartment at the plantation house; the people of the house took it unhesitatingly for Mrs Higginson, till I denied the soft impeachment, then for Mrs Lieut Colonel—that large & smiling brother being a bachelor.

DEC. 20

I think it is partly from my notorious love of children that I like these people so well. I habitually called my company in the 51st "the infants" much to my lieutenant's amaze; but these people who never know their own ages till they get past middle life & then select with the utmost precision an age & a birthday—these people prolong the privilege of youth. Their dialect is immature & childlike. Take this dialogue just outside of my tent.

"Hi, hi, get out of de vay."
"Hi, Willy, boy, where oo going."
"Going to de quattermatter." (quartermaster)
"Quattermatter *kill oo.*" (tremendous joke)
"No, no, sa, get out of de vay."

82. The New York *Tribune,* founded by Horace Greeley in 1841, was a daily newspaper identified editorially with Republican antislavery sentiments; TWH's "Letters from Kansas" appeared there in 1856. *Frank Leslie's Illustrated Newspaper,* a weekly founded in 1855, flourished during the Civil War, when its staff of field artists made battlefield sketches that were transferred to woodblock engravings and then printed, within two weeks of the events they depicted, thus offering the public timely visual representations of the war.

I am bothered nightly for new *countersigns*; their range of proper names is so limited, unless as the Adjutant suggests, I begin on Scripturals. At first they did not seem however to recognize the variations; one night an officer asked a sentinel if he had the countersign yet? & was indignantly answered, "Should tink I hab um; hab um for a fortnight." Which seems a long time for that magic word to last. Tonight I thought I would have "*Fredericksburg*" in honor of the rumored victory,[83] using the rumor quickly, for fear of contradiction. Later in the evening, in comes a Captain, gets it, goes out & returns, stopped by the guard who say his countersign is not correct. On inquiry, it proves that the Sergeant of the Guard, being weak in Geography, substituted the more familiar phrase *Crockery-ware*, which is with perfect gravity confided to all the sentinels, & accepted unquestioning by all, as the last result of military discipline. Oh life, life! what is fiction beside thee.

Talking of the age of our recruits, a fine looking man came to the tent door & claimed exemption by reason of age, & on inquiry into statistics, calmly stated that he was *eighty*—Gen$^l$ Saxton's code is comprehensive, but I confess I was a little startled, & was graciously pleased to assign him to attendance on hospital. Perhaps he may be forty five.

I should think that they would suffer & complain these cold nights, but they never do, though I hear a good deal of coughing. I think the red breeches must keep them mutually warm. At any rate they multiply fire light, I often notice that an infinitesimal fire with one soldier standing by it, looks like quite a respectable conflagration, & a circle of them *must* dispel dampness. I cannot abide these red trousers & shall get others by & by.

Last night the water froze in the Adjutants tent, but not in mine, which is closer, & had a fire in the evening in Fever & Ague.

The day has been mild & beautiful. I really think the blacks do not feel the cold so much as we do; & they say so. On the other hand, in drilling in some very hot days, they have seemed to suffer more from heat than I did. But they do dearly love fire and at night will always have it if it be possible, even on the minutest scale, a mere handful of splinters, to warm the fingers, appears to satisfy them. I suppose this is a natural habit for the short lived coolness of an outdoor country, & one thing that encourages it is the ease with which they get chips of very resinous pine, that can be lighted from a match or lamp & burns like tar barrel splinters giving a strong heat. My mode of life at present is this—wake at reveillé 6½, rise from that time to 7 (breakfast call)—breakfast about 7½, superintend guard

83. On December 13, 1862, the Army of the Potomac suffered a stinging defeat at Frederickburg, Virginia, enduring over 12,000 casualties in a single day of failed assaults on Confederate positions.

mounting at 9; then give instructions to the officer of the day & to the Provost Sergeant who has charge of the guard tent prisoners & of all fatigue duty. Then sign requisitions & passes, answer questions, inspect the Surgeon's report & the consolidated morning report of the companies. This last is my newspaper & daily mail; I look forward to it eagerly; if a single recruit has come in I always want to see how it looks on paper. Hear complaints; do any scolding; look at work going on; a new well sweep, a new guard house, a building on the plantation to be fitted up as a hospital & so on. Have an eye to the company drills, which are going; & so till dinner $12\frac{1}{2}$. After every meal the Adjutant & I always stroll down on the river bank to look for steamers & see what time of tide it is—this is an unfailing sedative. From 2 till near 4, now & henceforward battalion drill & at $4\frac{1}{2}$ dress parade, $5\frac{1}{2}$ supper; then back to tent, light spitfire & easy writing business &c in the evening till 10 or so, when I go to bed. And so on every day, these three weeks now, without any feeling of fatigue or monotony. Sometimes I ride about the plantation on horseback, but have not been to Beaufort since the first day & don't really care to go. Gen. Saxton, the only person there whom I care to see, comes down here every day or two at dress Parade & I can make all needed arrangements.

As I grow more acquainted with the men, their individualities emerge more & more, & I find first their faces, then their characters, to be as distinct as those of whites to me. It is very interesting, the desire they show to do their duty & to improve; the more they think about it, the more the importance of the thing comes home to them; they say that we cannot stay & be their leaders always & that they must learn to depend on themselves, or else relapse to their former condition. Last Sunday the Chaplain read to them some extracts from the letters in the N.Y. papers about their own expeditions, and then some about the battles of the colored regiment in Kansas;[84] & they were thoroughly stirred up. They are very ready to be attached to their officers & in some companies there is quite a beautiful relation existing between them & I think on the whole the youngest officers seem to do best with them.

Today we hear that the Circassian is in, & a large mail will be up tonight. Reports of Burnside's[85] having taken Fredericksburg, after severe fighting. It is singular to get news in this dim gradual way—first a sort of nebular formation, then gradually condensing, after the steamboat comes up the river.

84. The 1st Kansas Colored Volunteers (later 79th U.S. Colored Troops) entered combat at Island Mount, Missouri, October 29, 1862.

85. Major General Ambrose Everett Burnside (1824–1881), commander of the Army of the Potomac, was disastrously defeated at Fredericksburg (see note 83 above).

Besides the superb bough of uneatable bitter oranges which decks my tent pole, I have today hung up a long bough of finger sponge, which I found by the river side. As winter advances, butterflies gradually disappear; one species lingers, three others have vanished. Mocking birds are abundant, but rarely sing; once or twice they have reminded me of the red thrush. All the negroes say it will be much colder, but the white officers do not think so because last winter was so unusually mild, with only one frost.

On the first of January,[86] we are to have ten oxen barbecued, think of that: or not properly barbecued, but roasted whole. Square tables are to be built all through the edge of the grove, adjoining the camp, with accomodations for about 1000, but we expect several times that number here. Molasses & tobacco are also to be provided largely. Touching the length of time required to do an ox, no two appear to agree—accounts vary from 2 hours to 24. We shall have enough to try the gradations of roasting, & suit all tastes from Miss Abbott's to mine. But fancy me proferring a spare-rib, rare done, to some elegant lady visitor—, for all the superintendantesses will visit us; including Dr Rogers hopes, his unfair little friend, Miss Charlotte Forten,[87] the quadroon teacher, who lives near Beaufort.

Whatever are we to do for spoons & forks & plates? each soldier has his own & is sternly held responsible for it by Army Regulations. But how provide for the multitude? Is it customary to help to tenderloin with one's fingers? I ask, none answer. Fortunately, Major Strong superintends not I. Great are the advantages of military discipline. For any thing disagreeable, detail a subordinate—the talismanic military words are *detail* and *draw*. For anything that Uncle Sam can give "draw" on the Quartermaster. For any thing that men can do, get a "detail" from the Adjutant. I can conceive of a man's remaining in the service till he loses the power to lift a finger for himself, or spend a dollar.

This is all I have time for.

86. On January 1, 1863, President Lincoln was expected to issue the Final Emancipation Proclamation, having issued the Preliminary Emancipation Proclamation on September 22, 1862, in which he gave the rebellious states 100 days (i.e., until January 1, 1863) to rescind their secession and undertake voluntary emancipation of their slaves.

87. Charlotte Forten (later Grimké) (1837–1914) was a graduate of the Higginson Grammar School in Salem, Massachusetts and later a teacher there; a water cure patient of Dr. Seth Rogers in Worcester, Massachusetts, she became his devoted friend. Forten came to teach the contraband slaves at Port Royal in October 1862 and remained until May 1864—essentially the same period as TWH. She published accounts of her experiences there in the *Liberator* and *Atlantic*, and kept a journal, several volumes of which detail her service on the Sea Islands. See *The Journals of Charlotte Forten Grimké*, ed. Brenda Stevenson (New York: Oxford University Press, 1988), 382–449.

## CHRISTMAS DAY DEC 25[88]

> We'll fight for liberty
> Till the Lord shall call us home
> We'll soon be free
> When de Lord shall call us home.

This is the hymn the slaves at Georgetown S.C. were whipped for singing, when President Lincoln was elected—so said a little drummer boy as he sat upon my tent's edge, last night; & he showed all his ivory as he said "Dey tought *de Lord* meant for say de Yankees."

Last night at dress parade, I had read Gen¹ Saxton's Proclamation for the first of January. I think they understood it, for there was cheering in all the company streets after parade was dismissed. Christmas is the great time of year for these people[89] & as we had no programme for today, how do you think I celebrated Christmas Eve? very simply. I omitted the mystic half past eight curfew which we call *taps*—it is a couvre feu[90] literally—& let them sit up & burn their fires & have their little prayer meetings as late as they desired—and all night I waked at intervals & heard them praying & chanting & clattering heels. It does not seem a very heinous Christmas dissipation.

Dec 26 Christmas Day passed with no greater excitement for the men than shooting at marks, which they took extremely well.

My *Excitement* was greater—on Thanksgiving Day certain Lieutenants had us (the Adjutant & me) to dine: so we were to repay the compliment. It was an exquisite day & dinner a little belated, so after gathering some rose buds we went down to bathe. The tide was full & smooth & it was lovely there & after bathing we lingered to watch the gambols of some of the soldiers who plunged in farther down stream & tried to convince themselves they liked it as well as we. Meanwhile a great sail boat from Beaufort glided down stream & made for our landing. Out sprang two fine looking officers, some of our frequent visitors, I thought—and another look revealed Dr Rogers and James—I could not have dreamed how happy I should be in seeing them & to have them for a Christmas present, just in time for our dinner too—it was amazing—so as my birthday was made

---

88. In Anna's copy of the journal, this December 25 entry is copied before the December 19 entry; I have relocated it to its proper chronological order.
89. It was common throughout the South to allow slaves at least a few days of leisure at Christmastime, and customarily a weeklong holiday from Christmas to New Year's; parties, dancing, and all kinds of revelry were the rule.
90. The English word "curfew" derives from the French *couvre feu*, which literally means "cover fire."

happy by a mail, this Christmas Day was made happy by two friends—& they looked so nice and so handsome that every body was delighted with them & the Dr's assistant & James' Lieutenants, were equally pleased at being thus superseded—They are profuse in their praises of every thing—& perhaps of our *table* above all—James rolls his eyes and says "Is this *war*"? as each new embodiment of oysters & Indian corn is placed before him—and last night, in James' own company "de shout" was got up in the most demonstrative style I have ever seen & both novices were wild with amazement.

Except that James brings me no letters, only messages, from my old regiment, I had nothing to ask for. They also bring the good news, today confirmed by a later arrival, that Gen$^l$ Saxton is not removed. It has not been really supposed that he was, because it was previously understood that Gen Seymour[91] was to relieve Gen. Brannan.

Two different sets of colors for us,[92] from different sources, have arrived, & are to be presented at New Year's.

I see that Frank Leslie's Magazine of Dec 20 has a highly imaginative picture of the swearing in of our first Company, & also of the skirmish in which they figured.[93]

## Camp Saxton. New Year's Eve.

My housekeeping at home is not perhaps on any very extravagant scale. Buying beefsteak, I usually go to the extent of two pounds. Yet when this morning the Quartermaster inquired how many cattle I wished to have killed for roasting I answered composedly "Ten, & keep three to be fatted." Fatted, quotha—Not one of the beasts has one ounce of superfluous flesh. Never was seen such lean kine. As they swing on vast spits, composed of young trees, the fire light glimmers through their ribs, lantern like. But they are cooking, nay are cooked. One at least is taken off to cool & will be replaced tomorrow to warm up. It was cooked three hours & well done, for I tasted it. It is so long since I tasted fresh beef that I may have forgotten;

91. Brigadier General Truman Seymour (1824–1891).

92. "Colors" are the two silken flags every regiment of infantry was required to have, the first being the flag of the United States (stars and stripes), with the name of the regiment embroidered in silver on the center stripe, the second a blue flag with the arms of the United States embroidered in silk at the center and the name of the regiment, on a scroll, beneath the eagle. Yellow fringe was around the edge of the latter. See *Regulations*, 436.

93. *Frank Leslie's Illustrated Newspaper* (December 20, 1862), 200. See the gallery.

but I fancied this to be successful. I tried to fancy that I liked the Homeric repast; certainly it was all far more agreeable than I expected. The doubt now is, whether I have made sufficient provision for my family; I should have roughly guessed that ten beeves would feed as many million people it has such a stupendous sound; but Gen. Saxton's estimate for tomorrow is 5,000. & we fear meat will run short, unless they prefer bone. One of the cattle is so small, I am hoping it may turn out veal.

For drink we aim at the simple luxury of molasses & water, a barrel per company. Liberal housekeepers may like to know that for a barrel of water is allowed three gallons of molasses, half a pound of ginger & a quart of vinegar, this last being a new ingredient for my untutored palate though the rest are amazed at my ignorance. Hard bread with more molasses, with subsequent tobacco, complete the repast destined to cheer but not inebriate.

On this last point, of inebriation, this is certainly a wonderful camp. For us it is absolutely omitted from the list of vices. I have never heard of a glass of liquor in the camp nor of any effort to keep it out. A total absence of the circulating medium might explain the abstinence, but not the non allusion to the subject. The craving for tobacco is hourly and constant, like that of a mother for her children; but I have never heard whiskey even wished for, save on Christmas Day, & then only with a hopeless far off sighing as you on that day might have visions of strawberries. I am amazed at this total omission of the most inconvenient of all camp-appetites.

I do not think there is great eagerness for tomorrow, as a day, for they know that those in this Department are nominally free already, and also they know that this freedom has yet to be established on any firm basis. Still I expect a large gathering of people & a cheerful time.

January 1. A happy new year to civilized people—mere white folks. Our festival has come & gone with perfect success, and our good Gen. Saxton has been altogether satisfied. Last night the great fires were kept smouldering in the pits & the beeves were cooked more or less, chiefly more; it does not really take more than 4 hours, during which time they are stretched on great stakes made of small trees, and turned by main force at intervals. Even the night before I carried a small piece to supper in my fingers, from the first cooked, & there is really nothing disagreeable about the looks of the thing, beyond the scale on which it is done.

About ten these people began collecting, steamboats from up & down river, sent by Gen. Saxton to convey them, & from that time forth the road was crowded with riders & walkers—chiefly black women with gay handkerchiefs on their heads & a sprinkling of men. Many white persons also, superintendents & teachers—two of the Wares[94] & Edward Hall, a young minister whom Dr Rogers admires. Edward Hooper[95] in Captain's uniform & Dr Rogers' pretty little Quadroon friend, Charlotte Forten, who is here as a teacher. But most of these superintendents do not interest me much & seem rather secondrate & inefficient.

My companies were marched to the neighborhood of the platform & collected sitting or standing, as they are at Sunday meeting; the band of the 8th Me regiment was here & they & the white ladies & dignitaries usurped the platform—the colored people from abroad filled up all the gaps, & a cordon of officers & cavalry visitors surrounded the circle. Overhead, the great live oak trees & their trailing moss & beyond, a glimpse of the blue river.

The services begun at $11\frac{1}{2}$—prayer by our chaplain—President's proclamation read by Dr W H Brisbane,[96] a thing infinitely appropriate, a South Carolinian addressing South Carolinians—he was reared on this very soil, and emancipated his own slaves here, years ago. Then the colors were presented to me by Rev Mr French,[97] who received them in N.Y. for us, unknown to us & had that fact very conspicuously engraved on the standard—a fact which saves the need of saying anything more about the Rev[d] Mr French. But whatever bad taste was left in the mouth by his remarks was quickly banished. There followed an incident so simple, so touching, so utterly unexpected & startling that I can scarcely believe it when I recall it, though it gave the key note to the whole day. The very moment Mr French had ceased speaking & just as I took & waved the flag, which now for the first time meant anything to these poor people, there suddenly arose, close beside the platform, a strong but rather cracked &

94. Harriet Ware, who came to Port Royal to teach school in April 1862, accompanying Edward Philbrick's wife Helen; her brother, Charles P. Ware, came soon thereafter as a superintendent.

95. Edward W. Hooper, a young Harvard lawyer, was among the original members of the Gideonites; he served as personal aide and secretary to Edward L. Pierce, then became a captain on the staff of Gen. Saxton when the Sea Island plantations were reorganized administratively under the scheme by which the proceeds from the Cotton Fund supported the Port Royal Experiment.

96. Dr. William Henry Brisbane, a native Sea Island planter and convert to abolitionism, he abandoned South Carolina in the 1830s, but returned later after his political awakening to buy back his slaves and convey them to freedom in the North; in 1862 he was appointed as federal tax commissioner in Beaufort, supervising the sale of confiscated Confederate plantations.

97. Rev. Mansfield French, former preacher, teacher, college president, and recently the editor (with his wife Austa) of *The Beauty of Holiness*, a small monthly evangelical journal.

elderly male voice, into which two women's voices immediately blended, singing as if by an impulse that can no more be quenched than the morning note of the song sparrow—the hymn

> "My country 'tis of thee
> Sweet land of Liberty

People looked at each other & then at the stage to see whence came this interuption, not down in the bills firmly & irrepressibly the quavering voices sang on, verse after verse; others around them joined; some on the platform sung, but I motioned them to silence. I never saw anything so electric; it made all other words cheap, it seemed the choked voice of a race, at last unloosed; nothing could be more wonderfully unconscious; art could not have dreamed of a tribute to the day of jubilee that should be so affecting; history will not believe it; & when I came to speak of it, after it was silent, tears were everywhere. If you could have heard how quaint & innocent it was! Old Tiff & his children[98] might have sung it; & close before me was a little slave boy, almost white, who seemed to belong to the party, & even he must join in. Just think of it; the first day they had ever had a country, the first flag they had ever seen which promised anything to their people,—& here while others stood in silence, waiting for my stupid words these simple souls burst out in their lay, as if they were squatting by their own hearths at home. When they stopped there was nothing to do for it but to speak, & I went on; but the life of the whole day was in those unknown people's song.

I spoke, receiving the flags & then gave them into the hands of two noble looking black men, as color guard, & they also spoke, very effectively, Prince Rivers & Robert Sutton.[99] The regiment sang Marching along & Gen. Saxton spoke in his own simple & manly way, & then Mrs F D Gage[100] spoke to the women very sensibly & a Judge somebody[101] from

98. Old Tiff, a gentle, gray-haired slave in Harriet Beecher Stowe's *Dred: A Tale of the Great Dismal Swamp* (Boston: Phillips, Sampson, 1856), took care of two small white children, Teddy and Fanny Peyton, after their mother's untimely death, raising them to be proud of their old Virginia ancestry; eventually he took them to Canada.

99. Corporal, later Sergeant, Prince Rivers, later a member of the South Carolina Constitutional Convention, and a member of the state legislature; Corporal, later Sergeant, Robert Sutton, later court-martialed for an alleged act of mutiny (which, however, TWH and his officers disbelieved), then pardoned and restored to his place in the regiment (see below, September 5, 1863).

100. Mrs. Francis Dana Barker Gage (1808–1884), abolitionist and missionary, who assisted General Saxton in recruiting black enlistments when the 1st South Carolina was initially authorized.

101. Judge Stickney, according to *Army Life* (p. 61).

Florida & then some gentlemen[102] sang an ode & the regiment the John Brown song & then they seemed to have a very gay time; most of the visitors dispersed before dress parade, though the band staid to enliven us. In the evening we had letters & so ended one of the most enthusiastic & happy gatherings I ever saw. The day perfect & nothing but success. Now I must stop—

P.S. I forgot to say that in the midst of the services it was announced that Gen. Fremont was appointed Commander in Chief & it was received with immense enthusiasm. It was shouted across by the pickets above—a way we often get news.[103]

Jan 7th I take great delight in writing down at leisure moments the songs & hymns of these people, often as graceful & beautiful as those of Scotland. Think of coming on such a flower as this, for instance.

> "I know moon rise, I know star rise,
> Lay dis body down
> I'll lie in de grave & stretch out my arms
> Lay dis body down."[104]

What ages of exhaustion these four words contain. Rivers of tears might be shed over them. All their music is in this plaintive strain, & all the jubilee is for another sphere. When I hear a new one in the evening, I run out of my tent. The other night I caught this, sung with the intensest zest & clapping of hands for an hour. One circle of men revolving steadily & shaking hands with an outer circle.

> "One more valiant soldier here
> One more valiant soldier here
> One more valiant soldier here
> To help me bear de cross—
> Hail, Mary, Hail
> Hail, Mary, Hail
> Hail, Mary, Hail
> To help me bear de cross."[105]

This is all of it, but they repeat endlessly, or improvise. I was just interrupted by a soldier who once before asked a loan of $1.75 to be married on.

---

102. According to Charlotte Forten, this was Mr. H. G. Judd, singing a hymn he had written. *The Journals of Charlotte Forten Grimké*, 430.

103. The news was false, as other picket news frequently was; TWH seems only slowly to have learned to discount such tidings.

104. "I Know Moon-Rise," *Army Life* (p. 199).

105. "Hail Mary," *Army Life* (p. 90).

Now he is almost at the point of it & says "Now Cunnel, I want to get me a *good lady*.["] I hope he will succeed.

## SCRAP OF ETHIOPEAN CONVERSATION

1. "Cato. whar's Plato?["]
2. Question by Colonel "Is that a good girl whom John Gardner is going to marry"? "O yes, Cunnel, John's gwine for marry Venus."
3. ["]I d'ont want my wife to be 'posed upon, for she's got heaps of character."
4. Prayer overheard on Christmas night (in the narrative style introduced by old Dr Pierce of Brookline) ["]O Lord, when I tink o' dis Kismas & las Kismas! Las Kismas he (I) dere in de Secesh & notin to eat but grits & *no salt in em*, Dis year in de Camp & *too much victual*"
5. New Years address of a Sergeant to me, with many bows. "I tink myself happy, dis New Year's Day, for salute my own Cunnel. Dis day las year I was servant to a Cunnel of Secesh; but now I hab de privilege for salute my own Cunnel."
6. Anxious husband to Dr Rogers about his wife, a laundress in camp. "Him sick, Sa, in he tent; him c'ant come to de surgeon, surgeon must go to he". And another who was just to be married, wished money to buy for *he* a pair of shoes, he being the bride.
7. James Rogers' first experience as officer of the Day, in going the rounds of the guard at night. Guard asks for countersign, James wishing to test him says, "*Bull Beef*." (The actual word being *Bay Point*, a neighboring promontory.) Sentinel. "Advance, friend Countersign correct." Next time, the blunder having been carefully exposed & corrected by the Captain, he approached the Sentinel in high hopes, who immediately on seeing him shouts triumphantly Bull Beef.

However they make the best sentinels I ever knew as a general rule; they take great pride in it & once assured of their duties & rights, will put a bayonet in the path of a mounted field officer, without hesitation, if he happens to enter the camp by a forbidden route. Several times they have stopped Gen Saxby (as they usually call him) to his great satisfaction. Indeed I allow them to be more strict about such matters than is necessary in a camp, as an educational influence on them. I labor constantly to impress on them that they do not obey officers because they are white, but because they are officers. & that the non commissioned officers must receive precisely as implicit obedience, & as we have very able non com's, they readily learn the lesson.

Before I came here the desertions & absences without leave were very numerous, but this is now stopped & I am gradually getting back the older absentees. Every day they come back now, & one of the best things that has happened to us was the half accidental shooting of a man who escaped from the guard house, by the men sent after him. He was wounded & afterwards died; & this very evening one of two others who escaped with him came & opened the flies of my tent, after being five days in the woods near by, almost without food. His clothes were torn, & he was nearly starved, poor foolish fellow & his punishment will be nearly nominal. Severe punishments would be wasted on these people, accustomed as they have been to violent passions in white men; but a mild inexorableness tells on them as on children & they dread the guard house very much. To sweep the camp all day instead of drilling which they like, & to lose the sociable fires & shouts in the evening, is very hard on them, besides soldierly pride of which they have a great deal.

The wounded man died, in the hospital, and the general expression was, "Him brought it on heself." Another man died of pneumonia the same day & we had the funerals as these people prefer in the evening. It was very impressive, a dense mist came up, with a moon behind it, & we had only glimmering lanterns as the procession wound along. The groups around the grave, the dark faces, the red garments, the straggling lights, the misty boughs, were weird & strange; they sang one of their own wild chants; two crickets sang also, one on either side, & did not cease their little monotone, even when the three volleys were fired above the graves. Just before the coffins were lowered, an old man whispered to me that I must have them altered, the heads must be to the west, to the setting sun, so they were turned, though they are in a place so veiled in woods that either rising or setting sun will find it hard to spy them.

We have now a good hospital, admirably arranged in a plantation building by Dr Rogers—a well of our own digging within the camp—full allowance of tents, all floored, a wooden cook house to every company, with sometimes a palmetto eating house beside—a large wooden guard house of our own building with a fire place five feet "in de clare" holding logs of that length, where the guard can dry themselves & sleep in bunks afterwards—also a great circular school tent, made of old tents, & thirty feet diameter. & were we sure how long we may stay here, we would already have had a regimental oven & bakery. This in six weeks since I have been here (all but the well & some tents) & we have increased from 490 to 740—beside 100 additional recruits now waiting at St. Augustine—& we have practised through all the main movements in battalion drill. The regiment is far more advanced than was the 51st when it went into its battle.

So yesterday being six weeks from my last visit to Beaufort I went in there on horseback, glanced at several camps & dined with Gen. Saxton. It seemed quite like a reentrance into the world, though I don't see that the world is very inviting. I liked Gen. Seymour, who was with Gen. Saxton & seemed very soldierly & simple, such a man as one would imagine to have been with Anderson in Fort Sumter.[106] He is somewhat conservative but thoroughly highminded & honest—very unlike what Brannan must be, though I have never seen Brannan. Gen Seymour has already prohibited the sale of whiskey to officers & though he rather disained the aid of blacks, will throw no mean obstacle in our way. Like Gen Saxton he seemed impulsive & like him, perhaps easily taken in. Perhaps soldiers are ill trained for judging character—but seeing what inferior men are around Saxton I can easily judge how Fremont has been ruined by his friends. Edward Hooper is by far the most prepossessing of the General's attachés, indeed the only one who can be called so. They are about to establish a paper[107] which I fear will do more harm than good as Mr French is at the bottom of it.

It is characteristic of this man that beside giving the impression every where North that he was our chaplain, he has allowed his name to figure in the inscription engraved on our flag staff in much larger letters than the regiment to which it is given. I saw him through, when I glanced at that inscription.

Nothing would induce me to remain in this Department in any but a strictly military position, so little attractive are the persons, & so many the small hostilities: but Gen. Saxton is absorbed in his great aims & hopes & too simple minded to believe in the possibility of such mixed motives as rule the minds of those around him. *A more stainless integrity I never met with.*

I observe this trait in him, which may be a result of military training, that he utterly rejects that system of divided responsibility to which Pres. Lincoln is so much inclined. If he adopts a system, he adopts it wholly, if he appoints a man, he trusts him wholly, & lets him manage his own department, almost unwatched. If at last the man is proved unworthy, he is dropped without mercy, but meanwhile much harm may have been done. I have absolutely my own way; he would displace my Lt. Col. or Major, if I asked it, & if I were like him, I would do it; but now I cannot make up my

106. Truman Seymour had served with Major Robert Anderson, commander of Fort Sumter, the Federal garrison at Charleston harbor, South Carolina, when Anderson surrendered it on April 14, 1861, after 34 hours of heavy bombardment, to Confederate Brigadier General P. G. T. Beauregard.

107. Possibly this is the Beaufort *Free South*, which, however, had been established several months previously.

mind to it; I find no fault with either of them, but that they will never be soldiers. Two officers he has dropped at my request, a Capt. for ill health, who is to be commissioned on condition of resigning, & a 1st Lieut. 6 ft 3 inches high, in whom I have no moral confidence & who is to have no commission but to return to his regiment. I[t] was very painful to me to have to humiliate this young man, he being utterly unprepared for it, but there was no alternative, & the removal of these two will be an immense gain to the regiment.

Jan. 8. This morning I went to Beaufort, (both times on this young man's affairs) & happened very fortunately on a review of the troops before Gen. Brannan. It is amazing how few regiments are *accurately* drilled, after the Mass[tts] standard, that is conform strictly to the official tactics of the army regulations.[108] The best regiments here, I find, are not as particular as I require my Captains to be; many points in the position of the guides & the officers, for instance, & the precise wording of orders, vary with every reg.t, while yet the "tactics" are perfectly explicit. This would even apply to the regular army because as Gen Saxton himself admits, West Point itself varies from the "tactics," which the best Mass[tts] regiments do not.

I wished my regiment there today, for amidst all the rattling & noise of artillery & galloping of cavalry, there was only one thing done in infantry drill which they cannot do & that rather a novel movement done by one regiment & thought a great affair, but which I can easily teach them. It is really just as easy to drill a regiment as a company, nay perhaps easier, because you have more time to think; but it is just as essential to be sharp & decisive, perfectly clear headed, & put life into the men. A regiment seems small when one learns how to handle it, very small, a mere handfull of men, & I have no doubt a brigade or a division would seem as small, so far as mere field movements go—but to handle it judiciously, that is another thing, & maybe a rare quality. So of governing it is as easy to govern a regiment as a school or factory & needs like qualities; system, promptness, patience, tact; moreover in a regiment one had all the admirable machinery of the army. Very ordinary men do it passably; the Col. whom I dined with today, out of three who invited me, is very inferior, a mere bar room politician from Maine.[109] Col. Bell[110] of New Hampshire 4th is a young

108. *Regulations for the Army of the United States, 1861* (New York: Harper & Brothers, [1861]).
109. Col. J. D. Rust (see March 24, 1863).
110. Col. Louis Bell, to whom TWH will later give his tent-frame and latch (only to rescind the gift shortly thereafter) when the 1st South Carolina is given marching orders and breaks up its camp (donating various materials to the newly-arrived New Hampshire

man, quite well educated & attractive; we are good friends, though he is not radical; Col. Hawley[111] of the 7th Ct. is very antislavery & his wife the most intelligent women I have seen, but they are going to Hilton Head; Col. Morgan of the 90th N.Y. just arrived here is very antislavery also & a noble man, just removed from Key West by Gen. Brannan for that; & another regiment sent from here, whose Col. had ordered the slaves back to their masters.

The report of a 6 ms armistice is rife here,[112] & deplored by all. I cannot believe it, but sometimes I feel very anxious about the ultimate fate of these poor people. After Hungary, one sees that the right may not triumph, & revolutions may go backward,[113] & the habit of inhumanity in regard to them seems so deeply impressed upon our people, that it is hard to believe in the possibility of anything better. I dare not yet hope that the promise of the President's Proclamation will be kept. For myself I am indifferent, for the enjoyment of my experience here has been its own hourly reward; but it would be terrible to see this regiment disbanded or defrauded.

A long screed of dry discussion this; I should not have put all my plums at the beginning.

A young men's society have invited me to *lecture* in Beaufort, which I certainly shall not do if I can help it.

Jan 12. 1863. Many things glide by, without time to narrate them. On Saturday we had a mail, with the President's 2d message, and on Sunday it was read to the regiment. The words themselves did not stir them so much, for they had been told so often they were free, especially on Jan. 1, & being unversed in politics did not know as well as we how great a thing it was.[114] But the Chaplain spoke very effectively to them, as he almost always does, & I talked to them a little afterwards & made them hold up their hands & pledge themselves to be faithful to those still in bondage which was quite impressive, beneath the great old branches of the live oaks. I heard afterwards that one man only refused to raise his hand, saying that his wife was

---

regiment), then has its orders countermanded on account of smallpox in the regiment (see below, February 18, 1864).

111. Col. J. R. Hawley, later Brigadier-General.

112. Later on (see April 6, 1863, below), TWH will acknowledge that this rumor and others like it often came from Confederate pickets across the river.

113. TWH heard Louis Kossuth, leader of the Magyar, or Hungarian, national revival, speak during a lecture tour in 1848 and admired him tremendously; Kossuth was to lead an independence movement that precipitated the severance of ties to the Habsburg empire, and to his becoming president of a Hungarian republic in 1848, but in 1849 Tsar Nicholas I of Russia aided Austria in a joint invasion of Hungary that quashed the revolution.

114. The phrase "this 2d. proclamation" is interlineated here in pencil.

out of slavery with him, & he did not care to fight. The others of his company were very indignant, and shoved him about a good deal, marching back to camp, calling "coward." It was all very hearty & will be a good thing to remind them of hereafter, which was one reason for doing it. With these simple natures it is a great thing to tie them to some definite fact; they never forget a marked occurrence, & are always willing to be held to a pledge.

It is this capacity of honor & fidelity that gives me such entire faith in them as soldiers. For instance they take the greatest pride in guard duty and make the very best sentinels I ever saw. No feeble or incompetent race could do this. We have had many amusing instances of this fidelity. One night recently it was very dark, an unusual thing here, & rained hard, so I put on my rubber clothing & went the rounds of the sentinels to teaze and test them. I can only say that I shall never dare to try it again & have advised my officers not to do it. Tis a wonder I escaped alive; such a charging of bayonets & clicking of gunlocks, & although they are not allowed to load their guns, yet some will do it, & in doing their duty as guards they would shoot a man without scruple. Sometimes I would test them by refusing to give any countersign, but offering them a piece of tobacco, to take which they would have to let me come nearer than the prescribed bayonet's distance; tobacco seems worth more than gold to them & it was touching to see the struggle in their minds but they always did their duty at last, & I never could persuade them. It hardly seemed right to try it—yet if they hv. a weak point, it is certainly more important for me to find it out.[115] It was so pitchy dark that not more than one or two knew me, even after I had talked with their next neighbor & it was easy to distinguish those who did. The others would be so surprised and frightened when they found it was de Cunnel, afraid they had done wrong. At last I came upon a man, near the guard house who stoutly insisted that my countersign was wrong. (It was Vicksburg in honor of a reported victory[116] & they found the word almost as hard as Vermont, which completely bothered them). No I could not pass in, "de countersign not correct," I tried persuasion, browbeating & tobacco all in vain; no, I could not pass. Finally I began to edge away & recede from the lines, meaning to come in somewhere else, where my pronunciation was better appreciated. Not a step could I stir. *Halt* shouted my gentleman, holding me at the point of the bayonet, & I wincing & halting.

115. The preceding sentence is interlineated in pencil, and so perhaps was added later, possibly by Anna as she corrected her copying, or else by TWH at a later date.

116. As in the case of the "rumored victory" at Fredericksburg (see December 20, 1863, above), this report was false; Major General Ulysses S. Grant had ordered his forces to retreat after failing to invade Vicksburg, Mississippi.

Several times did I try, with equal unsuccess, the rain pouring in torrents. It reminded me of that time in Chicopee where I spent an hour trying to get into a hotel after bed time & was finally stuck half way in the window with my heels in a temperature of $-10°$ outside. Call the Corporal of the guard, said I with majesty unwilling either to stay there all night or to yield my incog, "Corporal of de Guard" he shouted, while the neighboring sentinel at the prisoners tent was roaring with laughter. "Who am dat?" he called "am he a buckra" (white man) "Don't know whether he done be a buckra or not," replied my jailor "but I'se bound to keep him here till de corporal of de guard comes." When the corporal of the guard came & I revealed myself, the poor fellow seems transfixed with horror & appeared to expect immediate execution, but of course I praised him most highly & next day complimented him before the guard & recommended him to his Captain for promotion, & the whole affair was very good for them all. Hereafter if Satan himself should approach them in darkness and storm they will take him for "de Cunnel" in disguise & know they are expected to hold him at the point of the bayonet.

In many ways the childlike nature of this people shows itself. I have had occasion to virtually remove two officers—one for ill health, the other for moral objections & they were Capt & 1st Lt. of the same company. It was a company where there has been constant complaint of officers & justly—always neglected and ill used, compared with any other company in camp. I supplied the vacancies by two of the very best & most popular officers in the regiment—& yet the men sent a deputation to me in the evening, in a state of perfect wretchedness. "We's very grieved, this evening, Cunnel, all we company D boys, 'pears like we could'nt bear it, to lose de Cap'n & de Lieutenant all two togedder," All argument was wasted & I could only fall back on their personal confidence in me, & that they ought to believe that I should take care that they had good officers. Also I reminded them how James Rogers' company (which adjoins their's) had improved under his reign, which they at once admitted and promising that their new Captain should'nt be "*savage to we*", which was one thing they deprecated, I assuaged their woes; twenty four hours have passed & I suppose they have already discovered what a blessing will be the change for them, for it was the one company in the regiment which made me uneasy.

Another child like trait about them not so agreable, but which I think may throw some light on some things, is a sort of blunt insensibility to giving physical pain. They are cruel to animals, for instance in a way that reminds me of children pulling of flies legs, in a sort of pitiless untaught experimental way. Apart from this, I should not fear any wanton outrage in war from them; after all their wrongs I should far rather be in a captured city with them than with white troops—but for mere physical suffering I think they would have no fine sensibilities to conquer.

Yet their religious spirit grows more beautiful to me as I am longer with them—far more so than at first, when it seemed more a matter of phrase and habit. It certainly influences them on the side where pietists expect religion to be influential, on the feminine side; makes them patient & resigned. In the hospital, this is very marked; there is very little of the restless defiant habit of white invalids. Imbued from childhood with patience, drinking in through every pore that other-world trust which is the one spirit of their songs, they can bear every thing. All the white camps seem very rough & secular, after this, although their whole type of religious life is very foreign from mine. "A religious army," a "gospel army" is their favorite idea, & it interests me to see how they are unconsciously evangelizing our Chaplain who is more pliable than I, though he began from the same point. We have 100 recruits on their way from St Augustine, where the negroes are all Roman Catholics and it will be interesting to see how their type of character shows itself in that connexion.

Now it is time to go to bed, & I have just been out of doors, where the eternal stars shut down in concave protection over the yet glimmering camp, and Orion hangs above my tent door, giving to me the strength & assurance which these simple children get from their Moses & the prophets. Yet they do not ignore it, for the most fascinating of their many songs I have transcribed is this.

> I know moon rise, I know star rise
>   Lay dis body down;
> I walk in de moonlight, I walk in de starlight,
>   To lay dis body down;
> I'll walk in de grave yard, I'll walk thro' de grave yard
>   To lay dis body down;
> I'll lie in de grave & stretch out my arms,
>   Lay dis body down;
> I go to de judgement in de evening of de day
>   When I lay dis body down;
> And my soul & your soul will meet in de day
>   When I lay dis body down.

Jan. 13. I am comprehending what my beloved Sprague used to say that for every regiment enlisted there should be another enlisted to do its *writing*. I am now thoroughly immersed in muster rolls, pay rolls and monthly returns. This afternoon we are expecting the men not the officers to be paid off, & if we get through without cheating somebody it will be a miracle. My captains all have a general knowledge of the rolls, but are not good book keepers—& but for my adjutant who knows nothing of these rolls but is a first rate book-keeper I never could pull through.

Speaking of *Sprague* recalls the thrill with which I read, in Charlotte Hawes'[117] letter, of my old regiment formed into line of battle, in the early dawn, and my perfect cavalier riding along the line & telling them "in the uncertain future that was before them, to quit themselves like men"; How that man always throws an instructive touch of poetry into every word & act; & how strange it is that a wholesale flour store in Worcester should have reared the only man who ever enabled me to understand what Prince Rupert might have been.

In speaking of the military qualities of the blacks, I should add that the only point where I am disappointed is a point never raised by their critics—namely their physical condition. They look magnificently often, to my gymnasium trained eye, & I always like to see them bathing;[118] but there seems some pulmonary weakness in the whole tribe; pneumonia & pleurisy are their accustomed diseases; they are easily made sick & easily cured; childish organization again. There is not much serious illness in camp, but a great deal of coughing; the guard duty in these damp nights affects them decidedly more than white soldiers; & double quick they do not stand nearly so well, I fear. Probably this may be balanced by some superiority as regards summer exposures—but thus far my theory of the physical superiority of the civilized man is sustained not weakened by observing them.[119] But as to general availability for military drill & duty, it is merely a question whether they are equal or superior to the whites.

Of one thing I am sure that their best qualities will be wasted by merely keeping them for garrison duty. For *partizan* warfare they are admirably fit-

117. Charlotte Hawes was a young writer TWH had known in Worcester, Massachusetts, whom he encouraged and would introduce to the *Atlantic Monthly*; among her other contributions was one called "Invalidism," *Atlantic Monthly* 18 (November 1866), 599–605.

118. The phrase "such splendid muscular development" is interlineated here in pencil.

119. "The traditional glory of the savage body is yielding before medical statistics: it is becoming evident that the average barbarian, observed from the cradle to the grave, does not know enough and is not rich enough to keep his body in its highest condition, but, on the contrary, is small and sickly and short-lived and weak, compared with the man of civilization. The great athletes of the world have been civilized; the long-lived men have been civilized; the powerful armies have been civilized; and the average of life, health, size, and strength is highest to-day among those races where knowledge and wealth and comfort are most widely spread." Thomas Wentworth Higginson, "Barbarism and Civilization," *Atlantic Monthly* 7 (January 1861), 53.

ted, like adventure, have a great deal of dash and abundant resources. This I have well tested in expeditions which I have had to send to arrest deserters, before I broke up the practice which I have now succeeded in doing. (Before I came here, they came & went very much as they pleased, the officers say, but now they are quite punctual.) For instance I sent one of my best Lieutenants & my best (black) Sergeant, to search for certain deserters at a certain plantation. They divided the houses, each having a squad of men. You should understand that on plantations the negro huts are usually in a row, often arranged at an angle thus,[120] either for better circulation of air, or so that the eye can observe them better. The two squads divided the houses. Before the lieutenant reached his houses, every man within had taken to the woods. The sergeant's mode of operation was described by a corporal from a white regiment who was accidentally sitting in one of the houses. He said that nothing was heard until suddenly a red leg appeared in the door way & a voice said *Rally*. Going to the door he found a guard round every house, & not a person was allowed to leave till the houses had been searched & the three deserters found. This is Serg't Prince Rivers some of whose daily reports I have sent home—a splendid figure of a man, formerly an aristocratic coachman in Beaufort, who once drove Beauregard in his carriage from this plantation to Hilton Head. He was in the Hunter regiment & is an extraordinary man: one who makes Toussaint[121] entirely intelligible. He is the color bearer whose speech on N.Y. day is reported in the paper I send with this.

CAMP SAXTON. JAN. 19.'63

> "And first, sitting proud as a King on his throne,
> At the head of them all rode Sir Richard Tyrone."

I do not think I ever had quite so proud a day—You know James Lowell[122] says nothing is so good as Turtle Soup except mock turtle, & perhaps nothing is so stirring as real war except make believe war. Today, for the first time I marched my whole regiment through Beaufort & back. They did march splendidly, as all admit. The dear 51st did not compare with them. Margaret's prediction was verified, "w'ont Uncle Wentworth be in

120. TWH's sketch (as copied by Anna) is reproduced in the gallery.
121. François Dominique Toussaint L'Ouverture (1743?–1803), Haitian revolutionary who led a force that expelled British and Spanish colonial powers from the island in 1798.
122. James Russell Lowell, boyhood friend of TWH's older brother Thacher, later TWH's friend and literary associate as editor of the *Atlantic Monthly*, poet and critic.

bliss—a thousand men, every one of them as black as a coal.["] To look back on twenty broad double ranks of men, (for we marched by platoons) every polished musket with a black face at the side of it, every face steady to the front, marching on into the future; it was magnificent, and when we returned, marching by the flank, (that is in fours,) with guns at "support arms," & each man covering his file leader, (the prettiest way of marching in the world) the effect was as fine. I had cautioned them before we left, not to be staring about but to look straight before them, & with their accustomed fidelity they did it. One of them said, since, "I didn't see anything in Beaufort—every step *was worth half a dollar*," & they all stepped as if it were so. It was just the way my old company used to do in Worcester—only think of the difference—what character & culture did there—here the evoked self-reliance of a race does with drill & personal magnetism of course added in both cases. And whereas there, as rival Captains indignantly averred, we ["]had the whole town to blow for us," this was marching through throngs of prejudiced critics, officers & privates, who had all drilled as many months as we had weeks, & who were absolutely compelled to admit how admirably the regiment appeared. Dr Rogers & others rode about among officers who came jeering & contemptuous, & had to say at last "they do splendidly," one Captain in the N.H. 4th, the best drilled regiment here, & he bitterly pro slavery said in the hearing of our Lt Colonel, to a circle of officers, "There is nothing in this Department that can excel them." And indeed one of our recruits, who did not march with the regiment, watching the astonishment of some white soldiers, said, "De buckra soldiers look like a man *who done steal a sheep*"! i.e. I suppose sheepish.

You who have read this journal will acquit me, in previous sheets, of any careless or sweeping boasts of this regiment; but I will now speak freely & say, that if I could have one half the time for drill that many regiments now in the service have had, there is not one with which I would be afraid to drill. I know what I mean in saying this, for I know precisely what is to be accomplished, & what material I have to work with. It is all as simple as the multiplication table, & it is just as easy to drill soldiers as it is to teach arithmetic, if one has the requisite material & begins at the right end. And when I see what the officers of our army are, I count it a very slight thing to offer to beat them at their own weapons. To make war & win battles is a very different thing & you will not easily catch me in any boasting *there*. But if they can be won at all, these are the troops with which to win them.

I send you an article from the London Spectator, which is so wise & discriminating, so admirably true to our experience, that it seems as if written by one of us here. There never has been in any American paper, a prediction in regard to negro troops so wise & profound.

CAMP SAXTON. JAN. 19. '63

My men formed line at 1 & left camp about 1¼, marching the 3 sandy miles to the entrance of Beaufort at "route step,"[123] that is without music & left free to talk, laugh & sing. And sing they did, first the imported "John Brown song" & "Marching Along," & then their own peculiar songs, some of which were admirable marching songs & seemed to lift their feet directly along, as

> "All ye children go in de wilderness, go in de wilderness,
> All ye children go in de wilderness
> To wait upon de Lord."

and

> "We have some valiant soldiers here
> To help me bear de cross."

They were in the highest spirits all the way.

At this end of the city we met the band of the 8th Maine reg't, which has always been obliging to us, & had agreed to march with us & of course this at once charmed these musical creatures by its power, second rate band though it be, "When dat band begin for play in front of us" said since my splendid color bearer Prince Rivers, ex-coachman to Beauregard, "Good Heaven, *I left dis world altogether.*"

Then we marched through Beaufort & back as I have told you, and then to the parade ground where we drilled an hour, forming squares & reducing them[124] & doing other things which look hard on paper & are perfectly easy in fact—& we were to have had a review before the General, only he was called to Ladies Island[125] & couldn't get back in time, so he did not even see us at all. Then we marched back singing as before, & got to camp about half past five. Now it is ten o'clock & the whole camp is wrapped in the profoundest repose, in which I must share.

123. "Route step" is given in Casey, *Infantry Tactics,* as a pace of roughly 110 steps per minute, in which, however, the soldiers are not required to march in cadence, with the same foot, or in silence, and may carry their arms at will—e.g., slung on their backs (1:163–64).

124. Forming squares is a maneuver undertaken by infantry to defend against cavalry attack; it involves the wings of a platoon falling back, in a line, to form a right angle at either end with the main body of the platoon, then uniting with another platoon that has done the same, the two "bracket" formations now uniting to form a square. Reducing squares means returning from this square disposition of troops to the original line formation. See Casey, *Infantry Tactics,* 3:147–55.

125. Ladies Island is a smaller island, east of Port Royal Island, just across the Brick Yard Creek from Beaufort.

## CAMP SAXTON. JAN. 21.

Today brought a visit from Gen Hunter & his staff, on Gen Saxton's invitation; I thought it possible they might come to our Dress Parade at 4, but they came during Battalion Drill—so we were caught in our old clothes, literally. It was the first time we ever underwent a regular review, & I suppose we did pretty well—but of course it seemed to me they never did so ill before: just as I always thought that parties at one's own house seemed dull, even though every body expressed satisfaction, because one is so much more sensitive to small things. After performing various manoeuvres I formed square & faced inwards, & brought Gen. Hunter inside to make a little speech to the men which he did without ease or fluency but with great heartiness. He told them his only regret was that there were not 50,000 of them, & Gen. Saxton afterwards stated that 50,000 muskets were on their way for colored troops. They cheered him lustily & he seemed pleased & complimented the regiment, though its appearance was not at all equal to that at Beaufort last week. Two such perfect successes could hardly come together.

I was rather disappointed in Gen. Hunter's appearance, he seems like a kindly elderly gentleman in uniform, but nothing would indicate that marked ability shown in his original proclamation & his subsequent letter to the Secretary of War.[126] There is not Gen. Saxton's air of concentrated purpose—yet I can fancy him to be an abstract meditative thinker & they say he is. With him were divers young Lieutenants of the average aid-calibre, & two correspondents of Tribune & Times who seemed very friendly, but may nevertheless give very unfriendly notices, but what care we?

> "What care I how black I be
> "Forty pounds will marry me,"
>
> quoth Mother Goose.

and forty pounds of ammunition will establish our reputation or mar it, according as we happen to succeed or fail. Military fame is the poorest of all fames, because it depends upon the moment's turn of events, & they depend on a thousand things over which one has no control. Napoleon ought to have won at Waterloo,[127] by all calculation, but who cares?

126. Edwin McMasters Stanton (1814–1869).

127. Napoleon Bonaparte returned from Elba to rally his former soldiers and attempt to return to power in March 1815; the armies of various allied European powers defeated him soundly at Waterloo on June 15, and he was again sent into exile, this time on St. Helena.

Do you know that Gen Hunter has not yet visited Beaufort at all, but came from Hilton Head[128] solely to see us. I shall not be surprised if some outcry from the white regiments follows this. He promises us all we want, pay when we can get it, Springfield muskets and blue pantaloons. I am to send a requisition to Hilton Head for them at once.

All now betokens movement—iron clads at Hilton Head & 17 vessels with troops said to be waiting outside. Apparently an attack on Charleston. We may not have a hand in it perhaps—but meanwhile I am going on a trip along shore to pick up recruits & lumber. The Lt. Col. & Major have had all that fun before—now I am going to take my turn. I am to have under my command a large steamer the Ben Deford, & a small gun boat, to protect the former, in case we venture near any dangerous places. All this you will see in print, very likely, as it is all surmized in Beaufort, only they don't know where we are going, up shore or down. I have implored Gen. Saxton to be as mum as I am, & not a soul in this regiment has dared to ask me a word about it—but I have no aids, fortunately. I d'ont even say as much as Banks that I'm going South; but if you d'ont hear from me for ten days you may infer that I am deep in pine lumbers, or picking up Ethiopians with their little bundles on the banks of rivers.

Speaking of bundles, the long lost coat has this day appeared in a neat box & nothing to explain the delay. As the Dr's (let out) has been adorning me for a week, it was rather embarassing, but I at once politely refunded his & took my own, which is about a facsimile & one of Theo's[129] most perfect fits.

Being so near Georgia, I have thought it best to be provided with the summer costume attributed to Georgians—a shirt collar & a pair of spurs, & have accordingly purchased both those articles.

Enough for the present, I shall write again before I go lumbering.

CAMP SAXTON FEB 4th

It is not easy to begin journalizing again, after the stirring life of the last fortnight—which was very much like a chapter of Amyas Leigh,[130] but

128. Hilton Head Island, a large island south of Port Royal Island, at the entrance to the Broad River.

129. Theophilus Brown, a tailor; neighbor of TWH in Worcester, Massachusetts.

130. Charles Kingsley, *Westward ho! or, The Voyages and Adventures of Sir Amyas Leigh, Knight, of Burrough, in the County of Devon, in the Reign of Her Most Glorious Majesty Queen Elizabeth. Rendered into Modern English by Charles Kingsley* (1855; New York: Macmillan, 1900). Dedicated to Rajah Brooke (to whom TWH refers in his December 10, 1862, letter to his mother), this romance of chivalric adventure in the sixteenth century features, among

not much nearer to camp life than home life. It seems a little strange at first to be the undisputed master of 3 steamboats, one of them the largest I ever was on board of—but I had previously been part owner in several punts, wherries &c & found that the imagination could easily expand to a Great Eastern & all her crew if necessary,—so I governed my fleet with a mind calm & serene, & selected my rivers as coolly as if balancing between beef & mutton at dinner. I always thought a pirate's life must be fascinating, & so it is; & when I landed at Fernandina between my forays, I fancied Col. Hawley, with his placid Connecticut regiment, regarded me a little as the magistrates of the Orkneys did Cleveland.[131]

When you set (empty) houses on fire, do _you_ kindle on the windward or leeward side? there are advantages in each—& oh, how beautifully they blaze. Nothing benefits the manners like piracy, you should have seen the elegant courtesy with which I informed the three old crones who garrison St Mary's[132] for the secesh, (better than a regiment could do) that I should begin burning in the house _next_ to theirs, so that they, being women, should'nt suffer. Dr Rogers hoped their house would catch, but it didn't of course, the wind being the other way—but Dr Rogers was very much excited. You see the trouble is, at St Mary's, when you approach, the women come out & wave their white handkerchiefs & their long arms, then you land & the old crones tell you that no rebels ever come into the town, & that they are devotedly loyal, and show you a painting of Gen. Washington— & as soon as you leave the wharf the rebels fire into you; this has happened repeatedly, & in such cases it is one's duty to burn the town & we ought to have taken the old ladies to Fernandina & burned their house too, but I was too softhearted. All the other houses were empty but theirs is crammed with furniture from garret to cellar. They were so grateful to me that some of the soldiers declare that one of them wanted to kiss me—but this is scandal.

Nothing could be neater than our trip to Woodstock[133] 40 miles up the river—we left Fort Clinch at the mouth, after dark, & after grounding 8 times in the narrow channel, dropped anchor before Woodstock an hour before daybreak. I sent troops on shore with the Major,—boat after boat

---

other stirring scenes, one in which Amyas shouts, "Freedom to the slaves! death to the masters!" and proceeds to unshackle the enslaved oarsmen who man the Spanish enemy's ship (p. 363).

131. The Orkney Islands, off the northeast coast of Scotland, became part of Scotland in 1472.

132. A ruined town on the Georgia side of the St. Mary's River, just above Fernandina, Florida.

133. Woodstock, Georgia.

disappeared into the darkness & silence. I walked the deck an hour listening in vain for musket shots, & then going on shore myself after day light, found a line of red legs round every house in the village. We took a flock of sheep & lots of things useful for the army, 7 prisoners, a cannon & a flag; but passed by house after house stored with costly furniture from down river; pianos were a drug. We left fifty thousand dollars worth of lumber, such as cannot be bought for money now—Southern pine. I did not injure anything except the feelings of the inhabitants, who did chafe at the complexion of my guards—blackguards—though the men behaved admirably—even one who threatened to throw an old termagant into the river took care to add the epithet "Madam"—you would all laugh for 10 years if you could hear some of the descriptions the men give around the camp fires of their conversations with these women.

I took all the men we found in Woodstock prisoners, meaning them for hostages in case we got into any serious trouble on the river & then meaning to put all but one a shore farther down, but their friends attacked us so vehemently, there was no chance for chivalry. I felt ashamed of them, to keep them, they were such forlorn specimens, Falstaff's ragged regiment,[134] though the men say they are a fair type of the whole. I tried to make Col. Hawley at Fernandina take them off my hands, & offered to get his wife another piano, if he would, but the 7th Ct. have their full piano rations already & the bribe was vain. Even mutton didn't move him, so I brought them to Beaufort & the men were delighted. They said "Spose we leave dem dar secesh at Fernandina, Gen. Saxby w'ont see them." As if they were playthings. Only one of them was an upper crust secesh—him I took out of bed, with the most distinguished courtesy, he being a slight invalid, first having Dr Rogers feel his pulse & inspect his health with his most delicate & sympathetic manner on. "Allow me sir to examine your lungs"—then ausculating him as tenderly as if he were a dying saint—I sitting by, with as Cromwellian[135] an expression on my countenance as its natural benignity admits, and a stately daughter, too angry to sit down, standing with averted head in the background.

Still more stately was Mrs Alberti the widowed lady of the house & proprietor of the whole wealth of the premises. You should have seen her come out to meet me on the steps, as composedly as Goethe's Duchess met

134. TWH is likely thinking of Sir John Falstaff and the men levied to fight for King Henry IV (Ralph Mouldy, Simon Shadow, Thomas Wart, Francis Feeble and Peter Bullcalf) in William Shakespeare, *2 Henry IV*, III.ii.

135. Oliver Cromwell, English religious, political, and military figure, proverbially stern of mien, led the Parliamentary victory in the English Civil War, and called for the execution of Charles I.

Napoleon.[136] "To what am I indebted for the honor of this visit, Sir"? But our intercourse rose into something more than frankness when we parted—after I had just discovered the slave jail with its abominations & brought away its stocks & shackles. She & her husband, (born in Philadelphia & N.Y.) had "devoted themselves for years to training & elevating these poor people". (N.B. The late Alberti left at his death a slave chained to this floor, whom the widow unpadlocked & sold soon after.)

Mrs Alberti also owned my kingly corporal Robert Sutton & I took the liberty to introduce him "Ah" said she, after some reflection, "*We* called him *Bob*." Oh dear! it was all very dreamlike & funny beyond description.

Would you believe that during one of the pauses of our cavalry fight, in the midnight moonlit woods, there came wailing through the woods the most cracked of female voices, calling back some stray individual who had run out to join our assailants "*John, John, are you going to leave me, John*—are you going to let me & *the children be killed, John*.["] I suppose the poor thing's fears of gunpowder were genuine & serious, but it was such a wailing squeak, & so infinitely ludicrous that I could see my men showing all their white teeth with laughter, in the midst of the row. She & the children were so profoundly safe & John's risk so entirely for himself that the preposterousness was feminine & sublime.

It was easy to see how little it costs to be courageous in battle. There are a thousand things that require far more daring; the reason being that the danger does not come home so vividly to the senses, in battle; there is the noise & the smoke, & then besides, no matter how loud the bullets may whiz, so long as you are not hit, they don't mean *you*, & after they do mean you, it's too late to be frightened. To a person afraid of lightening, for instance, a severe storm is far more terrifying than a battle, because you sit *silent* waiting for the flash & wondering if the next will strike you—& you have not the excitement of flashing back again.

Our danger in such expeditions is not nearly so great as one would think, as we have cannon & the rebels have not, & they run away from them. But I think they would run away from our men, even without the

136. During the Battle of Jena in October 1806, while French troops were sacking the palace, "the Duchess Luise manifested that dauntless courage which has never been forgotten, and which produced a profound impression on Napoleon, as he entered Weimar, surrounded by all the terrors of conquest, and was received at the top of the stairs by her,—calm, dignified, unmoved. *Voilà une femme à laquelle même nos deux cent canons n'ont pu faire peur!* he said to Rapp." George Henry Lewes, *The Life and Works of Goethe: With Sketches of His Age and Contemporaries, from Published and Unpublished Sources*, 2 vols. (Boston: Ticknor and Fields, 1856), 2:358–59.

cannon—I should think they would—I should. They are perfectly formidable. That night in the woods they wanted to plunge off in pursuit of the enemy, which as it afterwards appeared, they might have done with safety; & coming down the river they were furious at being kept down below, "What for de Cunnel say *cease firing*, & de secesh blazing away *at de rate of ten dollars a day*"! They "supposed de Cunnel knowed best, but it was mighty mean to keep them shut down in de hold, when dey might be *shooting in de clar field*." They desired intensely to get on shore & fight it out.

My Major is a man of immense pluck and exceedingly valuable. He was once on the Police in N.Y. & acquired that willingness to front danger *alone* that a police man acquires.

You will see my official report[137] & I cannot possibly write much more. I did not there speak of the endurance of these men under wounds. After the battle at Township,[138] one of the men with two wounds in the shoulder, brought 2 guns back to the shore, where we bivouacked all night. Robert Sutton with three bullet wounds, stood guard all night on the shore, & did not report to Dr. Rogers till next day, another, with 3 buckshot in his neck, never reported to the Surgeon at all, for fear of being kept from service next day, but got a comrade to dig out the buckshot. Still another, who seemed dying, from a wound through the lungs, said nothing as they carried him to the vessel except to ask 3 times if "de Cunnel was safe." He is now getting well, as are all, they were only flesh wounds.

Dr Rogers is a treasure, & enjoyed the trip immensely as did James, though I kept him rather out of all dangerous parts of it, he complains. *I* never shall have a chance to risk myself much, they are all lecturing me all the time, & I have got quite used to putting my head in safe corners. I wore my iron plated vest too, which is very light & comfortable.

I dare say this expedition may have to last us some time, as Gen Hunter is bent on the advance towards Charleston or Savannah, & we are more likely to be left here for garrison duty. Gen Saxton is not anxious to make us prominent in the Charleston movement.

Dr Rogers & I landed at day break in Beaufort I carrying my report in one hand & the shackles from the slave jail in the other. As Dr Rogers said

137. "Report of Col. T. W. Higginson, First South Carolina Infantry (Union)," February 1, 1863, *The War of the Rebellion: A Compilation of the Official Records of the Union and Confederate Armies*, Series 1, Vol. XIV (Washington: Government Printing Office, 1885), 195–98.

138. Township Landing, about 15 miles up the St. Mary's River, where TWH had gone on a trial trip, and with about a hundred men made a midnight foray into the woods in the direction of a Confederate camp; his men came under attack from a detachment of enemy cavalry, and one soldier, Private William Parsons, was killed next to TWH.

a message from heaven & one from hell. I walked into the Gen.l's bed room & left him reading the report.

## COPY OF A LETTER

I received by one of our Fernandina men from his wife: showing the superior intelligence among the Florida negroes. I have several almost as well expressed.

FERNANDINA, FEB 18

My dear Husband

This Hour I sit me down to Write you in a Little World of sweet sounds. The Choir In The Chapel near Here are Chanting at the organ and their Morning Hymn across the street are sounding and The Dear Little birds are forming thair voices in Tones sweet and pure as angels whispers. but My Dear all the songs of the birds sounds sweet In My Ear but a sweeter song than that I now Hear and That is the song of a administring angel has come and borne My Dear Little babe to join in tones with Them sweet and pure as angels whispers. My Babe only Live one day. It was a Little Girl Her name is Alice Gurtrude Steward. I am now sick in bed and have got nothing to live on the Rashion that thay give for six days I can Make it last but 2 days Thay don't send me any wood They send the others wood and I cant get any I dont get any light at all you must see so that as soon as possible I am in want of something to eat I have nothing more to say to you but give my Regards to all the friends of the family send their love to you No more at pressant

Emma Steward

FEB. 13. 1863.

I have just read this letter to Dr Rogers whose first remark was—"and yet you thought me crazy for reading to these people Emerson's emancipation poem,[139] last Sunday."

Indeed I declare that we have some orators in camp whose choice of language has as much natural poetry as this. The wife may not have writ-

139. Ralph Waldo Emerson, "Boston Hymn," *Atlantic Monthly* 11 (February 1863), 227–28. Read at the Boston Music Hall, January 1, 1863, in a celebration of the Emancipation Proclamation, the poem presents the voice of an angry God declaring, "I break your bonds and masterships, / And I unchain the slave: / Free be his heart and hand henceforth, / As wind and wandering wave" (p. 228).

ten the letter herself, though I think she did—at any rate somebody wrote it & that somebody was black or at least not Anglo Saxon.

I know persons at Fernandina to whom I can write & see that she is made comfortable, till her husband gets his pay which will be very soon as we are all to be paid off in a week or two.

Since the Expedition I have not written much as I have been unusually busy: the sick list has been much larger, partly from the excitements of the expedition & partly because these are the sickly months of the year for the negroes, (but not for whites)—

Their prevalent disease, pneumonia or pleurisy, affects them especially now; the night chills injure them. As I have always said they have no *toughness*; but childlike constitutions & the way to treat them is to take them off duty *at once* & apply remedies & then they get well—24 hours delay risks every thing. Dr Rogers is admirable, but I have to mount guard over him to keep him from working too hard. He is delicate as you know.

We have had 4 inexpressibly beautiful days like May; the frogs & tree toads sing at night, the mocking birds add new notes every day & I have seen robins. All over the lawn between the plantation house & the river are starting up green lines of vegetation in sinuous figures, where borders of polyanthus or some such flower are planted. Better than birds or flowers, the Adjutant thinks, Miss Hattie A Somerby has arrived. On her permit to land the item of "occupation" is thus filled out "To be married to Lieut. Dewhurst, Adjutant of 1st Reg. S.C.V." She can stand such things without exaggerated blushes, a sensible fine-looking young woman of 29, who knew just what she was about in coming to live in camp, and makes no nonsense about it. The Adjutant went down to Hilton Head to meet her & brought her up in the boat & she had supper with Wm & Hetty, who being still lovers themselves, appreciate that condition in others.

Then Mrs Hawkes, the Dr's wife,[140] took the wandering, seasick, undaunted damsel to her arms & tent, where she still abides—of course the Adjutant was immediately a little sick & she takes care of him. She is rather refreshing, as naive & frank as Aggie,[141] of whom she often reminds me, & takes the whole affair precisely as that damsel would—imperturbably & with considerable enjoyment. If her second trunk comes tomorrow the wedding will be on Sunday—regiment in hollow square. Band of 8th Maine & all. General Saxton & all his female train of teachers are expected to appear & the happy adjutant yearns for a photographer & Frank

140. Esther Hawkes, wife of Dr. J. Milton Hawkes, assistant surgeon, 1st South Carolina Volunteers.

141. Agnes Gordon Higginson, favorite niece of TWH (daughter of his brother Stephen).

Leslie. It is funny to see how one of the most simple & modest of men can hold his course without remorse when planning eclat for his nuptials. It is all to be a matter of high art.

Probably it will interest Gen Saxton, as a study for his own espousal—the happy damsel-elect having shut her school house & gone back to Philadelphia for her trousseau. She is a Miss Thompson,[142] she 18 he 36. She was here on horseback on New Year's Day quite young & that is all I noticed.

## Feb. 15.

Well, the Adjutant is fairly & thoroughly married. The bride yearned for privacy & a few friends at Beaufort; but the bridegroom planned it like a campaign & I found him replete with views on the minutest particulars. This morning was foggy & the lady's trunk was at the bottom of a vessel's hold at Hilton Head 10 miles way, no matter, at 4 P.M. the trunk was here & the day was clear. The band of the 8th Me Regt appeared at Dress Parade; the men looked neat & soldierly in their blue uniform (having got rid of the wretched red trousers, which they hated) & all was well. After the usual parade I formed square, & the band marched on to the bride and groom & Chaplain; they entered & then a number of ladies & gentlemen from Beaufort entered also. Miss Somerby wore a sensible brown silk dress, low necked and no ornament but a few flowers & looked sufficiently well; she is what would be called "fine-looking." The men were quiet & interested; it was a still sunny afternoon & all went well. The Army Regulations do not provide for regimental weddings; as Colonel I was first to congratulate the bride, but omitted embraces, as not being specified in the Tactics. Mrs Hawkes promptly supplied my place, & ere long the pair were marched off, without the band, I got the regiment into line and dismissed them. Mrs Lieutenant George Dewhurst, is it not an aristocratic name?

Since Genl Hunter came & Genl Brannan went, all the military flunkeys have conceived an[143] admiration for Gen. Saxton & wish to be brigaded under him; they also come out constantly to visit us. Little care we. No news yet from Montgomery; his camp is laid out beside ours, though it is yet uncertain whether ours is to be here indefinitely. In spite of the essential agreement of our two Generals, there are yet sundry cross currents of influence, as always, I suppose, in these army matters. Never

142. Matilda ("Tillie") Thompson, who came to Port Royal in summer 1862 to teach, along with her brother James Thompson, a superintendent. She would marry Gen. Saxton on March 11, 1863.

143. The copy-text reads "an an" here.

was a great army probably with so many accidental great men; my respect for them diminishes every day, as I see better what they might be.

I have secured an excellent new Lieutenant from the 1st Mass Cavalry, a Haverhill man, N. G. Parker.[144] I wanted a cavalry officer, as it may prove a great convenience; these men are such horsemen that we can extemporize a cavalry force whenever we can capture the horses. He says that the splendid Col Williams became a sot & could not sit on his horse in one battle, though he was a perfect soldier otherwise. He was tyrannical, though not rough; Major Higginson[145] rough & odd very blunt & independant he said; Major Curtis rougher still. Caspar Crowningshield beloved by all his men. This regiment, more than any other, has kept up the absurd Beacon Street system as to promotion; not a Sergeant has been made Lieutenant, up to this time, from the battalion stationed here. This man is extravagantly recommended by his Captain Rand,[146] whose orderly Sergeant he was.—I have bespoken two other Sergeants from my old company in the 51st, Stephen Greene & Henry Stayner, both invaluable acquisitions. As for James Rogers he has surpassed my expectations & is the best Captain in the Regt already.

Just now as I was sitting in the Adjutant's tent with the future Adjutentess, James put in his bright face. Do you want to hear about Gen Washington? and thrust in a boy of ten, coal black & fatter than any thing you can dream of, who, instigated by James, made his manners & began in recitative, "General Washington he one great General, he govern he people well" & so on for a few sentences out of some school book ending "Liberty is de birt-right of all mans and must never be give up," after which being questioned as to the origin, of the same he replied, "Mr Hyde's son, sa, teach we," then displayed ivory enough to set up three elephants, was abducted by James, appled, & sent out of camp. Mr Hyde superintended this plantation & his son taught "We."

Some of these men have splendid memories, one sergeant who cannot read, calls the roll from memory. One of our ablest sergeants, a carpenter, paid his master $365 dollars a year for his time for several years, think of it! He used to make $2.50 a day, erected buildings on contract, &c, he & 6 others built the town of Micanopy on contract. Henry McIntyre is his name, a light mulatto. He would never learn to read, because it exposes them to so much more suspicion & watching. Finally he had to leave, because he named a child Wm Lincoln & it created such suspicion.

144. Second Lieutenant Niles G. Parker.
145. Major Henry Lee Higginson, 1st Massachusetts Cavalry, son of TWH's first cousin George Higginson.
146. Captain Arnold A. Rand, 4th Massachusetts Cavalry.

Uncle Tom is prosaic to the stories which any dozen men here can tell. There is a pretty little laundress here, a soldier's wife, Fanny Wright, who had a baby shot in her arms, escaping from the main-land in a boat. There is a family of Millers, whose mother a grand old woman was here New Year's Day; she attempted to escape from near Savannah failed & while her husband was receiving 500 lashes, collected 22 of her children & grandchildren & tried again—hid them in a marsh till night, then found a flat boat which had been rejected by the rebels as unseaworthy, put them on board & came forty miles to our lines. One of my officers saw them when they came in. The old woman stood up tall & erect with children in her arms & as they touched the shore, said "My God, are we free"?

There is another family of Wilsons of which there are several representatives in this regiment. Three or four sons deliberated about escaping & finally selected the youngest to remain & take care of the old mother. The others with their sister and her children came in a "dug-out"—they were five men in the boat, & they were shot at by the rebel pickets & every man was wounded. A little girl of nine (who was here on New Years Day) said, when they fired on "Dont cry Mother, Jesus will help you," & she began to pray, with the shots flying about. Capt Trowbridge was on the naval vessel which took them up; the mother & child had been living 9 months in the woods & the child would not speak to any one. He asked the mother if she would not let him adopt the child & she said "I would do anything for *oonah* but that." (oonah is the plural for *you*, they sometimes use it.[)] This mother is almost white, her father was white & her grandfather Indian; she said that the negroes in their prayer meetings at Savannah prayed that the Yankees might take the city & that when Fort Pulaski was taken,[147] thousands of slaves got ready to come to us. Capt Trowbridge has since seen a Savannah paper in which the Mother & child were described & a reward offered.

Gen Saxton is now much more sanguine about the success of the advance on Charleston, a very intelligent fugitive has lately come in, who says there are no obstructions in the river & the Monitors can ascend. He says that in a public meeting he heard Beauregard say that the place was *indefensible* and the people hissed him. It is possible that the man may have made his news as favorable as he could, but it has evidently encouraged Gen. Saxton very much, who was not previously very hopeful about this expedition.

Since our own *expeditious* (as the men always call it) we have settled back

147. Fort Pulaski, Georgia, at the entrance to the Savannah River, surrendered on April 11, 1862, after intense bombardment from Union forces under the command of Capt. Quincy A. Gillmore.

into drill and camp life more completely than at first seemed possible—at first it appeared like a butterfly's contracting its wings again, to reenter the chrysalis. Nothing can ever exaggerate the fascination of war; I hardly hear the crack of a gun without recalling instantly the sharp shots that spilled down from the bluffs at us, along the St Mary's, or hear a sudden trampling of horsemen without remembering the moonlight & midnight when we were suddenly stopped by hearing it before us, at Township Landing. I never can write about those wakeful but dreamlike nights of moonlight it was all too good. My report to Gen Saxton merely skimmed a few drops of cream & left the substance of the draught. As for the courage[148] & all that, it is infinitely exaggerated—to stop furious runaway horses, to enter a burning house, to plunge in a boiling ocean, requires far more personal pluck than to have "dem dar bullets let loose after we" as my men describe it; the danger is so invisible, it is not nearly so hard to disregard it; I know what I say. Bomb shells are far worse, but we have only fired, not received them. Oh such superb & grotesque eloquence as I heard from some of our orators on the forward deck, as we came home after the "expeditious."

Old Adam Alston for instance, James Rogers' company cook "When I heard de bomb shell, a-screaming through de woods like de Judgement Day, I thought—if my head was took off tonight, dey couldn't put my soul in de torments, perceps (except) God was my enemy! And when de rifle bullets came whizzing across de deck I cried aloud "God help my congregation! Boys load & fire!" This I wrote down at the time.

The more I become attached to this people, the more my desire grows to be transferred to some locality more permanently defensible than this. I mean for them. Should any peace, short of conquest, be adopted, it will be almost impossible to defend for freedom this mere fringe of islands & all these people must flee or be slaves again, in that event. But Florida is infinitely more defensible and if that can be once reclaimed for freedom it could be held indefinitely; it cost the U. S three hundred millions, it is said, to subdue the Seminoles, & I am satisfied that these people, having once tasted freedom, could sustain themselves there indefinitely. Indeed the white loyalists of Florida say that black troops alone can regain the state & hold it forever. This conviction gives me great hopes for this people, even should the worst occur. But if Charleston be taken, then the rest of the state must fall & it would give a new turn to the war. Since my expedition however my hopes rest, far more exclusively than before, on the employment of negro troops.

148. The word "required" is interlineated here in pencil.

## Camp Saxton Feb. 20

We are all delighted at an act of tardy justice, by which Gen. Saxton is put in command of the forces (3 regiments beside this) at Beaufort. It has always been his right, save when Gen. Brannan was here, his senior; but heretofore he has always been regarded only as a civilian, in respect to his functions, by the military officers here, so that in Genl B's absence, Colonels have taken command, & defied Gen Saxton's authority. Now this is settled by Gen¹ Hunter & these Colonels themselves are glad, for it simplifies things & they have no longer to try to sit on two stools. It is an amusing coincidence that today we have been perfectly thronged with visitors & they have been even unusually complimentary. Dr Rogers had two Mass^tts Surgeons & said at tea they were enthusiastic about our battalion drill. James & I exchanged glances which said "My dear Doctor, what *can* a surgeon know about drill? It amuses me also to hear Colonels & Majors of freshwater regiments say guardedly "Your regiment does much better than I expected" when they know & I know & they know that I know that their regiments couldn't form square forward on the centre even if there were to be an Adjutants wedding in the middle.

Many good things today, Gen Saxton's taking command, two boat howitzers for the "John Adams," 1000 Austrian rifles for us, first jasmines brought in, a dandelion reported, & chocolates for supper.

All day we have heard dull thundering, shaking even glass in windows. It is the Monitors, bombarding a fort in the Ogeechee River,[149] 40 miles away.

At Hilton Head a few days ago, (my first visit there) I went with Gen Saxton to see Gen. Hunter; an easy amiable elderly gentleman with his vest unbuttoned, that is the way he impressed one—more like Pickering Dodge than any one else I now think of; but whatever he says he does, "and no man can hinder we" as my negroes say in their song. He has just arrested Brig. Gen. Stevenson of Mass. (son of J. T. S.) & is going to send him to Washington, for having said that he would rather our armies should be defeated than that they should succeed by aid of negroes. Gen. S. has begged most pathetically to be let off, they say, and perhaps will be freed from arrest. I sincerely hope not—such men need discipline.

Gen Saxton calls this regiment my "mamelukes,"[150] & I am sure that he

149. Fort McAllister, an earthwork fortification on the Ogeechee River south of Savannah, Georgia, was first bombarded on January 27, and periodically thereafter; it finally fell on December 13, 1864, when Sherman's March reached the sea.

150. A "mameluke" is a member of a former military caste, originally composed of Turkish slaves, that ruled in Egypt from the thirteenth to the sixteenth centuries, and continued to be powerful into the nineteenth century.

is a perfect Mohammedan in his fatalism on the subject of it; his faith is absolute that every thing which occurs in the whole affair is the very finger of God. He told me with triumph yesterday that Montgomery had said there was one man whom he especially wished for Lt. Col. & now that very man has written from the Army of the Potomac, unexpectedly to ask for the place. You have no idea how many applications he receives, & I too, for commissions—one man writes that he is sixty years old, as if that were an irresistible qualification for a Captain.

Today, a Mameluke came to consult me about his claim on a certain house "It was returned over," he said, turning over being a military transfer "to a man who kep a liberty stable for cavalry horses, but it was understood that I was to be de possessioner."

Feb. 23. Letters have come & some newspapers with my report & no very stirring news else. Montgomery has come too, tonight, with 125 men as the nucleus of the 2nd regiment. He reports a poor state of things at Key West.[151] If even under Gen Hunter there is so much semi-secession among officers of different regiments, what must it be under McClellan yet in almost every regiment there are anti-slavery officers also, & the same difference exists among privates.

My friends seem anxious about my exposing myself; but they may be assured that I am kept under a tight rein in that respect already; never was a man so teased & badgered as I was on this last trip. I do not need it, because though naturally enjoying danger as much as most men perhaps, I am not such a fool as not to see the value of my life to this regiment & through it to the whole movement of which it is the beginning & now that I have tested my men & they me, I certainly am not going to curtail my work with them by any needless prominence. Usually I am not given to setting my heart on immediate results, but I should certainly dread even a wound were it ever so slight, if it obliged me to give up the reins but for a day. So I have every inducement to caution.

Spring advances, grass grows green, yellow and fragrant jasmines flaunt from tree tops in the woods, above white waxen beads of mistletoe, which I have never seen before. Birds multiply, snakes, frogs, things that James & I love; on other islands peas are two inches high; but it is a cold night nevertheless. The feeling I have this snowless winter is that while I wear thicker clothing than ever before in my life, there is some inner garment beneath them, which is thinner. The feeling is precisely correct, the inner garment being the skin, which here retains in winter its summer condition.

151. Key West, Florida, remained in Union hands through the war.

I am delighted to have Montgomery for though very likely his system of drill & discipline may be more lax & western than mine; still in actual service his experience will be invaluable. This is all I can say now

## ITEMS.

(Indignation checked by religious restraint.) "Ha-a-a, boy, spose I no be a Christian, I *cuss* you so"!

(Quartermaster's man threatened with chloroform for a surgical process) "O Quattermatter, Quattermatter! let me say goodbye to my wife & de chil'en. If de Doctor put me to sleep he never let me wake up."

(New recruits discussing the assistant Surgeon, Dr Hawks) "Who dat little buckra dey call de Sergeant"? (Surgeon) "He name Doctor Hawk" "I dunno whether he be Hawk or Buzzard, I know he secesh." (The only basis for this distrust was that he got our Hospital Steward, his brother-in-law, from the N.H. 4th regt, which our men think "de same one as Secesh," from its pro slavery reputation.)

## REFLECTIONS ON THE WAR.

Villard, Tribune correspondent, & Coffin, the "Carleton" correspondent of the "Journal"[152] were here yesterday. Both have seen all portions of our army, & Villard is familiar with foreign armies. Both say, our army is not an army, in the sense of an European army, but a mere collection of armed men. They want drill, discipline, subordination, and confidence in their leaders. Both attribute it in some degree, to democratic habits unfitting men for military subordination. I do not admit this, at all, but think the contrary, as I always did. I think the superior intelligence of our white men would secure the best army in the world in a cause which united them. It is *slavery*, not democracy, which has vitiated our army, like our politics. In every regiment here I find division among the officers about slavery. In a war against a foreign power they would be united.

Gen Saxton thinks (& many others,) that it is a great advantage in *this* regt, to have a distinction of race between officers & men—that it helps discipline &c. I do not think so, at all. The advantage lies in the more undivided enthusiasm of these men, & their local knowledge. For a campaign in Mass^tts I would prefer Mass^tts men. Between these men & me there is a

152. Henry Villard (1835–1900), formerly Washington correspondent of the New York *Herald*, joined the New York *Tribune* in 1862; Charles Coffin (1823–1896) was correspondent for the Boston *Journal*, using the pen name "Carleton."

social distinction, but I governed my Worcester company by precisely the same methods & with the same success. Other things being equal, I would rather command troops who were my neighbors and were men of education; the only reason I prefer these is because other things are *not* equal; viz personal enthusiasm & local knowledge.

Whether this is true of officers generally I don't know; & it may be that the test of a military organization is to give the maximum of support to an *average* officer; which can be done best possibly, by having the soldier socially inferior. Montgomery says "It requires a very strong man to bear close inspection—hence military rules interpose barriers between officers & men, for the good of both—nevertheless no one is fit to command, who needs to avail himself of these barriers for this purpose." To this I agree entirely. I found no more difficulty in combining familiarity with authority among my white company than in this regiment; & it was so with other officers who were fit for their place; & indeed I think that the elective system secured better officers & more willing obedience than in other non-elective regiments which I observed. I enjoyed being *under* Col Ward & Col Sprague, men whom I had not recognized in Worcester as my superiors except in military knowledge: & all the good line officers paid them equal deference—I am *sure* that democratic habits as such, promote subordination by basing it on intelligence, not on habitual subserviency. In this regiment the men most slavish are the poorest soldiers; those least slavish the best. Reminiscences of tyranny do not benefit any of them, except by the recoil.

Machines cannot make soldiers like mine. The very first object is to develop self respect. The Regulations say "all officers of whatever rank are required to observe respect towards guards"—& this is the principle relied on for making good guards. A guard obeys no orders save from the officers of the Guard & the Commanding officer. He may shoot his own Captain if he interferes with his duty as a guard. This educates self respect, & as each man is in turn on guard, each man learns it. I allow no man to stand with his cap off, talking to me out of doors; I explain that slaves do that—*soldiers* give a military salute, which the officer is as absolutely required to return as the soldier to offer. The better soldiers they become the more they are spoiled for slaves. I see that the latest rule proposed in the rebel Congress is to sell by auction all slaves taken in arms—but no rational man would buy them; they know too much.

This week all the troops at Beaufort were reviewed by Gen Hunter & Gen Saxton & in the afternoon they came down escorted by the Mass. cavalry to review this regiment. The men appeared admirably; the Generals were much pleased, & Major Somebody, sent direct from the War department to inspect this Dept, was much pleased also. Gen Hunter said they had improved so much since the last review—but the improvement was chiefly in the blue pantaloons & in having a half hours notice instead of being taken by surprise.

Gen Hunter did not review us, having done so before—but it was done by Gen. Saxton who was elegantly dressed & mounted & looked splendidly; we were all delighted to see him look as he ought to look.

Feb 28th As to insults or annoyance, I find that, as might be expected, it depends chiefly on the officers themselves whether they or their men are subject to it. Our Quartermaster who is obliged to mingle with the world, ask favors, incur collisions, bore with applications, compete with others, more than all the rest of us put together, told me today that there was only one person in the Dept who had ever treated him disagreably or made him remember that this was anything but a white regiment: on the other hand I have officers who with the best intentions cannot be sent on any official business but they return boiling over with resentment for slights received. My experience is like the Quartermasters, but I am less severely tested. He is a simple, good tempered manly fellow, who always takes fair play for granted & receives it. If an officer in a colored regiment mounts guard with a microscope for annoyances, he may receive them. My greatest discomfort is from overpopularity—too many visitors—too many applicants for office. If you could see the slouchy, dirty neglected white soldiers who stray out here & ask for a commission before they leave camp, you would understand why I prefer my own Maroons, who have at least learnt to keep their coats buttoned.

Gen Saxton told me that when he had on his shoulders all the immense business transactions of the Sherman expedition hither,[153] it seemed little, so long as he staid in his office—it was merely making the figures a little larger. But when he went out on the wharves of New York, laden with valuable property & he responsible for the whole, it seemed perfectly fearful. Just so with my responsibilities—it is just as easy to order 10 oxen wasted as a pound of beefsteak, just as easy, with the army machinery to manipulate a thousand men as a dozen—it is only once in a while when it comes over me that each of my units is a world that the responsibility is alarming. A man becomes insane, or his family suffers, or a Lieutenant's Irish wife behaves like the female who originally taught Satan his bad tricks, whoever it was, & then I find that the individual is the torment—the

153. Rufus Saxton participated in the expedition to Port Royal in November 1861, when a Union fleet under Flag Officer Samuel F. Du Pont seized the South Carolina Sea Islands.

multitudes giving no trouble, only that one feels they will all presently begin to do just so.

Flowers bloom rapidly, peaches, plums, wild shrubs, yellow jasmine flings fragrant clusters over the copses, the men who go for wood come back with great logs balanced on their heads & their hands full of daffodils & narcissi,—not that these are wild, but grow profusely about the plantation. Snakes, turtles, even a young alligator, think how delightful. New bird-notes every morning, but always it turns out the mocking bird. A lady brought me an aster & a wild cherry that grew side by side; but the most charming thing I have seen was a grove floored with bloodroot. I shall get some tomorrow, I have the new translation of Titan,[154] which matches well with spring & of which I dole out to myself a ration a day. I have not cared for any book before.

I have other dialect beside the negro to study. I have a Drum Major temporarily detailed from the 90th N.Y. now at Key West. He is an old Belgian who has been in a dozen armies & the state of whose brass buttons is a study for all American soldiers, so lustrous are they. His talk is a mixture of all tongues. "Co-lo-nel, I muss haf my deescharge & not return to Key West; dere is de yellow fever and then pop goes de weazel mit me; I haf no fear in battel, but de yellow fever is too much mit me."

Among Montgomery's recruits there is one handsome Mulatto with an Irish name & an unexceptionable brogue, with scarcely a trace of negro in it. I have not learned his history.

Mr Obadiah Oldbuck,[155] when he decided to adopt a pastoral life and assumed the provisional name of Thyrsis, never looked upon his flocks & herds with more unalloyed contentment than I on my flock of sheep. In Kansas they used to talk of a "pro-slavery" "colt" or an anti "slavery cow"—but the fact that these sheep are secesh sheep is the crowning charm. Methinks they frisk & fatten in the consciousness that they are no longer under the shadow of Madame Alberti's slave jail, but are destined to furnish mutton broth for sick or wounded Maroons. The slaves who once, perchance, were sold at the same auction with yon patriarchs of the flock, have now asserted their humanity & will eat him. Meanwhile the man who watches has a sharp bayonet with no crook to it, and I feel the mingled sensations of Ulysses & Rob Roy[156]—sheepstealers of less ele-

154. Jean Paul, *Titan: A Romance*, tr. Charles Timothy Brooks, 2 vols. (Boston: Ticknor and Fields, 1862).

155. Timothy Crayon (pseud.), *The Adventures of Mr. Obadiah Oldbuck . . .* (New York: Wilson & Co., 1842).

156. Sir Walter Scott, *Rob Roy* (Edinburgh: Printed by J. Ballantyne for A. Constable, 1818).

vated aims when I come upon these trophies of our own wanderings.[157]
March 4th This day the regiment begins to break camp, bound[158] for parts
unknown. It always seemed to me an act of unpardonable leakiness in
Banks to say that he was going *South.*

## HEADQUARTERS. JACKSONVILLE—
## MARCH 13. 1863

This pretty place, which we have retaken & now hold for the Government,
was the chief city of Florida & once had about 3.000 inhabitants & was
rapidly increasing in importance. It was held & evacuated a year ago by Gen
Hunter's orders—we came in on the anniversary (within one day) of the
evacuation. There are fine rows of brick houses, all empty, along the wharf,
& the houses & gardens are very pretty. My house, the chief one in the town,
is new & really magnificent, with beautiful gas fixtures & superb marble fireplaces. The streets are shaded with fine trees. About 500 people remain here,
men women & children, semi-loyal only. Many are very poor so that I shall
have to issue rations to them. Capt Rogers is Provost Marshal & has entire
charge of the people & houses, collects furniture from empty houses & locks
them up, has a patrol to prevent annoyance to the people &c.

My men have behaved perfectly well, though many were owned here &
do not love the people as you may suppose. There has been no wanton outrage. We can make the town a pretty strong position and I have sent the
Boston to Fernandina for four white companies & a battery in addition,
which Col Hawley has promised me. The streets are barricaded & we do
not go outside at night, but by day the rebel cavalry shew themselves beyond the hill & we go out to meet them, but they retire again. I was at first
much opposed to having any white troops under my command, but these
are desirous to come (7th Ct Regt) & the more I have, the more freely I can
act up the river, & range through the country. It is as beautiful a river as I
ever saw; we are 30 miles from the mouth, & it is a series of fertile banks &
occasional picturesque houses with a look of thrift very unlike South Carolina; more like the Kennebec.[159] Here are splendid quarters for the men
& storehouses &c—a whole street of brick buildings along the wharves.
Vessels can come up to the wharves at any time. Round the outskirts the
woods are cleared away for some two miles, for safety & beyond is dangerous ground. This is the only post on the main land in the Dep't of the South
all the rest are islands. With this place held, Florida could be conquered by

157. The copy-text reads "these wanderings trophies of our own wanderings."
158. The word "bound" reads "bounds" in the copy-text.
159. The Kennebec River in Maine.

five regiments & at any rate, Fernandina & St Augustine become very safe places. I only hope its evacuation will not be again ordered. You cannot conceive any thing prettier than the effect as we sailed up the beautiful stream, to this pretty town at eight A.M. the children all running out to meet us, the men & women gazing in amazement. All were polite, some over-joyed, some secretly cursing; some of the women hate the black soldiers, others say they have known many of the men all their lives, & it does not seem like being among strangers. It is so funny to go into a strange city & go to housekeeping in another's man's house—Col. Sunderland,[160] a rich lawyer—whether the Union or Confederate troops have been here, this has been the Head quarters, but entirely uninjured. Brick kitchen adjoining with every convenience & lingering pickles, a brick office opening out of my private room, & accessible by another door from street. The office is lined with great empty book cases, & we have furniture enough for the house. The field officers &c are with me and my faithful William is Major Domo.

(I am writing one letter & dictating another as the boat is almost leaving.)

Companies go out on the dangerous direction & after a while the rebel cavalry perhaps appear & fighting begins—or firing at least. Messengers gallop down & tell me & I mount my horse & ride to the scene of action, & usually the rebels have all disappeared; so that I have not yet seen one of them; they do not seem daring & my men are very willing to advance.

One U.S. gunboat will remain here most of the time & be a great aid. With this we can safely hold the position, & as reinforcements arrive, can move more freely. The place is one of the healthiest in the country—in summer always cool at night, & not over 86 by day. Roses and heliotropes luxuriate every where; I send geranium leaves from a great bush in front yard.

The "Boston" will probably return at once from Fernandina & you will hear again ere long as I shall send her directly to Beaufort.

DIRECT TO JACKSONVILLE. FLA
VIA PORT ROYAL
S.C.

HEADQUARTERS JACKSONVILLE
MARCH 16. 1863

Sitting with the windows open, in a soft June evening, the air full of the shrilling of insects & of the cadence of flutes & violins from the street by the water side, where the men's quarters are.

160. Sunderland was a New Yorker, and "reputed author of the State ordinance of Secession" (*Army Life* 113).

How many new night associations these forays have given me. The night at "Township" on the St Mary's, for instance, when I sat on the doorstep in the dying moonlight waiting an attack till morning. Like it, but more intense, was the first night here, the most terribly anxious night I ever passed; we were all perfectly exhausted, the companies were posted in various parts of the town, all momentarily expecting attack. My temporary quarters were in the loveliest grove of trees, and as I sat & nodded on that door step, the mocking birds sang all night like nightingales, in the sweet air & among the blossoming trees. Since then we have arranged our defences & sleep soundly.

In respect to personal courage I have learnt nothing new, & adhere to the belief that war has not so much harder tests than peace. But the anxiety of a commander is something for which peace affords no parallel, not even in Waldo,[161] running to the head of the stairs when any one came in the evening, lest it should be some messenger of accident on the Railroad. This of itself would be enough to keep me from any desire for high military responsibility & if it is so with one of my easy temperament, what must it be to those as conscientious & more excitable? I can understand how Burnside felt. So far as love of adventure goes, it must yield less & less enjoyment as one goes up—were I a private, I could do many things & run many risks which I ought not now to incur. I would go out by night on scouts. I have power, responsibility, rule a city absolutely, adjudicate arrests of prisoners & restitutions of old women's cows—plan defences, go on well-escorted reconnaissances, but the propensity for personal scrapes is partially corked up. Sometimes I envy our chaplain, the most erratic of mortals, who comes & goes at all hours, like a wild man, galloping on a lean horse, wearing a pistol in each side his belt & a rifle on his shoulder, making all manner of desirable discoveries by incurring risks which no regular officer would have a right to venture. Even Sunday gave no respite. "Is it not Sunday,"? asked some critical officer as he dashed in, after his wont. Nay, quoth his Reverence, it is the Day of Judgement!

I have won my silver spurs,—a pretty pair, which turned up somewhere & which the Quartermaster has turned over to me. As I spend half the day on horseback they are not misapplied.

Beyond the town there is a sort of Debateable Land, like that of the Scotch mosstroopers,[162] a broad cleared valley. We feel very brave on our side—& the other party very brave on theirs, but neither yet ventures

161. Waldo Higginson, one of TWH's older brothers.

162. Mosstroopers were raiders operating in the bogs on the border between England and Scotland in the seventeenth century.

far on the other's preserves. With the control of the river which we possess, it is not an object for us to march directly into the interior. Still from day to day they edge a little farther back & we a little farther forward. And I think they are more anxious about their camp than we about the city.

The men take with philosophy like the officers the change from the scantiness of tents to spacious & stately rooms. It is odd to spread again after contracting. There is no house in Worcester, scarcely any in Boston (where houses cover less ground however luxurious they may be) which equals that I live in, & now we are getting together furniture (for safe keeping of course) so that it seems less bare. A large office, with every convenience opens out of my private room on the one side—a dining room on the other. The Lt Col, & Major, Dr Rogers & others have large rooms, & there are rooms unused as yet. A brick building in the rear, but connected, has servants quarters on a large scale, There are but two stories, above is a cupola where the Post flag floats. Some luxuries d'ont *go*,—the gas, the bathing room, the billiard room even most of the balls being absent—but nothing is really injured, as every successive regime has preserved the royal residence for its own interest.

Of course infinitely funny things constantly occur. Every white man woman & child is wheedling & professes Union sentiments—Every black ditto believes that every white ditto is a scoundrel & ought to be shot were it not for discipline. The Provost Marshal ( James Rogers) & I steer between these as we can. Then the distinction between legitimate and illegitimate plunder is naturally hard to enforce. I am consoled by Capt. Stedman U.S.N. of the Paul Jones (a Charlestonian by birth) who says the white soldiers plundered 100 pr ct more at the first occupation of the city, & that the officers then sent home thousands of dollars worth of furniture &c, whereas we only use it for safer preservation. But the scenes!

Rush of indignant Africans. A white man in woman's clothes has been seen going into a certain house—undoubtedly a spy. Farther evidence discloses the Catholic priest, a peaceful little Frenchman in his professional apparel.—Anxious female enters—some sentinel has shot her cow for a rebel—the Colonel commanding cannot think of paying the desired $30. Let her go to the Quartermaster & select a cow from her herd. If there is none to suit her, let her wait till the next lot comes in, that's all. Yesterday's operations gave the following total yield—30 "contrabands"—18 horses, 3 mules, 11 cattle, 10 saddles & bridles. 1 new army wagon. At this rate we shall soon be self supporting cavalry.

Where complaints are made of soldiers, it almost always proves that the women have insulted them most grossly, swearing at them &c. One unpleasant old Dutch woman came bursting with wrath, & told the whole narrative of her blameless life amid sobs—"Last January I run off two of my black people from St Mary's to Fernandina (Sob) then I moved down there myself, & at Lake city I lost six women & a boy (Sob)—then I stopped at Baldwin for one of the wenches to be confined (Sob)—then I brought them all here to live in a *Christian country* (Sob, Sob) Then the *blockheads* (blockades i.e. gunboats) came & they all run off with the blockheads (Sob, Sob, Sob,) & left me, an old lady of 46, obliged to work for a living, (chaos of Sobs without cessation.)["]

When I found what the old sinner had said to the soldiers I wondered at their self control in not throttling her.

### MARCH 20 MIDNIGHT

For the last twenty four hours we have been sending women & children out of town, in answer to a demand by a flag of truce,[163] the first we have received. It was designed no doubt to intimidate & in our ignorance of the force actually outside, we have had to recognize the possibility of danger & work hard at our defences. At any time by going into the outskirts we can have a skirmish, which is nothing but fun; but when night closes in, with a small & weary garrison, there sometimes steals into my mind, like a chill, that most sickening of all sensations the anxiety of a commander. I should not speak of this were it not passed; this was the night generally set for an attack if any, though I am pretty well satisfied they have not strength to dare it—& the worst they could really do is to burn the town. But tonight instead of enemies appeared friends—our devoted civic ally Judge Stickney[164] the brain of Florida, & a whole Ct regiment, the 6th, under Major Meeker,[165] & though the latter are aground 12 miles below, yet they give us strength, & hereafter I can breathe more freely. I only wish they were black, but now I have to show not only that blacks can fight, but that they & white soldiers can work in harmony together.

I send by this mail some copies of a map of Jacksonville by which you will see how the city lies; the creek which passes round it is easily defensible

163. When one army wishes to hold communication for any reason with enemy troops (as here, to warn women and children to evacuate before an assault, or to exchange mail, etc.) a messenger approaches the guards or pickets showing a flag of truce. Lieut. Col. A. H. McCormick's March 17, 1863, letter and TWH's reply may be found in *The War of the Rebellion: A Compilation of the Official Records of the Union and Confederate Armies*, Series I, Vol. XIV (Washington: Government Printing Office, 1885), 839.

164. Judge Lyman Stickney.

165. Major L. Meeker.

& the main approaches lie all on one side, which is protected by two forts we have run up.

Unless we are attacked during the night & things change their aspect, I shall send away the "Burnside" tomorrow and besides you will hear again through the Boston in a day or two. The report is that Gen Hunter will be here tomorrow, which will make still another chance to send. There is a mail on the Boston for us, but I have not seen it.

Up the river the other night, a detachment captured some lovely horses, almost racers, & the finest has been assigned to me I paying the good price $125 for him, he is a sorrel named Rinaldo, belonged to a rebel cavalry officer & is perfectly trained, very fleet & perfectly gentle. By an odd coincidence he was reared by Col. Sammis, former master if not father of my young orderly Albert, who regards Rinaldo as a sort of foster-brother,— younger brother I suppose by the severity with which he rides him. The only trouble is that one's rides are so limited by the narrow limits of the dominion, a good part even of this being encumbered with prostrate trees to keep other people from riding!

## March 22. 1863

Last night was one of unbroken quiet, the night before there was firing & cannonading all night, expecting an attack from the enemy, which proved only a reconnaissance by perhaps fifty men who kept us stirred up all night. It was intensely dark, which increased the perplexity.

Every day makes us more impregnable & now the enemy has drawn back & there is no more skirmishing & I think we shall be let alone unless we march out to meet him. This is Sunday; the bell is ringing for church & Rev. Mr French, a not very pleasing Beaufort Magnate, is to preach. This afternoon my good Quartermaster starts a Sunday School for our little colony of Contrabands now numbering 70.

### SUNDAY AFTERNOON

The bewildering report is confirmed & in addition to the 6th Ct. Regt. which came yesterday—appears part of the 8th Me Regt. The remainder with the Col. (Rust) will be here tomorrow probably—& report says then Gen Hunter. If the latter, very well. Otherwise I shall be superseded in command of the post & my troops placed in a close contact which will defeat all my plans & their success. It is just what I begged *not* to have done. Now my hope is that we may be allowed to go to some point higher up the river, which we can hold for ourselves. There are two other points which in themselves are as favorable as this, & for getting recruits, *better*. So I shall hope to be allowed to go. To take posts & then let white troops garrison them—that is my programme.

What makes the thing more puzzling is that the 8$^{th}$ Me Regt, has only brought ten days rations, so that they evidently are not to stay here, & yet where they go or why come here, is a puzzle.

Meanwhile we can sleep sound o' nights & if the black & white babies do not quarrel & pull hair, can do very well.

## JACKSONVILLE FLORIDA MARCH 24

I remember Charles Devens[166] saying that he never had felt such unutterable relief as when Col. Baker[167] arrived on the field at the battle of Ball's Bluff.[168] Not that he brought very strong reinforcements with him, but simply that he lifted the load of responsibility off Devens' shoulders; and after that he had merely to fight & obey orders—not command.

Something of this feeling has been mine for twenty four hours. When the Delaware approached the wharf with the 8th Maine Regt & Col Rust (my superior offier) I had to send him the message that I was very sorry I couldn't receive him handsomely, but the fact was we were in the midst of a fight. The rebels were just then beginning to shell us for the first time with a big gun they have got on a locomotive: but it didn't last long. Then he took command (though it is a queer affair & he may only be here a few days. Nobody knows until Gen. Hunter comes, which he may not do)— and instantly a load fell. It is odd too chiefly a matter of imagination, he leaves almost all to me, regards himself as a visitor, takes command because he can't help it, is a mediocre, (a heavy Maine livery stable keeper) has smelt no powder & sleeps on board the steamboat; nevertheless the fact that he is in command, not I, makes life seem mere play.

The woman on board ship went on combing her hair during an alarm of shipwreck—because that was the Captain's business—& this is the way one feels on being superseded or as it is delicately called *relieved* in command.

You understand that the Senior officer has to take command & that

166. Col. Charles Devens, Jr. (1820–1891), an attorney and outspoken critic of slavery who volunteered at the outbreak of the Civil War, and led the 15th Massachusetts at the Battle of Ball's Bluff, Virginia.

167. Col. Edward Dickinson Baker (1811–1861), U.S. Senator from Oregon, who was shot dead by a sharpshooter in the Battle of Ball's Bluff.

168. On October 21, 1861, Union troops were caught disorganized in open ground and suffered great casualties at Ball's Bluff, on the Virginia side of the Potomac River.

there was no way of sending me reinforcements without a senior officer I being junior to all the Colonels. Only the 6<sup>th</sup> Ct has an absent Colonel, & if he returns soon, as is expected, he will supersede both Rust and me. That is Col. Chatfield said to be a fine officer which Rust is not.

Oh how these Conn. & Me boys long for active service, from which they have always been kept back. One of the Captains said pithily last night "I enlisted for the war though I *have never got to it yet*"—So one of my new Lieutenants, from the Mass Cavalry, apoligized for a little nervousness by saying that though he had been eighteen months in service, he had not grown so familiar with fighting as we had!

It is odd how used one gets to alarms, especially when "relieved" by a senior officer. Last night Montgomery said "Tonight the town will be shelled." He is commonly so little apprehensive that it meant more from him than it would from most men: it was based on their known wish to destroy the town, & their having shelled us during the day. I said, "they w'ont dare," went to bed with my clothes on and never waked from half past nine to six.

Montgomery is splendid, but impulsive & changeable never plans far ahead, & goes off at a tangent. The last tangent is to leave us tomorrow— go up the river 30 miles on a steamer & strike directly for the interior, where the slaves are leaving the rebels to watch us here. What makes the project odder is that in forty eight hours or so we i.e. the S.C.V. hope to be under weigh to take & occupy some upper point, so that by waiting he could strike off from us. But off he goes tomorrow unless he changes his mind. His only anxiety is that his men will get their feet so blistered; for they are all Key West men—that island is only 8 miles by 2 & that is the longest distance they have ever walked in their lives.

The band of the 8<sup>th</sup> Me is going about serenading; it really seems like a garrison town. For twenty four hours[169] I commanded part or the whole of 4 regiments quite a brigade.

People are coming into town—shops opening few and small. "Society" consists of a nest of sallow singing semi-secesh spinsters, just behind my head quarters, who are haunted day and evening by lieutenants naval & military. I received my share of blarney on the day of first arrival, & have since kept clear of it.

Have I written of my handsome secesh horse Rinaldo, a strong yet slender & graceful sorrel with a white line down the face & the proverbial two white feet. A cavalry horse, belonged to a rebel officer perfectly trained, without a trick, goes like the wind & is pulled up with a touch. Foster

169. Copy-text reads "twenty fours," an evident slip of the pen.

brother of my orderly, both raised by Col Sammis, a rich old slaveholding refugee who has returned with us. Col S sold him to the rebel officer for $275 & I have him for $125 the Govt price.

March 25. Last night Montgomery thought they would *not* shell town & they did. Now shelling the town sounds very formidable, but something depends on whether it is done by a popgun or a battery. Last night it was no battery but one 32 lb rifled gun—the only one the rebels have in the state or are likely to have. The same size with that which we have, also on a platform car. They fired seven shell, & stopped soon after the gunboat opened fire in reply. Three passed through houses in town, one doing serious damage by tearing away a musquito net from a bed. It was not so damaging as a severe thunderstorm & far less exciting to the nerves, though the shells were well thrown.

March 28th We are ordered to evacuate this Post. Just as our defences are complete & all in order for the transfer of part of our forces up river, to other points, we are ordered away. Every military and naval officer here takes the same view of the order—but it is useless to criticize; there is nothing to do but to go. We have so daunted the rebels that we can go out 4 miles in any direction with one or two companies only, & the big gun with which they once played bombard us they now dare not bring within range of the city (2 miles). The possession of this place gives the key to Florida, & the present garrison can hold it & spare us to go up river and yet we must go. We must also leave the Union population here to the persecution consequent on a third evacuation; for the same thing has been done twice before. It is the first time I have been thoroughly subjected to that uncertainty of counsel which has been the bane of the war; it defeated us in this case, just in the hour of success—but thanks to my natural buoyancy, I can stand it. What is to be done with us I have no intimation.

Col. Montgomery has just returned from up river, as far as Pilatka,[170] he landed incautiously & was fired upon. Lt. Col. Billings who was with him was wounded in both hands a bullet passing through each and in the hip—no one was killed—on the other hand they brought down 13 rebel soldiers whom they surprized asleep on picket. Montgomery took all their guns then shook one on the shoulder to wake him. "What is it?" quoth the sleeper. "You are prisoners" said Montgomery. "No," said the man explaining, "we belong to Westcott's company" (a noted guerilla force) "Yes" said Montgomery, "*but we d'ont.*" So they were all taken, with their horses and arms.

A fuller order has come today, signed by Gen. Seymour, now Gen.

170. Palatka, Florida; the skirmish took place on March 27, 1863.

Hunter's Chief of Staff, & strongly opposed to us—recalling us to Beaufort, so we shall settle down at Camp Saxton once more. How like a dream all this life of daily skirmishes & nightly alarms will then appear. Did I write of the Battle of the Clothes Lines? A company of the Maine 8th was out scouting with one of our best men for guide & sent back word that he had discovered a rebel camp, with 22 tents; they had seen the officers & men & it might be possible to capture it. So Col Rust let me go with 4 companies. It was a beautiful open pine wood where we had never been before. We marched on for several miles, sometimes stopping to explore forward, when all the long line of skirmishers & the reserve would lie down in the long thin grass & beside the fallen logs till one could not imagine a person there; then at a word like Roderick Dhu's men,[171] all would rise again & the green wood be peopled with armed life. At last we divided & I sent a detachment round the head of the creek to surprize the camp on that side while we cut off their retreat—cautiously we stole nearer & nearer and at last came out on a solitary house where clothes had been hung out to dry on the fence!

This was our victory. It may be that the men were not imagining, for it may have been a picket station; we captured one house & a quantity of inexplicable *bits* which the man said a friendly blacksmith had bequeathed to him; we hung them across the horse and as I rode back on him they clanked like broken chains, so came we triumphantly back through the lovely woods joking at the scare for which we were glad not to be responsible. But for our early departure, I think the 8th Me would never hear the last of the jokes cut thereon—one being that the officer who saw the tents must certainly have been "three sheets in the wind" which is one of the cant phrases for inebriation.

More thoroughly exciting was a march & artillery skirmish the morning before. We went 5 miles out towards the rebel camp—5 of my companies 4 of the 8th Maine & 4 of the 6th Ct. My men were in the middle with a 10 lb rifled cannon on a platform car in front the long line of skirmishers spread across the woods, five paces apart, white—black—white, forming one harmonious line; & probably each crow thought his own young one's whitest, at least I preferred my own. They seemed to me far more regular

---

171. Sir Walter Scott, in *The Lady of the Lake* (1810), has Roderick Dhu demonstrate to Fitz-James the complete ease with which his troops can conceal themselves from foes: "Down sunk the disappearing band; / Each warrior vanish'd where he stood. / In broom or bracken, heath or wood; / Sunk brand and spear and bended bow, / In osiers pale and copses low; / It seem'd as if their mother Earth / Had swallow'd up her warlike birth" (V.ix). Sir Walter Scott, *Poetical Works*, ed. J. Logie Robertson (London: Oxford University Press, 1904), 253.

& steady in their advance than the brave but undisciplined white troops each side, who fought each for himself. The 8th Me. skirmishers especially got much too far forward, & halting when we had gone as far as I judged prudent, they could not be recalled. At last they were got back & meanwhile certain lowering puffs of smoke, two miles farther on the railroad showed the dreaded locomotive battery with its 64 lb Blakely gun,[172] coming slowly in our rear. They kept it at this distance for fear of our getting a force behind to tear up a rail & so capture it. We were retreating with our smaller gun which could however carry as far. Soon began the artillery duel; there would be a little puff of smoke from the distance & I would bid all the men lie down in the ditches each side of the track—then a dull report & then came the iron messenger, usually thrilling through the air just above our heads (for they work the gun splendidly, having an accomplished artillery officer) & bursting its great fragments, but hurting no one because of the ditches. The men grew quite indifferent to it very soon, & I was glad they should see that artillery the most formidable arm in appearance is really evaded more easily than any other. The Maine 8th who did not lie down escaped less entirely, two were killed & 2 wounded, while we were unscathed though ten times as many shell passed over us, because we were directly in the track. Meanwhile our little gun would fire back shells exploding directly over[173] the monster, who stood vague and lowering in smoke and distance, so that with my glass I could only see a vague Dantesque image. At last she stopped firing and since then she has never again come so near. The shells were huge conical masses larger than a man's head; often they did not explode, & then were formidable in one place only—but moving slowly and showing a light it is possible to dodge them by day or night & therefore every one soon becomes comparatively indifferent to a simple cannon throwing shell, however powerful it may be.

ON BOARD STR JOHN ADAMS
MOUTH OF ST JOHN'S RIVER
MARCH 30. 1863

Here we are in an easterly storm, 2 gunboats & seven transports, unable to get out over the bar, and liable to be here for days—for with any thing like an east wind, this bar is impassable. All the boats are crowded with passengers, refugees & their furniture, contrabands &c going to Beaufort or Fer-

172. A rifled cannon used extensively in the Civil War, especially by the Confederate army, with a reputation for considerable accuracy.
173. The copy-text reads "directly of."

nandina & this morning it seemed as if our expedition were to end where the Burnside expedition began. But the storm is abating, we are in an excellent harbor, & though on some of the boats there is much discomfort, I think we can worry through. This is just where we lay waiting for the John Adams, on our first arrival & that was much harder than this from the anxiety lest her delay should make the whole expedition a failure. Now, nothing can take away from this regiment the credit of another successful expedition; & if the men can only be made comfortable, a few day's delay makes no difference.

The only time since I entered the service when I have felt within the reach of tears was when after the men were all on board at Jacksonville, I walked back among the burning buildings (set on fire by the white soldiers, not by mine) & picked a tea rose bud from the garden of my Headquarters. To think that this was the end of our brilliant enterprise & the destruction of my beautiful city was a sadder thing than wounds or death,—as for defeat I have not yet known it—and knowing the triumphant hopes felt by all the loyal Floridians & the corresponding depths of their disappointment—and the apparent aimlessness of the evacuation, it was doubly hard. But this did not last long—"tomorrow to fresh fields & pastures new." It is my first experience of the chagrin which officers feel from divided or uncertain counsel in higher places; and I find I can stand it. As for the men their buoyant spirits are proof against every thing. I tell them "it is just as well to go somewhere else as to stay at Jacksonville, where there was latterly nothing to shoot at but *rebel heels*; ["] & a joke always has more effect on them than a thousand arguments. Their little sorrows are usually like those of children—once make them laugh, & the cloud is dispelled. Mean while on board the transports with white troops, there is general grumbling & dissatisfaction. Every Captain of a transport who has once taken my regiment wishes to take it again in preference to whites.

Some of the Floridians think that after the taking of Charleston or Savannah we shall be sent here again; and I think this magnificent river is virtually abandoned by both parties. Yet I have thought so much about Pilatka, I cannot but think that I shall some time go there; & tap that treasury of slaves & sugar. Indeed I fancy that part of the charm of Florida to me is in its saccharine products; are you aware that neither Maple Sugar nor the most scientific Stewart is comparable to the ordinary cane molasses which every little squatter here makes for himself. It has a flavor of its own, it never cloys, it foams in the tumbler when mixed with water, & old settlers say there is no excuse for drinking whiskey in Florida, for one can always drink Syrup. It is singular that it is not exported, for unlike maple syrup it can be kept all the year round in any climate.

*120*

Our orders now are simply to return to Camp Saxton & we must necessarily put in at Fernandina on the way, to leave many people & much property; which will lighten our vessels and make our people more comfortable.

I told you in my last Journal that Montgomery had brought in 13 rebel prisoners (pickets;) I did not add that he also captured the Lieutenant, who afterwards escaped by aid of a crowd of female friends who came to take farewell. He crawled away behind their skirts, then ran & would not stop though Montgomery raised his pistol. But M. would'nt shoot, for he said he could'nt kill him in his sister's presence—a very characteristic touch. His revolver is unerring—the other day he shot an alligator in the eye, the only part visible. James Rogers is a splendid shot & did the other day something I never saw done before. Shot a turkey buzzard on a bough & *left it there*, making ineffectual efforts to fly. He wanted one to stuff, but it did not fall, or not for a long time, though it was evidently shot. It would have been pathetic had the bird been more attractive; indeed it was rather so, as it was, to me. Somehow I never feel any impulse to fire a shot: but on the other hand the death of a man does not seem to affect my sensibilities in the slightest degree; it does not *reach* me, when it happens although in advance I have a nervous desire to guard against it. Indeed I can conceive that a man might be perfectly fearless in himself & a mere poltroon as a commander: especially when worn by watching & care, Major Anderson,[174] for instance, I consider to have had the severest trials of the war; I do not wonder his health is gone.

We have on board a delightful old pilot 70 years old, who has been on all our trips; a perfect old philosopher, who knows every nook on the coast from Maine to New Orleans, & who once tapped, talks forever, with the raciest personal adventures. Capt. Gomez he is—was of course born in Salem, in *Clam Shell Alley*, in a part of the city called *Button hole*—His mother could not read and whipped his sister for venturing to study grammar at school—"What business have poor folk's children to *learn Grammar?*—I'll Grammar you—it's Billy Gray's folks that *learn Grammar*.["] He never learned to spell, & has a way in writing letters of putting a word in several successive spellings, to give his reader the choice, as volley, voylly &c. He formerly lived in Jacksonville among other places & was delighted to go there & get back a chest of tools: he is a brave little old thing too and staid on deck when I drove all others under; & when Montgomery was sur-

174. Maj. Robert Anderson (1805–1871), who endured 34 hours of bombardment at Fort Sumter, April 12–13, 1861, before surrendering; elevated to Brigadier General in honor of his heroism.

prized at Pilatka & Lt Col. Billings wounded old Gomez tried to work the gun himself. The rebels managed that matter well—the houses at Pilatka are just on the wharf & Montgomery landed rather carelessly, when they suddenly had a volley from a garden close by. Colonel Billings was just climbing up the wharf, had both hands up at the top of the ladder, & a buckshot went simultaneously through the fleshy part of each hand without touching the bone. He incautiously turned to retreat & a spent ball hit him lightly on the hip. So he brought home three slight wounds, two of which clearly belong to the Major & me—both of whom have been exposed much more than the Lt. Col & feel a little envious. Such *little* wounds, you know and yet they are wounds & save the necessity of any larger one. We try to treat him pleasantly, but we think it rather grasping in him.

I may as well say that there are several different theories about the cause of our withdrawal. (1) that they simply need every available soldier in S. Carolina (2) that they must have the transport vessels which we necessarily detained (3) that it is simply a thwarting of our career by Brig. Gen. Seymour now chief of Staff to Maj. Gen. Hunter and one of the Brannan stamp (4) that Gen Hunter has advices of an important move from Savannah to dislodge us. This last would be the most satisfactory explanation, but can hardly be admitted, because *we* had advices.

Since writing this I have seen a person who left Beaufort 24 hrs. after the news of the evacuation of Jacksonville. He says it was not 20 minutes before Gen Saxton had his steamer the "Flora" under weigh for Hilton Head to see Gen Hunter & get the order rescinded. (It would not be the first time he has done so) But he could get no information even about the cause of the recal—he urges Gen Hunter even to let us stay *alone* at Jacksonville if necessary, but he was resolute against it. This does not surprize me, perhaps, so much as you; and it is possible by the time we get there that the recal may be regretted even by its author.

The only person wounded at Pilatka, beside the Lt Col. was one of our priests & apostles, old John Quincy, cook of our crack company & a man whose eloquence has the scream of the Arab in it, & he looks like a Bedouin.[175] He was shot in the foot very badly but may save the foot; he takes it very quietly, saying that "there must be wounds." Only he feels a little natural indignation against his wife, to bring whom from Pilatka he joined in the expedition as a volunteer. She originally would not escape with him because she would not leave her trunk & now he has decided to leave *her*. He is the man who said "When I heard de shell a screaming like

175. A Bedouin is a member of any of the nomadic tribes inhabiting the deserts of North Africa, Arabia, and Syria.

de Judgement Day, I cried—Lord! help my congregation. Boys! load & fire." Several times when we have expected a fight or an expedition we have contrived to call out John Quincy for a speech beforehand—but now we must leave him at Fernandina till his foot gets well.

Today most of the companies have gone on shore, to quarter in deserted fisherman's huts till the bar is passable; they have built up fires & gone to housekeeping with their wonted promptness. One of them had shot a black pelican such as fly all about us here, & put his hand in its enormous pouch. "Dat same as quart" he said; "Hi! boy," said another, "neber you bring dat quart measure in *my* peck of corn." It was a piece of their usual quick repartee—& very appropriate as their pouches sometimes hold 11 quarts.

March 31. Expect to cross the bar & reach Fernandina tonight.


HEAD QUARTERS 1ST REG S.C.V.
ADVANCED PICQUET STATION
MILNES PLANTATION. PORT ROYAL I.
APRIL 6TH.

Here commenceth a new chapter in this strange life. This morning we had reveillé at 4 A.M. & before noon were encamped amid fresh fields and pastures new. No more Camp Saxton—no more forays with the Steamboats—no more stately garrison life & daily skirmishing at Jacksonville. No imprisonment in Fort Pulaski, which was what we most dreaded, but a wild free breezy life over this beautiful North end of the island—the main camp 7 miles from Beaufort, 9 miles from our former camp, & our outer picquet line spreading for nearly ten miles along the shore of the creek which seperates us from the main land. The chief access to that creek is by the Shell road, a hard beautiful road, straight broad level & wooded all the way, beside which we are encamped. Along this road the rebels must come, almost inevitably, if they dare an attack on this island while Charleston is besieged. They may or may not—the duty of our pickets being to watch the river day & night, resist any attempts to cross, at the same time warning Gen Saxton by a mounted courier & falling back when necessary, on the fortifications which protect the Town itself.

Riding out two miles or so farther on the shell road one comes to a causeway,[176] then to a tide stream[177] of 200 yds; then beyond is another causeway & the rebel pickets beyond. But after being on the mainland at

176. A raised roadway allowing passage over water or marshland.
177. A stream that drains and floods coastal areas at low and high tides.

Jacksonville, it seems so safe & remote to see pickets across a stream, where a dash is impossible, that it is not at all alarming. They may endeavor to surprise & capture a picket or company—in which I think they would fail. To advance in force is what I cannot expect; if they do, there will be ample notice as the thing implies time & noise. A mounted orderly, from the Mass Cavalry is kept at each of the four outlying stations—& 3 here at head quarters. As you will see by my map, just beyond this camp there are creeks each side so that an enemy could only advance along a causeway, which a few could defend against many & there are cypress swamps all the way back to Beaufort where we could defend ourselves & harass the enemy immensely. So I think they will hardly venture.

Meanwhile life on picket is rather a picturesque & fascinating life; consisting for me chiefly in galloping through miles of lanes with sprays of immense wild roses, pale & fragrant, meeting overhead; & trees of white cornel gleaming out at intervals, fantastic masses, snowy surprises. My quarters are in a plantation house, with immense fireplaces for the evening, & rose bowers for the day; There are four rooms & a piazza & we have it all to ourselves. At Seabrook's plantation, 2 miles off where we have a picket, but where we have not yet been, lives Charles Follen, though strangely enough it was not till today that I knew him to be in this Dept at all. I think he must have kept out of Beaufort as effectually as I.

April 7<sup>th</sup> This morning I rode to Seabrook & along to the Ferry—across the creek there are here & there men & horses—mere picquets & they shouted to our men when first put on, being just within shouting distance in a few places—but our men were mum. It is pretty on the other side, less level than here with pine woods rising to bluffs; & the negroes think it a sort of Pisgah view of the promised land & long to go in & possess it. Seabrook's plantation or "Rice Bank" is one of the prettiest I have seen; there I saw Charles Follen & also his assistant, a keen, black eyed, white toothed young man who proved to be young Silva, son of our host in Fayal, and a draughtsman for Charles F when architect. *Both*, it seems, wish for commissions in one of these regiments, & I at once offered C. F. a vacant lieutenancy in James Rogers' company which he as promptly accepted. Oddly enough within half an hour on the same ride I met still another Mass<sup>tts</sup> acquaintance, of whom I did not know that he was in this Dept & to whom I should have offered the same commission, had not C. F. filled it.

We have heard heavy firing all day & even during last night; & it is said that the attack on Charleston began at 3 P.M. Sometimes news has been obtained very early by the picquets at the Ferry calling it across—but sometimes great lies also—as of the 6 months truce, a while ago. When my company went on duty today, they called from other side "Has your Doctor sold his white horse yet"? thinking we were the 6th Connecticut, whose turn would come next, & whose Dr had a horse which a Flag of Truce wanted to buy. Little they knew that our surgeon's complexion was black (for we commonly speak of ourselves as colored officers)—and that of his horse sorrel.

It is a part of my usual luck that my blooded horse came to my hands before this life began, for my former old discomfort would have made it impracticable.[178] But Rinaldo enjoys it all & if he can get one of the other sorrel racers beside him, his speed is only limited by my will, at least thus far; for I have never trusted him on such occasions to the top of his bent, & he is to be ruled with a touch. Here the shell road is harder than our roads, & the lanes are very different from the heavy sand near Camp Saxton & far more agreable riding.

If there is no attack made—& I expect none—I shall have a lazy time here, compared to any previous service. It seems quite queer not to be in an enemy's country where we can forage for ourselves & help ourselves to little conveniences!

ADVANCED PICQUET STATION
PORT ROYAL ISLAND
APRIL 12.

Sensations follow us. Several days ago I was waked about $5\frac{1}{2}$ by cannon shot which we at first attributed to some gunboat going round the island, though it seemed too continuous. As the day previous I had alarmed the family by tumbling off the scanty shelf bequeathed me by my predecessor Major Filler for a bed, I checked all alarm when soon after 6 a cavalry courier dashed in breathless to say that a small armed steamer the "Washington" was aground near our farthest station & the rebels firing through & through her. I sent couriers at once to Gen. Saxton & to the gunboat Paul Jones the other side of the island, & soon put Rinaldo to his speed for the scene of action, 5 miles away. Approaching I met man after man who had escaped from the wreck across almost impassable marsh; poor fellows, some with literally only shirts on, but all with every garment pasted to their

178. TWH's meaning is somewhat obscure here, but perhaps he means that he is lucky to have acquired Rinaldo no sooner than the time when he and his regiment returned from Florida and went out on picquet (i.e., *just* "before this life began"), since some chronic physical ailment, now in remission ("my former old discomfort") would have prevented him from riding horseback before now. It appears, in his letters of 1864, as illness takes a toll on his energy and he prepares to leave the army, that he suffers from a chronic gastrointestinal disorder, which he may have been prone to suffer in the past as well.

bodies with mud. When I reached the spot, (having to wind cautiously along the picket paths, as the rebels had shelled the shore afterwards) I saw the looming wreck aground beyond a half mile of marsh, out of which the forlorn creatures were still floundering. It was a mixture of war and Robinson Crusoe.[179] Our irrepressible Chaplain & others coming up, I sent him with a white flag & 4 men out on the marsh for some wounded men whose cries we could hear; I also went out part way; but it took all the morning to get them all; our last achievement being the pilot an immense black man with a wooden leg. Another gunboat, which had originally accompanied this one, came back & got the last. It seemed the boat was not aground but at anchor & as usual inexcusable carelessness had been shown: for they had heard the rebels all night making preparations for something in the opposite woods.

This was Thursday; since then I have been beseeching Gen. Saxton to make that last gunboat come and take the cannon from the wreck, it seemed so shameful for the rebels to get them & we had no way to prevent it without cannon. Finally yesterday the rebels went to work on the wreck, out of our gunshot, brought back their original battery, had boats or pontoons at that point—also at another point, the Ferry itself, the latter evidently for a feint. Still it might be the long talked of invasion; so we had an afternoon & night of it I assure you; courier after courier in all directions. Gen. Saxton has such splendid plans for the defence of the island, he c'ant bear not to have it attacked—& just at this time four regiments arrived from Charleston, on the avowed ground that they heard Beaufort was taken & burnt, & they wanted to see what could be saved. So up came 6 cannon & various companies of regulars, & bivouacked uncomfortably near us, while we, used to "scares" at Jacksonville slept soundly, after arranging to send away in an ambulance, in case of attack, Mrs Dewhurst & pretty little Charlotte Forten, Mrs D's quadroon visitor, she who once taught the Higginson grammar School in Salem & is our Daughter of the Regiment. But our first nocturnal cannonshots made the rebels quit the wreck & withdraw their light batteries from the shore—and that was all. In the misty gray of the morning I rode out to the Ferry amid rose scents & the song of early birds—hearing for the first time the Chuck-Will's Widow, the Southern Whippoorwill, whose peculiar note I at once recognized. There all was quiet & I sent the batteries home. I never gave an or-

179. Daniel Defoe, *The Life and Strange Surprising Adventures of Robinson Crusoe, of York, Mariner: Who Lived Eight and Twenty Years, All Alone . . .* (London: Printed for W. Taylor . . . , 1719), concerns a shipwrecked Crusoe and his attempts to salvage a few stores and utensils from the wreck with which to eke out a tolerable existence on a remote island.

der to an officer of regulars before, & though it was only a juvenile little lieutenant, fresh from West Point, who had come out on the boat from N.Y. with me, & then threatened to quit the service because he could not bring with him a basket of Champagne,—still it seemed rather presumptuous. To be sure I have habitually under my command a company of the Mass. Cavalry detailed at pickets & that too seemed odd at first,—but "tout arrive en France."[180]

A corporal of cavalry with whom I was riding the other day told me a story of Henry Higginson to put beside Midshipman Frank's "all ready Sir to fire the ship." Once there was an advance beyond this Ferry a year ago to fire a bridge & the Mass. Cavalry went along—almost their only smelling of powder in these parts—& Henry being reproved by Gen. Stevens[181] for exposing himself somewhere, only stammered out—"P-p-pooh! They w'ont hurt *me*"! a piece of assured invulnerability which became a byword in the corps—the only good volunteer regiment I have seen, by the way, outside my own camp. And their place of encampment the Barnwell plantation, is a piece of pastoral beauty beyond anything I have seen here—a live oak avenue that is a dream of England as one rides through it.

This afternoon brought Gens Hunter and Saxton & a host of aids—the first named as easy & chipper as if his one chance of immortality had not tumbled to pieces within 24 hours—for the troops are all back & the Charleston expedition over! Nothing was said of our inexplicable recal from Jacksonville, nor of this more recent failure, but he seemed to think the locust blossoms over the house very pretty, as they undoubtedly are, & sat by the window a little while with his vest unbuttoned & then went goodnaturedly off. Well, I pay respect to my superiors, & d'ont make criticisms—but I believe I monopolize this abstinence, in this department. Gen. Saxton thinks we may be ordered to Florida again & I think he would'nt dislike to go with us, but it seems so stupid to go there again that I can hardly expect it. The only reason ever given for our recal is that all the troops were needed here—

First saucer full of strawberries today—

APRIL 13

Leisure I never have—especially never since we went to Jacksonville; here my life is more positively enjoyable than at Camp Saxton, because the re-

---

180. "Everyone arrives in France."
181. Brigadier General Isaac Ingalls Stevens (1818–1862), who commanded the post at Beaufort in 1862.

gion is so beautiful & I spend every morning, without exception, in the
saddle. On the other hand there is no interlude so soothing here, even with
a tangled desert garden full of roses & magnolias—as the stroll down to
the river bank before & after every meal at Camp Saxton. However it is so
entirely different both from that Camp life & the life at Jacksonville & also
from the semi-naval life of our expedition, that it will last for a long time. It
is part of my usual lucky star that this regiment has seen less of the joyless
monotony of war—of its dirty & dreary stagnation—and also of the arduous life of marches—than is usually the case. We have had but one day
of knapsack marching—the day we left Camp Saxton & came here. On
the other hand few regiments so young have been so much in the face of
the enemy or been placed so continually in advance. This is regarded as
the most honorable post in these islands, and usually regiments are here
for 10 days at a time only, but we are camped here & may stay indefinitely,
or be ordered away at any time.

We have had a good specimen, just now, of the advantage of colored
soldiers in local knowledge. One of our most important stations is called
the Brick Yard—on an island seperated by a small creek from this island.
Picquets have been there two years without discovering how horses could
pass over to the island—& it is only since we came here that the passage
has been found; some of the men extracting it from the people on the plantations. I rode across with perfect ease at low tide, & we are to take a cannon over, which has been supposed impossible.

The life of the owners of these beautiful plantations was peculiarly divided. Beaufort was their winter & summer residence—their Seaside and
City in one. They spent December out here, then those who had children
to be educated went into town till April—spent April on the plantation
again—then into Beaufort till December. Those who had no children to
educate staid out from December to May. This seems English, as does the
plantation life generally, so that it is no wonder if Englishmen are attracted
by it—

The only book I shall associate with these times, because the only one I
have read, is Jean Paul's Titan, which I have taken a few pages at a time, for
these 6 weeks, & it still holds out, especially as I am just coming to the Roman part which is the most beautiful.

Col. Littlefield of Illinois who is now here wishing to raise a black
brigade, is a good instance of the current popularity of the thing. He is a
Cavalry Colonel, (higher pay than infantry) & is not only willing to
exchange for equal rank in a black infantry regiment—but to be its Lt. Col.
or Major—such is his interest & faith in the enterprise. He wants, however,
to raise a Brigade, & is one of the most prepossessing officers I have seen.

Tonight the Major has come back from Beaufort & says on what I know to be good authority that there has been no quarrel between Gen Hunter & Admiral Dupont,[182] but both agree that the attempt was hopeless, though the Monitors were beyond Fort Sumter, & they could read the time on the city clocks 10 minutes of 12—think of that. Robert Small, the pilot, cried to think of being so near & yet obliged to give it up. It does not surprize me, for Gen. Saxton told me beforehand that Admiral Dupont considered it a "forlorn hope", but of course every body feels somewhat depressed, except perhaps myself. I should not be surprized if we were sent back to Florida, though I believe we are gaining credit here. I have just heard that a squad of cavalry was sent, the night of the alarm to make the round of our pickets, along some 15 miles of shore; they spent the whole night & reported that they could not get within 30 yards of a single man without being challenged. This the sergeant of the squad told Major Strong today.

Dusky Flowers of Speech—

1. "What for dat Chaplain made preacher for? He is the fightingest more Yankee dat ever I saw."
2. (Filial Sorrow) on returning from the expedition, "Cappen, my old father done dead & somebody tief my big rooster."
3. (Shaksperian.) "Where is your gun?" "Cappen, I took dat gun, & I put it in Cappen tent. Den I looked, and de gun not dere. Den Conscience says, Cappen must have giv dat gun to some other man. Den I say—Conscience, you reason correct."
4. "Cappen Is been a sickly pusson ever since de *expeditious.*"
5. (How are you today?) "Not quite so well, bress de Lord." (and again) "Not superior, tank God"—
6. [(]After Dr Rogers had drawn some tents over men asleep on deck.) "Dat Doctor's got de bulliest heart."


ADVANCED PICQUET STATION
MILNES PLANTATION
APRIL 17.

I wonder if I can find time to describe something of the picturesque summer life into which we are settling down. Four companies of the regiment

182. Rear Admiral Samuel Francis Du Pont (1815–1865), who led the successful expedition to capture Port Royal, South Carolina, in November 1861. On April 7, 1863, he moved against Charleston with a squadron of 7 Monitors, an armored gunboat, and the New Ironsides, withdrawing after two hours of bombardment, his vessels having suffered great damage.

are distributed at different points, 2 or 3 miles away; six are here, encamped on a breezy field, the field officers living in the plantation house
near by—a little house with four rooms & the Doctor's closet and a large
piazza all immersed in a dense mass of waving and murmuring locust
blossoms. Upstairs the Adjutant & his wife & opposite them the Major &
Chaplain. Below, the Kitchen & dining room in one where William &
Hetty reign; then my office, with my bed on one side consisting of a broad
wooden shelf & some blankets—& a great open fire place, with bricks for
andirons, to be used on chilly evenings. Then the Doctor's little box, opening on a piazza, the front door of the house borrowed as a door to it & no
windows, but an opening into locust blossoms by day & a shutter at night.
Doctor's floor carpeted with pine needles, so that the whole room is
scented. Outside are the negro houses & sundry rambling sheds, to ac-
commodate our many horses; though Rinaldo lives in a little house close
by the door, where I can go and give him salt at any time, which he eats like
sugar. By the house are sundry tents belonging to officials, dotted among
the trees. Our mess is large & very pleasant; I have grown quite attached to
the Major who is always sunny & obliging, very energetic & industrious, &
as daring a man as I ever met; then there is the Chaplain an eccentric genius with a good deal of brilliancy & perfectly unexpected in word and
deed; Dr Rogers; Dr Minor[183] his assistant & Lt Bingham the Quartermaster,[184] two as true, pure hearted & manly young fellows as the world
can show. Then there is Captain Rogers & the Adjutant & his wife; he always steady, unassuming, & equal to all he undertakes, & she taking life always on the sunny and sensible side. With two or three more women as
bright & pleasant our little household would be quite a model.

We breakfast at 7—then the couriers come in from different directions
with written reports of what happened during the night, sometimes
merely, all quiet along the Coosaw,[185] sometimes a boat coming up to
shore, or picket fired on, a battery suspected as erecting. This is my morning paper, my Tribune or Journal; I consolidate it & by 9 have sent off a
courier to Gen. Saxton, with my daily statement. Then I call for Rinaldo
& away to visit the pickets; at Seabrook we keep a nice little sailboat which

183. Dr. Thomas T. Minor, assistant surgeon of the 1st South Carolina.
184. First Lieutenant J. M. Bingham.
185. "'All quiet along the Potomac' they say" was the first line of a poem by Ethel
Lynn Beers entitled "The Picket-Guard," *Harper's Weekly* 5, 257 (November 30, 1861),
766; later better known by the title "All Quiet along the Potomac," it was set to music and
became a popular camp song among both Union and Confederate soldiers. The Coosaw River separates Port Royal Island from the South Carolina mainland where the
Confederate pickets were stationed.

I brought from Jacksonville, sometimes I take that & cross to some island which we do not picket & which we & the enemy both approach cautiously, they especially, for they have never shown daring except in hopes to find us napping. Sometimes I am back to dinner, sometimes a little in rear of it, sometimes dine out, though that is never very inviting. In the afternoon, writing commonly, dress parade & a little drill at 5; then pick some rose-buds or see if any more of the small magnolias have opened their cloying flowers; tea at six. Lazy evenings, piazza, fireside, chess, a mail, a few more choice pages of "Titan", my only book which I carefully husband; & sound sleep, unless there are pickets to be visited by night, riding under the solemn starlight through the pine woods amid the nocturnal noises of which the "Chuck-Will's Widow,["] the whippoorwill's Southern cousin is the wildest & most frequent. Last night I went out on board the wreck of the George Washington to see where her guns are, stealing out among the creeks & marshes with muffled oars, watching each movement lest some other visitor should be seeking the wreck also, listening breathless to all the marsh sounds, black fish splashing & little wakened reed birds that fled wailing away across the dim river, equally safe on either side. We have spent a good deal of watching on those guns, though we have not been on board the wreck before; but today a gunboat is at last coming to remove them; & then we shall have no excuse for danger unless I let the Major go & surprise a picket somewhere which he is always dying to do. I am sure from what I saw last night that they do not keep very wide awake or they would have fired on us, even at long range from the shore, for they hanker after the wreck as much as we, & we made noise enough to be heard at Fort Sumter. My men are horribly addicted to coughs & colds & it is always the victims of Catarrh who seem most eager for any enterprize requiring pe-culiar caution. As soon as we were under weigh one poor boy next me be-gan to wheeze & I turned indignantly upon him; he saw his danger & meekly said "I w'ont cough, Cunnel," & there he sat choking for two hours, grasping his gun with never a chirrup. But two wretches in the bow of the boat I could not reach; so stopping at our last picket station, at some risk, I dumped them in mud knee deep & took a substitute from the post, who after the first ten minutes coughed louder than both the others. Handkerchiefs, blankets, overcoats suffocation in its direst forms were tried without effect, but apparently the rebel pickets slept through it all & not a shot was fired at us. I think they were asleep, for certainly across the level marshes there came a nasal sound, as of the (Conthieveracy) in its slumbers: It may have been a bull frog, but it sounded like a human snore.

If we remain here long in peace my entomological tastes will rapidly revive. Such immense & lustrous butterflies I have never seen except in dreams; & not even dreams had prepared me for sandflies. Almost too small to be seen they bite worse than musquitos & leave more lasting soreness. They are almost incompatible with Dress Parade; fancy me standing motionless, with my face a mere nebula of these little wretches, torrents of tears rolling down my expressive countenance, from mere muscular irritation. They are however a valuable addition to discipline as they abound in the guard house and render that institution an object of unusual abhorrence. Thus do the weak things of the earth confound the mighty.

Without sandflies & with as good a bathing place as we had at Camp Saxton, this would be a pretty good Paradise for a summer camp. But nobody has a conception how long we are to stay here. Today we hear, that the troops are ordered back to Charleston. Strategy is destined to be as mysterious here as on the Potomac.

## APRIL 19

Thermometer 82° at noon yesterday in shade, 90° today as we dined on the piazza; a cool west wind blowing all the time too. No good bathing place here, but I am trying to contrive one. Thin clothes sadly needed.

This P.m. the Chaplain being away, Corporal Thos. Long has preached. He who went 10 miles into the interior, behind the enemy's camp at Jacksonville, to burn a bridge. He conducted all the services with very little impropriety of language except that he always said Epiopians for Ethiopeans. He said "If each one of us was a praying man, it appears to me that we could fight as well with prayers as with bullets, for the Lord has said that if we have faith even as a grain of mustard seed cut into four parts, you can say unto the Sycamore tree, arise & it will come up." Also he said "For if God says *I shall say*, I will not be harmed. Hell may roll with all its indignation of wrath & I shall be safe."

This morning I met a Flag of Truce at the Ferry—who wanted to send a communication yesterday but couldn't as we could send no boat off at low tide. It turned out after all that they were under orders to hold no official communication with officers of this regiment. Is'nt that an honor? They asked courteously if there was no other officer with whom they could communicate: I said of course not, I was in command. I told them it was their own loss, as it was they who had the letter to send. That we had never had occasion to send a Flag of Truce, but that at Jacksonville their friends were very willing to send them to us; having sent three within twenty four hours, to our great inconvenience, when one would have done as well. They were perfectly well bred young Southerners, Capt Loundes,

Capt Kirk, & Lt Washington:[186] they apologized for troubling me for nothing.

The best thing is that this Brig. Gen. Walker[187] on whose staff they are, is an old friend! He is that Lieut. Walker U.S.A. who was sick at the Water Cure[188] & liked me because of my physique & my abolitionism, he being a desperately pro-slavery invalid: who afterwards met me in Kansas as Capt Walker, with a cavalry company to arrest Redpath[189] & me, & would'nt do it for old acquaintance sake—& here he is across the river, face to face with me again. What an odd little world this is, so constantly the same Dramatis Personae jostle against each other.

I have just heard the soldiers say "Dere's no prisoner on parole for us. Dere's no flags of truce for us;" & it is just as well to have it so, for they are really a great bother & no benefit to those who fight in earnest as this regiment does.

One thing is certain; I have now had under my command white troops from five different states, in connexion with colored ones, & there has been no quarrelling or chafing as yet from Maine, Mass, R.I. Ct. & Pa. This is creditable all round. At the same time it always makes me anxious, for if a quarrel should arise, even slight, the whole slumbering hostility would awaken instantly & might be the destruction of all of us.

Now that the troops are ordered back to Charleston, I suppose we are anchored on this picquet station here till that expedition is over. Montgomery is ill in the hospital. This regiment has never been so healthy.

We have still trouble about countersigns. One of Gen. Saxton's aids now issues them from some geography or dictionary of battles great & small. Our poor sentinels call Carthage *Cartridge*, a word with which they are more familiar, and popularize the classic Concord into Corn Cob. What then can they make of Chapultepec & Wagram? The same is however almost equally true of the Germans & Irishmen who abounds in these

186. Capt. James Lowndes, assistant adjutant-general; Lieut. George S. Worthington, aide-de-camp. No Captain Kirk is mentioned in General Walker's letter about this incident, cited in note 187.

187. Brigadier-General W. S. Walker, commanding at headquarters of Third Military District, Pocotaligo. In a letter to Brig. Gen. Thomas Jordan, April 20, 1863, Walker states that he regarded it as "offensive and insulting" that his Flag of Truce had been met with someone (TWH) "obnoxious to the well-known sentiments of the authorities of the Confederate Government." *The War of the Rebellion: A Compilation of the Official Records of the Union and Confederate Armies*, Series I, Vol. XIV (Washington: Government Printing Office, 1885), 903.

188. Walker had been under the care of Dr. Seth Rogers in the fall of 1852 at the Worcester Hydropathic Institution. See Rogers, "A Surgeon's War Letters," 389.

189. James Redpath, correspondent for the *St. Louis Democrat*, a Free Soil newspaper.

white regts. James Rogers' men keep up their bright sayings. One said criticizing an invalid, "I think, Cappen, he's in a *Casuptious*" (Consumption.)

James Rogers has great luck in drafting men—he had 17 good recruits within two days.

I have authority from Gen S. to draft on these islands, but I d'ont care to do it. So James goes with a squad of men & warns them "If you don't wish to be drafted tomorrow you had better *volunteer* today." Then he leaves his Sergeant who stretches the point a little farther, "Dese yer drafted men aint no account. Dey d'ont get no leaves of absence. Dey has to go & stay with Cunnel Montgomery, on a Point. We call 'em *Bucks*; & dey stay there while our regiment goes & does all de good tings." So they come & *volunteer* for James' company. My men also call Col. M's regiment "De rheumatism regiment," because so many appear to be crippled. The truth is however with these men that the drafted do just as well as the others. Indeed it seems to be so with the whites; there are several regiments of drafted men here from Pa. and their behavior is said to be unusually good.

## April 23

Col Sammis, a large pleasant goodnatured Floridian, formerly very rich & a large slaveholder, very much beloved by his slaves—former owner of my orderly & of Rinaldo—has just been here. He has seen a woman just from Jacksonville, who says not half the city is burnt, after the repeated burnings. My headquarters are not. He says the rebel pickets watched the putting off from the wharves of the last steamboats, but did not fire on them. Now almost all troops have left Florida & he thinks they will not try to reoccupy it. Gen. Seymour assures him that Jacksonville is to be occupied once more—when the second Charleston expedition,[190] now supposed to be only a feint, returns. Gen. S. says it was all Gen. Hunter's own doing, recalling us, but that all troops were needed here. Though they certainly have not done much.

I hope you have not been troubled by the attack on me by "Conservator" in the Evening Post. As to the putting on shore of furniture &c at Jacksonville I certainly did it; for it was a choice between furniture & life. The crowding, on board those boats, was fearful, & nobody suffered more by it in the end than those very people whom I had partially relieved by clearing the vessel. I had my men busy removing the cannon that morning,

190. A naval attack on Fort Sumter commenced on April 7, 1863; Union vessels were severely damaged and withdrew. After this failure, and the repeated penetration of the Union blockade of Charleston Harbor, President Lincoln relieved Rear Admiral Du Pont of his command on July 6, 1863.

while the town was already burning, & when I came to put the men on board ship, I found one half the hold of my principal vessel full of an immense accumulation of furniture. The Captain entirely refused to take on more than 3 companies & I had six to place there; so the only possible way was immediately to put on shore whatever could be got at, leaving only the trunks of the people. As it was, we nearly had a pestilence on board that vessel solely from overcrowding & had to put all the soldiers on shore at the mouth of the river & cleanse out the ship.

In case of storm all the rest of the furniture & the horses must have been thrown overboard, & that might have been called cruelty too. D'ont you know a woman will sooner lose her life than her featherbed. Of course I tried to discriminate as far as I could, but there was little time to discriminate, with the vessels lying at the wharves of a burning town, ammunition on board every vessel & a rebel force outside. And finally every chair & table was taken up on the Boston, where there was a good deal more room, & which lay at an adjoining wharf. Nothing was really left behind; only I refused to take it on my vessel.

Moreover, though it sounds very fine to talk about "Union" citizens, the people who made most noise were avowed secessionists until they thought we were the strongest; & then were afraid to stay because they had gone too far. One family of semi-ladies in the house behind mine who had confessed themselves secessionists to me, had *five wagon loads* of their furniture brought by our only three wagons, when it was hard to get teams to save the sick from the hospital & the cannon from the forts. They had played & sung & flirted with the young naval officers & wound them round their fingers—though entirely without charms. Now they are in Beaufort, in one of the best houses, & have appeared in the streets with secession aprons. Montgomery's Quartermaster is one of their chief admirers. On the other hand some of the real Union people of Jacksonville could not get a team to haul their furniture, so overwhelmed were we with work. Not that Col. Rust meant any special harm, but he was unequal to the terribly difficult task of evacuating a town in a hurry & carrying away the inhabitants.

As for the burning, the place was only very partially burnt, but the perfect insubordination which the attempt showed was outrageous, though not strange to any one who knows our regiments. Good, brave, hardy fellows, intelligent too, but with no more discipline than so many calves. Col. Rust is so unpopular that all but two of his officers have just resigned, & some said openly that they burnt the houses because they thought he didn't wish it.

Of course I shall not write any correction of that report about "Cruelty

&c" because I never believe in contradicting falsehoods; it only keeps them alive. Dr Rogers who first entered his protest as Surgeon against my filling half the ship with furniture, & through whom Capt. Boehme first protested, wants to write something, & I told him he might, provided I was not required to help him.

You know it is not my habit to worry, especially about personal matters, & it is *such* a piece of luck that the public should not charge all the burning on my men, as was to be expected, that I am willing to be thought as bad as "Brute Butler"[191] for a time, if that will buy justice for them. But I expressed the hope in Jacksonville that I might be kept out of the way of "Union" people in rebel communities; if you trust them, they betray you—once refuse their wishes & they denounce you. For one who proposes to fight in earnest it is of course difficult to steer clear. Especially with these colored troops who have good reason to distrust almost the whole of them & who represent the only real Union population of the South.

Do you see the Boston Commonwealth, edited by Conway & Sanborn[192] (this is said to Mother & Anna.) It was flat originally, but is now becoming very able & I advise you to subscribe for it.

Now it is dark, the night insects are shrilling, the "Chuck-Will's Widow" wails, the mockingbird dreams in music & I have ordered Rinaldo, to go & visit the pickets along the Ferry station, pacing slowly along narrow paths down to the projecting points of river bank where my black statues silently watch the paler stream; or out on the causeway where they crouch breathlessly listening to those who crouch as breathlessly aross the narrow channel, seperated a stone's throw in their bodies & more than the distance of life & death in their purposes. N.B. D'ont be frightened; they never fire across.

There was a chance at one time of Charles Follen's coming into this regiment, but some private obstacles came in the way, & it is not to be.

### April 24 —

It is odd to read the papers; we read loud to each other the narrative of our own adventures & agree that no one need say we are not kept supplied with

191. Major General Benjamin Franklin Butler (1818–1893), accused of corrupt practices while military governor of Louisiana in 1862, called "Beast" or "Brute" Butler by his enemies.

192. The Boston *Commonwealth* was a Free Soil newspaper, edited by Moncure Conway and Franklin Sanborn (the latter had been, with TWH, part of the John Brown conspiracy).

new novels! Dr Rogers has sent word to have his little Bell[193] fed on the Arabian Nights[194] altogether & never read a newspaper.

We have nothing to complain of for on the whole this regiment gets rather more than less than its due—but the details are chiefly fabulous, so few men can discribe what is before their own eyes.

April 26.

The Camp here, with six "company streets" of tents looks very pretty, for there is a line of even green awnings before every tent, all uniform-making a sort of little cool bazaar in each company street, under which the men sit and clean their guns, mend their clothes, read their primers &c, & it is all picturesque. Entirely their own idea, too,—one company, my pet Floridian "G" always foremost in everything, led off also in this—& all the others followed.

Yesterday one of my Sergeants & a private were scolding at a sentinel, very improperly, & this morning I sent for the private from the guard-house to scold *him*. "Why, Cunnel, it was dis yer way—I came through the bushes & I heard our Sergeant cussin,—I d'ont know whom he was a-cussin, but I came up just to *help our side*, and I cussed too, and den I found it was de guard-man & I knew we ought not to cuss him." They always call the sentinel the "guard-man," & it is generally recognized that he is not open for what Jack Downing[195] would call "cussing & discussing."

Last night in visiting a picquet at a station where an alarm was created by a boat adrift, last week, a man thus described what he would do, in case a boat came along. "First I shoot and den I shoot and den I shoot again, & den I creep-creep up near de boat and see *who dey in 'em* (who in it) and spose any body pop up he head, den I shoot again. Spose I fire forty rounds, I tink he hear at de camp and send more mans." This was a daring fellow named Paul Jones, quite worthy his namesake.

193. Seth Rogers' wife was named Bell.

194. *Arabian Nights Entertainments* or *The Thousand and One Nights*, a collection of stories written in Arabic, derived from Indian, Persian and Arabic sources, available in various English translations, and appealing strongly to the Western vogue for "oriental" folklore.

195. Jack Downing was a comic vernacular character, the prototypical "Yankee," who initially appeared in Seba Smith, *The Life and Writings of Major Jack Downing of Down-ingville, Away Down East in the State of Maine* (Boston: Lilly, Wart, Colman, & Holden, 1833). Various other writers (such as Charles Augustus Davis) also adopted the Jack Downing persona for their writings, and Seba Smith later added to this collection, finally publishing *My Thirty Years Out of the Senate, by Major Jack Downing* (New York: Oaksmith & Company, 1859), which followed Downing from his first innocent observations on the Maine state legislature to the Mexican War and the national political scene of the 1850s.

Last night I visited picquets by moonlight from $8\frac{1}{2}$ till 12, a lovely night, and happened in upon a wedding at one of our stations. As I came up, a straw carpet was spread outside the door of one of the little cabins, and a semicircle was formed outside, of white soldiers and black for an artillery squad is stationed there—white soldiers with coats unbuttoned & black with them buttoned, for this is a cardinal point with me, you know, & my test of the condition of a regiment, & if a man begins with swearing & stealing, bad practices grow & you always find him at last with his coat unbuttoned. Out stepped the bridal party he out of uniform altogether in "citizen's dress" of dark frock & white vest & pants (I thought of arresting him instantly for violation of army regulations 115 "soldiers must wear their uniform &c["])—the bride in entire white, countenance excepted which in the moonlight was a perpetual shade, poor thing; there are times & seasons where black is not becoming, though infinitely neater on Dress Parade. There they stood, Gabriel & Lerinda, on their carpet at their door, the extremes of society meeting on that common footing, so to speak. The chaplain performed the ceremony quite tenderly & thoughtfully much more so than at our Adjutant's more imposing nuptials. Then Capt. Trowbridge & I shook hands with them & before I left the white vested approached my house and suggested wedding cake—"Cake ready, Gabriel," "Oh yes Cunnel, he done bake" so presently out came a little waiter of modest but not despicable cake, & then the everwandering Chaplain rode off with me to the pickets through the glimmering woods, in a silence broken by the occasional rustle of an opossum or the "*Who's go dar*"? of a watchful sentinel. (I have thought of printing a translation of the Tactics, like the Surinam Bible, into Negro-English.)

I should add that when Capt. Trowbridge sent for the chaplain, Gabriel added "Tell the chapman to come for sure, for I 'zackly in a hurry." His reverence however, forgot the espousals at the appointed time & was galloping off in his erratic way two or three miles in the opposite direction.

A family whom we brought from Jacksonville were sent over the lines by order of Gen Hunter yesterday rather against Gen Saxton's will, as they were very unwilling to go. *We* did'nt handle the affair, as we "d'ont communicate"—& Gen Saxton will not *receive* any communication by the way except through us. An extra family of 13 to feed did not seem to meet with any warm enthusiasm over there, but they were polite to them. Newspapers were exchanged with late dates from Charleston and Savannah crowing over the defeat of our forces, as was to be expected, but still owning to a good deal of anxiety, especially about food. Still we saw no indications of want of food in Florida, I must own, so far as essentials are concerned; any quantity of cattle & hogs & corn to be found there & this soil is so easily worked & things grow so fast, it is hard to imagine starvation. Yet the Savannah paper says[196] (April 16) "Fail in the provision crop, or let it be only what it was the past year & there is no telling what manner of destiny awaits us."

The rebel officers had two black men with them, one of whom whispered to a white soldier that Gen. Walker had withdrawn most of his forces from the opposite side; but it may not be true. Certainly we see & hear less of them—only a few men at each picket station. Both sides merely watch each other & have done so for a long time.

I suppose Lt. col. Billings will be a hero at the North. A wound is a wound no matter if one stumbles into it, as was undeniably the case with him. For myself I could spare him forever; he is absolutely worthless to me.

## May 2ND

One of the men to the Quartermaster who had tried long to explain something to him. "You know, Quattermatter, no use for nigger to try to comb he wool straight, he always short & kinky. *He brains short too*, Sa." (As you may infer from the remark, he is very bright in his answers, like the Irish, however blundering in comprehension.) One good story at Jacksonville I think went untold: the story of the *goose*. In one of our hottest skirmishes, [(]which we called Company K's skirmish, because that company are composed of South Carolinians, & never highly esteemed, did really the best skirmishing we have ever done,) it was noticed that one of the advancing line appeared to move with difficulty. (I should explain that skirmishers are deployed about five paces apart.) It soon appeared that he had come up with & captured a fine *goose* & not wishing to lose it, could find no way to hold it but *between his legs*, so he went on, deliberately loading & firing & occasionally advancing, with the goose writhing & struggling & hissing in this natural pair of stocks. Both came off unwounded & finally retired in good order, when the affair was over; but I think a cooler thing is hardly recorded. Another fellow on the same occasion came blubbering to his Captain, as the skirmishers were drawn in, & said "Cappen, make Cæsar give me my *cane*." It appeared that he during an interval of the fighting had helped himself to an armful of rebel sugar cane (which they delight to chew) the Roman hero, during another interval had confiscated it, whence these tears of the returning warrior.

Our life here is an English rural life with a limited amount of female society & a dash of war thrown in. Without blithe, childlike Mrs Dewhurst I

---

196. The copy-text here reads "papers says."

d'ont know what we should do; her merry laugh & frank simplicity refresh us all the time; it is like having Aggie in camp, though she looks more like Louisa Cabot.[197] We meet at breakfast—scatter to our various rides, all disguised as duty, & bring back experiences at dinner time. Today I brought in an opossum, with the young clinging to the natural pouch provided for them—Dr Rogers a six foot snake round his neck. (not alive.) Dr Miner some great white water lilies, larger & less fragrant than ours—& Mrs Dewhurst, to complete the specimens, the drollest little black baby.

The rebels have left us undisturbed for some time, & unless we alarm them some night, there is not much chance for excitement just now. But on the *vigilance* of the picquets (which is inexhaustible) the whole safety of the island depends. The white Regts had been in the habit of coming here, ten days at a time, now for two yrs & had become rather easy in the discharge of their duty—picquet was regarded as a sort of play time. To my men it is a serious matter. They will hardly even sleep in the daytime when posted at picquet stations, though it is rather expected that all but one at each post will do this. "D'ont truss 'em" they say of the rebels: that is a favorite expression of theirs.

The snake above named was called the thundersnake by the men, of which I could get no explanation save "speck he look like streak lightnin, sa." They are much more afraid of snakes than of alligators which, they say, seldom attack men even in the water but are afraid of them. I have seen a dead alligator 6 ft long, but there is a live one 18 feet long in a cypress swamp not far from here, which I am going to visit.

Speaking of snakes, my courtmartials are over. Gen Saxton complained that I arouse the sympathies of the court too much for the offenders—& as they *didnt know the wives*, they were too tender; cutting down the offense from Desertion into Absence without leave & deciding that the 2 month's imprisonment, part of it in irons, was penalty enough, beside the disgrace; so they were restored to the reg't (the wives having long since left this Department)—but Gen S. told the men they ought to have been shot & made them resign, so I am rid of them; which is all I care for; poor weak fellows, they would have been splendid officers without their wives—two Irish fiends, one swore worse than all my officers put together & the other never opened her lips and was the most formidable tyrant of the two. Those two brave men whom I had seen stand to their guns in the hottest fire on the St Mary's were like whipped spaniels before those women.

I am afraid to quote the things the paymaster said of this regiment, but

197. Probably Mary Louisa Higginson Cabot, TWH's niece (daughter of his brother Francis J. Higginson), who married Francis Cabot.

Mr Page has sent it all to the Tribune they say. I am ashamed to be so praised; it is such a reproach on this undisciplined unbuttoned mob we call an army. I hope it will never be my lot to write military memoirs; I should have to dip my pen in stronger superlatives than I ever mixed before.

Here is the latest Beaufort anecdote. There is a N.Y. regiment here which calls itself Les Enfans Perdus or the lost children, being composed of all nations—officers chiefly French. One of these, the Adjutant, was criticizing some of Gen. Hunter's late movements & some one in joke threatened him with Fort La Fayette. "Vas dat you say" he cried in a rage, "ven you say *La Fayette*, take off you hât" (suiting the action to the word.) "Ven you say *Vashington*, take off you hât" (uncovering again.) "Ven you say *Huntare*, do as me, Ah-h-h" (griping his hat over his ears with both hands, grinding his teeth & running away in an ecstasy of despair.)

You may fancy from this that there is no enthusiasm felt here over the failure at Charleston & the evacuation of Jacksonville.

## MAY 7

It is a funny life we lead here, even beyond the average fun of this oddest of planets. From the time we first went to housekeeping by taking down the front door of the house to complete therewith the Dr's little snuggery, everything has been upside down. I undress according to the weather, if it is bright moonlight I turn in very thoroughly; if it is very dark & a trifle rainy I undress as Suwarrow[198] did when very lazy—take off one spur. One wakes up in the middle of the night & has a horse saddled to go & inspect pickets, or is waked up with some difficulty, to be told that somebody is somewhere firing at something, which always settles itself like Napoleon's unanswered letters.[199] Then the morning arrangements are peculiar. I fitted up a bathing place in a creek which somehow got appropriated by the company laundresses; but I have my revenge for I bathe in the family washtub. After all the kitchen has the advantage, for they use my napkin to wipe off the table. For food it is impossible to get chickens here

198. "It is said that Suwarrow, even in peace, always slept fully armed, boots and all. 'When I was lazy,' he said, 'and wanted to enjoy a comfortable sleep, I usually took off one spur.'" Thomas Wentworth Higginson, "Physical Courage," *Atlantic Monthly* 2 (November 1858), 735.

199. According to Ralph Waldo Emerson in "Napoleon; or, The Man of the World," in *Representative Men* (1850), Napoleon made it "his practice, when general in Italy, in regard to his burdensome correspondence . . . to leave all letters unopened for three weeks, and then observed with satisfaction how large a part of the correspondence had thus disposed of itself, and no longer required an answer." Ralph Waldo Emerson, *Essays and Lectures* (New York: The Library of America, 1983), 735.

save in the immature shape of eggs & other fresh meat seems out of the question. For drink we chiefly imbibe Florida syrup which we take exclusively from a whisky bottle. The pretty fluid is so effervescent that it sometimes pops out the cork, like ale, at dinner & leaves a blot of syrup on the ceiling of the piazza.

It is not at all unhealthy here yet, & I do not suppose it will be on these islands; & yet I think Dr Rogers & I are the only officers in the reg't who have not been sick since we began. He keeps up wonderfully, by dint of great care & the Major says I appear to be "tough as a pine knot.["]

May 8—Today we had an adventure. The Major & I rode to the Ferry where Jas. Rogers was on picquet & there at the opposite point of the long causeway were two men: The rebels sometimes come down there, but I saw that they were beckoning & were black. It seemed so improbable that they could have eluded the picquets, we suspected a trap; but James wanted to go over & I let him go in a dugout, paddling across alone, as it would only hold three. My great fear was that there might be rebels in the bushes on the causeway who might have made these men come out as a ruse and would fire on him—but I made four men come out to our end & point their guns over the little breast work, all ready to fire & watched, intensely anxious, through my glass, till he had safely touched shore & off again & when we got them on our side I made my men give three cheers, just as they did when they had destroyed the "George Washington" a while ago. It proved that the men had come from 100 miles in the interior. Just as we got them the twenty horsemen came along as usual at noon, to relieve their picquets, & must have wondered what we were all doing out there, but perhaps they do not know till this moment, as the fugitives had dodged round the causeway at low tide, somehow; We found they had been at the place since morning, but the men on duty had been afraid of a trap, & indeed it seemed hardly credible that their picquets should not have watched better. It is quite a manly thing in James, & gives him two recruits of his own capturing.

Yesterday Gen Hunter came up from Hilton Head to review the troops at Beaufort, & I rode as one of Gen. Saxton's Aids. About 5,000 troops only were reviewed & nothing really looked well except Gen Saxton who always looks elegantly on horseback—& his escort the Mass^tts cavalry. There is always a Southern inelegance about the equipages here, carriages, harness, saddles & horses. When Major Gen. Hunter & his attending ladies had scrambled across the lumber schooner Jotham P Jones to get ashore; there was an absurd contrast between Gen. Saxton's personnel & the vehicle into which he tucked the dames. Then said he in a courtly way, to Capt Lowe, the post quartermaster—"Now, Captain order down the rest of the carriages.["] Whereupon Captain Lowe meekly responded, "This is the only one, Sir" & the remaining damsels had to walk or go crowded.

I had some talk with Gen. Hunter afterwards. It is hard not to like him when one is with him; he seems so goodnatured, generous, and impulsive. He impresses me as being by habit lax, indolent, vacillating & forgetful; but as capable of being on a given occasion prompt, decided, and heroic. So far as principles of action go, this war has nothing more to teach him, his defects are more hopeless because they belong to his temperament and no conversion can extricate him from them. With the tonic of a strong moral influence always beside him he could be easily held up to the standard of a great man; as it is while he is asleep, the devil sows tares, & that is a large part of the time.

You can scarcely imagine how little is said here about the Charleston expedition. It took such a interminable time to prepare for it; people here felt such a languid confidence in it; & the failure came so soon; that every body has acquiesced in a sort of stupefied way, & now the chief interest seems to be in getting furloughs. The Army & Navy are very distinct departments & d'ont criticize each other much & I suppose really that there has been less excitement over the whole thing than at the North.

## MAY 10

Such fun as we have had over the newspaper accounts of us. I just told Dr Rogers it was fortunate that novels were still published, that there might be truth found somewhere, since history certainly affords none; but he says if things go on so much longer we c'ant even put faith in novels. We have just seen the scrap about our picket firing—two negroes wounded—two butternuts[200] biting the dust—all sheer fabrication. Occasionally they fire a little, at very long range & my men fire back, & that's all about it—except Gen. Hunter's pithy endorsement on the back of Gen. Saxton's letter— "Give them as good as they send—D. Hunter, Maj. Genl. Commanding"—that was to the point.

The great drawback of these Southern col'd regt's will always be the severe burden of writing they throw on officers, both field & line. I spend hours daily, & much vitality needed for other things, in doing writing which every Col. of a white reg't has one or more clerks detailed to do; the same with my Quartermaster, the same with my adjutant. This is in-

---

200. "Butternut" was a colloquial expression for a Confederate or a Southern sympathizer.

evitable; in addition in this particular case, the Lt. col. & the Major are not naturally bookkeepers, any more than drillmasters (neither of them could drill either the reg't or a company ten minutes without some serious mistake—& if we were in battle & I were injured, a Captain would have to take command); The Sergeant Major, the only other person I can ever call on for aid in writing, is sick, & not efficient when well, & has his own work beside. If col'd regt's were not easier to drill & discipline than white ones, all their officers would die, except those who had happily never learned to write.

I d'ont wish to be severe on my field officers—Maj Strong I should be very sorry to lose; he has no turn for drill & his health is delicate, but he is the soul of courage, full of enterprise & resources, always amiable always ready to work. Lt. Col. Billings is absolutely worthless.

It is Sunday noon & a wedding party is sitting under the trees, awaiting the Chaplain. One soldier a good looking youth in uniform coat & festive white pants & gloves; & two young girls, jet black, in low necked white muslin dresses, shirt sleeves, straw colored sashes, with good figures, not too stout which they are apt to be & of the handsome shade of black. Many have a *grimy* black, which is repulsive looking as if it would come off—but with many the color is a very deep wine colour which to my eye is very handsome in its way; the skin being smoother & finer grained than ours, (Dr Rogers observes) both in the men & the women; their arms are particularly handsome, because labor seems to develop them without making them wiry or hairy or sunburnt. We have had many recruits lately & Dr Rogers often calls me in to admire their fine physique or to see the common marks of the lash.

Last Sunday there was a funeral on this plantation & during the whole sunny day a great prayer meeting of women sat under the great live oaks before my window & sang hymn upon hymn—an old Deborah[201] leading off, gesticulating and beating time with her whole body & calling on each woman present by name. In the afternoon old men came from the various plantations & I let the soldiers march there, instead of to our usual meeting. The women all looked neat, with handkerchiefs round their heads.

As for the wedding, this is one of the days in the quarter when they go to be married "by de book" as they call it; often letting a mere social ceremony suffice for a time.

My poor Lieuts. O'Neil & Stockdale[202] have fared hard. After 48 days

201. Deborah was an Old Testament judge and prophet who aided the Israelites in their victory over the Canaanites.

202. Lieut. James B. O'Neil and Lieut. William Stockdale both resigned on May 2, 1863.

imprisonment they were tried by court martial—convicted not of desertion but of absence without leave & set at liberty as punished enough. This Gen. S. attributes to my being too mild on them in my evidence & saying too much in their favor; but he made them resign & Gen. Hunter dismisses them from service as incompetent & worthless and they forfeit all their pay, & all this because two women, who had been soldiers wives for years, couldn't make up their minds to go to New York alone! At any rate they will not return to the reg't of which I was at one time afraid.

The rapid multiplication of colored regiments is of more *personal* importance to me than to all the rest of the nation, for it is taking a load of personal responsibility off my shoulders. There is no doubt that for many months the fate of the whole movement for colored soldiers rested on the behavior of this one regiment. A mutiny, an extensive desertion, an act of severe discipline, a Bull Run panic,[203] a simple defeat, might have blasted the whole movement for arming the blacks—& through it the prospects of the war & of a race. Now the thing is so far advanced that Africa holds many shares in the lottery of war & should the 1st S.C.V. prove a blank, others will not. The Tribune correspondent said to me the other day, "This is the only *regiment* with which the public has become familiar; in all other cases they have known at most the Division or the Brigade. (It is amusing to see, even now, how they all call my 850 a Brigade.) I have had enough of this notoriety & am very willing to be merged in an army of such regiments!

## ADVANCED PICKET
## MAY 25

Two things in the way of compliments for the regiment have turned up lately, better than the average. Col. Littlefield (30 reg. S.C.V.—in future) says that Secretary Chase[204] told him the Cabinet at Washington kept their whole action in regard to enlisting colored troops *waiting* to hear from us in Florida, & when the capture of Jacksonville was known, the whole question was regarded as settled, the policy avowed, and Adj. Gen. Thomas[205] sent out on his mission. This is, I think, the best expression of the importance of our action that has yet occurred.

203. In the First Battle of Bull Run, July 21, 1861, exhausted Union troops in a state of confusion fled the battlefield.

204. Salmon Portland Chase (1808–1873), Secretary of the Treasury in Lincoln's cabinet.

205. Brigadier General Lorenzo Thomas (1804–1875) was sent to organize black regiments in the Mississippi Valley.

The other is the saying of one of our men who was asked if he belonged to Col Montgomery's regt. "No," said he proudly, "I'se belong to *Colonel Higginson's regulars.*" This is the triumph of self-respect, with a witness!

Col. M, with some officers for the 30 regt, is to sail in a day or two for parts unknown, to recruit his numbers. I wish him success most heartily, though his career here has disappointed me; at least he has not been so generous & noble as I hoped. But then he has had a good deal to try him in the delays he has met with; he is very ambitious, and impatient constitutionally in regard to system and order, for which I am rather a stickler. Our whole method as to discipline is so different that perhaps we are as well apart. In carrying on war we should not differ much, except that my plans would be more tenaciously adhered to, less flexible.

Only think of a pic nic here the other day Mrs Lander[206] got me up at the Barnwell place the most beautiful on the island & I helped her a good deal. It was got up for a young Mr Hay[207] Pres Lincoln's Private Secretary, a nice enough young fellow, who unfortunately looks about 17 & is oppressed with the necessity of behaving like 70. He wrote about Ellsworth & some foolish thing in the Atlantic,[208] & is staying with Gen Saxton. Mrs Lander spent the whole day arranging—with one of our own gay young Paymasters, & Mr Page the blundering Tribune correspondent. Mrs. Dewhurst & I went over early; & it was entertaining to see the Ex actress's eye for effect—a table cloth here, a scarlet lined coat there, Miss Brown's curls in an available vista, & blackberries & black sentinels in the back ground. About 4 came the band, the officers, the young ladies, Gen Saxton without his livelier half, Mr Hay laboring not to appear new mown. It went off better than the average—the place was beautiful, old trees & a view across

206. Jean M. Lander (née Davenport) was the widow of General F. W. Lander, and formerly a stage actress.

207. John Milton Hay (1838–1905), Lincoln's assistant secretary, oversaw the President's correspondence and dealt with visiting politicians; he came with Lincoln from Springfield, Illinois.

208. John Hay, "Ellsworth," *Atlantic Monthly* 8 (July 1861), 119–25. Ephraim Elmer Ellsworth was a military reformer who organized the United States Zouave Cadets of Chicago, a volunteer militia company, in 1859, and later another company in Springfield, Illinois—where he was nominally a law student in Lincoln's office. The Zouaves' colorful uniforms and military élan brought them wide popular renown, and Ellsworth became a celebrity; after Lincoln's election he was appointed a Lieutenant in the army, but soon threw up his commission, electing to raise a volunteer regiment in New York, the First Fire Zouaves, or Eleventh New York, and on May 24, 1861, led them across the Potomac from Washington, D.C., to occupy Alexandria, Virginia. He was shot dead by a hotel keeper when he tore down the Confederate flag from a hotel, and his death occasioned widespread public anger and grief. Hay does not appear to have made any other contribution to the *Atlantic*.

Broad River to the rebel shore, a great sail cloth laid down to dance on, Gen. S. leading out Mrs L. in lingering widow's weeds; his dancing as direct grave and simple as his policy, hers graceful as if she were sweeping the boards, technically so called. We all like her, she is so off the stage what she was on it, simple, earnest, high-minded, sensible. We had blackberries & *milk* & after this pastoral entertainment galloped home through the wood paths by the young moon.

I forgot to tell Mr Hay for old Abe's delectation that the little drummer boys of Mrs Dewhurst's school all nodded eagerly when she asked if they knew who was President of the United States. On her requesting them to name him, they burst out in eager chorus "Uncle Sam."

I send one of the certificates which Sergt Wm Brandon has a passion for giving his recruits; no two are alike. There is something sublime in the opening. *"Here is a strayed Man,"* what an epic beginning, what a picture. Fancy him going round in these times to pick up all of this class. The mysterious signature "S.C. African foundation" is an epithet he has devised for himself, because he was the first black soldier enlisted in this Department.

How could I ever tell you all the funny things I hear. Yesterday a noble looking old woman, as stately as Mrs Le Baron, came to explain gravely to me the wrongs her son endured from a bad wife, which culminated in the following ignominious scene "Dey got *a-tangling*, sa, and *she took his foot and kick he out of de door"*!

I get so accustomed to hearing the use of he & his for she & hers that I insensibly fall into it myself.

The heat is not yet oppressive save sometimes at noon & there is commonly a western breeze all day; always at night. Soon, they say, we shall have more rain. The regiment is healthier than ever before & in better condition except as to nicety of drill, which always suffers from active service & picquet duty. We have had 70 recruits since leaving Jacksonville & thrown out some 30 for disability. Our aggregate a few days ago was 860, the largest it has ever been—this includes sick, absent and all. Today it is 853.


ADVANCED PICQUET STATION
MAY 17.

Let me see, if I have not forgotten all my literary arts, whether I cannot coin my Captains into sentences.

1. *Captain Trowbridge.* The brawn & health of an Englishman; a prize fighter by nature & an abolitionist by grace. Ideas and sentiments gradually su-

perinduced on a coarse organization. Having commanded black troops earlier than any of the rest, and taken them at their lowest, he does not feel the respect for their personal feelings that we do, mimics their own dialect to them, calls them "boy," patronizes them & in general seems like a goodnatured overseer, who will resent every tyranny but his own.—A mason by trade & a "brick" himself; too ponderous to be quick, but irresistible; as indomitable as a steam engine & as incapable of being hurried. Lived in Brooklyn N.Y. where he was, undoubtedly, foreman of a fire company, though I never heard any one allude to it.

2. *Captain James.*[209] An Englishman by birth, a Welchman by nature, neat, prompt, faithful, choleric, accurate, thorough—mounting guard over his company like a lioness over her young; as incapable of caring for the rest of the regiment as Calhoun or Randolph[210] for the rest of the Union, would go without his breakfast & see a whole army do the same, rather than that his worst drummer boy should have only half rations of sugar to his coffee. Always at sword's points with every other Captain; always in high favor with his Colonel & the Surgeon. His company the second best in the regiment, because he thinks of it and labors for it every waking moment.

3. *Captain Heasley*[211]—a Pennsylvanian & a thoroughly equable, invariable, & average man, one whom I always find in every emergency or non-emergency in precisely the same place, whom I can scarcely conceive of ever blaming or praising. I have never perceived that it made the slightest difference in his aspect or intonation whether I sent him on some dangerous expedition or left him in camp to guard knapsacks. His person has the same unobtrusiveness & neutral coloring with his mind; you would not notice him if he were in the same room with you. Yet there is nothing stolid or indifferent in all this; he is moderate even in his moderation.

4. *Captain Whitney*[212]—a tall slender young man with fair hair, mildish face, & character not quite formed; has inclinations after culture, has Byron[213] & a guitar, knows a few ladies & wishes to know more. I have never

209. Captain William James.

210. John Caldwell Calhoun (1782–1850), South Carolina politician and political theorist who advocated states-rights and slavery, opposing the Compromise of 1850 in his final weeks as Senator; John Randolph (1773–1833), Virginia politician who was an important proponent of states-rights doctrine.

211. Captain Alexander Heasley.

212. Captain H. A. Whitney.

213. George Gordon, Lord Byron, English Romantic poet (1788–1824) whose work was immensely popular in America, although widely condemned for immorality on account of both his poetry and his scandalous life; young men who aspired to Byronism often held themselves to be in rebellion against conventional morality, in defiance of fate, and in search of high heroic feeling.

quite understood how he coped with his company, which is the only rough one in the regiment, made up of sailors & quartermaster's men. Yet he does it, very tolerably, and they did in Florida, the best fighting we have ever accomplished, though there is not a Floridian among them.

5. *Capt Metcalf*[214]—the model captain of our model company; yet one can see in him only a quiet, good looking, gentlemanly young man, with an air of culture & refinement, which he acquired on a travelling confectioner's cart in Massachusetts. Where he got his secret of perfect & unerring success, I do not know—he has a first-lieutenant even superior to himself & his company is of better materials than any other. But these do not explain that universal superiority shown at every point—drill, discipline, equipments, sanitary arrangements, company writing—which all concede to Company G. It must lie largely in the Captain.

6. *Capt. Dolly.*[215] The antipodes of the last named; our one thoroughly rough diamond, a Maine lumberman, scarcely able to write his name, coarse, swearing, not without a tendency to drink;—yet a decided favorite of Dr Rogers from the first glance, even to me, though strange to say, I never heard him swear. But there is a kernel of true & kind manhood below, & he is very faithful to his men in all essentials & they to him; though a neat & satisfactory company it will never be.

7. *Captain Randolph*[216] was omitted; he should have ranked third. Our oldest Captain, with streaks of gray in his beard & of sincere fanaticism in his brain; a physician originally & a man of ideas & eloquence; could march on bayonets himself with a joy too eager for him to make his men march steadily with him. Too unmethodical to be efficient, too fussy to be thoroughly respected; a grandmother instead of a father to his men. He came out of the "Roundhead Regt." of Pennsylvania, but he dates back to the original Roundheads himself.[217] In Jacksonville when a prisoner whom he had taken asserted that he was promised a trial by Capt. Randolph, the latter heard the claim with unfeigned amazement. "I promised him," quoth he "*nothing*, except the Day of Judgement & Periods of Damnation!"

8. *Capt. Tonking.*[218] Petty, precise, prim, priggish—an Englishman with all national attributes left out except an intense love of forms and neatness. His company alone wears white gloves at Dress Parade, & they are al-

214. Captain L. W. Metcalf.
215. Captain George Dolly.
216. Captain W. J. Randolph.
217. Roundheads were supporters of the Parliamentarians during the English Civil War, so called because of the close-cropped hair of the Puritans.
218. Captain James H. Tonking.

ways spotless. Full of little punctilios, without an atom of tact, he drives his best men into insubordination by perpetual teazing. Perfectly courageous, but with a kind of coolness more irritating than any excitability. I have myself seen him, under fire, stop his men's firing and put them through the manual exercise[219] in order to keep them cool. So utterly does he fail of his effects that his is the only company in which I should fear a panic. He has a few qualities which if they could be unscrewed & used seperately would be inestimable. But he is a man of outsides.

9. *Capt. Rogers.* A great sunny force in the regiment, with his handsome young face, great dark eyes always rolling, great white teeth always smiling; enjoying every moment, revelling in his men as a girl in her paper dolls; the only Captain who can frolic with his men,—who all adore him. Perfectly fearless, perfectly buoyant, almost boyish, he is a favorite every where. Sometimes he forgets or neglects duties, but it is always because preoccupied with some other duty. Accomplishes more every day & with less effort, than any other Captain. I have had a glimpse, but very seldom, of corresponding depths of depression and gloom.

10. *Capt Thibadeau.*[220] Our youngest Capt., and was our best lieutenant. Promotion almost spoiled him, because his ambition is intense & he has no patience; a Canadian Frenchman by birth, with all the excitability of his race, but in its most dangerous form—a speechless irritability that locks itself inside. At every disappointment he shuts his lips & grows dogged. Incurs censure deliberately and refuses to defend himself. Of the most daring courage, but allows his men no rest, nor himself either, so that all he accomplishes is done with an immense expenditure of force. He never smiles in dealing with his men, rarely praises, is habitually sarcastic, & when exhausting himself on their part creates in them the impression of perfect indifference.

ADVANCED PICQUET
MAY 29 — 1863

Ever since I made my officers understand that they were to be kept down to a valise apiece, & no stealing, they have delighted in inveigling me into any small luxuries, a chair, a desk &c; & my exhibiting a sheet at last produced a thrill of triumph; & now that Montgomery's regiment is just off (which did stealing for a dozen) James Rogers has just seduced me into an

219. The manual of arms, basic exercises in the controlled manipulation of a soldier's weapons.
220. Captain J. H. Thibadeau.

enchanting musquito netting, lace, wash "blonde" (as Mrs Dewhurst instantaneously designated it) of whose Jacksonville origin there can be no reasonable doubt. I feebly suggested "hospital", to which destiny all mattrasses were long since devoted; but it was finally settled that it should invest my humble couch till we set up a camp hospital; & I assure you that the transparent drapery caught up in the middle over a vista of crimson blanket, quite enhances the beauty of the apartment. For other furniture we have two secretaries & a very few chairs & stools—flowers everywhere, a pelican's wing three feet long & various military appurtenances beside the regimental flag. Then the white walls are covered with clever heads in pencil by a Lt Richardson of N.H. & there is an admirable map of the whole picquet region by Lt Crowningshield[221] of Boston, Caspar's brother.

My distinction about stealing is that I approve of public stealing so much as to disapprove of private. And in respect to officers' luggage, I d'ont care how comfortable they make themselves in camp, but in removing from one camp to another, the public cannot transport more than the prescribed allowance. I have never owned more than a valise myself, & find it harder to keep the officers in check than the privates; for the weight of a knapsack is a natural limitation.

Gen. Hunter's new letter to Jeff. Davis[222] is a very unfortunate one, like many of his impulses. The threat to execute his prisoners unless J. D. revokes, would only make the latter smile for he must know that it would never be carried out—because public sentiment would not sustain it. But public sentiment will sustain retaliatory acts & the threat of those carries a weight which the more extravagant threat only impairs. I am sorry he has done it. Not that this whole discussion carries any great interest in this regiment, as we never have come within any risk of being taken prisoners & know J. D's threat only as a wholesome tonic. Nothing is better calculated to make men feel in earnest. The privates have never heard of the order, but they know their late masters well enough without it. I suppose if captured they would doubtless be sold, until retaliation takes place; but I have no idea that they would do any of the officers much damage for they would *know* Gen. Hunter would retaliate.

I am not at all sure that some of Gen. H's pro slavery staff have not urged him up to this measure that it may defeat itself. Nothing amazes me

---

221. Lieutenant Francis W. Crowningshield, 2d Massachusetts Volunteers (Infantry).

222. Jefferson Finis Davis (1808–1889), President of the Confederate States of America. On May 1, 1863, the Confederate Congress passed a resolution stating that captured white officers of Northern black troops would be put to death or otherwise punished for inciting insurrection.

so thoroughly as to see the men with whom these anti slavery Generals sur-
round themselves, though Gen. Saxton's has been gradually purified &
they have always treated us perfectly well; as have Gen. Hunter's to our
faces, though sometimes thwarting us behind our backs. But they have annoyed & insulted Gen Saxton to that extent, that he has just gone to Washington to get the assurance of control in his own department. I am glad of
it; his honest face will carry conviction with it, if he has decent men to deal
with. If he once did a dishonorable act I should forever lose my faith in him
& with it in human nature—as I once heard old Samuel Hoar say of
Charles G Loring.[223] I wonder what saucy things little Mrs Tillie[224] will
say to old Abe. Do you know she can imitate perfectly her husband's handwriting. Gen Hunter's, Pres. Lincoln's, Gen Scott's,[225] Mr Seward's[226] &
even the sacred Mr Spinner's who signs the Greenbacks. I have seen them.

It is quite nice to have a private telegraph; we have just heard of a
steamer coming in at Hilton Head, which may bring a mail. The latest rumor from Beaufort is (not by telegraph) that Montgomery's Expedition is
given up & he ordered to stay here, which would be hardly credible in any
other department, & will be a great disappointment to him.

We have lost our first officer—Lieut. Gaston,[227] who was accidentally
shot by one of his own in a little reconnaissance across the river yesterday.
He and James & 20 men went; the rebel pickets were retreating & giving
free passage when Gaston was shot through the heart by the gun going
off. James felt it very much as he was very fond of him, & close by at the
moment. I was watching them across the ferry through a glass—at daybreak—in such a driving rain that the glass was blurred & I could not tell
who fired the gun or why they came back. It is singular how little emotion
I feel at such times, sympathetic as my nature is—the death of a man beside me falls off from me as if I were marble & excites no more sensibility
than when a tree falls & yet at any other time I should feel it very much
more. Tonight we had funeral services here just at dusk & it was one [of]
the most impressive funerals I ever knew; the chaplain was in one of his
best moods of utterance & so perhaps was I; & the closing hymn "Jesus live

223. Charles Loring was a Boston lawyer active in the antislavery movement.
224. Matilda "Tillie" Saxton, née Thompson.
225. General Winfield Scott (1786–1866), who resigned as chief military commander of Union forces on November 1, 1861, following the defeats at First Bull Run and
Ball's Bluff.
226. William Henry Seward (1801–1872), former New York Governor and Senator,
now Lincoln's Secretary of State.
227. First Lieutenant R. M. Gaston, killed at Coosaw Ferry, South Carolina, May 27,
1863.

& reign forever" was really magnificent, led by Uncle Adam Allston[228] one of our saints & a splendid leader in these songs—often he is too excited, but today the emotion sobered him & he stood waving his arms & gesticulating with the music, he was wonderfully graceful & solemn. The air is the original John Brown hymn, but more varied. One verse is very close to it & more impressive.

> "My body's bound for de mouldering of de clay
> And my soul's marching on."

The coffin was all filled with flowers & all was touchingly *real*. Just at the beginning up rode Mrs. Lander & Mr Page, Tribune correspondent. The latter looked at it as an item; but Mrs L. was exceedingly affected by it; I was so absorbed in our men that I forgot all about her widowhood. It would have affected anybody, though, there is something so plaintive about the whole condition of these grown up children, at any time; a——— ———would shed rivers of tears over almost anything they do, whether they laugh or cry; there is a sort of mute appeal about them unknown to themselves. It is very hard to punish them, they seem like dumb or blind babies, or maimed animals. There is infinitely less of the defiant or dangerous element about them than I expected; very few *devils* in the regiment; but the same soft texture which nothing but the contact with gunpowder seems to harden.

May 30. Went down in the early morning, a few of us, to take Lt Gaston's remains to the beautiful green quiet cemetery around the old Episcopal Church. It is small, high walled with stone & filled with old monuments of stately Carolinian families Middleton, Barnwell, De Saussure, all buried in masses of green shade. As I sat in the empty church, the doves cooed into the window & the mocking bird trilled & then the cavalry bugles rang through with their shriller sound, & then I walked out again among the luxurious Southern growths, & thought there could not be in a strange land a sweeter resting place for a discarded body.

HEADQUARTERS. 1ST S.C.V.
BEAUFORT S.C. JUNE 16. 1863

Here we are under canvas again—for how long nobody knows; but all seem to enjoy it the officers like being brought together again & I feel like a matronly hen with her family at last under her wing again. They seemed so

228. Corporal Adam Allston.

innumerable too, I thought I had never seen so many soldiers in the world as at our first Dress Parade. I had only had 4 companies for so long; & then again the reg't had never been so *availably* large, we have discharged so many men surgically unfit & got new men in their places; it makes a great difference. I have not myself lived in a tent save for a night or two, during more than 3 months & at this season one enjoys it; the waking & going to sleep are lovely & through midday all the sides are taken up & one does very tolerably.

There is a Reg't on either side of us, on the great parade ground where we are, the 174ᵗʰ & 176ᵗʰ Pa. both drafted reg'ts, chiefly German; & the 52ⁿᵈ Pa. a 3 yrs reg't has just removed. The three together are about the size of mine (860). The two former return in a fortnight or so, & then the parade ground will be turned over to colored troops, who will soon have things their own way in this Department; as indeed they seem likely to do elsewhere.

Matters here are perplexed; Gen Saxton was amazed at Gen. Gilmore's[229] being put in Command of the Dep't, (being his junior officer) & at once resigned the military command of the Post, retaining only his civil functions—which it is thought may end in putting him in command of the Dep't, instead of Gilmore. Meanwhile the forces here are under command of Col. W. W. H. Davis of Pa. a good officer, (Senior Col.) editor of a Democratic, almost Copperhead[230] newspaper, but so very kind and obliging to me that I hardly know what to make of it only that it is very convenient and pleasant. He was in the Mexican war under Cushing; Gen Gillmore I have not seen, but I have had no trouble with any official yet & expect none with him. Strange to say I have experienced more annoyance & discourtesy from Montgomery than from any pro slavery functionary in the Department. He is now down near Georgia making some capital raids. If he were only as noble & generous, in thought as he is daring & successful in action. As it is, he will never rise above a brigand. His hatred of control makes it hard for him to believe that a regiment which is well drilled can be fit for action. Whereas I believe that want of self control will demoralize our men and want of drill will unfit them for *regular* warfare when needed. He thinks me straitlaced & red-tapish—I think him fitter to command a hundred men than a thousand.

I write with an immense spike of yucca in my tent, there must be almost

229. Major General Quincy Adams Gillmore (1825–1888), assigned to command the Department of the South on July 10, 1863.

230. During the Civil War, a Copperhead was a Northerner who sympathized with the South.

a hundred blossoms & it grows wild—the *spicata* not *filamentosa*, but they are much alike only this is less moony than Margaret Fuller's favorite.[231]

## HEADQRS 1ST S.C.V.
## BEAUFORT S.C.
## JUNE 27. 1863

It is almost the first of July & there has been as yet none of that insufferable heat one hears about—only a *relaxing* heat from nine to four or so & almost always a cool breeze at other times. On the other hand there has been almost no *fascination* of climate—none of the soft, sweet, musical days of our Early Spring, none of the regal fulness of our June. I do not think it is a mere fancy,—for it has occurred to me so often,—that there is the same temperament in the climate and in nature here which I have noticed in Southern women—passion & fire, without fineness or depth. The range of elements in our Northern zone seems infinitely greater, hence a combination more rich, more pliable, more inexhaustible.

Meanwhile my large family sun themselves & are happy, work cheerily when needful, and bask like lizards beneath their shelter-booths of Evergreen. They are now perfectly healthy, while almost all the officers, except myself, feel more or less the subtle effect of climate. This makes a great difference; I mean the health of the men; an officer learns to live so much in others & these men, seeming more like children, affect one's sympathetic nature more. It is a singular sort yet un-analyzed. I am conscious of but little affection for individuals among them, if a man dies in hospital or is shot down beside me, I feel it scarcely more than if a tree had fallen, of course if the tree is a fine one I am sorry; but over their *collective* joys & sorrows I have smiles & tears, I shrink from exposing them to danger, I cannot fling them away, they suggest emotions of cowardice *for them*, which I could not personally feel. It would be agony to meet them again after a battle, with half the number gone. Probably it is like the love of animals for their young; they cannot count, do not subdivide affection into fractions. Brute mothers will die for their collective progeny, but you may take them one by one, without notice; no bird cares for a single egg, only for the eggs. I like to go round the tents of an evening & hear them purring & know that they are happy, and happier for seeing me pass. Sometimes there is a sublime elo-

231. [Sarah] Margaret Fuller (1810–1850), was a celebrated writer, editor, and social activist. Her "Yuca Filamentosa" can be found in *The Essential Margaret Fuller*, ed. Jeffrey Steele (New Brunswick, New Jersey: Rutgers University Press, 1992), 50–52. TWH noted Fuller's love of flowers in his biography, *Margaret Fuller Ossoli* (Boston: Houghton, Mifflin and Company, 1884), 18–19.

quence about them, that thrills me with impressions of immortality, but more commonly they are just children, & when they are earnest it is their *dumbness* that is pathetic, what they bear in silence with the hopelessness of centuries of wrong—that touches. When they speak about small things there is such a jumble commonly, all pathos puts on the robes of comedy. "Cappen Scroby (Trowbridge) he acvise me not for marry dis lady, 'cause she hab seven children,—what for use?—Cappen Scroby can't lub for me, I must lub for myself, and I lub he." Meanwhile *he* stands by, an unattractive female, impenetrably black, in an old pink muslin dress, torn white gloves, & a bonnet beyond the wildest dreams of Irish girl, & descended through generations of tawdry mistresses. It is impossible for an inexperienced person to appreciate the *variety*, physical & mental among those equally black. There are men & women in this camp, soldiers & laundresses, who to my eye are beautiful—complexions clear & rich like wine, handsome regular mouths, eyes full of expression, forms noble & graceful; these traits scattered among many, if not united in one. Sergeant Prince Rivers is as superb as a panther, whose *tread* he perfectly possesses. Hetty wife of my orderly is as essentially ladylike and refined as Sarah Butman, & if she did not, unlike most of her race, stand in need of the dentist, she might safely be called a charming person. It must be remembered that the texture of the negro skin is peculiarly smooth & fine; the strongest men in my regiment have arms which would make the fortune of an English belle, in all but color, round & satiny, without a trace of hair. It is certain that every separate type of physical humanity has it's own points of beauty.

One of our prime favorites is dear old York, our "Uncle Tom", who takes care of Dr. Rogers, a perfect type of well-bred respectability as to the outward, & inwardly a saint. In Sunday services, when we wish to get particularly near to Heaven we have Uncle York sit upon the platform during the services, or make a little prayer. Imagine our dismay when he dropped some hints, the other day, that he had not always been so beatified, and had had his period of wild oats. At length the officers, probing him farther, began to approach the details of these early transgressions. The veteran shook his head over the retrospection—& confessed. "*Used to dance,—and tings.*" What the *tings* were which come in as milder etcetera after the one great remorse of dancing, we shall never know.

Have I ever said what is the favorite reading-primer of our drummer boys? McClellan's Bayonet Exercises.[232] Large type—short words—subject intelligible—pictures fascinating; it combines all merits. "*Ac-*

232. George Brinton McClellan, *Manual of Bayonet Exercises: Prepared for the Use of the Army of the United States* (1852; Philadelphia: J.B. Lippincott, 1862).

vance, re-treat, leap to de front, leap to de rear" and so on. Think of the great dethroned idol, banished from all other temples,[233] still reigning in the primary schools of the blameless Ethiopians!

## BEAUFORT. S.C. JULY 7. 1863.

We are settled here on the Parade Ground, for an indefinite time, since the garrison left here is not more than sufficient to guard the island, indeed scant for that. Two companies are at Hilton Head for fatigue duty for ten days, & two on picquet leaving only six in camp, so I did not keep my chickens long under my wing. Still I enjoy it here, I like to perfect details always and fuss over my Camp as I used to do over a vase of flowers or an Atlantic article. A camp is a sort of landscape gardening or model farm, there is always some small improvement to be made, an additional trench for water, shade for sun, an increased vigilance in sweeping. Then I like to take good care of the men, to hear them purr. So far I have always plenty of resources in the absence of active service, & in the present great stir of the department,[234] we hope to take some share, though as I said, I expect the regiment as such to remain here.

General Gillmore having ordered away Col. Davis' brigade, Gen. Saxton to the joy of all, has consented to take command of the Post again—for which the Colonel (White) who wd. hv. otherwise succeeded, is grossly incompetent. Every one likes & admires Gen. Gillmore thus far—he is dashing, cordial, approachable, fair, decided & has the prestige of success, with that immense visible activity of temperament which always commands enthusiasm, sometimes exaggerated. So far however he shows organizing as well as executive power & behind his bluff frankness keeps his own secrets admirably. Ten regiments went in one night from St Helena Island to Folly Island,[235] & neither regiment knew that it was going till the middle of the afternoon. He has very few troops to act with, but he will evidently make every man of them tell & the rebels must look sharp to know where they are or what doing. But his general plan speaks for itself. Folly Island gives a fair chance at Morris Island; to have Morris Island is to have

233. McClellan, general-in-chief of the Union forces, who had a history of political feuding with the Lincoln administration and battlefield ineptitude, was relieved of his command by Lincoln in September 1862.

234. General Gillmore had taken command of the Department of the South on June 12, 1863; he planned another attack on Charleston (which had successfully resisted naval assault in April), this time from land.

235. St. Helena Island is near to Port Royal Island; Folly Island is up the coast, near Charleston.

Fort Sumter, & that is to have Charleston.[236] There is a feeling of hope in his success, far beyond anything that existed in the Hunter time. That had grown to be so old a story before anything was done.

As yet none of the colored reg'ts are ordered to Folly Island & I don't expect to be—but we may be employed on certain collateral matters. I shld. regret this—but that for the present it is likely to be chiefly an artillery fight at Folly Island & there will be a great deal of hard fatigue duty. As for my officers & men they wd. of course rather go anywhere than stay anywhere.

I never have any ennui, because I always have enough to do, which is perhaps a blessing in red tape. The men are healthy, but many of the officers ailing. I hold out excellently, have my usual good appetite & digestion, & fare tolerably well. Dr. Rogers has yielded at last, & gone into town tonight to stay some days at Mrs. Lander's kind home, away from the cares of camp, & if possible from the enervations of noon which always wear upon him. He will not I hope be ill, but will go North at any rate very soon, not returning till autumn. He was very delicate when he came & the wonder is that he shld. hv. done so well. But I do not see why any healthy person should not be healthy here, unless compelled to over exertion; there is always a breeze so far, except from eight to four sometimes; often it blows all day. We have a great corn field on one side the Camp & a great open common on the other: no miasma or impurities near, & salt marshes almost encircling us. There were 13 deaths in the reg't in February & only 3 in June, so you see how much healthier the men are.

I rarely see any person from the Mass[tts] 54th[237]—they are brigaded with Montgomery's under him, by some management, not of their choosing. Montgomery has been a sore disappointment to me & to General Saxton, with whom he is at sword's points; I do not desire to be brigaded with him, because he would chafe so much at being under me & I should have such hard work to coerce him into my notions of civilized warfare. He had one of his men shot without trial, the other day, for desertion, & was about to shoot two more when Dr. Rogers' wonderful power of influence made

236. Morris Island is the next island up from Folly Island, closer in to Charleston Bay. Fort Sumter stood on a man-made granite island at the entrance to Charleston Bay, guarding access to Charleston; it was fired upon by Confederate forces on April 12, 1861, and surrendered by the Union two days later, marking the onset of the war. Retaking it was thus both militarily desirable and symbolically important for the Union cause.

237. The Massachusetts 54th, commanded by Col. Robert Gould Shaw, was a regiment composed of free blacks from the North, celebrated for their heroic assault on Fort Wagner, South Carolina (a Confederate earthwork fortification guarding the entrance to Charleston harbor), on July 18, 1863, in which they lost nearly half their number, including Shaw.

him change his plan. Yet he is not a harsh or cruel man, but a singular mixture of fanaticism, vanity, and genius.

HEADQRS. 1ST S.C.V.
BEAUFORT. S.C. AUG 22. 1863.

As the Arago[238] came up to the pier on Thursday, at Hilton Head, sudden movements were observed among the soldiers detailed for duty on the wharf: arms were raised, fingers pointed, glances interchanged & an evident mutual proclamation of "de Cunnel". No cheering, they seldom cheer, but Nature in vindication of the oppressed, instead of tongues gave them teeth, & the end of the pier might presently have been a procession of elephants, so magnificent was the display which spread along the line. There, quoth I to the officers who stood with me on the deck, did you ever see a white regiment receive it's Cunnel like that, & they universally said or sighed or swore they never did.

This was a detachment at work down there. When I came out toward the Camp in Beaufort, after a short pause, a little girl on a sand bank began jumping & gesticulating to her brother down below "Johnny, de Cunnel's come"; I found she was a soldier's child though I didn't know her. As I approached the Camp, the elephants resumed their procession. I went along the edge & greeted the officers & then went for limited "howdies" (probably a kindred word with howdahs)[239] among the men. They were just falling in for a review; there was nothing vociferous; there never is, only an universal dropping of the business in process, to shake hands & say "Cunnel, sa," "How's you, sa" "How's you little family sa." "Bress de Lord sa, for see my Cunnel once more". "Hab waited for you comin', sa, with eyes ob expectatious" & so on, though I think no single flower of speech on my return impressed me so much as that wh. dismissed my departure "You's a mighty big rail out ob de fence, sa".

Among the officers the feeling of relief was very perceptible. So many were sick, so many changes of command had taken place, what with dismissal, promotion & sickness, that the whole atmosphere of the thing was

238. TWH had been wounded in battle and gone home on a furlough since his last entry in the journal.

239. A howdah is a seat fitted to the back of an elephant or camel, often with a canopy; an Urdu word, derived from Persian or Arabic. TWH's etymological speculation here seems motivated by his habitual association of blacks with other exoticized races, and with elephants, rather than any linguistic reasoning; "howdy" is simply a shortened informal version of the familiar greeting "how do you do," as he previously acknowledged in a letter to Louisa Storrow Higginson (April 22, 1863).

forlorn & gloomy. Fortunately it reached the borders of the ludicrous & made me hilarious & jubilant to the last degree, & as a very little inquiry showed that nothing was really wrong that a few days of steady sway would not set right they brightened up very soon. Certainly there is a formidable amount of sickness, & my new Lt. Col. & Major must both go North—still I feel perfectly well & with a decided exhilaration of spirits.

There is no reason to suppose we shall be ordered to Morris Island, as Gen. Gillmore has now all the troops he can use. The feeling exists now that the resistance to be offered after the fall of Sumter may be greater than was expected so that many months may pass before Charleston is taken. Fort Sumter is said to be badly breached.

I hv. been writing part of this with the mercury at 97° in my tent, but a shower has brought it down to 79°. The nights are cool & damp. We live well—fresh fish, white sweet potatoes, squash, beans, eggplant, hominy & I have now chocolate for a year's supply, I should think.

It shld. hv. been said that I got to camp just in time to put on my sword for a review of the few regiments here—the first time we hv. been in line with white troops. We had the left of the line—the second post of the four, & the regiment appeared very well, marching of course far better than any: nobody can doubt that where colored troops are concerned. Col. Van Wyck (56th N.Y.) the Congressman of the famous Investigating Committee, was in command of the brigade & the review was before Gen. Saxton.

Dear old York our Uncle Tom, was in bliss with his spectacles, so thoroughly Tiff-like as to link him to both novels.[240] He sent his thanks to "de lady"—"tell her 'stremely obliged to her indeed". It was even more of an event than the recent arrival of his wife from the main. She has come from Darien Georgia, with no less than $1300.00 in *silver* which she has somehow saved or picked up—think of that! She is said to be as fine in appearance as he & is now in Beaufort where she was, he says, "a native liver". Probably they met in his impure youth when he "used to dance—and tings."

I think I feel better than I have since coming down here last winter—it is perfectly inexplicable that I should feel so well. It is a beautiful place, too, this South Carolina, spite of all I said when I was at home. My two companies on picquet are ordered back & I hope for the two at Hilton Head— I have got rid of some poor officers & acquired some good ones; & we hope for new tents & Springfield muskets. So it costs nothing to be jolly & I surely

---

240. That is, to both of Harriet Beecher Stowe's antislavery novels, *Uncle Tom's Cabin; or, Life Among the Lowly* (Boston: J. P. Jewett, 1852) and *Dred; or, a Tale of the Great Dismal Swamp* (Boston: Phillips, Sampson, 1856).

am. It is an exquisite evening cool, with moonlight & music all over the camp. We are now on the river bank, high above the water, with large pine trees between us & the edge.

HEADQRS. 1ST S.C.V.
BEAUFORT S. C.
AUG. 26. 1863.

No symbol but the hen & her chickens can describe the pleased condition of a regimental commander when he gets his family together again. To-day I had my first battalion drill save the enforced one at Inspection t'other day, when a little Lieutenant of Regulars hauled us over the coals very judiciously & usefully. Today the marching in line was perfectly wonderful, "Every step was worth a half a dollar." Some of the Companies were rather impaired in appearance, then, & so on, but they will soon come up.

I find that soon after they were paid only $10 per month, desertion began again, the men saying that they had not been treated fairly nor paid what was promised.[241] About 20 went during my absence, though none since my return. Before this, desertion had long been almost annihilated. I suppose they thought as the President had proclaimed the doctrine of Retaliation,[242] they wd. act upon it. "Intensely human" again.[243] But it will not be hard to stop it.

There is no increase of sickness among the officers, now, nor is our work hard. The weather decidedly comfortable. I hv. had a floor to my tent & a pretty penthouse over it of poles & gray moss, which we use a good deal—this keeps off the sun, & I have scarcely ever had such comfortable quarters. All goes very well in the regiment, shorthanded as we are; but the change in the mess is quite painful. Every one of those whose society I es-

241. TWH gives a narrative account of "The Struggle for Pay" in Appendix D of *Army Life* (pp. 267–76). During the last months of his military career and for some time thereafter TWH campaigned for the fulfillment of pecuniary promises made to the black soldiers, writing numerous letters to the editors of newspapers.
242. President Lincoln formally ordered on July 30, 1863, that the government of the United States would "give the same protection to all its soldiers, and if the enemy shall sell or enslave anyone because of his color, the offense shall be punished by retaliation upon the enemy's prisoners in our possession."
243. "General Saxton, examining with some impatience a long list of questions from some philanthropic Commission at the North, respecting the traits and habits of the freedmen, bade some staff-officer answer them all in two words,—'Intensely human.' We all admitted that it was a striking and comprehensive description" (*Army Life* 232). A slightly different account of this incident is given by TWH in "Intensely Human," chapter 6 of his *Part of a Man's Life*.

pecially enjoyed is gone; Drs. Rogers & Minor, the Adjutant & wife, & the Quartermaster; one deceased, the others absent sick or on detached service;[244] then the Lt. Col. is dismissed, the Major absent sick, & the mess is reduced to the Chaplain & little Dr. Schofield.[245] I look with longing to October when they will be back, or some of them. Dr. Minor may be recalled any day.

I enjoy the locality better than any we hv. ever had, we are near the edge of a curving bluff, fringed with pines & overhanging the river; below the bluff is a hard narrow beach where one may gallop a mile & bathe at the end of it; we look along the curve to Beaufort & the few vessels that come & go.

To appreciate the following one must know the first lessons in drill. The very first question asked my Lt. Col. was—"What is the position of a soldier without arms"? which he cd. not answer & report says no other question was asked. So Capt. Rogers asked it of one of his men & wrote down the following in return. It is a ludicrous travestie of the passage in the tactics & you must read it (Anna)[246] to Gen. Phelps as the fruit of our instructions.

> Position of a Sojer widout no gun.
> "Heels extendin' a inch apart.
> Toes extendin' not quite a-elbow.
> Body extendin' right plump.
> Hands extendin' down side of pants.
> Little finger extendin' seam of breeches.
> Head flare to the front, extendin' on de groun' fifteen paces.
> Hat square on de head["]

> Horace Delaney Co F. 1st S.C.V.[247]

244. J. M. Bingham (Quartermaster) died on July 20, 1863, from effects of exhaustion on a military expedition; G. W. Dewhurst (Adjutant) and his wife, along with Dr. Rogers, were, as TWH had been, absent sick; Dr. Minor was detached for service elsewhere.

245. Lieutenant-Colonel Liberty Billings, of whom TWH had thought ill from the start (see November 24, 1862, above) was dismissed for incompetence by an examining board, July 28, 1863; Major Trowbridge was absent sick but returned shortly (see September 23, 1863, below).

246. Anna Higginson (1809–1892), TWH's unmarried older sister.

247. Casey, *Infantry Tactics*, 1:25:
> Heels on the same line, as near each other as the conformation of the man will permit;
> The feet turned out equally, and forming with each other something less than a right angle;

I have made a change in officers for the better, carrying out that process of sifting which has been necessary fr. the beginning. I am gradually raising the tone. It is not hard to impose on Gen. Saxton, and some very incompetent persons obtained position here. Indeed it is hard for the most penetrating person to detect in advance who will be a good officer.

Today has been a cool comfortable New England September day.

I observe that the men, as they get farther from their old condition, lose it's ways & some of its picturesqueness; for instance their *shouts* are less frequent & less serious, they show more levity during the process & make the dance more of a jig. I hope they will never grow so civilized as to lose their piquant use of personal pronouns. Just now I heard one fr. the company streets improvising an imaginary General orders. "Headquarters No 1. General order No 162; Heretofore no man must fry he meat, must always boil he."

Major Trowbridge is still Major Scroby, Captain Thibadeau, Capt. Stevedore, the Chaplain Mr. Chapman & Mr. Chapel, Lieut. Merriam[248] Lieut. Mary Ann. We hv. a new Lieut. Childs[249] of juvenile look & soft manner & one of his company was trying for his name this morning. "Dunno he name, sa, speck he name Lieutenant Baby, sa." It seemed incredible that it shld. be serious, but I verily believe it was. They have the same unconscious satire on the plantations & Mr. Eustis[250] is Mr. Useless.

My ordnance Sergeant, a jewel of a man, London Spalding, always denigrates Bayonet Scabbards as Bayonet Scavalry, as if with some subtle dragoon associations.

I hv. just talked with a very bright negro just in fr. Savannah, wh. he left

The knees straight without stiffness;
The body erect on the hips, inclining a little forward;
The shoulders square and falling equally;
The arms hanging naturally;
The elbows near the body;
The palm of the hand turned a little to the front, the little finger behind the seam of the pantaloons;
The head erect and square to the front, without constraint;
The chin near the stock, without covering it;
The eyes fixed straight to the front, and striking the ground about the distance of fifteen paces.

248. Second Lieutenant E. C. Merriam, formerly of the 8th Maine Regiment, joined the 1st South Carolina on November 17, 1862.

249. Second Lieutenant Asa Child, formerly of the 8th Maine Regiment, joined the 1st South Carolina on August 7, 1863.

250. Frederick A. Eustis of Milton, Massachusetts, one of the first members of the Port Royal Mission, was superintendent of a Ladies Island plantation which he inherited but earlier refused because of his antislavery views.

however Aug. 9. He says they are all ready to evacuate & go up country when Charleston is taken, wh. they think only a matter of time. That it was the general rumor there that Rosecranz was then in Georgia.[251] That it was all false about the ladies going down on steamboats to see the rebel ram—only men went. That within a month they hv. begun to forbid the negroes fr. going to see the troops drill, for fear they should learn it & be all ready to go into the colored regiments—isn't that a good commentary on the bug bear of them arming their slaves?[252]

## Aug 30. 1863

Taking an aft'n ride just now after a day's rain I came upon a picturesque out of the way plantation to which a number of families had been sent after one of the raids up the river—people newly arrived, for whom there was no house room anywhere & to whom old tents were assigned instead. They were in a lovely place, under great live-oaks draped with moss; but the moss streamed with moisture & the people looked a little comfortless as they squatted by little fires before their tents. I stopped by one tent to speak to a pretty child who sat assiduously watching over a pot of boiling hominy, when an old white bearded man looked out from the tent & claimed her as his grand daughter. I asked if they were comfortable, he said the tents leaked & the nights grew chilly, but when I asked if he was sorry he came away fr. the main land, his old face brightened all over. "No, tank God, Massa, neber sorry, noting but glad, *too much* glad; no man neber did better ting dan fetch we poor people out ob de land ob bondage". This from a man upon the verge of eternity, who had left all the habits & associations of his whole life behind, & who (if any one) would have all to lose & nothing to gain by the change,—would seem a testimony worth all the sacrifices any one cd. make, to win. If freedom were worth all this to him, what was it worth to the bright little girl who sat with not only her hominy but a life of womanhood before her.

## Aug. 31. 1863

Last night I waked up cold in my tent & finding the double blanket over me insufficient, added my heavy overcoat & cape & was none too warm. To-day is a perfect New England North Easter: mercury 63°

251. Brigadier General William Starke Rosecrans (1819–1898), commander of the Department of the Cumberland, was maneuvering in Tennessee, not yet in Georgia.

252. Although the idea of the Confederate Army enlisting blacks had been occasionally proposed and considered, it did not happen until 1865.

HDQRS. BEAUFORT
SEPT. 5. 1863.

When Robert Sutton was tried & condemned, I thought to myself—some day, I shall perhaps sit in Court-Martial on his condemners & shall try not to retaliate. So now I am sitting in judgment on Col. Sammons, who presided in that court. However he is a good natured old soul a farmer by nature, a road-contractor by profession & a Colonel by misfortune. I expect that he will be acquitted of everything but blunders & a little injudicious swearing. But the tediousness of Court martial is beyond expression. The essence being that *every word* shall be reduced to writing. The presiding officer is Col. Van Wyck, he of the Congressional Investigating Committee, a strong determined sharp eyed man with spectacles that are an investigating committee in themselves. & the contrast between his keen impatient country lawyer ways, always willing to cut every knot by a free & easy chat all round—with the accurate propriety of the Judge Advocate, a nice boy from West Point, utterly inexperienced in worldly affairs, as ignorant of all that is unmilitary as Van Wyck is regardless of all that is military—is very entertaining. Nothing is more simple than the whole army method of doing everything, if one will only give one's mind to it, & Court-Martials are an accurate & admirable, though most tedious, method of sifting out the truth.

Especially when I hv. all my regimental work to do. However everything flows very smoothly & if we can only keep still for a while, all will be in nice order again. As for staying still I fancy now it will not be a hard thing for a time. Genl Saxton who is just back fr. Morris I. shakes his head over Gillmore's prospects. There is no other nut so easy to crack as Sumter; we can destroy Charleston, no doubt, but as to holding it, that is another affair. There is a rumor of a severe battle impending, but I hv. no expectation of it. The sudden arrival of 38 surgeons & 5,000 *beds* puzzles everybody, unless there are on their way to Gillmore vast re-inforcements besides those now known. Gen. S.'s visit to Gillmore didn't *seem* anything more than one of our accustomed military picnics wh. took the place of war here under the Hunter dynasty. It was two boys spending Sat'y afternoon together & one showing the other all his playthings; Gen. Saxton was allowed to light the 300-pound gun as much as he wanted to. I think he enjoyed playing with Quincy Gillmore very much.

Meantime my black children with their smaller playthings of the same sort, sing & laugh & sleep & drill through these cool & lovely Autumn days. Every body says the season is wonderfully healthy & there is no unusual illness in any of the regiments. None of my officers show any signs of illness except those who broke down in my absence, & for myself I continue well & happy, & in a few days, the Court Martial over, my work will be light.

Recurring to courts martial & military procedure, I am freshly impressed every little while not with the excess of it in the Army but with the need of it. Perhaps I naturally like it—ever since the early epoch when my brothers used to lie awake on cold nights & conjecture whether I had not somewhere an inventory of the bedclothes in the house. But I have much oftener been struck with the want of it than with any superfluity. For instance: there is just now a contest between Gen. Saxton & Col. Montgomery as to the right to officer the latter's regiment, which each claims. It is referred to the War Department for decision; so the War Dep't writes back saying that there is not on file in Washington *a copy of the instructions issued to either of the two* & requesting copies from them! Thus of these two most important documents—one of which (Gen. S's orders) forms the historic basis of the whole organization of our colored army, no copy was put on file. Give us double rations of red tape henceforward, say I.

## MINUS HAMILTON AGED 88 (?)

one of those who came down on Montgomery's Combakee Raid.[253]

"De people was all a hoeing, hoeing in de rice-field, Massa, when de gunboats came. Den ebry man drap dem hoe and leff de rice. De massa he stand and call "run to de wood for hide, dem Yankee come, sell you to Cuba, run for hide"! ebry man he run, and, My God!, *run all toder way.* Massa stand in de wood, peep, peep, faid for truss (afraid to trust) he say "run to de wood" and ebry man run straight by him to de boat.

["]De brack sojers dey so *presumptious,* dey came right ashore, hold up dere heads. First ting I know, dere was a barn with ten tousand bushels rough rice, all in a blaze, den Massa's great house all cracklin up de roof. Didn't I keer for see em blaze? No, Massa, didn't keer, lor, Massa, didn't keer notin' at all.—*I was gwine to de boat.*

["]De brack sojers dey so presumptious (3 times)

["]Ole woman & I go down to boat, den dey say behind us, "rebels coming, rebels coming," ole woman say, "come ahead, come plenty ahead." (Meaning come along fast) I hab notin' on but my shirt and pantaloon, ole woman one single frock he hab on & one handkerchief on he head; & I leff

253. Colonel James Montgomery went up the Combahee River, South Carolina, raiding Confederate property and stores on June 2, 1863.

all-two my blanket tie up on de bank, and run, for de rebel come: and den dey *didn't* come, didn't truss for come.

"I'se 88 year old, massa. My old massa Loundes keep all de ages in a big book & when we come to age ob sense, we mark 'em down ebry year, so I know.

["]Too old for come? Massa joking, neber too old for leave de land o' bondage. I old, but great good for chilen, give 'tousand 'tank ebry day. Young people can go through *force*, massa, (forcibly) but de ole folk hab to go slow."


Hᴅꟼᴀs. 1ˢᵀ S.C.V.
Sᴇᴘᴛ. 12. 1863

When I am tired & jaded in the evening nothing refreshes me more immediately than to go & hear the men singing in the Company streets. There is such a world of trustful peace in it, I feel as if they were a lot of babies in their cradles cooing themselves to sleep, the dear blundering dusky darlings. They are so unconscious of the best & most graceful things in their songs, it seems a grasping at something that has some time rolled over their heads; and the *time* of their singing is something so ideal & perfect that the harshest voices have a fascination. Just now they were singing something faster than their usual time, which I had never before heard: it was

     1. "Weeping Mary feed my lambs,
     Feed my lambs feed my lambs
     Weeping Mary feed my lambs
     Sitting on de golden altar

     (Then) 2. Paul & Silas—feed my lambs

     3. Doubting Thomas—feed my lambs[254]

& so with other scriptural worthies & there was such a perfect rhythmical refrain about the whole that it was as fascinating as a Virginia reel. Then comes in a grander strain

     Roll Jordan, roll,
     Roll Jordan, roll,
     Roll Jordan Roll,
        To help me bear de cross

254. This song does not appear in chapter 9 of *Army Life*.

One more valiant soldier here        (Great<br>
One more valiant soldier here        variety of<br>
One more valiant soldier here        Cadence)<br>
To help me bear de cross<br>
Then Hail, Mary, Hail &c<br>
To help me bear de cross

Still there is no doubt that as their military habits develope, these chants disappear & the regular Ethiopian melodies of the North[255] become more common.

Sept. 15. I have a pomegranate & an orange neither quite ripe, before me; that sounds seductive, but it does not look so. There are also ruby acorns from the live oak, & some lovely feather-grasses. The flowers are more abundant & beautiful now than ever before—less yellow than with us at this season; those which I most enjoy are a great twining Convolvulus, white with a pink centre & a high delicate Gerardia that empurples the fields. When my imaginary leisure days come & my semi-imaginary (so they seem) field officers return, I may become a field officer in a literal sense myself & try to make some transplantations round my tent. I hv. already the prettiest trellis of moss to shade the main tent fr. the sun. It was curious to notice, that the only regiment which ever planted anything round it's tents was a foreign one called the Lost Children or Enfans Perdus from the variety of nationalities, the 100th N.Y. They had a little garden round almost every tent.

I see Mariotti the new Times man whom I remember of old at Cambridge, being freshly arrived, burst out in amazement at the buttonless condition of our American army. This morning I had occasion to go before a board of officers, four of them—a Lt. Col., a Captain, & two beside. All should have been in full dress. Not one had his coat buttoned, only two had anything to designate rank & indeed one of these was absolutely out of uniform, in civil costume. They were no doubt as good officers as the average—but I thought of Lt. Col. Maggi's dismay "Good Heaven! Colonel! is it possible that in the American army Captain come to officers' meeting in his sleeve-shirt"?

Apparently all American officers in white regiments (except from

255. So-called "Ethiopean melodies" were the vastly popular tunes, ostensibly derived from traditional African-American folk music and featuring comic dialect, that white performers in blackface circulated in the North—songs like "Jump Jim Crow," "Zip Coon" and "Ole Dan Tucker." In *Army Life*, TWH says that these "ditties" "took no hold upon the mass," being sung only by "a few youths from Savannah" (pp. 221–22). See below, April 21, 1864.

*168*

Massachusetts & a few Batteries) have the proverbial souls above buttons.[256] I'm sure I wish they hadn't.

CAMP SHAW.[257] SEPT. 23. 1863

Well, the agony is over & I've got a Major back, perfectly bursting & overflowing with health & spirits,—& I haven't been sick! Thanks to the
magnificent October weather we have been enjoying, I suppose; I don't
think I could have done so many men's work, even for these few weeks,
without it, but now I am safe. Dear, bluff, tender, ponderous, indomitable "Scroby", caught by fate from the fire companies & ward
meetings of New York,—a bricklayer by profession and a brick himself,
as I said once before—a born "rough" tempered by a passion for
Methodist hymns & a splendid voice for singing them; "Scroby" came to
hand on the very day his furlough was up, (the only case on record;) &
henceforth I can take a holiday every other day if I wish, and spend the
intermediate day in tormenting my Captains. For, look you, if we are to
stay here and get into good condition, then we must *be* in good condition,
if we are to have inspections & brigade drills, then drill & inspection it
must be, and if the men are on fatigue duty all the morning, they must be
making themselves pretty all the afternoon. "Captain Jones, are you
aware, Sir, that I have absolutely discovered a man in your rear rank, at
today's inspection, with his canteen under his haversack instead of over
it, and still another with his coat unhooked at the collar, *unhooked at the collar* sir, after all my efforts. What *is* this regiment coming to. We might as
well be white"!

I can compare it to nothing but a bird pruning her feathers, or a cat lick-
ing her kittens, the constant labor of keeping a regiment in perfect condition. Here are eight hundred men & every one of them every Sunday
morning at farthest must be ascertained to be provided with every article
of clothing, buttons, shoestrings, letters & figures on his cap, gun complete
with bayonet, bayonet scabbard, cap pouch, cartridge box, cartridge box
plate, cartridge box belt, cartridge box belt plate, gun sling, canteen,
haversack, knapsack packed to perfection, forty cartridges, ditto percus-
sion caps; and every one of these articles polished to the highest brightness

256. George Colman, the Younger, *New Hay at the Old Market: An Occasional Drama in
One Act* (London: Printed by W. Woodfall for T. Cadell, and W. Davies, 1795), scene 1: "I
had a soul above buttons."

257. After Robert Gould Shaw was killed in the assault of the Massachusetts 54th on
Fort Wagner, the new camp of the 1st South Carolina, just outside of Beaufort, South
Carolina, was named in Shaw's honor.

or darkness, as the case may be, and worn or carried precisely in the prescribed manner

Then every corner of the camp must be presentable for inspectors &
commanders like the Gods "see everywhere" or should do it; hospital, sta-
bles, guardhouse, cookhouses, company tents, must all be brought to perfection & every square inch of this "farm of four acres" must look as nice
as an English lawn, twice a day. All this *beside* the discipline & the drill & the
regimental & company bookkeeping, except as they all connect themselves together, because if you once make perfection the standard in a regiment, though you may not reach it, you can probably reach as near as to
any particular grade of imperfection which you accept. On many points I
am happy to say, the standard is here far higher now than ever before; and
it is one compensation of being out of active service that it can be brought
higher. The great trouble with volunteer officers is in their standard; they
have no such high aims, as to the details, as regular officers have, & hence
the immense inferiority in the condition of their men. The young regular
officers whom I have seen usually study four times as much as volunteer
officers of the same grade, & the criticisms & suggestions of regular 2d
lieutenants are usually worth more than those of volunteer colonels.
Stephen[258] might pooh at this but it is true.

I reaped the advantage of one crotchet at the visit we had from an official inspector. We had a storm the night before & the morning of the day
appointed was a hard rain, with occasional liftings, barely long enough to
"police" the camp. At nine oclock, the hour appointed, the regiment was
in line on the parade ground, fully equipped, *in a steady pour*; in about ten
minutes up rode little Lieutenant Sanger, said nothing about the weather,
except to offer that the men might have their overcoats, which I declined,
as he could not then inspect their equipments; & he went through his business, with intervals of sunshine & rain—he sharp eyed & thorough as
usual—for the whole morning. Ever since then, I hear, he has been cele-
brating the event, saying it was the only time he had ever found a regiment
in line in the rain to receive him. It seems rather absurd that so simple a feat
should go unperformed.

Don't imagine from what I say that this regiment is in tiptop condition,
far from it, some companies are in a very slovenly state but it is because
they need a change in their officers which ere long, I trust, will occur. But
we have taken a fresh start towards a better condition than ever before—
indeed it takes a year in the service to know the ropes.

Sept. 26. I wish I had time to tell you of the daring exploit of a squad

258. Stephen Higginson, TWH's older brother.

part of whom were my men who penetrated up the Combahee to the RR. & read telegraphic despatches for 5 hours![259] All are back safe, of mine, save the Chaplain & one soldier, prisoners, the first we have ever lost. The plan originated with Capt. Bryant[260] of the *4th* S.C. one of the most daring scouts in these parts.

One corporal went without food 5 days & could retain none for two days more.—7 days in all—he was chased in the marshes & came in without throwing any of his equipments away.


HEAD QUARTERS
1ST S.C.V.
CAMP SHAW NOV. 6. 1863

How long an interval there has been to my journal; it is now five weeks since I first gave up duty, & I have sent only notes & notelets since then.

Now I am growing strong again: the truth is I never have got up my strength since I was wounded in July,[261] but when I came back in August there was so much to be done that I worked for a month or more on my nerve power & thought I was all right, & when the Major came to relieve me I at once collapsed.

As I grow better no tongue can tell the comfort that man is to me; I see the manhood in him growing every day & in return I rest upon him as on a granite floor; never was there more solid reliable manhood inside of one uniform, & in spite of all deficiencies of education he has grown right up to his promotion[262] & every drawback I feared has diminished or disappeared. It is so new to me to have a field officer who can really help me that I hardly know how to use him. All the officers in the regiment feel the growth in him & treat him with a hearty respect.

Several promotions & changes have been made, all improvements, except the loss of Captain Rogers[263] whose resignation has been accepted

259. In *Army Life* TWH reduces this feat to "an hour or two" (p. 231).
260. Captain J. E. Bryant belonged to the 8th Maine, according to *Army Life* (p. 230).
261. While on an expedition up the Edisto River, South Carolina, July 9–11, 1863, TWH's boat, the *Enoch Dean*, came under fire from a Confederate battery on a bluff along shore; a ball apparently grazed his side, doubling him over and causing a serious contusion. The injury seemed minor at first, but recovery came slowly, and he finally sought a furlough to speed his recovery.
262. Previously a Captain, Trowbridge had been promoted to Major on August 11, 1863.
263. James Rogers was engaged to marry Annie Earle, whose mother lobbied determinedly for her future son-in-law to return to Boston rather than have her daughter join him in the camp.

*from Washington* thanks to the unconquerable energies of his future mother in law, who finally enlisted even Gov. Andrew[264] in his behalf. Her object was to save her daughter from coming out here to be married—his was to finish his college course & it comes rather late for that. He is now at the new Convalescent Camp at St Augustine, whither they send homesick officers to cure them by contrairies—getting them farther from home. So I don't know how he likes this tardy acceptance of a resignation which Gen. Gilmore refused in the summer.

I suppose we shall remain here this winter unless we go on some expeditions—yet I suppose if I asked for it the regiment would be ordered to Morris Island. Personally I should like this as being the scene of immediate action & because I should at once have command of a brigade (being Senior Colonel of colored regiments). But they do work the colored soldiers so unmercifully there that I will not *ask* to victimize my men by going. I think Gen. Gilmore desires to do strict justice, but these men do *work* so much better, especially in summer, & while this is so, I am willing to stay here where though the men are worked quite hard enough, it is more directly in the line of military duty.

Next Monday we go out on picquet for twenty days, taking our turn with the other regiments.

I have been a good deal associated here with Col. Van Wyck of the famous investigating Committee—a strong, active, inquisitive man, & like most volunteer Colonels, rather indifferent to the technicalities of military duty. They let the patriotic spirit which no doubt brought most of them into the war stand in lieu of all nice attention to the work they have in hand, & hence the whole drill discipline & military appearance of their regiments run behindhand—their books get into confusion, & sooner or later the soldiers or their heirs suffer. In case of Col. Wyck, the irregularity is so great that the Col. himself has never been either commissioned or mustered into the service, & that every act he has ever done as an officer is illegal. If those who have suffered from his political scrutiny get hold of this, there will be a pretty storm.

My men are jolly as ever & just as funny. Their aspirations expand—they have now a building association, with a view to the purchase of land, also a literary association, with the end chiefly, of learning the art of writing. The latter came near getting into trouble the other day. The President sent in his resignation, and as no one present at the meeting chanced to

264. John Albion Andrew (1818–1867), a radical Republican elected Massachusetts Governor in 1860, serving until 1866; he was a vigorous supporter of Lincoln and the war effort, and of black enlistment.

know what the word *resignation* meant, it very nearly produced a storm. They suspected an insult.

Nothing can exceed the sageness and piquancy of the things I often hear, if I could only write them down. The other day I asked a sergeant about a man in his company "A'int got no sense, Cunnel—senseless man—he's smart enough, but *aint got wisdom to tote 'um"*—that is has more sail than rudder, or perhaps I should say more rudder than sail—not wisdom enough to tote or carry the smartness.

Just now they have a song in camp, which is really quite a daring reference to dignitaries. It is sung sarcastically.

> "Ten dollars a month"!
> "Tree ob dat for cloting"!
> "Gwine to Washington
> "To fight for Linkum's darter"!

What suggested throwing the responsibility of their impaired pay upon Linkum's imaginary darter I d'ont know, but I've no doubt Old Abe would enjoy the joke. Their nonsense is as inscrutable as children's, you can never get behind it & find where they get the combination of ideas.

## CAMP SHAW. NOV 13. 1863

Today is inexpressibly beautiful, like one or two peculiarly delicious & memorable days I remember in Fayal—& in a degree like the softest, haziest, most tender & tremulous mornings of latter April with us—more than like our Indian summer which is a drier air. There is a perpetual chatter of jackdaws, a black glossy bird, intermediate between the blackbird & crow in size, which congregates in immense flocks at this season, soaring & alighting in great armies, though not whirling over & over each other.

## NOV. 21

The above is all I have had time to write, since the regiment went out on picquet a fortnight ago. I have staid here, at the camp, with a few dozen cripples, partly to spare my strength & partly because there was a job of writing for me to do that cd. be best done here. I meant it for a sort of vacation, though it has hardly proved such: besides that I knew Scroby was dying to run the machine for himself out there & I thought it would do him & the regiment good.

The first morning it seemed pretty forlorn though—we had a few days of real cold, & severe wind which blew the sand white & smooth & in the

early morning the few lingering tents gleamed like Arctic snows as the column moved away over the level plain, and as we few went inward to our
stoves again it seemed like Sir John Franklin.[265] Then we had soft weather
once more & now lovely moonlights. I have been anxious about Dr. Rogers
who has had vertigo, & I hv. moved him in town & there was my young
cousin Frank in town to be looked after & kept in books & milk; sick officers coming back, an evening lesson in tactics at Gen. Saxton's, (of the field
officers of the regiments here)—then a Brigade Drill to be observed—&
writing in plenty. Once I have been out to the Picquet Station & over to
Barnwell Island where there has been some skirmishing of late; that night
I slept on the floor in Dr. Minor's room, I remember, with the largest rat I
ever saw patrolling the floor before the bright firelight between us. It is a
charming place still & they gather camellias instead of magnolias in the
deserted garden.

The men enjoyed the change, all the evening before there was a gurgle
of glee through the whole camp, & long before daylight we were waked
with songs & laughter; nothing can ever be too early for *them*. I remember
noticing a bit of their lightheartedness. I sent for 8 wagons fr. Beaufort &
they sent 14 because they said all those wd. be necessary to bring the other
regiment in (the 56th N.Y.) so we might as well have them to go out. I would
not however let the men send their knapsacks by wagon, because they do
not march a great deal, & the practice is very important. One captain however let his men put theirs in, through mistake, & I coming along, straightway ordered them all out again. Upon this the men looked a little
disconcerted, till one, heaving up the big black burden, shouted consol-
ingly *"Ebry man he own hoss"* i.e. (his own) which practical witticism created
a general guffaw, & the knapsacks were resumed with perfect cheerfulness.

They are very piquant & very impressive in what they say. There is now
much discussion about owning land which they greatly desire to do—&
there is a Building Association in the regiment in which Sergt. Rivers is
leader. There is a party among the white people here, represented by Edward Philbrick[266] (who owns several plantations & has done much good
by conducting them well) which opposes the sale of land to the colored
people, thinking that they will do better for a time as tenants. I do not think
so, nor do the colored people generally & Sergeant Rivers looked really
sublime when he summed it up in conversation the other day—"Every

265. Sir John Franklin (1786–1847), an Arctic explorer credited with discovering
the Northwest Passage; he published a *Narrative of a Journey to the Shores of the Polar Sea, in the
Years 1819, 20, 21, and 22* (London: J. Murray, 1823), and *Narrative of a Second Expedition to the
Shores of the Polar Sea, in the Years 1825, 1826, and 1827* (London: J. Murray, 1828).

266. Edward S. Philbrick was among the first party of Port Royal missionaries.

colored man will be a slave, & feel himself a slave until he can *raise him own bale of cotton* and *put him own mark upon it* and say *Dis is mine!*["]

The Philbrick theory is that the people have a peculiar distaste for raising cotton (which is true, chiefly from association) and will raise corn instead & live by fishing & selling eggs & chickens & let the lands go to waste. But I find they are all sharp enough to see the vastly greater profits to be made on cotton at present rates & they all say they shall plant cotton & buy their corn.

I believe I have a constitutional affinity for undeveloped races, though without any of Thoreau's anti-civilization hobby.[267] I always liked the Irish & thought them brilliant. It is the fashion with philanthropists who come down here to be impressed with the degradation & stupidity of these people. I often have to tell them that I have not a stupid man in the regiment. Stupid as a man may seem if you try to make him take a thing in your way, he is commonly sharp enough if you will have patience to take him in his own. Dr. Rogers declared always that they are all Emersonian & that it is only because we do not meet them on high enough ground, if they fail to understand us. A figure, a symbol, they always comprehend, & sometimes when they seem dullest, they have a meaning of their own. Today Abram Fuller, certainly one of the poorest specimens of brain we have had, if not the poorest, came for his Discharge Papers, he having been discharged for physical disability. After I had explained to him that he was no longer a soldier & told him how to get his pay by these papers, he said looking at me in a sort of unintelligent way "I in dis army still, Cunnel." Oh, dear, thought I, you certainly are hopeless, & began again to convince him that he was discharged from the army, & no longer responsible to me &c, when he stopped me with "I mean to say, dat I in dis army still" with a kind of flourish of the hands, & at last I felt my own head "growing thinner" as the men say when a thing dawns on them, and I fathomed that he meant that in the great warfare for freedom he wished still to be counted on, though discharged from the 1st S.C.V. He had completely shot over my head with the fineness & elevation of his ideas & left no resource for my Caucasian intellect except to employ him as my private tutor. It is not the only time I have had just such a rebuke.

We have very pleasant winter quarters, if such they are destined to be (& just now all seem perfectly stationary in this department, & the men have acquired the habits of soldiers sufficiently to be content wherever they

267. Henry David Thoreau, evidently judged by TWH to have a naive or sentimental investment in the primitive; TWH's essay on "Barbarism and Civilization," along with other writings, had argued that men could become civilized without being enervated.

are.[)] They do not pine after Florida, as they did last winter. Of course they would rather be going on expeditions all the time, those are their high-tides & festivals, those the eras by which they date. "I'se been a sickly pusson ever since de last expedit*ious*."

We have a very pleasant mess again ornamented not only by Mrs. Dewhurst, frank & handsome as ever, but by Mrs. Chamberlin, our new Quarter*mistress* a pretty amiable little lady, who looks about eighteen & has the sweetest little baby, six months old.[268] They take to camp life as if born here, & the little thing in a scarlet cloak & hood with long sleeves is toted round all day by the black nurse to the delight of the whole camp. She is the grand-daughter of the regiment, & is rapidly becoming familiar with Dress Parade, Guard mounting[269] & all the daily pageants; never cries, & goes to anybody. The other evening, going to their tent, while Mrs Quartermaster was looking up some envelopes for me, I heard a great cooing and murmuring in the back tent and asked if the baby was still awake? Oh yes, go in; & pushing in I saw no glimpse of any baby, until Mrs. C. quietly pulled away the counterpane of her bed which hung to the floor, and hauled out the camp-made cradle, where lay the little lady, perfectly happy & wider awake than anything but a baby possibly can be & looking as if the seclusion of a dozen parental couches would not suppress or discourage her. Since this I have had no solicitude about that small household.

## CAMP SHAW. BEAUFORT S.C. NOV. 24. 1863

A year ago today I arrived here & took command. The regiment is on picquet & I detained here now on a Court Martial, but I celebrated the anniversary in my own thoughts. How differently I now feel; then it was the threshold of a great experiment, which was to mould the destinies of the colored race & the fate of the nation; and I seemed the chief person on whom the burden lay. Now the experiment is tried, the case settled, this particular body is lost in the multiplicity of colored regiments & we are in the shadow of comparative privacy. How I longed for that privacy, last winter, sometimes; as Mr. Page truly said, there was no one brigade or division, even, in the army that attracted for a few months the attention this

268. First Lieutenant G. M. Chamberlin, formerly of the 11th Massachusetts Battery, was the new Quartermaster, as of August 29, 1863, replacing the deceased J. M. Bingham; his wife joined him in camp with her infant child.

269. Guard mounting is a ceremony performed when camp or garrison guard are relieved of duty, and a new guard takes their place; inspected by their officers, the two guards exchange places. *Regulations for the Army of the United States, 1861* (New York: Harper & Brothers, [1861]), 49–53.

regiment did; it was under microscopic observation—a single misstep, a defeat, a mutiny, would have annihilated the whole prospective colored army. I am only grateful to have honorably lived through that glare of no-toriety & to be out of it now. Now my duties are only the ordinary ones which absorb or shld. absorb every Colonel—to bring to perfection, more & more, every item of business, discipline & drill; to scrutinize buttons & gunlocks & messpans & morals; to be armed at all points & be sharper eyed than the sharpest Inspector who can visit us. At present I can truly say that the regiment is in more perfect condition than ever before, & that I daily & nightly wish that some first class white infantry regiment (if such a thing there be among volunteers) could be sent to this post to give my men a higher standard. As it is, they are in danger of growing conceited, for want of adequate competitors.

Today, for instance, some of those left in camp were looking at a Brigade Drill of the four white regiments. "Dese yere white sojers may do well enough" was the pitying conclusion *"but dey can't march"*, and it was simply true. Two of the four colonels had admitted the same superiority in march-ing to me, of their own accord a few nights before. There is an imper-turbable perfection of *time* about my men's marching which I have never seen equalled yet—*that* is a natural gift, but it is also a powerful auxiliary in producing that perfect alignment which drill is required to complete.

To change the subject; today I dined on a roasted opossum. Done to perfection, done *brown*, with such *crackling* as Charles Lamb in his visions of roast pig only dreamed of,[270] I found it a dish of barbaric fascination. Bear meat is delicious, it is like beef that has been fed on honey; alligator steaks are a kind of racier fried-halibut; but I see that 'possum is one of the great compensations of Nature, given to elevate & idealize the lives of these un-sophisticated Africans. What does Abolitionism, what did Mrs. Kem-ble[271] know of 'possum? They feel, these poor people what it is to them, &

270. Charles Lamb, "A Dissertation Upon Roast Pig," *The Essays of Elia*, in *The Complete Works and Letters of Charles Lamb* (New York: Modern Library, 1935), 108–13. "There is no flavour comparable, I will contend, to that of the crisp, tawny, well-watched, not over-roasted, *crackling*, as it is well called—the very teeth are invited to their share of the pleasure at this banquet in overcoming the coy, brittle resistance—with the adhe-sive oleaginous—O call it not fat! but an indefinable sweetness growing up to it—the tender blossoming of fat—fat cropped in the bud—taken in the shoot—in the first in-nocence—the cream and quintessence of the child-pig's yet pure food—the lean, no lean, but a kind of animal manna—or, rather, fat and lean (if it must be so) so blended and running into each other, that both together make but one ambrosian result or com-mon substance" (p. 110).

271. Frances Ann Kemble, known popularly as Fanny Kemble, was a renowned Eng-lish actress who came on tour to America in 1832, retiring from the stage in 1834 to marry

speak of it with a kind of unctuous reverence. Doubting whether to send a savory morsel of it to Dr. Rogers, in town, we consulted Uncle York, the veteran, his personal attendant, as to whether he would probably eat it if sent. Uncle York opened his eyes, eyes that had seen generations of possum, and answered with smiling certainty "Eat um, sa? *Oh* yes Sir. If he eber taste um, he eat um *sure.*" And the thing was sent.

Other savory bits we have occasionally, marsh hens shot among the reeds & young partridges, captured in ingenious traps the children make. Lee, (our blackest) brought three females & a male, beautiful birds which he caught at one fell swoop, & found the rest of the brood all laboring to get them out. Lee's eyes rolled with delight & he gave us a piece of sentimental ornithology "De *man*" (pointing to the male bird) "call dese same ones" (pointing to the females) "*Chloe*"! Sure enough that sounds like the cry of the male bird, but it seemed odd to have all the die-away romances of Daphnis & Chloe[272] revived by Nature for a little black urchin's aviary.

It is well we occasionally get these, for with eggs at 50 or 60 cts & milk at 10 cts pr. quart & chickens nowhere, we need some such accessories though by the way Daphnis & his Chloes were in this case begged for Hetty by William, as pets, which perhaps completes the circle of tender sentiment.

HEADQRS. 1ST S.C.V.
CAMP SHAW. DEC. 1. 1863

There is certainly something very gipsy like in this camp life. This morning I had an Official Inspection & a Court Martial; this afternoon a Brigade Drill; the first in which the regiment has taken part, & which went off very nicely. This evening passing the Quartermaster's tent I heard the Major's fine voice singing Methodist hymns (for Scroby has been all things, from Bowery boy[273] to Methodist class leader) and Mrs. Quartermaster's sweet

---

Pierce Butler, owner of a rice and cotton plantation in the islands on the Georgia coast, at the entrance of the Altamaha. Over her husband's strenuous objections she published her journal of the American stage tour in 1835, but not until 1863 did she publish *Journal of a Residence on a Georgian Plantation in 1838–1839* (New York: Harper & Brothers, 1863), in order to add her voice to the opposition to slavery. She had left her husband and children in 1846 and divorced soon after, eventually returning to the stage.

272. Ancient Greek pastoral romance by the poet Longus, featuring two young people whose sexual desire awakens, leads to love, and eventually to marriage.

273. The "Bowery Boy" is a stereotypical character from nineteenth-century American popular literature and drama, so named from association with the Bowery, a street in lower Manhattan in New York City, then a famous and somewhat disreputable gambling, prostitution, and entertainment district. The Bowery Boy, introduced in the play by Benjamin A. Baker, *A Glance at New York: A Local Drama in Two Acts* (New York: Samuel

innocent voice chiming in. So I went in to the small cot; a fire was burning pleasantly in the back tent, & a scrap of red carpet made the floor magnificent. Scroby sat on a box, Dr. Minor on a stool, Mr & Mrs Q. M. & Mrs Dewhurst & Capt. Whitney on the bed; the baby was under the bed. Baby had retired for the night, was suppressed, overshadowed, sat upon; the singing went on & the little thing had wandered off into her own land of dreams, nearer to heaven perchance than any pitch their voices cd. attain. Presently another officer was sent out for, to sing something or other; with the pause the suppressed innocent began to cluck and coo; it's the kitten, said somebody; it's *my* baby said Mrs. Chamberlin cheerily with the true young-maternal emphasis on the pronoun. Up got the bed-sitters for a moment; totty was hauled out wide awake & untroubled as usual, and sat in one or another lap during the rest of the singing, sometimes winking at the candle, but chiefly attending critically to the songs, with that rapt Sistine Madonna earnestness of eye and mouth which the cheapest human baby so easily gets up; how much more a bright eyed little darling like this. Not a sound, did she make, except one little soft sneeze, which led to an immediate flood tide of red shawl, submerging all but the head. After a little, I drew off the singers, because I knew from observation that Baby had carefully watched the Inspection & the Brigade Drill during today; and a period of repose was obviously necessary.

Hdqrs. 1ST S.C.V.
Camp Shaw. Dec. 19. 1863

Our Camp is coming to be one of the most picturesque. The men work with great taste & facility in building screens & shelters of light poles, filled in with the gray moss that hangs from the live oaks everywhere; all the officers have vestibules of it before their tents which are perfect shelters from wind & rain; the company cooking places are fenced round in the same way, & in some of the company streets there is a screen before the line of tents the whole length. The Sergeant at the entrance of the Camp has a bower and we are getting up a Schoolhouse or "Praise-House" of the same, for school & prayer meetings, of some thirty feet diameter. I have always had rather a knack at these decorative matters, but the men lead me entirely & get up just what they please, within certain restrictions.

***

French & Son, 1848), was characteristically a lively and irreverent rascal, streetwise and daring, known for wearing the costume of a volunteer fire department (such fire companies were essentially gangs at the time, with fierce rivalries among themselves).

### Dec. 26.

The Praise House was inaugurated Christmas Eve by a voluminous Prayer Meeting conducted as they usually are by the greatest saints & scamps of the regiment; the way of things everywhere. These leaders appear be designated by a handkerchief round the head, & there is a peculiar tie of this which is known technically as "Going tro' de lonesome valley" as it represents the preliminary stage of grace. One sees young women at work in the fields with the lonesome valley on their heads & it is accompanied by a total abnegation of all clean clothes up to the day of baptism, which thus has a special efficacy. However most of our leaders are past this symbol; and one of their functions is to enact a sort of Greek chorus in the play, filling out the pauses of every speaker with unflinching zeal. One man, the other night, got up & began "Sleep am de ruin of many souls".—"*Bress de Lord*" burst in the chorus—"*Pray for dem*". And so it went on, not as last Christmas all night, but till 9 Pm.—the usual bedtime of the children being 8.

Christmas Eve there was a ball in Beaufort to which my fashionables went; Christmas Day there was a prize shooting here & I gave them a football. There was also a fair at one of the churches in Beaufort which they patronized largely; so they had a pretty good time. The ball on Christmas Eve had one incident which shows how far the feeling of color may be ignored. There was some dispute about a partner between one of our men & one of the 54th Mass (Colored). Two of the Mass. Cavalry took the part of the latter, saying he was *from their state*; whereupon some soldiers from the regular artillery took up the cause of our man: it seemed at first as if there would be a regular fight, particolored on each side; not ranging by colors but by states; however it was quieted somehow. I don't know why the regular army should side with South Carolina, but it always leaned that way, you know, even in white times.

To match this small alienation between these two belligerent states I am happy to record a munificent present to us from the officers of this same Mass^tts cavalry, in the shape of a fine flag staff, the handsomest in town, which they, being ordered to Hilton Head have today presented to us. This is quite an addition, as we happened to be without any & on the 1st of January we want it.

### Dec. 28.

After all the Christmas present which our men have enjoyed most has been their service on the Provost Guard in Beaufort. A new Provost Marshal has just been appointed—one of my Captains,—& the Guard (or local Police) is furnished from my regiment every other day. As the "reliefs" go round, on those alternate days, stationing the sentinels under charge of a black corporal, the black soldiers are successively dropped & the whites picked up, gradually changing the complexion like Lord Somebody's black stockings darned with white, until at last there is only a "relief" of white soldiers obeying the "Support Arms" "Forward March" of my corporal. This is rather dramatic, but what pleases the men is that it is the only military duty hitherto withheld from them, and then it is a sort of self government, guarding the peace of their own town. And thoroughly they do it. It is said the guard house never was so full within human memory as after their first night of service; and one young reprobate, son of a prominent philanthropist here was much aggrieved at being taken to the lock-up merely because he was found drunk in the streets. Why, said he, the white corporals always showed me the way home!

For other entertainment there was a grand ball at Gen. Gillmore's quarters, at Hilton Head, on the night before Christmas Eve. I yielded to a gush of ill-advised benevolence & let my two other field officers go instead of myself, and perhaps, like Charles Lamb with his boyish cake,[274] shall always repent it. They say it was a beautiful affair, & there were actually some 50 ladies, of whom our pretty Mrs. Chamberlin was rather the belle, the Maj. Gen. Commanding taking her down to supper. The party fr. Beaufort went down in a steamer with Gen. Saxton & returned at 12.

On Christmas Evening there was a little party at Gen. Saxton's which went off very pleasantly—charades, games, music, jugglery &c. It was odd in the charades to see what I hv. often noticed, the impossibility of judging who possess dramatic ability. Capt. Saxton the mildest & timidest of men was more free & easy in assumed parts than he ever was in his own, while Mrs. Lander who never before saw a charade, but was bred to the stage from childhood was seriously embarrassed by timidity—though awkward she never could be. This interested me for I remember in my essay on Physical Courage[275] to have chronicled the same thing about some eminent English actress.—Another surprise was the success of Gen. Saxton &

274. Charles Lamb, in "A Dissertation Upon Roast Pig," tells how, upon returning to school after a holiday, he "in the vanity of self-denial and the very coxcombry of charity, schoolboy-like" gave his aunt's gift of plum-cake to a beggar and soon regretted his "out-of-place hypocrisy of goodness" (p. 112).

275. Thomas Wentworth Higginson, "Physical Courage," *Atlantic Monthly* 2 (November 1858), 728–37. Considering the "dependence of many persons' courage on habit," and their consequent timidity when out of their normal sphere of action and in unfamiliar circumstances, Higginson avers that "it was probably from the same cause, that Mrs. Inchbald, the most fearless of actresses, was once entirely overcome by timidity on assuming a character in a masquerade" (p. 731).

wife in interchanging characters. She the smallest woman I ever saw, almost, appearing as a Lilliputian[276] officer & he as a strongminded wife. Their costuming or "make-up" was admirable & when she (he) finally caught him (her) up in her (his) arms for protection & ran out of the room the applause was enthusiastic.[277]

I have been deep in Court Martials this month, trying the gravest cases & musing on the mixture of all pursuits into which war initiates one. Issues which at home are only entrusted to the Supreme Bench have been before us & I only the second in rank in the Court; several Capital cases hv. been tried & we are just finishing that of Col. Van Wyck of the[278] famous Investigating Committee of Congress, on a charge wh. if proved will dismiss him from the service in ignominy. The rules of Court Martial are however so much more formal & careful than those of civil courts that one may venture among them with less risk of error.

HDQR. 1ˢᵀ S.C.V.
BEAUFORT S.C. JAN. 20. 1864.

I have at last got my tent in the only comfortable form, dispensing entirely with poles & cords & substituting a light frame just like that of a house, over which the canvass is tightly strained. This gives a regular room 16 x 9, 9 ft high at the ridgepole 4 at the eaves; there is a proper door, & extreme luxury may even add a pane of glass for a window. In front there is a pretty vestibule of poles & moss, the width of the tent & half as long, with a canvass roof—this has a settee where people can meet & William has a little table in the corner for his primer & writing book. This moss is the feature of our camp, next to the cleanliness in which the Chief Inspector pronounced it to be first in the Department. All the officers' tents have this vestibule, some far more elaborate than mine & most of the Company streets have screens of the same at the edge of the sidewalk before the tents. It is astonishing what rapid progress soldiers make in the art of comfort. If my men were removed to some wholly new place with only tents & equipments, they wd. make themselves more comfortable in three weeks than they were all last winter.

It is done imperceptibly too. Last winter we had a constant striving after bricks with teams & flats & yet cd. only get chimneys for the company cookhouses & a very few officers. This year we hv. no such good locality for

276. Lemuel Gulliver, protagonist of Jonathan Swift, *Gulliver's Travels* (1726), is shipwrecked on the island of Lilliput where the people are six inches high.
277. The bracketed words in this sentence are TWH's own.
278. The copy-text here reads "the the."

bricks, can never spare the teams, have no flat-boat and there is not a tent in the regiment without a chimney. Where they came from, who brought them, when they came into camp, I actually cannot imagine—& yet there they are.

This is one thing that is giving us our wonderful improvement in health this winter. Last year on the 6th of February the sick list was 129 through Feb. & March it averaged 96. Today it is 18 just on the edge of the sickly season. To be sure, a good many unfit persons hv. been discharged within the year but not more than in the average of regiments.

Today the land sales are taking place in Beaufort & the men are intensely interested. Soldiers buy paying only one quarter cash, but they hv. speculators to bid against. My orderly & 3 others bid in a house for $900 today on wh. they hv. paid $50 each. Another of my men bought a house for $900 & has since been offered $1200 for it. Robert Small got a valuable estate for $600, no one bidding against him. I believe a great fortune might be made by investing here, for it will certainly be a depôt for years to come.

Thanks solely to General Saxton through Charles Sumner[279] the *plantations* are not to be sold by auction in this way; but divided into 20-acre lots & pre-empted; that is, each man records his claim, paying part the money, & has the lot at $1.25 per acre, after it is surveyed accurately. Some of our officers will buy land in this way. This plan has been adopted by the President over the heads of the Tax Commissioners here, who would have let it go to speculators. Everything yet really effected here has been really traceable to General Saxton, who while exercising the highest functions of a legislator & solving the most important administrative problems on the face of the earth, is yet always secretly pining after a command in the field, which would simply place him among a mob of Brigadier Generals, all destined to be forgotten in a month after the war ends. I hv. told him this & he has owned it, but he says it is the natural result of his military education. But he has to admit that all great soldiers have found their career as Conquerors culminate in legislation at last.

Emerson says no man can do anything well who did not feel that what he was doing was for the time the centre of the universe.[280] I thank heaven that I never yet have supposed for a moment that any brigade or division in the army was so important a trust as my one regiment—at least until the

279. Charles Sumner (1811–1874), radical antislavery activist elected to United States Senate in 1851 from Massachusetts, he was prominent among those who called for permanent confiscation of Rebel property and its distribution to former slaves.
280. "A true man belongs to no other time or place, but is the centre of things." Ralph Waldo Emerson, "Self-Reliance," *Essays: First Series,* in *The Complete Works of Ralph Waldo Emerson* (Boston: Houghton, Mifflin and Company, 1903), 2:60.

problem of negro soldiers was conclusively solved before all men's eyes.
How much of petty anxiety & mean solicitude has this not saved me—for
mere military life is a circle so small & so fascinating too, that it requires a
larger aim, as politics do, to keep one from being hopelessly belittled. The
privileges & pleasures of rank are so subdivided & adapted & brought directly home to every man, that when one is once[281] within the charmed
circle, one can easily understand how a great crime might be committed
for the sake of antedating a commission a single day.

I have read Hosmer's & Hepworth's books[282] & think the former far superior—it is simple, modest, graphic & gives the rarest of points of view,
that of a cultivated man in the ranks—while the other writer seems conscious and shallow in comparison & has far too much philosophizing, of a
cheap sort, with wonderfully little personal experience of facts. Still, both
have value. Hosmer's estimate of Banks seems extravagant, & I doubt if
his strategic plan was so systematic & well fulfilled. Military plans very seldom are & are apt to come *after* the events supposed to exhibit them.

HEADQUARTERS 1ST S.C.V.
JAN. 25. 1864

This morning I had from General Saxton what some persons might think
a very handsome offer. He told me that he had information that a certain
Col. Littlefield a rather shallow personage who has been for some time trying to raise a regiment, & had temporary command of the Mass. 54th had
gone to Washington recommended by Gen. Gillmore for Brigadier General, with the understanding that he was to return here with the command
of colored troops. That this was "an outrage" as he was perfectly unfitted
for the place and it belonged to me on the ground of seniority in command, as well as on other grounds, and if I would write to Mr. Sumner or
Mr. Wilson,[283] stating my claims, he would accompany the letter by the
strongest representation he could make. That he has always intended to

281. Copy-text reads "when is once."
282. James Kendall Hosmer, *The Color-Guard: Being a Corporal's Notes of Military Service
in the Nineteenth Army Corps* (Boston: Walker, Wise, and Co., 1864); George H. Hepworth,
*The Whip, Hoe, and Sword: or, The Gulf-Department in '63* (Boston: Walker, Wise, and Co.,
1864). As TWH mentions in his January 10, 1864, letter to his mother, Rev. Hosmer was
his brother Stephen's pastor in Deerfield, Massachusetts, and he surmised that it was
Stephen who had sent him the book. And in another letter to his mother, January 14,
1864, he added that he had received Rev. Hepworth's book from Henry Michels, who
was Hepworth's congregant.
283. Henry Wilson (1812–1875), Republican Senator from Massachusetts, wartime
chairman of the Senate Committee on Military Affairs.

urge my promotion & if he could have got leave to go to Washington, it was one thing he should have effected. &c &c &c

I told him with some indignation that if I cd. be made a Major General by writing a note ten words long to a Congressman I certainly would not do it; that I never yet had asked for any position in life & never expected to; that a large part of the pleasure I had had in commanding my regiment grew out of the perfect unexpectedness of the promotion. That if it were to be a matter of intrigue probably I could muster as many backers at Washington as any other Colonel—but that this was not my way nor the way of my house. That last Spring I heard that an effort was being made by Gov. Andrew & others to push me for a Brigadiership, but that I had heard no more of it & had never asked a question &c &c &c. Upon which he said that *he shld. feel just so, in his own case,* & was not surprised that I did; but that in most cases these promotions were not effected unless a man made some effort, himself, & he feared it would be so in this case. And there we left it.

We hv. all known well that Littlefield & Montgomery were running this race, & one reason why I was glad not to be at Morris Island was to keep clear of the whole affair. On the whole I shld. decidedly prefer Col. Littlefield's promotion over me to Col. Montgomery's, because L. is amiable & very conciliatory, whereas M. is very quarrelsome. L. has no experience of any value, unlike M., while as to attainments in drill, or power of discipline, there is little to choose. Most profoundly do I hope never to serve under either, because when one has a certain standard, & has been so long under a man like Saxton, it wd. be hard to be under an inferior man.

The amount of it is that military promotion is precisely like political: there is much that is disagreeable in the rivalries of both; while both are redeemed by conspicuous instances of men like Sumner & Andrew, who rise by sheer merit, without lifting a finger.

I saw six months ago that if I wanted promotion, I must go to Morris Island, because there as Senior Colonel I shld. hv. commanded a brigade, & it wd. hv. been hard for Gen. G. to pass me over, if I did decently well. But as I remember writing then, it seemed wrong, by any effort of mine, to take the men where they wd. be so very hard worked, & this, with my love & admiration for Saxton kept me here. And I shall always be glad I staid, if I see every officer promoted above me—I remember too well the longings expressed by the men of the 2d S.C.V. (when I was at Morris Island) that they cd. be permitted to return to Beaufort,—& the pleasure I then felt in not having carried my men there.

It would be pleasant if I were to be rewarded for this by having a larger command in Beaufort: but if other colored reg'ts come here (the 8th U.S. is expected) Gen. S. thinks somewhat of encamping them beside us &

brigading them under me. You understand that a brigade comprises fr. two to five regts—usually 3 or 4 & the majority of brigades in the army are commanded by Senior Colonels, who still have the rank & pay of Colonels though they do temporarily the work of Brigadiers.

We had today the most interesting drill we have ever had. Our officers happening to be scarce, I dispensed entirely with them & had battalion drill with every company commanded by a Sergeant. Not a white face but the Major, Adjutant & self. The Sergeants did splendidly; I gave more explanation than usual, but we all agreed that the movements had never been better done. I purposely did the harder movements, in "Casey"—"Division Columns" & "Oblique Square"[284] Their *style* was quite equal to the average of my officers; & it will have an admirable effect in commanding the respect of the men for officers of their own color. This is not like the educated colored officers of Louisiana,[285] remember; half of these men could not read & most of the remainder had learned it since entering the regiment.

## Camp Shaw. Jan. 29. 1864.

I think I never saw any one but General Saxton who was so essentially simple & noble that he could dare to *complain*. Complaint in him is the protest of a manly nature, too transparent to be diplomatic, against the perpetual annoyances which have hampered his whole career. Having done the Administration a greater service, in my judgment, than any man in America, by his practical vindication of their special policy of Emancipation, he can scarcely get a letter answered or a request fulfilled. Now, as from the beginning they simply tolerate him, while reaping the fruits of his success. In this Department it is no better. At this *post* he has it all his own way; but there has been a steady tendency, under Gen. Gillmore, to strip & belittle this post,—such as under Hunter never occurred. He seems a kind of military Cordelia,[286] whose torturers are not his children. An added regiment

284. Instructions on marching divisions in columns can be found in Casey, *Infantry Tactics*, 2:187–229; squares, formed as described above (January 19, 1863), may, under the pressure of immediate cavalry attack, be formed obliquely (i.e., with acute and obtuse angles rather than right angles) in less time, as described in Casey, 3:151–55.

285. Perhaps TWH is thinking of the noted bravery of the 9th and 11th Louisiana and the 1st Mississippi, who defended the Union fort at Milliken's Bend, Louisiana, on June 7, 1863, or (more likely) the role of the Louisiana Native Guards (some of whom were men of wealth and culture) in the failed assault of May 27, 1863, on Port Hudson, Louisiana.

286. Cordelia, the youngest of Lear's three daughters in William Shakespeare, *King Lear* (1604-05), refuses to secure her father's favor by flattery as her sisters do, and therefore loses his favor despite honoring him truly as they do not.

is promised to his small garrison; instead comes an order, taking one away; the cavalry go, each battery goes in succession; now an order comes removing all the Gov't horses for some spasmodic project of mounted Infantry at Hilton Head; the result of which is that shld. there come another cold snap, the hospitals cannot be supplied with fuel without burning fences or shade trees: nor can the offal of the town be carried to a healthy distance. On the other side he is equally tormented by the Tax Commissioners, who entirely refuse to carry out the instructions he has obtained fr. the Pres't, dividing the land for pre-emption.

With him & Gen. Gillmore personally there is no trouble, for Gen. G. evidently wishes to have matters go smooth. But they are very seldom brought together, most of the intercourse necessarily passing through Gen. G's staff, a race of very little men, who seem to take a real delight in vexing Gen. S. about small things; the same men were here under the former administration, & know Saxton's sensitive points & still reach them. This makes me hate all arbitrary power more than ever, this military life, because I see at what a price of possible injustice its efficiency is bought; even if you hv. one of Carlyle's ideal kings,[287] he can only work through staff-officers, & even if he bowstrings them for every act of tyranny, that does not recompense the victims. Even I have often, for the sake of discipline, to sustain my officers in acts which I severely condemn & how many such acts may pass unseen I have no way to tell. How much more then with Gillmore's larger responsibilities & the disadvantage that nobody credits him with really caring much about anything that does not bear on his engineering plans. A smart, driving railroad conductor, suddenly lifted into dominion, that is the way he always impresses me; bent on achieving his purposes & perfectly indifferent to persons, white or black; whereas General Saxton, equally energetic & determined, would step out of his way to avoid injuring the humblest child.

If Saxton had been placed in command of the Department, I do not know that he would have shelled Charleston though I am by no means sure that he would not—but I know that the general administration of the Department would have been completely transformed. And as to mere

---

287. Thomas Carlyle, in *On Heroes, Hero-Worship, & the Heroic in History* (1841), argued that a country perfectly subordinated to "the Ablest Man that exists there," a man who embodies "whatsoever of earthly or of spiritual dignity we can fancy to reside in a man," would be "the perfect state; an ideal country." "Alas, we know very well that Ideals can never be completely embodied in practice," Carlyle conceded. Thomas Carlyle, *On Heroes, Hero-Worship, & the Heroic in History*, ed. Michael K. Goldberg et al., *The Norman and Charlotte Strouse Edition of the Writings of Thomas Carlyle*, ed. Murray Baumgarten et al. (Berkeley: University of California Press, 1993), 169–70.

military ability, I hv. infinitely more faith in the comprehensiveness of his ability than in Gillmore's, who is a mere specialist, except in the item of energy, & that they have in common.

In this general upheaval which war gives, one learns anew how small the circle of the world is, & how limited the Dramatis Personae. It seems as if I knew everybody who came down here & as if all whom I know were coming. This morning brought to my tent a little old fat bald grayhaired man, accompanied by a young boy & at last I recognized Robert Carter, whom I knew well at Cambridge, when he consulted me as to the economy of marrying Ann Augusta Gray on his post office salary of $200 a year, & afterward announced to me his purchase of a pair of young eagles whose butchers' bill was longer than his & his bride's. Since then he has been Tribune Correspondent & Eagleswood professor & now comes here as Clerk in the Treasury Department. Within an hour after, I met in Beaufort Edward Philbrick, with whom Carter used to walk over to Brookline & who certainly did not look more than thirty today while Carter looks sixty five. So uncertain are time's changes.

## Jan. 30. 1864

Just now a soldier was here, defending himself against his Captain's complaints & said indignantly "I aint got colored-man-principles, I'se got a white-gentleman principles. I'se do my best. If Cappen tell me to take a man, if de man be as big as a house, I'll *clam hold of him* till I die, inception I'm sick." Corporal London Simmons, this was.

They have some phrases as poetic as the Portuguese. The reverberations of the noon day gun, which are often very beautiful, they call "bush-take-um", meaning that the land takes up & echoes the sound. In describing a particularly severe whipping, the Major has heard them say "Mausr *trow de stick* till de bush take um." To "throw the stick" is to whip, & this was done till it echoed again. The phrase is pretty, though the thing be ugly.

I am not sure if it was one of our men who said when asked insultingly, "What are you, anyhow" answered "When God made me, I wasn't much, but I's a man now.["]

At any rate one of our men made an answer that cd. not be improved, when on Provost duty in Beaufort & arresting somebody who asked his authority—"Know what dat means"? said the Sergeant pointing to the stripes[288] on his arm, "Dat means *Guvment*" Volumes cd. not have said more.

288. The word "chevrons" is interlineated here.

It was quite amusing the other night, after a party at Dr. Hayden's, to hear the officers say anxiously "Got the countersign? Got the countersign? The donkeys are on guard tonight & we must look out for our lives." After a party at Gen. Saxton's the guard before the house would not let an ambulance be brought from the stable for our ladies, because the driver hadn't the countersign. Perhaps you are not aware that military fashionables ride to parties in ambulances in as matter of course a way as in sleighs or hacks at the North! The 8th Maine flag raising was really a pretty & tasteful affair, the camp was beautifully decorated & the prettiest dining hall built of moss & floored with sea sand set round with palmetto leaves. I escorted Mrs. Lt. Colonel Wheeler who is the belle of Beaufort & wears a riding habit with a double row of gilt infantry buttons ("I") in front, to correspond to her husband's rank! When I get home I shall devote myself to amending Mary's[289] costume accordingly!

The party at Dr. Hayden's was a surprise, got up by ladies, he being a bachelor & a good soul. He heard of it about noon I believe, so that the real surprise came next morning when he found that one of his visitors had carried away his new hat.

## HDQRS. ADVANCED PICQUET. PORT ROYAL I. FEBRUARY 1. 1864.

I am so glad that I came out with the regiment today, after many valetudinary doubts. It has been perfectly delightful. First the setting off in the misty morning, just about sunrise, though when we were once on the wide parade ground neither sun nor Camp nor anything else was visible; nor even from one end of the regiment to the other could one see, & when I rode on a little way & looked back there was only a moving mysterious line, looking rather awful in the dimness & a swaying of multitudinous weapons that might have been Camel's necks & the whole thing a caravan crossing a desert in a haze of dust not vapor: off on one side waited the train of wagons, for us to pass—another dim mystery—; & so we swayed along till we came out upon the "shell-road."

I had forgotten what a jubilant thing it is to go out on picquet or in from picquet or anywhere else with our men; they were at the top of exhilaration, there was one broad grin fr. one end of the line to the other; it might now have been elephants instead of camels by the ivory & the duskiness;

289. Mary is, of course, TWH's wife, Mary Elizabeth Channing Higginson. She was the daughter of Barbara Higginson Perkins Channing (who was TWH's first cousin) and Dr. Walter Channing.

they came on at "route step" at a great pace, chattering & laughing & singing. At the entrances of plantations & at cross roads the farm people crowded to see us pass; every one had a friend & a greeting. "How you do, Aunty." "Huddy, budder Benjamin." "How you find yousef dis mornin, Tittawisa['] (Sister Louisa) rang out to everybody known or unknown. Venerable matrons courtesied laboriously to every body with an answering "Bress de Lord, budder"; grave little boys, blacker than ink, shook hands with our laughing & utterly unmanageable drummers; & one pretty mulatto girl ogled & coquetted & made great eyes, as Thackeray[290] would say, at half the young fellows in the battalion. Meantime the singing was brisk along the whole line, & reining up for them to pass, successive waves of song drifted by—first John Brown, of course, then "What make ole Satan for follow me so", then "Marching Along", then "Hold your light on Canaan Shore" then "When this Cruel War is over" then one which always calls out the greatest zeal in these marches

> "All true children gwine in de wilderness
> Gwine in de wilderness, gwine in de wilderness
> True believers gwine in de wilderness
> To take away de sins ob de world
> (*Hoigh!*)

a sort of Irish yell.
All their own songs had verses improvised as usual, & mingled in the oddest way;—the commonplace of today with the depths of theological horror, thus

> Gwine to de Ferry—(Chorus) Oh de bell done ringing
> Trust, Believer—Oh de bell done ringing
> Gwine to de landing—Oh de bell done ringing
> Satan's behind me—    " "  " "  " "
> Tis a misty morning—    " "  " "  "
> O de road am sandy—    " "  " "  " "  "
> Hell done open—  " "  " "  " "

And so on indefinitely. The little drummer boys strode ahead, with the officers' waiters, a jolly crew, always joining in the nearest song. At the head of all walked, by some self imposed pre-eminence a respectable Elderly female, one of the company laundresses, with a large bundle balanced on her head & a long handled tin dipper waving in her hand, like a sword.

290. William Makepeace Thackeray, author of numerous novels featuring dramas of courtship and coquetry, among them *Vanity Fair* (1847–1848).

Such a medley of fun, war, music & picturesqueness no white regiment in the world could muster, & so we marched our seven miles out here, beneath great pine cones dropping & budded jasmine streaming over trees & bushes & weird bunches of mistletoe in blossom high up among the branches.

The day grew warm & sunny so that we were grateful for a cooler breeze this afternoon; it is like loveliest June; mockingbirds busy in the trees around the house, an apricot in blossom by the piazza & the officers whom we relieve carrying off all the japonicas from the garden. All windows are open, children are exploring & shouting round the house, & we cleaning up & going to housekeeping inside: it is like moving out to a country seat & I'm glad I sang with the men "I can't stay behind.["]

Feb. 2. One thing I should mention to the credit of the regiment, that there was absolutely *no* straggling, the whole body was together, & in as much shape as is required by "route step", the whole time; whereas I literally never met a white regiment, in relieving picquet, which was not spread in little squads of two & three over several miles of ground.

## CAMP SHAW AGAIN. FEB 7. 1864.

Great are the uncertainties of military orders. Since we were ordered away from Jacksonville we hv. had no such surprise as came to us on Wednesday night. It was our 3d day on picquet & we had just got nicely settled—men well tented & with good floors & in high spirits, officers at out-stations all happy, Mrs. Lieut. Stone[291] coming to stay with her husband, we at headquarters just in order, house cleaned, moss garlands up, camelias & jessamines in ten wash-basins, baby in bliss; our usual run of visitors had just set in, two Beaufort Captains & a surgeon had just risen from a late dinner after a flag of truce, Gen. Saxton & wife had driven away but an hour or two before, we were all sitting about busy with a great fire blazing, Mrs. Dewhurst had just remarked triumphantly "Last time I had but a mouthful here, & now I shall be here three weeks"—when

——In dropped like a bombshell, a despatch announcing that we were to be relieved by the 8th Maine the next morning, as Gen. Gillmore had sent an order that we should be ready for departure from Beaufort at any moment!

Conjectures, orders, packing of trunks, sending away couriers to out-stations, were the employments of the evening; the men received the news with cheers & we all came in next morning.

291. Wife of First Lieut. Henry A. Stone.

Whether we were glad or sorry was not quite clear. Of course there was exhilaration in the thought of moving, especially as it was understood that a new Florida Expedition was on foot. On the other hand my impaired health & strength—our having but one Surgeon—and the uncertainty under whose command we were to be placed, were all great drawbacks. To go to Florida was delightful—but to go under General Seymour?

From that moment to this we hv. expected at every moment a telegraphic order to move, until we hear today that the expedition, whatever it may be, has gone without us & for two reasons, first that Gen. Saxton remonstrated so strongly & second that we had small pox in the regiment, as if we were ever without it. But these rumors are mere gossip, like the rest, & we know nothing. Still it does not seem likely that we shall now be ordered away.

6. P.m. Another surprise! An order to remove camp to the Entrenchments, about a mile out on the Shell Road. Still another! On enquiry, it turns out that our camp is *not* to be moved, but that we are simply to furnish details at the Earthworks, instead of Provost Guard & other duty.

Our greatest fear has been of being posted at Hilton Head & going no farther. One Lieutenant, an Irishman, in deprecating this remarked, If we are ordered away anywhere I hope it will be either to go to Florida or else stay here!

CAMP SHAW. FEB. 11. 1864.

On the 4th inst. I found the bloodroot in bloom; there is a quantity of it just outside our camp lines. Last year also I found it early in February; two war winters rolling over it's head & just the same white creature here as in Massachusetts. It symbolizes military life though, whose forms & pageants are all innocent enough to look at,—baby watches Dress Parade every day—till some morning unearths the ensanguined root of it all. Well, if Nature has room for the bloodroot, I suppose it has room for us.

For three days, now, we have watched the river every day & every little steamer that came up to coal brought out spyglasses & conjectures, & "Dar's de Fourth New Hampshire" for when that comes we go. Meanwhile we hear stirring news from Florida & the men are very impatient to be off. It is remarkable how much more they are soldiers than last year, & how much less home-bound men—the South Carolina men I mean, for of course the Floridians wd. wish to go to Florida.

In every way I see the gradual change in them, sometimes with a sigh as parents watch their children growing up & miss the droll speeches & the confiding ignorance of childhood. Sometimes it comes over me with a pang that they are growing more like white men; less naive & less grotesque. Still I think there is enough of it to last; & that their joyous buoyancy will hold out while life does. This morning after a forlorn chilly night on picquet that would have wearied out any white men, I noticed the company which had been out, marching by the camp to discharge their guns; they were at the highest pitch of spirits & singing one of the few native songs which are not hymns—not that anything can be jollier than their hymns. But this relates to one of their two *secular* myths—Becky Lawton being the mysterious subject of one "Rain fall & wet Becky Lawton" of which I can only trace that if people are bad it is thought the rain will not fall on their graves. The hero of this "Hangman Johnny" is an equal enigma, you never can make them do more than roar with laughter & say they "don't know nottin" about him. But these men were singing as they marched along, to a perfectly inspiring refrain that seemed oddly contrasted with the lugubrious subject.

> O dey call me Hangman Johnny
> O ho, o ho
> But I neber hang nobody
> O hang, boys, hang
> And we'll al hang togeder
> O ho, o ho,
> But dey neber hang nobody
> O hang, boys, hang,

Some of the officers thought there was a line about "De buckra sogers work for money" but I couldn't make the chorister Sergeant own to this. He shook all over though when I endeavored to get at the genealogy of Hangman Johnny.

I believe I never wrote abt the prisoner our men took in the Battle of the Bloodhounds. He was a specimen of what our men call "de clean cracker", or the unadulterated poor white. Thus

Where do you live? "O a piece up yonder."

What County? "Dunno about what county, I live in *Pickens's Deestrict*." (There's Southern life for you—his geography lies in the name of his Congressman.[)]

Many men left there? "O yes, there's right smart of shavers there yet."

Have you ever been mustered into the army, ever signed yr. name on the muster roll. It turned out, of course, that he couldn't write & few of the company could. "But" he added "some of our sergeants are *right smart scribes*". I believe I could say that of ours.

I did not see the shaver in question, but our officers were struck, as usual, with the superior material in our men over these scrimped sallow forlorn crackers. In them there seems poverty in grain, in our men it seems merely a few, sometimes solid, sometimes thin—which they express themselves by saying "I feel my head growing thinner" as they advance in knowledge.

Dear old Uncle York leans in the doorway of Dr. Minor's tent, with his broadbrimmed white hat on, like a retired seraph in easy circumstances. Along comes little Ben, Mrs. Dewhurst's page, $2\frac{1}{2}$ ft. high, & swaggeringly says—Come, Uncle York, gwine to school? and the blessed veteran gets down his primer, dogs-eared now as far as four syllables & away they go to the moss-house where Mrs. D. holds sway over drummers & divines.

The singular mingling of the military & scholastic in all their training! Today some of the men were drilling with unspeakable delight, the fattest little boy of five or less, in McLellan's Bayonet Exercises. There he was with his plump little legs stretched to their utmost range in a correct & knowing stride—"Leap to de front", "Ac-vance" (advance) "Retreat", "Leap to de rear" in which case he invariably fell head over heels, still clinging to a piece of bread which he was steadily munching throughout. If you could see the profound gravity with which some of these urchins give the military salute! Most of the women give it also, & no doubt it will be permanently grafted into their emancipated manners.

## Camp Shaw. Beaufort S.C.
## Feb. 18. 1864

Oh the sublime uncertainties of military command! After being ordered in from picquet, to be ready at a moment's notice—after the subsequent ten days of uncertainty—after watching every steamer that came up the river to see if the 4th N.H. were on board, at last the regiment came. Then followed another break—there was no transportation to take us. At last a boat was notified. Then General Saxton (as anxious to keep us as the regiment to go) played his last card in *Small Pox*, telegraphing that we had it dangerously in the reg't (N.B. all varioloid,[292] light at that & we *always* have it.) In vain; the order came back to leave behind the sick & those peculiarly exposed, & embark the rest next day. Great was the jubilee—the men were up I verily believe by three in the morning & by eight oclock the whole camp was demolished & in wagons & we on our way. The 4th N.H. soldiers swarmed in, every board was swept away by them; there was a time when

---

292. Varioloid is a mild form of smallpox, occurring chiefly in those who have been vaccinated or have already had the disease.

*colored boards* if I may so express myself, were repudiated by white soldiers but that epoch long since passed. I gave my new tent frame, even the *latch*, (the glory of the Camp) to Col. Bell, ditto Lt. Col. to Lt. Col. Down we marched the men singing John Brown & Marching Along & Gwine in de Wilderness; women in tears & smiles lined the way. We halted opposite the dear General's we cheered, he speeched, I speeched, we all embraced symbolically & cheered some more. Then we went to work at the wharf, vast wagon loads of tents, rations, ordnance & what not disappeared in the capacious maw of the Delaware. In the midst of it all came riding down the General with a despatch fr. Hilton Head. "If you think the amount of small pox in the 1ˢᵗ S.C.V. sufficient, the order will be countermanded." "What shall I say"? quoth the guilty General, perceiving how preposterously too late the negotiation was reopened. "Say, Sir," quoth I "say that we are on board already & the small pox left behind, say we had only thirteen cases, chiefly varioloid & ten almost well." Our blood was up with hard work & we would have held down Maj. Gen. Gillmore, commanding Department, & all his staff upon the wharf & vaccinated them all by main force rather than turn back. General Saxton rode away & we worked away. Just as the last wagon load but one was being transferred to the omnivorous depths of the Delaware—which I should think wd. hv. been filled ten times over with what we had put into it—down rode the General again with a fiendish joy in his handsome eyes, struggling with a look of penitence & pity. "The marching orders of the 1ˢᵗ S.C.V. are countermanded"————————————"Maj. Trowbridge" said I ["]will you give my compliments to Lieut. Hooper, somewhere in the hold of that steamboat, & direct him to set his men at work to bring out of the vessel everything which they have carried in!["]————

"You will return to your old camping ground Colonel" said the General placidly. "Now," he added with serene satisfaction, "we will have some brigade drills"! Brigade Drills! Since Mr. Pickwick with his heartless tomato sauce & warming pans,²⁹³ there has been nothing so aggravating as to try to solace us who were already as good as on board ship & under

293. Charles Dickens, *The Pickwick Papers*, ed. James Kinsley (1837; Oxford: Clarendon Press, 1986). In chapter 34, Serjeant Buzfuz, attorney for the plaintiff, Mrs. Bardell, in the trial of her suit for breach of promise of marriage against Samuel Pickwick, her former tenant, introduces into evidence two notes Pickwick had written to her—one asking her for "Chops and Tomata sauce," the other advising, "Dont trouble yourself about the warming-pan" (p. 521). Buzfuz labors to interpret these ordinary notes as coded professions of love, then berates Pickwick, describing him to the jury as a shameless deserter who "comes before you to-day with his heartless tomata sauce and warming-pans" (p. 522).

weigh—& in imagination as far up the St John's as Pilatka at least—with Brigade Drills.

Never did officer ride at the head of a battalion of more woebegone, spiritless, disgusted wretches, than I marched back fr. Beaufort that day. "When I marched down to de landin'" said one afterwards, ["]my knapsack full of feathers. Comin' back, *he lead*"! As if the disappointment itself were not sufficient—to return to our pretty camp, accustomed to it's drawing-room order—& find it a desert! Every board gone fr. the floors—the screens torn down for the poles—all the little conveniences scattered—& to crown all, a cold breeze such as we had not known since New Year's blowing across the camp & flooding everything with dust. I sincerely hope the regiment wd. never behave after a defeat in battle as they behaved then. Every man seemed crushed, officers & soldiers when they broke ranks, they went & lay down like sheep where their tents used to be or wandered disconsolately about, looking for their stray belongings. The scene was so infinitely dolorous that it gradually put me in the highest spirits; the ludicrousness of the whole affair was so complete. Nothing was wanting. The horrible dust blew till every officer had some black spot on his nose which paralyzed pathos. Of course the only way was to set them all at work as soon as possible, & work then we did, I at camp & the Major at the wharf; loading & unloading wagons & just reversing all which the morning had done. The New Hampshire men were very considerate & gave back most of what they had taken, though many of our men were really too delicate or proud to ask or take again what they had once given away to soldiers or to the colored people. I had no such delicacy about my tent frame, latch included & by night things had resumed much of their old aspect & the men's cheerfulness was in part revived. Yet long after I found one first Sergeant, sitting crying with his handkerchief at his eyes, a Florida man, most of whose kindred were up the St. John's. It was very natural that the Florida men shld. all feel so, but it shows how much of the habit of soldiers they hv. all acquired that the South Carolina men, who were leaving their families for an indefinite period, were just as eager to go, & not one deserted though they knew it for a week beforehand.

No doubt my precarious health makes it easier for me, *on reflection*, to remain here—than for the others. At the same time Florida is fascinating & it offered not only adventure but the probable command of a brigade—& certainly at the last minute there was hardly[294] a sacrifice I wd. not hv. made rather than wrench myself & the rest away fr. the Expedition. But it is a great thing for a commander that he *has* to think of others & forget him-

294. Copy-text reads "was a hardly."

self; & as it has always been my way to live in the present, it is easy now. We are of course thrown back into the old uncertainty, & if the small pox subsides (& it is really diminishing decidedly) we may yet come in at the wrong end of the Florida Expedition.

Feb. 19 Not a bit of it! This morning the General has ridden up radiant, has seen Gen Gillmore who has decided not to order us to Florida at all, or withdraw any of this garrison. Moreover, he says that all which is intended in Florida is done—that there will be no advance to Tallahassee & Gen Seymour will establish a Camp of Instruction in Jacksonville. Well! if that is all, it is a lucky escape for us & I wd. far rather stay in Gen. Saxton's camp of instruction here. It may be a fortunate small pox after all, that kept us here.

But oh! how cold it is. Mercury 25° at 7½ today and only 38° at noon. With a high wind!

## Camp Shaw. Feb. 23. 1864.

There was a sound of revelry by night at our pretty ball, in a new great building, beautifully & laboriously decorated. All the collected flags of the garrison hung round & over us as if the stars & stripes were devised for an ornament alone, & the array of uniforms was such that a civilian became a distinguished object: much more a lady. The belles of the 1st S.C.V. Mrs. Dewhurst & Mrs. Chamberlin, who are really the prettiest as well as most pleasing women I have seen in the Department, were there in full array; Gen. Gillmore was there for a short time with an impressive female in blue silk; Gen. Saxton & his wife; Major Hay the President's late private secretary, an elegant little fellow, with the aplomb picked up in Washington among the diplomats whom he affects. All would have gone according to the proverbial marriage bell, had there not been a slight possible shadow over all of us from hearing vague stories of a lost battle in Florida,[295] & from the thought that the very ambulances in which we rode to the ball were ours only until the wounded or the dead might tenant them.

Gen. Gillmore only came, I supposed, to put a good face on the matter—for although he is not a man of the sentiments, still we all knew his[296] military reputation could ill afford so damaging a blow & he certainly cares enough for that. He went away soon & Gen. Saxton went;

295. At Olustee, a depot on the Florida, Atlantic & Gulf Railroad, about 50 miles southwest of Jacksonville, Florida, troops under the command of Brig. Gen. Truman Seymour were soundly repulsed by Confederates under Brig. Gen. Joseph Finegan on February 20, 1864, suffering more than 1860 casualties.

296. Copy-text reads "he."

there was a rumor that the "Cosmopolitan" had actually arrived with wounded; but still the dance went on. There was nothing unfeeling about it; one gets used to things; & it seemed not unnatural to cross question an officer just from Jacksonville as to whether the casualties numbered more or less than a thousand, and then to moot the other question whether on a lady's card one stood engaged for the tenth dance or the twelfth, when suddenly, in the midst of the dances—

—There came a perfect hush, the music ceasing, a few surgeons went hastily to & fro, as if conscience smitten (I should think they might have been)—there "waved a mighty shadow in", as in Uhland's Black Knight,[297] & as we all stood wondering we were 'ware of General Saxton, who came hastily down the hall, his pale and handsome face more resolute even than usual, & looking almost sick with anxiety. He had just been on board the steamer, there were 250 wounded men just arrived & the ball must end. Not that there was anything for us to do, but the revel was mistimed & must be ended:—it was *wicked* to be dancing, with such a scene of suffering near by.

Of course therefore we broke up, though with some murmurings & some longings of appetite, on the part of some, towards the wasted supper. Was there not really, however, something that we could *do*. I had asked several of the leading surgeons & they all replied that everything was provided for, three hundred spare beds in hospital & everything in abundance at the wharf. With this I had to be satisfied though I have since heard fr. Lt. Col. Strong that when the boat touched the wharf not an ambulance nor a surgeon was there to meet them, to the unbounded indignation of the surgeons on board.

But when I went on board, an hr. after this, the transfer was being effected with some promptness—though why all the men only moderately wounded were not taken off then instead of leaving all but 50 on board till morning, is a part of the same questionable mystery. Night is a far better time to remove wounded men—no sun, no dust, no delaying crowd in the streets, no loungers nor starers, & then moreover the "Cosmopolitan" (which is expressly a hospital boat) was imperatively needed at Jacksonville for another load. It is very possible however that there was some explanation of the delay, but the surgeons thus far consulted agree with me; & every month increases my distrust of the medical department as here administered.

On board the boat among the long lines of wounded, black & white

297. Ludwig Uhland, *The Songs and Ballads of Uhland Translated from the German* (London: Williams and Norgate, 1864).

mingled, there was the wonderful *quiet* which usually prevails on such occasions. Not a sob or groan, except from those undergoing removal. It is not self control, but chiefly the *shock* to the system which wounds, especially gunshot wounds invoke, & which almost always keeps the patient stiller at first than at any other time.

A company from my regiment waited on the wharf, in their accustomed dusky silence, to render aid; & I longed to ask them whether, with what they saw they still wished that we had been there. I confess, in presence of all that human suffering, that *I* could not wish it, but I shld. not hv. wished to suggest the doubt to them.

I found our kindhearted ladies, Mrs. D & Mrs C. on board the steamer, but there was nothing for them to do & we walked back to Camp in the radiant moonlight; Mrs. Chamberlin more than ever strengthened in her blushing woman's-philosophy "Don't care who wins the laurels,—so long as we don't."

As to the fight itself, I do not know how much will be made public, but it is useless to disguise that it was an utter & ignominious defeat—not ignominious as to the men who behaved well, but as to the generalship which cd. be caught in a shallow trap in a dangerous country. Gen. Gillmore last night threw the responsibility as he did after Fort Wagner[298] on Gen. Seymour—but he it was & he only who diverted 10 000 of his 20 000 men, upon a secondary enterprise perfectly understood by the enemy, who had an interior line of railroad by which he cd. be confronted with a superior force at any point. Knowing the country as I do in Florida I hv. always held that to penetrate it for any distance was a thing to be attempted with the greatest caution—the enemy possessing the greatest advantages if disposed to use them. There was nothing to be gained by victory beyond a member of Congress; while the loss includes more than a thousand killed & wounded, half in the enemy's hands—four or five cannon—& large supplies of stores destroyed by fire to keep them fr. the enemy. Now our troops are falling back on Jacksonville & we are likely as not to be kept fr. farther advance.

The difference between this Florida movement now & ours a year ago is this. Then there were large supplies to be had in Florida (now much diminished) large hopes of negro recruiting (not now aimed at) & greater safety, because the RR. communication with Charleston & Savannah, then incomplete, is now perfect. I had the advantage moreover in my men

298. Battery Wagner, on the northern tip of Morris Island, was assaulted by troops under Brig. Gen. Truman Seymour on July 18, 1863; spearheaded by the black troops of the 54th Massachusetts, whose numbers were decimated, the assault failed miserably.

of an intimate knowledge of all this very region, which no regiment now with Gen. Seymour possesses.

One aspect of the case I often think of is the impression which our friends of course have, from the last letters, that this reg't is in Florida, which might lead to great anxieties. If for instance it shld. appear fr. the rebel accounts that a Colonel of a colored reg't was killed (the Commander of the 8th U.S.) I might again read my own obituary as I did a year ago.

I did not put in what several officers say that the 54th Mass. & 1st N.C. really saved the affair fr. being far worse than it was, by making a charge & driving back the enemy for a time under cover of which our troops retreated. On the other hand it is said that the 8th US Colored, being entirely raw, did not stand well. No doubt you will be duly informed of the latter in Gen. Seymour's report—whether the former fact appears is more questionable.

HEADQRS. DV. PICQUET. FEB. 25. 1864.

Here we are, established on picquet again, with weather as lovely as before & the season a little more advanced during the three weeks—& only a little, because of the interval of cold. I have just been wandering about. The encircling woods are draped with that "net of shining haze" which belongs to our Northern May: the wild plums are in bloom all around the house, a small white profuse blossom, tenanted by murmuring bees. There are peach blossoms also; & the yellow jasmine is opening some of its multitudinous buds, climbing over trees & waving from bough to bough. In the garden the magnolias are bare & the remaining japonicas are blighted—but the myrtle & petisporum are in bud & there are fresh young ferns & garden-snowdrops in the tangled beds, fast reverting to wilderness. In this wilderness the birds are busy; the two main songsters being the mocking bird & cardinal grosbeak, which monopolize all the parts of our more varied Northern orchestra, except the tender & liquid notes, here unattempted by any, unless by some stray bluebird. Jays are as busy & loud as with us in autumn, & I noticed the shy & whimsical chewink for the first time today. Sparrows & wrens there are many, not known to me, & not conspicuous in voice.

In doors, the picquet headquarters seem like the temporary abode of some party of young surveyors in time of peace, with a little female society thrown in to mitigate the free & easy ways without taking fr. the outdoor quality. A large low dilapidated room, the walls darkened with successive sketches or scrawls of many regiments, most of the window-glass broken, & an immense fireplace in which perennial embers smoulder all day, & bright flames flicker night & morning. The walls have the old-world picturesqueness wh. comes from the profuse display of objects of use— flags, swords, pistols, belts, rifles, spyglasses, gauntlet gloves, canteens,— all hung carelessly here & there; while wreaths of moss above the windows & a great cluster of holly & evergreen over the high mantle—indicate more deliberate decoration. The furniture (brought with us) is decidedly varied, & when the room is filled with ten people or so at evening writing, reading, sewing, card-playing, it seems very pleasant; nor less so by day, with officers & soldiers streaming in & out on various business; baby in her scarlet cloak & her stately observant serenity; people coming up on horseback, their hands full of jasmine; & the sweet sunny air penetrating through all the windows, that are always open even when they are shut. From the neighboring camp there is a suppressed & perpetual murmur— louder voices & laughter re-echo from the woods near by—& sometimes from some other part of the woods where the relieved guard are discharging their pieces, there comes the hollow & reverberating sound of dropping rifle-shots, as of skirmishing, the most unmistakable & fascinating association that war bequeaths to the memory of the ear.

Feb. 29. We certainly came wonderfully near having a sufficiency of these delightful associations of rifle shots. But for a few trivial cases of varioloid, we should certainly have been in that disastrous fight. We were confidently expected for several days at Jacksonville, & Gen. Seymour told Col. Halliwell that we being the oldest colored reg't would have the right of the line, or the foremost place. Of course we should, & should probably hv. lost severely, as the 54th did, though there were only three officers wounded there & slightly,—unlike the other colored reg'ts engaged. This was certainly missing danger & glory very closely.

HEADQRS. ADV. PICQUET.
FEB. 26. 1864.

I have said before that the first black man killed in US. uniform was named John Brown; it was before this regiment was organized, he belonged to Major Trowbridge's Company at St. Simon's Island. He was son of our saint, old York Brown; & Uncle York believes profoundly to this day that his son & no other is the hero of the song which the men are always singing!

Old York is a saint who is a saint. We have another saint who is a sinner—old James Cashman equally prominent in the prayer meetings & in sharp bargaining; he is a sort of caterer for our mess & makes about 50 pr. ct. profit. Major Trowbridge & his newly arrived wife met him yesterday & the Major wishing to give Mrs. T. some knowledge of Southern high life, hailed him; "Jim, how much wife you got"? "*On'y but four, sa,*" answered Jim regretfully. I don't know who the 3 others are or have been, but I know No 4. to be a nice looking young girl who is perfectly devoted to the veteran, & dances her baby at him in triumphant delight.

Maj. Trowbridge has a keener ear for oddities of language than any of us & his knowledge of these people's ways & phrases is far more complete: he imitates them in perfection. Yesterday he saw a very old woman & asked her age. "Maus'r," said she "I tell you no lie. In de first earthquake I was den fourteen"! This awful revelation of antiquity, this intermingling of personal autobiography with the great convulsions of geology, seemed perfectly stupendous; & then the intricate difficulty (on a more modern hypothesis) of finding *which* earthquake, real or imaginary she meant, seemed like Emerson's suggestion of hitching one's wagon to a star.[299]

Just now a man came & asked Dr. Minor what time "*de omelet*" was going to town—meaning the ambulance. Some of them, more nautically educated, call it the *admiral*.

## H.Q. Advanced Picquet.
## March 7. 1864.

I have to chronicle the most startling ebullition on the part of our saintly Uncle York; the Doctor's beloved. He was actually seen kicking violently, with his removable leg, at Pete, the Major's boy, who eluded the attack by jumping off the piazza & running away shouting with laughter. The veteran himself relaxed into a smile, softened into anxious gravity when I upbraided him with this carnal manifestation.

It appeared that the boys occasionally amuse themselves with a habit Uncle York has of soliloquizing aloud, & this morning he was heard to ejaculate, while grooming a horse "You must wake, snakes, and switch you tails"—which cabalistic incantation, repeated suddenly in his ear by Pete, led to the above ebullition.

Uncle York's explanation of the remark is "I was only remarkin' a man I used for know in Darien",[300] which may or may not throw light upon it.

299. "Now that is the wisdom of a man, in every instance of his labor, to hitch his wagon to a star, and see his chore done by the gods themselves"; "Hitch your wagon to a star": Ralph Waldo Emerson, "American Civilization," *Atlantic Monthly* 9 (April 1862), 502–511 (quotations p. 503); also *Society and Solitude: Twelve Chapters,* in *Emerson's Complete Works,* New and Revised Edition, Vol. VII (Boston: Houghton, Mifflin and Company, 1891), 32, 33.

300. Darien, Georgia is a town at the mouth of the Altamaha River.

The Major's boy Pete is exceedingly bright: he has picked up Gullah[301] dances from native Africans, leads the boys in "shouts", & decorates the school tent very prettily on his own plan. He is rather hard to wake in the morning & when the Major's boot is thrown at him with or without the owner's foot, he pleads apologetically that it is bad luck to wake de fus' time you are called. "Sometimes ghosts do call 'um", he adds in explanation, which implies the necessity of a wholesome caution.

Pete says Uncle York once told them that he once walked from a certain point to Darien, twenty miles, "discoursing" to himself all the way, & that he had finally to stop outside of Darien "to end de discourse". In this & many other points he constantly reminds me of Socrates,[302] only that Socrates, as it would appear, never did end.

ADVANCED PICQUET. PORT ROYAL I.
MARCH 13. 1864
AN EXQUISITE SPRING MORNING

Just now a soldier was here, very young, whose face I did not remember, though it was peculiarly bright; I asked Maj. Trowbridge who it was. He said it was a boy named Sammy Roberts whom he once brought fr. Amelia Island.[303] As the Major & Com. Goldsborough[304] were talking on the beach, with this boy's old father, the urchin went peeping about in a most inexplicable way, till the father noticed it. "Hi! Sammy, what you's doing, chile"? "Daddy" said the youth "don't you know Maus' always tell us, Yankee *hab tail*,—I ain't seen no tail, Daddy"!

The Major & I were talking over some of the funny things on our Edisto Expedition[305] after we got the slaves on board—the little boy with

301. The Gullah were a group of people of African ancestry living in the Sea Islands and coastal areas of South Carolina, Georgia, and northern Florida, whose life in geographically isolated communities fostered the development of not only particular cultural practices (like dances) but also a creolized language, based on English but including vocabulary and grammatical peculiarities from various African languages as well.
302. Socrates (469–399 BC), a Greek philosopher.
303. Amelia Island, Florida.
304. Either Captain John Rodgers Goldsborough (1809–1877), who commanded the *Florida* in 1862 and was senior officer of the Union blockading squadron off Charleston, or Captain Louis Malesherbes Goldsborough (1805–1877), who commanded the Atlantic Blockading Squadron and then, when this command was divided in October 1861, the North Atlantic Blockading Squadron.
305. In preparation for the attack on Battery Wagner, Maj. Gen. Quincy Gillmore sent the 1st South Carolina Volunteers on a diversionary maneuvre, an amphibious expedition against a railroad bridge on the South Edisto River, July 10, 1863.

no rag of clothing except the basque waist of a lady's dress, wrong side before, with long whalebones perceptible—the enraptured female who
blessed the Lord that now she would have salt victuals, anyhow;—& he
mentioned some things I did not see. When I was wounded & lying in the
berth, the Major bustled about for a fan & found but one, which was in the
hands of a fat old aunty, just brought on board, who sat on an enormous
bundle of her goods, in everybody's way, fanning herself violently &
breathlessly ejaculating "Oh! Do Jesus! Do, Jesus"! in the course of which
the Major abruptly grabbed the fan & left her still pursuing her pious exercises.

Before this, when he went on shore in a boat at Wiltown Bluff,[306] after
the battery was silenced, he asked the first man he met, how many soldiers
there were with the battery? "Maus'" said the old man stammering "I c-c-
c—"—How many troops are there up there, shouted the Major with his
mighty voice & all but shaking the poor old thing in his eagerness for the information. "Oh Maus'" recommenced he "I c-c-c-c-*Carpenter*",—holding
up eagerly an old hatchet which he clutched as his treasure—as if his profession excused him from all military observations.

At this very moment the burly Major is just swinging in the hammock
on the piazza & talking with a squad of women whom he brought fr. St.
Simon's island & who stand in their clean Sunday array, erect & stately as
Nubians, recalling past days. He is asking them now about Mrs. Kemble,
whose neighbors they were & they are putting together their scraps of
reminiscence about her which amount to only two though they lived on
the next plantation & one of those two at least would make a sensation
among polite readers, perhaps, if appended to the next edition of her
book. "Use to row boat, sa, I seen her"—"I neber seen her wid de boat sa,
but I seen her wid de oars"—"Use to row boat *well*". Then was extorted
the last item of biography—the one other trait sufficiently impressive to
reach the next plantation—the narrator half covering her face with her
hand & turning slightly away "Used to stop & pull up she stockns-an'-
garters *anywhar*. Right in de 'treet (street)!"

What a singular commentary on the compensations of the universe,
& the way in which the seeds of the finer instincts are sown broadcast
throughout the human race, that these poor creatures whose utter
abasement she has delineated for the world to read, should have been
slyly criticizing her all the while for an inelegance which was serious

306. Willstown Bluff, about 20 miles up the Edisto, at its confluence with the Pon Pon
River, is where TWH found his way blocked by spiked timbers sunk across the river's
neck as well as a Confederate battery. The battery withdrew when TWH landed his
troops and took control of the area.

1. Col. Thomas Wentworth Higginson. From Thomas Wentworth Higginson, "The First Black Regiment," *Outlook* 59 (1898), 523.

2. "Soldiers on review, South Carolina." 1st South Carolina Volunteers on dress parade, January 1, 1863, assembled to hear the reading of President Lincoln's Emancipation Proclamation. LC–BH82201-341. Courtesy of the Library of Congress.

3. (a) Sgt. William Bronson, (b) Sgt. Henry McIntyre, and (c) Sgt. Harry Wilkins. From Thomas Wentworth Higginson, "The First Black Regiment," *Outlook* 59 (1898), 526, 529.

FLAG PRESENTED BY CITIZENS OF NEW YORK
TO 1st S.C. VOLUNTEERS.
THE COLONEL COMMANDING,
CHARGING PRINCE RIVERS AS COLOR BEARER
NEVER TO GIVE IT UP.

Page 1.

4. From Luther Goodyear Bingham, *The Young Quartermaster: The Life and Death of Lieut. L. M. Bingham of the First South Carolina Volunteers* (New York: Board of Publication of the Reformed Protestant Dutch Church, 1863), opp. p. 184. Higginson mentions this engraving in a letter to Louisa Storrow Higginson, January 22, 1864: "I send some copies of 'the Young Quartermaster['] with a remarkable engraving of a certain Colonel which you may recognize." See p. 349 below.

a.

b.

c.

5. (a) "Company A of the 1st South Carolinian (Colored) Volunteers taking the oath of allegiance to the U.S. before Gen. Saxton, at Beaufort, S.C.—From a sketch by Col. G. Douglas Brewerton, A.D.C." (b) "A Detachment of the 1st South Carolinian (Colored) Union Volunteers, under the command of Col. Beard, repelling the attack of Rebel troops in the vicinity of Doboy River, Georgia—From a sketch by Col. G. Douglas Brewerton, A.D.C." (c) "A Detachment of the 1st South Carolinian (Colored) Union Volunteers, under command of Col. Beard, in the U.S. transport steamer Darlington, Picking off Rebel sharpshooters concealed in the trees on the banks of Sapello River, Georgia.—From a sketch by Col. G. Douglas Brewerton, A.D.C." From *Frank Leslie's Illustrated Newspaper* (Dec. 20, 1862), 200. "I see that Frank Leslie's Magazine of Dec 20 has a highly imaginative picture of the swearing in of our first Company, & also of the skirmish in which they figured." See p. 74 above. Courtesy of the Library Company of Philadelphia.

6. Brigadier General Rufus
Saxton. From Thomas Went-
worth Higginson, "The First
Black Regiment," *Outlook* 59
(1898), 530.

*The Baby of the Regiment*

7. Mrs. Chamberlin and Annie Chamberlin, the "baby
of the regiment." Courtesy of the Houghton Library,
Harvard University.

8. "Scroby." Capt. (later Maj.) Charles T. Trowbridge,
Quartermaster. Courtesy of the Houghton Library,
Harvard University.

In describing the tent I omitted to describe the Camp Stove, not yet set. A singular structure — all funnel, no bottom.

A funnel ending in a tunnel which is simply clapped down in a box of sand & there you are. A slide in one side admits your fire & gives draft. In such an edifice I dwell & such an one is being upreared beside me by the adjutant who proposes to bring hither his bride, who, if she be as capable and intelligent as she looks in photograph, will grace it very well.

9. Page of Higginson's journal (Anna Higginson's copy), showing sketch of camp stove: "A singular structure—all funnel, no bottom." See December 5, 1862 (p. 62 above). Courtesy of the Houghton Library, Harvard University. MS Am 784(20).

the "negro" huts are usually in a row, arranged at an angle thus □□ either for better circulation of air, or so that the eye can □□ observe them better. The two squads divided the houses. Before the lieutenant reached his houses, every man within had taken to the woods. The sergeant's mode of operation was described by a corporal from a white regiment who was accidentally sitting in one of the houses. He said that nothing was heard until suddenly a red leg appeared in the door way & a voice said "Rally." Going to the door he found a guard round every house, & not a person was allowed to leave till the houses had been searched & the three deserters found.

10. Page of Higginson's journal (Anna Higginson's copy), showing diagram of slave cabins: "on plantations the negro huts are usually in a row, often arranged at an angle thus." Courtesy of the Houghton Library, Harvard University. See January 13, 1863 (p. 88 in the present edition). MS Am 784(20).

11. Map drawn by Higginson, from letter to Louisa Storrow Higginson, February 16, 1863, showing road from Beaufort to Hilton Head, with Camp Saxton in between: "Today I am going down to Hilton Head for the first time." Courtesy of the Houghton Library, Harvard University. bMS Am 784(782).

12. The Sea Islands of South Carolina (Port Royal–Hilton Head area), map from Elizabeth Ware Pearson, *Letters from Port Royal 1862–1868* (Boston: W. B. Clarke Co., 1906). Courtesy of the Library Company of Philadelphia.

enough from their point of view to remain a tradition of her for twenty years!

We could extract absolutely nothing else concerning her except that she had two daughters & one was named Sarah. All these women had husbands or sons in this regiment, whom they came to visit. One is the mother of Sammy Roberts, the youth who speculated on the taillessness of Yankees.

Prayer of Thomas Long of Co. G. who preached today to the regiment:—taken down by an officer.

"Let us all pray.

[‘’]Our Heavenly Father, we come before you to ask of you to bless us— here we are in thy presence this afternoon & we feel that we are unworthy to come before you, but we come a chosen people & seek thy blessing. May our hearts be filled with love divine, like our dear Jesus—wilt thou look down in mercy upon us in our great baptism of suffering, & bless us as we each one of us need. Help us to feel, we beseech thee the wants of us all, both colored & white, & we pray, O Lord, that we may be permitted to visit our friends in the Slavery land & deliver them from slavery chains & bring them into the way of freedom & the light & truth & Oh Lord we beseech thee today to bless us & do more for us than we can ask or expect, & finally save us all for Christ's sake, Amen.["]

ADVANCED PICQUET P.R.I.
MARCH 16. 1864.

I have not yet had time to write of our alarm on the night of the 11th which was quite lively while it lasted, though it lasted longer in Beaufort than it did here. In the middle of the night I was wakened out of the profoundest sleep by the sentinel before the house, who said that there was artillery firing at the Ferry, $2\frac{1}{2}$ miles distant. I got on the piazza in time to hear the last report of a cannon with the Explosion of a shell. Now this was an ominous thing because there is no battery near the Ferry, either light or permanent, nor was there any conceivable reason why they should open on us there in the middle of the night unless they had made up their minds to throw pontoons across & advance on Beaufort, in which case this is precisely what they would do. Any such deliberate attack I have always rejected as utterly improbable, the difficulties for them would be so great & the object so small, Beaufort being valueless to them, as there are no magazines or stores for them to destroy, while the gunboats would drive them out directly, and completely hem them in. On the other hand it was just high tide, precisely the time for them,—& there had also been some very mysterious & puzzling demeanor on the part of my old friend Gen. Walker[307] about a Flag of Truce; & it seemed as if this might be the key to it all. However there was nothing for me but to get all the men quietly into line, send off the big Major on his big horse to the point of interest, post a company to command a causeway between here & the Ferry, & await events. This being a central position & my reserve but small, & attacks rarely coming single, my place is here, by the telegraph wire, with my ears open: for if I trotted my men to the aid of an attacked picquet in one position, the rebels might presently trot in from another.

So I got the men into line & got all the horses harnessed or saddled, ambulance ready for the ladies, & so on. Mrs. Dewhurst put more in one trunk, her husband declares, than she ever got into two before. Mrs. Chamberlin was warned by the experience of a former smaller scare, on which occasion she came beaming out with her lovely face, & said excitedly "I tried to stay up stairs, but after I heard the roll of the drums, I couldn't stay." "Have the drums beaten"? said I—"I hadn't heard it" ["]Oh yes,["] said she, ["]for ten minutes['] & she looked like Joan of Arc.[308] I stepped to the door & found that Uncle York whose first impulse is to meet every crisis by building a large fire, had one already roaring up Dr. Minor's chimney, & that was the longest roll that was sounded! But this time she simply looked sweet & suggested nothing, until at a later period she heard a sound of marching men on the other side of the house which proved eventually to be a vocal Grand March of frogs in a neighboring marsh. Meanwhile Mrs. Trowbridge came from her tent in her accustomed best bonnet & best composure. As for Baby she raved with delight at being suddenly uncribbed & thrust into her little scarlet cloak & hood & brought down at an utterly unauthorized hour to a piazza with lights & people & horses & general chaos. She crowed & gurgled & talked & gesticulated & shouted her advice on the military situation as freely as mother gives it, or the Springfield Republican, or any other unheard Cassandra.[309] But for some slight obscurity of language, I suppose the whole rebel force might have been captured upon her suggestions; certainly I should far rather fight under her orders than under Gen. Seymour's, just

307. Confederate Brig. Gen. William Stephen Walker (1822–1899), in command of the military district between the Ashepoo and Savannah rivers.

308. St. Joan of Arc (1412–1431), who, as an illiterate young girl, had been inspired by the voices of saints to undertake the heroic mission of liberating France from English domination.

309. In Greek mythology, Cassandra was endowed with the gift of prophecy but fated never to be believed.

as Dr. Holmes[310] advised Mary by all means to stick to her homeopathic medicine chest in her private practice, rather than dabble with one that might hurt somebody.

Everybody behaves well, capitally; nobody committed the mistake once made by an excited soldier of our Qrmaster's former regiment, who was found during an alarm endeavoring to put his own boots on another man's feet.

Within half an hour a messenger came puffing in from the Ferry, astride the poor relics of what was once a horse, such as they furnish for picquet purposes. His account was that a battery of several guns had come down to the Ferry opposite, & without asking any questions opened fire on the house at the edge of the river where our picquets, or their reserve, remain—firing one shell through the house & 7 others unpleasantly near—but they had now entirely stopped & there were no signs of an attempt to cross. Long before this I was satisfied from this cessation of fire that nothing serious was intended. I telegraphed accordingly to Gen. Saxton & we kept up for another hour during which reports came back from the front that all was profoundly still: the Lieutenant commanding at the Ferry had coolly taken his men back into the house that had been attacked, & nothing more had happened. So the men were dismissed to sleep with their clothes on—the ladies went upstairs, baby relucantly receded into the ignoble cradle, & peace prevailed till we all met in high spirits at breakfast next morning.

Next morning it appeared by putting things together that a few guns had been fired on the other side at $9\frac{1}{2}$ which we had heard but thought nothing of; that then there were rockets & then the battery came down. Also that later in the night, there was quite a demonstration of boats at Caper's plantation which is almost in the opposite direction from the Ferry—some half dozen rebel boats, which were bothered greatly by the tide, grounded, landed on a sort of peninsula & tried to find a picquet which was not there & finally retreated without a shot. This also was mysterious.

This would all be hardly worth the telling, but that the affair had put all Beaufort we found, in a far worse alarm; the wind favoring they heard the artillery practice, also saw rockets; all the troops were turned out, traders

310. A lifelong family friend, sometime neighbor, and fellow *Atlantic*-contributor of TWH, Dr. Oliver Wendell Holmes had published debunking lectures on *Homoeopathy and Its Kindred Delusions: Two Lectures Before the Boston Society for the Diffusion of Useful Knowledge* (Boston: W.D. Ticknor, 1842). Presumably at some point he had been called upon to discourage Mary from enlisting others in her enthusiastic dabbling in animal magnetism, electricity, hydrotherapy and other outré medical fads.

packed up their goods, and a light battery patrolled the streets, ready to re-pel attack fr. any quarter.

The question was afterward whether the artillery attack was a genuine scare on the rebels' part. I mean that they were scared, and the boat affair a mere afterthought of theirs; or whether the artillery part was a mere cover to a boat attack previously premeditated.

Next day there was a Flag of Truce & Capt. Barnwell, a courteous young Captain fr. the other side, was asked for information, as it is usually the understanding that the picquets will not fire or be fired on. He only an-swered, smiling, "You gentlemen are training your Buckinghams (which, it seems, is now their cant phrase for colored soldiers) to shell us from the gunboats, & this little bombardment was our only way to retaliate". He ought to have added melodramatically

"Off with his head—so much for Buckingham".[311]

Even this was not quite satisfactory—but the day after brought some men from the mainland, slaves, who reported that it was all a concerted plan. The shelling was expected to draw our picquets to that part of the is-land—and the boat-loads of men, (two companies) which came down all the way from Pocataligo,[312] were to land at Capers's & make a raid across the island. But that part of the attack was delayed by the puzzling naviga-tion & cross currents of these muddy creeks—& our picquets wouldn't re-treat & so they went ignobly back without firing a gun: & if a gunboat had happened round that way, would have been terribly cut up. Nobody was hurt on our side; & it shows the steadiness acquired by our men that no-body on our side fired a gun all along the line.

The next night we had no alarm, but a dance in the parlor, with a capi-tal fiddler from the regiment & one officer acting as lady.

Gen. Saxton is now on a Court Martial & I was to have taken temporary command of the Post but Brig. Gen. Birney[313] came here just in time, with one of his Maryland Regiments the 9th US. that of which Storrow H.[314] is Chaplain. Gen. B. came out here very promptly & rode along part of the picquet lines with me. He seems superior to any volunteer officer I have met, both as soldier & man, a martinet & a moralist at the same time, one fit to command colored troops or any others: a fine looking officer of 45,

311. "Off with his Head—so much for *Buckingham*," *History of King Richard III* . . . *Alter'd from Shakespear, by Mr. Cibber* (1721), in *The Plays of Colley Cibber*, ed. Rodney L. Hay-ley, 2 vols. (New York: Garland Publishing, Inc., 1980), 1:128.

312. Pocotaligo, South Carolina is about 25 miles upriver from Port Royal Island.

313. William Birney (1819–1907), became recruiting officer for black troops in Mary-land in 1863 and reported with them to Hilton Head, South Carolina in February 1864.

314. Storrow Higginson, nephew of TWH (son of Stephen Higginson).

hair slightly gray, great courtesy & cultivation in his manner,—son of Jas. G. Birney,[315] once prominent,—brother of Maj. Gen. Birney[316] of the Army of the Potomac. So many incompetent men have crept into the command of colored troops, it is pleasant that the Brigadiers should be such men as Wild[317] & Birney. It reconciles me the more to the possibility of leaving the service, that it should be coming into such hands.

The 9th US. is a very fine looking regiment & the officers appear well. The men have different songs & ways from our men, & their type of religious enthusiasm seems different. Our men are chiefly Baptist & those Methodist; the former is certainly better for the body, as involving at least one complete ablution in each lifetime. The 9th US. men are farther divided into two subdivisions, in this regard, the Holy Jumpers & the Holy Rollers. The difference between them is that when under conviction, the Holy Jumpers jump & the Holy Rollers roll: a division decidedly more palpable than most sectarian barriers.

MARCH 27. 1864

From today's Sermon by Private Thomas Long. Co. G. acting Chaplain.

"We can remember, when we first enlisted, it was hardly safe for we to pass by de camps to Beaufort & back, 'lest (unless) we went in a mob & carried our side arms. But we whipped down all dat. Not by going into de white camps for whip um; we didn't tote our bayonets for whip um; *but we lived it down by our naturally manhood*; and now de white sojers take us by de hand & say Broder Sojer. Dat's what dis regiment did for de Epiopian (Ethiopian) race[.]"

"If we hadn't become sojers, all might have gone back as it was before; our freedom might have slipped through de two houses of Congress & President Linkum's four years might have passed by & notin been done for we. But now tings can never go back, because we have showed our energy & our courage & our naturally manhood.["]

"Anoder ting is, suppose you had kept your freedom widout enlisting in dis army; your chilen might have grown up free, & been *well cultivated* so as

315. James G. Birney, an abolitionist from Alabama, pioneering leader of the Liberty Party.

316. Maj. Gen. David Bell Birney (1825–1864), an Alabamian who was, nevertheless, one of the most ardent enemies of slavery among Union army generals.

317. Edward Augustus Wild (1825–1891), an outspoken abolitionist and advocate of black enlistment, he recruited "Wild's African Brigade" which was organized at New Berne, North Carolina in 1863 and initially served in Charleston Harbor, South Carolina, then transferred to Virginia where he commanded all black troops in the vicinity.

to be equal to any business, but it would have been always flung in dere faces—"Your fader never fought for he own freedom"—and what could dey answer? *Neber can say that to dis African race any more,* (bringing down his hand with the greatest emphasis on the table.) Tanks to dis regiment, never can say dat any more, because we first showed dem we could fight by dere side."

He also said "Notin makes you more trouble dan dat red flag you keep wagging out of you mouf" (the tongue)

## ADDRESS OF A LETTER

Mrs Sarah Clark
Fearnandina Flo. (Fernandina Fla.)
Frome your brother P. T. R. (Peter)
Parsons one of Hutzel Salms (Uncle Sam's)
Soldiers 1ˢᵗ S.C. Vols. Co G.

### CAMP SHAW. BEAUFORT
### MARCH 28.

Came in from Picquet today; the 9ᵗʰ U.S. relieving us. It was quite pleasant to be relieved by a colored regiment & to feel that perhaps the men would be restrained by discipline from injuring the picquet stations as the white soldiers do. We got the kitchen white washed this trip & bequeathed it to Storrow & his friend Armstrong, as a solemn charge to whitewash the parlor also, for which we had collected the lime & borrowed the brush—there being two on the island.

I rode in from Picquet with Mrs Dewhurst & Mrs Chamberlin, in advance of the regt—the ride was lovely, the young leaves coming out every where on the underbrush of the pine wood—and the clover & grass springing up here & there, soft & delicate as the baby's cheek, and often spangled with violets. The horses danced gaily along & it seemed almost as pleasant to return as to go out. I enjoy the camp in some respects—as one enjoys a great nursery, I like to hear the humming & cooing all round. Our mess is just as pleasant at mealtimes, but the evenings are comparatively isolated & I miss the great gay dilapidated room with its vast fireplace & the wood fire which I never wearied of re-arranging. It was as near as one could get to a baronial hall, with retainers coming & going & the part of the principal Baron by yours respectfully. However I have no doubt that in 24 hours it will seem equally pleasant here.

I saw in town a sight singular & painful. In front of the Provost Marshal's office in the busiest part of the main street of the town, stood upon a box a well dressed man, large & commanding in appearance, & with gaping gazers all around: He was sentenced by Court Martial to stand there two hours daily for a week, with the inscription on his breast "I sold liquor to soldiers" & with a 24 lb ball & chain attached to his leg; after which he was to be fined $500 or be imprisoned 6 months, & then sent from the Department forever. But Gen. Saxton in pity for his wife, who is here took off the inscription & the ball & chain & let the rest take its course. I felt it the more from the fact that I was on the Military commission which tried him, though I happened to be unable to attend the trial. Popular indignation sustains the verdict, partly because of the enormous price at which the man sold the surreptitious whiskey ($12 pr gallon) & partly because he came down here as a preacher and like most of that class, exhorted & cheated on alternate days; it is most remarkable how badly all the clerical envoys have turned out; I literally have not known an exception; the only preacher who is really respected here is a young lawyer from N.Y. the acting Post Chaplain who can only be "acting" because he has never been ordained. In this very case the two leading divines of the town Rev. Dr Peck & Rev Mr French, went to the Provost Marshal & tried to get the man discharged without trial, because of the scandal to the church, Sunday School &c in which Brother McRae[318] had been prominent.

The man excited my sympathy & showed some character by the way which he took to shun facing the ignominy of this standing pillory. He stood bending over a little blank book or diary in which he was writing busily all the time. He looked as far removed from the world as St Symon Stylites on his pillar.[319] Indeed there was something inconceivably remote & foreign in the whole scene—the man wore a broad brimmed hat, long straight overcoat & high riding boots and seemed to have stepped out of Puritan days; I should not have been surprized, in riding up, to find a scarlet letter on his breast.[320]

It seems, very inconsistent, this punishment, with the fatal liberality with which government allows whiskey regularly to officers & even to sol-

318. James A. McCrae, a missionary.

319. Simeon was the first and most noted of the Christian pillar-hermits, religious ascetics who aspired to sainthood by isolating and exposing themselves atop columns. TWH likely read Tennyson's poem, "St. Simeon Stylites" (1842). See Alfred Lord Tennyson, *The Poems of Tennyson*, 3 vols., ed. Christopher Ricks (Berkeley: University of California Press, 1987), 1:593–604.

320. TWH alludes to Nathaniel Hawthorne, *The Scarlet Letter* (1850), a novel wherein the heroine, Hester Prynne, an adulteress, is made to wear a scarlet A on her breast as a sign of her sin.

diers. Every regiment here but mine, draws its rations of whiskey for officers & men or did till Gen. Birney took command—and as every few days
Gen. Saxton is free from his Court Martial duty, I suppose they can get
their requisitions approved on those days. Gen Birney will not do it—he &
I being of one mind on that point—while it is almost the only point on
which Gen Saxton & I do not agree.

General Birney is a new sensation here being far stricter than Gen. S.
with I fear, a slight tendency to overdo. Unless this fear be realized I think
he will prove a[321] splendid officer. The impression now is that he is to remain here under Gen. Saxton, & command the five infantry regts now
here, while Gen. S commands the post.

Our pet "Dominie"[322] the Reverend Storrow Higginson thinks he
(Gen B) is not *practical* & I attach much weight to his opinions of character,
finding them unusually discriminating; & as Col. Bailey, a wild slap-dash
free & easy Westerner from Grant's Army, made it his crowning praise of
the Dominie himself "just exactly the Chaplain we need—*so practical*"!—
I think his criticism may pass, even if the critic's own antecedents have
been something of the dreamiest.

ADVANCED PICQUET STATION
APRIL 9TH 1864

Here we are again. It is a rainy morning, so dark that I have just put out my
candle at $9\frac{1}{2}$. The baby & two kittens are sitting on my strip of carpet before
the great fireplace & business & talk go on busily around. Baby & kittens
are trying mutually to comprehend each other, she pats them & squeezes
them & chatters to them endlessly, & they struggle away & sit up just beyond her reach, & gaze bewildered at her; & how it is that they, being so
much younger & smaller, can crawl & she c'ant, is an unceasing puzzle to
her mind usually settled by drawing them back by the tail. We were suddenly notified at breakfast time on Thursday to come out that morning &
relieve the 9th which was ordered to Hilton Head; we had been in only ten
days, but there was no other regt which could be safely sent, the three others being merely the fragments & recruits left behind of re-enlisting "veteran" regiments, so called, though they seem to me very unworthy that
name.

The men, always ready for change, enjoyed the suddenness of the order
& the march out was as jolly as usual. Storrow rode along with us a good

321. Copy-text reads "a a".
322. A Scots term for cleric or schoolmaster.

way & was in perfect delight with the merry singing from "Dixie"[323] to "de bell done ringing"—my chief fun came this time from the Drum Corps among whom there is wit & frolic & deviltry enough to set up a legion of Topsies.[324] Every woman who came to the road-side must be greeted (never indecently) or shaken hands with; every squad of little urchins straight & black as so many lead pencils, must be hailed, in prospective sympathy, with "Dar's de drummers for *de next war*"; Every horse & wagon with "Halt! hoss! Advance, cart, & give de countersign"! Then came a tremendous quarrel among them as to who had grown most within the year, & little Davy Wright, the best drummer of the lot, was derided into madness by the others for claiming to be taller than his last year's altitude. Finally he towered above them in indignation. "You dunno not'n about it—you dunno whether a feller's grown—you dunno not'n 'cept about *eatin*. Feller might grow as high as dat tuft of grass & you wouldn't know it." Evidently he felt that to watch his growth required some peculiar concentration of the perceptive faculties like astronomy, with a withdrawal from all merely selfish pursuits. Finally in the squabble one of them dropped half his ration of bread which threw the whole battalion into some confusion & when at last it was recovered in a very dusty state, & the derision was turned on the proprietor, the leading sergeant remarked in indignant vindication "Dat man wouldn't forsake he piece of bread!" which seemed a fine touch of chivalry, as if one ought to cling, even in disgrace & dirt, to the loaf which nourished one in its better days.

Arrived here, we for the first time found things better than we left them—house whitewashed (which we began) and tolerably clean; the camp was really very pretty thanks chiefly to Storrow's taste. How long we are to be here, of course we do not know.

I believe I register jokes which bear on others pretty freely & I ought not to ignore those which occasionally turn up at my expense. They say "on the line" which means in camp phrase among the line or company officers

323. "Dixie" was a patriotic song, thought to have been composed by Daniel Decatur Emmet, a noted early blackface minstrel performer, a member of Dan Bryant's troupe. It was most popular in the South, sung by Confederate soldiers as an anthem; TWH had earlier noted (September 12, 1863) that his soldiers were growing less likely to sing their own songs and more apt to adopt "the regular Ethiopian melodies of the North," and this seems to provide evidence for his observation. See also April 21, 1864, below.

324. Topsy was a character in Harriet Beecher Stowe's *Uncle Tom's Cabin* (1852), who exemplified the degenerate amorality thought by Stowe and others to be the product of enslavement; because of her humorous rascality she was a popular feature of the numerous stage adaptations of the novel that were performed throughout the country in the following years.

as distinct from the more exclusve "field & staff" that after what we call our second return from Jacksonville (i.e. from the wharf leading towards that city)—when the dust blew furiously across the camp and begrimmed us fearfully as usual,—the Colonel remarked rather critically to Captain Sampson,[325] "Captain, you must excuse me if I recommend a little soap & water applied to the countenance, I have myself applied it with excellent effects." "Ah, sir?" replied Capt. Sampson, with perfect courtesy, "*I should not have perceived it*"! upon which the Colonel, consulting a larger looking glass than his usual dentist's hand mirror, discovered an ample field for labor upon his own ingenuous countenance.

They have another story against me which I claim the merit of having first told myself. At the ball the night after the battle of Olustee, I was promenading with one of our belles, when a certain gallant Captain entered with a stout widow much older than himself, with whom he boards & to whom he is quite attentive. "There," said I, "is Capt. B with Mrs E—he seems quite devoted." "Devoted" quoth my fair one indignantly, "*He had better be attending to his mother*"! Ah said I innocently, *I did not know she was in this Department*! upon which my companion looked at me, evidently doubting whether this was a touch of real or affected stupidity; and I am never likely to hear the last of it among our mess.

## On Picquet. Apr. 11. 1864

We had a funny turmoil the other night. I was playing 4-handed chess in the parlor, when I heard an odd voice, unmistakeably counterfeit, inquiring for me at the door. Uncle York in his courteous way was asking the applicant in, and indignantly rebuking the boys Pete & Lee, for their disrespectful chuckling "Dese yere young debbils,—ain't got no manners. Walk dis way Ma'am". Going out, I discovered an elderly black lady in large cap & bonnet, who stated that she had just come from the main land: and on being brought into the parlor we soon recognized our pretty Mrs Chamberlin. Turning again upon the attendants, she began to talk wildly & run at them, on which ensued a perfect Babel. Some thought her a ghost, some an insane woman & some a secesh spy. "Give me one stick" roared Uncle John our cook, as he sprang for the bushes; Pete the Major's Topsyish boy drew a knife as he ran, the sentinel loaded his gun (it was about dusk) & the mysterious visitor ran about, wild with spirits, so that Uncle York ejaculated "I don't know what he be, but I see he *fly* off dat piazza." I was really anxious for her safety they were all so excited & when

325. Captain William W. Sampson.

she disappeared & they came together again, it was great fun to hear their comments in the kitchen. At first the supernatural theory prevailed, & Pete recurred to former superstitious terrors in this same locality "I bin a tell you, all las' summer, dere's *tings* here,—& now you know it." "But we know," said Uncle York in his stately pious way "dat de Savior he come in de form of a person," evidently feeling that each new avatar should be treated reverently, however improbable the form. But Uncle John was a skeptic as to that theory, & fell back very seriously on the theory of the Secesh spy. "I don't fear a man" quoth he "but never had no opinion of dese yere old women, no way." And finally they settled down into the agreement that they were disappointed in the Colonel, he had not met the occasion with the judgment & decision which they would have expected—for here had he allowed the goblin or spy to slip away from him after all & go at large instead of being captured securely till morning. The thing has never yet been cleared up to their satisfaction.

Uncle York was telling, the other day, about a master with whom he had deposited his odd earnings & who died without refunding them, so that they were lost altogether. Uncle York finally officiated in driving to the grave, and as the vehicle jolted over the roots in the woods he says "I didn't care how much I jolt he—*I pure tink of my money all de time.*" This use of the word pure is genuine old English.

The woods are beautiful now, I rode yesterday into a great tangled swamp, set with large trees & more vine than trees, interlacing all the gnarled live oak boughs & the pines that counterfeit the writhed shapes of live oaks, with a thousand intertwisted sets of cordage, just beginning to put greenness on; the level floor spread with new ferns & the stiff fan-shaped leaves of the Spanish thorn or Yucca spicata, while the distant openings were blocked with masses of wild plum bushes, a mass of emerald. Everywhere through these woods run lines of trench & dyke, ancient plantation landmarks, soon looking venerable as does everything where vegetation is so swift & rank: & there is even this early a sort of steaming fervor of vegetable vitality that pervades the atmosphere, although one always misses the delicate & spicy odors of Northern woods. The same want of finer & mellower attributes marks everything, sights, sounds, & scents, & this is the compensation for increased luxuriance, as one goes toward the tropics. It is the difference between the odor of magnolias & of new made hay.

Change on change—the 8th Me, 4th NH, 55th Pa leave here today, the 56th N.Y. tomorrow & as these are *all* the white reg'ts at the Post we can only wonder what colored ones, if any, are coming to take their places. If none, then part or the whole of ours must go in—so large a picquet force cannot be spared. The plain inference is that farther aggressive operations are to cease, in this department & all spare strength be carried to Virginia.

Be that as it may I look at it with the waning interest of one whose term is drawing to a close. Every warm & sunny day now teaches me that I cannot safely stay more than a month longer: & if I once go away, it is not probable that I shall ever return, for various reasons, health first.

ADVANCED PICQUET. P.R.I.
APR. 17. 1864

It gives an autumnal tinge to this beautiful opening Spring to think that I shall, in a few weeks, leave it perhaps forever. Still my mind turns naturally to home associations & all other beauty has a vague & alien look; I cannot bring it near to me.

It seems settled now that General Gillmore & the 10th Army Corps, comprising almost all the white soldiers, will be withdrawn & most of the Department garrisoned with Colored soldiers. Only one white reg't & that a poor one is left in Beaufort, & no other is expected. The 29th Conn. & 26th US., both colored, are at Beaufort also.

The rebels are always complaining that our men will not talk across the river as the white picquets do; but they (the rebels) are much less abusive than last year. Our men also talk more to them, though it is as a general rule forbidden, & they reconcile it to their consciences to speak at all by never under any circumstances speaking the truth to them. Thus

What regiment are you?
Answer. Hundred thirty third Benighted States.
Where's the First South Carolina?
Answer First Souf done gone to Jacksonville.
What pay do you black soldiers get?
Answer. Hundred and six Dollar a month!

And so it goes on; not disclosing certainly any truth which could give aid & comfort to the enemy.

This is not much more piquant however than a conversation between Lieut. Hooper[326] of this reg't & Rev. Mr. French the other day. Hooper is the frankest & most straightforward Englishman who ever wore a Crimean medal.[327] Mr. French is the high priest of the department, tall, erect, autocratic, evangelical, determined, unscrupulous. There has never yet been

326. First Lieutenant Charles W. Hooper.
327. The British opposed Russia in the Crimean War (1854–1856), attacking Russia's Crimean Peninsula in the Black Sea.

a General in this department whom he could not wind round his finger, & I will back him for telling lies against any saint of any sect now going.

Mr. French. Glorious tidings, Lieutenant Hooper, 30,000 colored soldiers are ordered to this department!

Hooper. Bully!

Mr. French. *Amen!*

How I wish you could hear Mr. French greet Storrow as "Brother Higginson".

The men have just been paid, those who wished, after 4 months delay, at $7, & I am glad to have it over. They behaved very well, that is there was no insubordination, though only about a third took the pay. All the officers approved their taking it & explained to them that the acceptance of this wd. not affect the prospect of getting the whole—but they reasoned very shrewdly about it; saying that they at first had $13 then $10 now $7 & if they signed the rolls for this, perhaps next time there would be only $4 paid them and so on. The general feeling was that they wd. rather serve for nothing than take less than the contract. One said "We's willing to serve for not'in, but the Guvment ought not for insult we too, by offering seven dollar." Several said "it's the *principle* we look at." Another said "If we take it, it's because our chilen need it, but it *takes de sojer all out of we*, to be treated so unjustly." The companies being scattered, on picquet, there was more chance for independent action, & as a general rule it was very marked that the best companies & the best men in the companies which declined. Of the three companies which unanimously declined, two were the two best in the regiment in soldierly morale—while the only one which unanimously received it was by no means so good an one. In several companies a dozen or twenty men took the pay & it was almost a joke to see what a poor set these usually were—all the guardhouse members & the regular invalids & shirks, while the really valuable men stood aloof. To this of course there were marked exceptions.

One must be actually among these men to realize how wicked wanton & suicidal is such injustice, especially a time when the most wretched white recruits are paid great sums in bounty; & it would have been a most unhappy day to me had I not just received satisfactory accounts of the bill which has passed the Senate & provides for my men the full pay fr. the enlistment, which will repay them for their sorrows when it comes in a lump.

ADVANCED PICQUET STATION. P.R.I.
APRIL 21. 1864.

A very old woman died on the plantation, day before yesterday, & yesterday there was a great gathering & singing at the funeral. Afterward it settled down, or unsettled, into the most tumultuous "shout" I ever remember. It was a moonlight evening & the dark cabin was crammed with a mass of human beings male & female, old & young, all revolving in a circle, singing in faster time than I ever knew on such an occasion before, more like a "break down"[328] than any religious chant, & keeping that wonderful accuracy of time which makes all their dancing so fascinating. In all the corners of the room the people who were squeezed out of the circle were jerking & footing it by themselves, so were those on the doorstep, & every white spectator's foot came soon into play; it is impossible for any one who has an ear not to partake the rhythmical excitement. It was strange to contrast this scene with similar dances in the equally smoky hovels of the Portuguese peasants—only there the dance was slow though secular & here riotous though pious; most of the younger women were smiling as they swayed or ducked or whirled, & such was the admixture of ingredients that old James Cashman, the greatest hypocrite in the regiment, (he who had "on'y but four wives, sa")—James left the house in dudgeon saying *"Too much goat shout wid de sheep."*

You must remember that the church members here generally disapprove of unsanctified dancing quite as rigidly as the same class in Evangelical churches at the North, & it is quite instructive to see what an outlet the same propensity finds in these most exciting festivals, where there is absolutely nothing except the words of the song, to distinguish it from the wildest revel of Bacchanals. And yet so singularly are the religious associations intertwinable that although they will at any time get up a "shout" on application, & show it off eagerly before strangers & look at you with broad grins, it is yet thoroughly identified with their most genuine religious emotions. The Shaker dancing[329] I fancy is not real dancing, but only the ghost of it—a solemn & self sacrificing rite, like dancing in good society but the "shout" is an enjoyment per se, and even tends to excess, like opium. It is a part of their earliest training too, & it is not uncommon, in riding about the plantation to find three or four mere babies, from three to six years old, seriously "shouting" on a door step. I have noticed too that the one pet song of these children is almost always the most grimly melodramatic of the elder incantations.

"What make ole Satan for follow me so?
Satan ain't got notin to do wid me!

328. Noisy, energetic American country dance; the "Negro break down" was a staple element of plantation fiction and blackface stage entertainments.
329. A distinctive part of the worship practices of the Shakers (a millennialist and revivalistic Christian sect that practiced celibacy and communal living) was a group dance, accompanied by singing, that could be quite lively.

(Chorus) Hold your light! Hold your light!
Hold your light on Canaan's shore.

It seems pathetic that these little innocents (straight & black as so many short lead pencils) should thus early appreciate the peripatetic habits of the evil one.

It is as strange to see some of our Sergeants, tall & stately men, with stentorian voices, full of absolute command, relaxing into this hilarious festival, & to catch sight of their august chevrons revolving in the mass. This however is not common. The Florida men, especially, eschew the whole affair, & there is a small clique of rather stylish youths from Savannah who know all the Ethiopian melodies & play violin, violincello, castanets, tambourine, or anything. I have never in my life seen dancing so perfectly graceful as that of our Commissary Sergeant, who would pass for white, with Mrs. King,[330] one of the laundresses a little jet black woman who can read & write & has taught a little school.

We had a wedding in the regiment a few Sundays ago, but I was not well & did not go out—I mean it was literally in the reg't, in hollow square. The men still come for my consent to be married, as they used to ask their masters, & I always annex the provision, that they must get a good wife. I think they rather incline to what they call a "settled woman", which means a widow, more or less authentic. "Him do court one settled woman" is a common observation.

H.Q. Advanced Picquet. P.R.I.
April 25. 1864

Mrs. Chamberlain & I have just filled a large vase (namely a tin wash basin) with the freshest rosebuds, & the thought of my rapidly waning days on this pleasant military picnic makes me wish to write something more.

The scene on sunny mornings here, for an hour or two after breakfast, is like the descriptions of English Castle life in the country. From all the out stations couriers or officers are here on horseback, coming, going, or waiting, & the pleasant piazza, is thronged with officers, orderlies, ladies in riding habits or arranging flowers, & the omnipresent, observant Baby with her pretty mulatto nurse & her red hood. Then a background of prancing horses, a waiting ambulance or "omelet" as the men call it, scattered tents, live oaks, trailing moss, emerald plum bushes, my crimson blanket hung out to air, & a dark blue pacing sentinel. The preparation & distribution of

330. Susie King Taylor (b. 1848), the wife of Sergeant Edward King of the 1st South Carolina Volunteers, whose memoir is cited above.

orders & despatches makes a whirl of business for a little while; then everybody disperses right & left & we subside into a rather lazy day.

Last night our attendant urchins got up a "shout" around a tree just by
the house, four of them stamping round & round & singing with a rhyth-
mic footfall & sometimes with a hollow clapping of hands & they happened upon one of the oddest chants that even *their* taste for the religious
melo-dramatic has produced. After their favorite "What make ole Satan
for follow me so" which is the special cradle hymn of these dusky innocents, they brought out the same old offender in a disguised aspect.

> I see de ole man sitting
> Glory Hallelujah!
> He sit in de chimley corner
> Glory Hallelujah!
> He wash he face in ashes!
> Glory Hallelujah!
> He call he name Jesus
> Glory Hallelujah!
> But I know he by de *clump-foot*
> Glory Hallelujah
>
> Chorus  Hold your light—brother Benjie—hold your light!
> Hold your light on Canaan's shore.

Later. It is the warmest day we have yet had in this cool Spring & a thousand soft arrows shoot through me & take all my strength away. I am now
making all arrangements for going & am wholly content to go, although I
shrink from *facing* the separation so entirely that it requires an effort for me
to go over to the camp & I am reluctant even to see a soldier—it is so hard
to wrench one's self away from the habit of months, now fast growing to be
years. I never yet saw a chapter in life which was not good, no matter what
people called it, but this turning of the leaf is a trying epoch—& all such
things tempt to cheat one's self & others, by making believe that perhaps,
after all, one isn't really going to remain permanently. However this is now
generally understood, though General Saxton entirely repudiates the suggestion & says I may take 6 months furlough but *not* resign. But he is always
reasonable & if it is necessary for me, I know he will acquiesce.

All I wait for, now, is to see the April monthly business through, & then
I can go at any time, for my private preparations would not take more than
a day. The transportation is likely to be rather irregular for it is understood
that the Fulton & Arago are to be taken off & that the regular 8 days' intervals will be abandoned: but unless some unexpected delay should occur, I
expect to leave here by May 10th.

# THE
# *War Letters*
## OF
# *Thomas Wentworth*
# *Higginson*

*"a bouquet on every bayonet"*
To Louisa Storrow Higginson
Worcester. Aug. 4. 1861


*Dearest Mother*

I hope you have got back to Brattleboro[1] & health again, since your experiments in other places seem unsuccessful. It seemed such a pity you should be sick in Pittsfield.[2]

Two days this week have been made exciting by the return of troops; the look of Col. Jones' 6th Regiment[3] was peculiarly wild, every man wearing a little red skull cap more or less faded, with or without a tassel—surmounting the worn & faded gray uniform. I do not think the Zouaves just from Africa[4] could have been a wilder spectacle, than those thousand scarecrows tramping in order through our streets with a bouquet on every bayonet. Dr. Martin[5] whom you know, has lost 30 pound of flesh & come back the very handsomest man who ever wore an uniform.

When the daughter of the regiment—a little Jones girl—was being placed on her horse—a black man here carried her a bouquet, saying that it was an acknowledgement for her father's *hospitality* in going to the defence of Washington.

Several of the men had kittens in their knapsacks.


1. Brattleboro, Vermont, TWH's mother's home and location of a popular water-cure and health resort.

2. Pittsfield, Massachusetts, in the Berkshire Mountains.

3. Colonel Edward F. Jones, 6th Regiment Infantry, Massachusetts Volunteer Militia (3 months).

4. French Army Zouaves, first organized in Algeria in 1831 and composed of tribesmen from Zouaoua, later admitted Europeans to their ranks and fought bravely in the Crimean and 1859 Franco-Austrian wars; their distinctive and colorful uniform featured baggy red pants, a blue vest and sash, and a blue tasseled red fez. A celebrated object of curiosity in American newspapers and magazines, the Zouaves inspired numerous volunteer drill companies in American cities, which imitated the eye-catching uniforms, with variations; some of these Zouave units volunteered and fought in the Civil War.

5. Dr. Oramel Martin, 3d Battalion Riflemen, Massachusetts Volunteer Militia (3 months).

We had Col. Leonard's regiment[6] on their way *to* the war, also, & the "John Brown War Song" was sounding through the street all the evening. It is a Methodist tune very plaintive & impressive, yet easily sung & they *all* sang it. "John Brown's body is a mouldering in the dust" (3 times) "And his soul's marching on."

> (Chorus) *"Glory Glory Glory Hallelujah*
> *"As we go marching on."*
> "He's gone to be a soldier in the army of the Lord." &c &c[7]

And they make up verses on other subjects, keeping the fine chorus. I never heard anything more impressive & it seemed a wonderful piece of popular justice to make his name the war song.

Mary sends love. T. W. H.

*"people must act up to their consciences"*
## To Louisa Storrow Higginson
## Worcester. Nov. 1. 1861

*Dearest Mother*

You will never take a hopeful view of anything, I see, till you give up that unfortunate Springfield Republican. In every war there must be ups & downs, mistakes committed, valuable lives lost (as we foolishly call it)—defeats sustained. But these very defeats often produce good in the end. The defeat at Manassas[8] was just what we needed, & it may yet prove so with this.[9] It is of immense importance to know, as we now do that our raw troops may be as cool even in retreat as veterans, for that is the point where veterans usually have all the advantage. The recollection of this will be an immense strength in the next decisive battle, when it comes. Charles Devens smoked a segar quietly perhaps to reassure his men, during the whole time & his men moved as quietly as if on parade. How sublime is such quiet courage—worth how many sacrifices. Yet that was by no means a superior regiment in material or in officers, Devens was much depressed about it when he went away. It was infinitely inferior to the one just gone, & to many of our regiments.

6. Colonel Samuel H. Leonard, 13th Massachusetts.

7. Julia Ward Howe's poem, "Battle Hymn of the Republic," was printed in the *Atlantic Monthly* 9 (February 1862), 145.

8. Confederate General Joseph E. Johnston loaded his troops onto cars of the Manassas Gap Railroad to carry them to Bull Run, where they were a decisive factor in the defeat of Union forces on July 21, 1861.

9. The Battle of Ball's Bluff, October 21, 1861.

Think too of this remarkable fact that while of the British army in the Crimea the majority died within a year or two from want of proper sanitary arrangements, here the health is better among every regiment than at home. It is a singular fact that the war is said not to have raised the price of gunpowder, because the amount used does not exceed the amount ordinarily expended in field sports. And so against the losses in battle we must set the lives saved from home diseases & dangers. Usually the camp is far more dangerous than the field.

I suppose the present policy is to keep things as they are on the Potomac & send naval expeditions to different points on the coast. This is a saving of life, as compared with great general engagements.

The tendencies all are toward a more emancipatory policy;[10] the instructions to the naval expedition[11] go as far as any one can ask, for I should not approve a general & indiscriminate arming of slaves, & this goes all lengths but that. This too tends to shorten the war & spare life, by attacking slavery in it's one indefensible point.

For some time I hv. been making up my mind that antislavery men were leaving the war altogether too much in the hands of Democrats & Irishmen, & that if we expect to control it's conduct or settlement, we must take part in it ourselves. No prominent antislavery man has yet taken a marked share in the war, & as I am satisfied that there are a great many in this & other states who would like to go if I do, I have made up my mind to take part in the affair, hoping to aid in settling it quickly.

I have authority from Gov. Andrew to take preliminary steps toward raising a regiment, which when formed will be placed under charge of an US. officer—probably Capt Saxton[12] of the naval expedition, who is an antislavery man. At any rate the Colonel is to be satisfactory to me & I to be under him.

Mary has of course taken this with her usual courage, seeing it not to be a fever of the blood but a conviction of duty. I hope the same will be the

10. TWH may be thinking of General Frémont's unauthorized emancipation proclamation in Missouri, August 30, 1861 (which was, however, modified by President Lincoln), or of Lincoln's pending proposal for compensated emancipation of slaves in Delaware (offered November 26, 1861); but he may also be interpreting events in a more general way.

11. In October 1861 President Lincoln directed that a naval expedition be launched which became the Port Royal Expedition; under Brigadier General Thomas W. Sherman and Flag Officer Samuel F. Du Pont a huge flotilla left Hampton Roads, Virginia, on October 29, to seize control of Port Royal, South Carolina.

12. Captain Rufus Saxton (later General, and TWH's commander) participated under Brigadier General Thomas West Sherman (1813–1879) in the Port Royal Expedition, which seized and held the Sea Islands of South Carolina in November 1861.

case with you also, dearest, for what is the use of having children who are good for anything unless you are willing to have them used? My habitual impression of the uncertainty of human life is so strong that Mary declares I regard crossing our Main st. among the carriage wheels as being far more perilous than a battle,—& I certainly do regard it as very dangerous,—but I have always had a remarkable faculty of falling on my feet, & having got through Kansases & Court Houses unharmed,[13] have the most entire faith in my having the same faculty here. I observe that the men whom bullets hit are usually men who have forewarnings beforehand, but my forewarnings are all the other way, & all that troubles me is leaving Mary in female hands (Margaret, Ann, Mrs. Hall & Charlotte Hawes,) although I have made up my mind that a man has no right to make this home duty paramount to all others. Fortunately she is growing rather better, though not so well as when I went to Kanzas.

As for the duration of the war, I have not the slightest idea that the Free States will hold out three years, but think they will acquiesce in a separation before that, rather than hold on longer. Nor do I think that the Confederacy can possibly sustain itself for even that time, for want of money.

I am limited to three companies in Worcester County & the others are in certain localities elsewhere, which I have partly designated. It will probably be a month or so before we cd. go into barracks & possibly New Year's time before we would get off.

This is all I can write now, but I shall write again soon, before long

Ever thine
T. W. H.

Mary sends her love & says that she always feels most strongly that people must act up to their consciences & be left free to do so. If men feel that they must go to the war, women must not try to prevent them, but quietly submit & hope for the best. That she thinks Margaret & Ann will take very nice care of her.

I may add that of course Margaret with the enthusiasm of her years, is very anxious that I should go, & promises to do her very best.—& nobody can do better when she is thoroughly roused to a thing.

---

13. TWH had assisted in the arming of antislavery settlers in Kansas in 1856, at some risk to his safety; in 1854 he had led a mob that tried unsuccessfully to rescue a captive fugitive slave, Anthony Burns, from the Boston Courthouse.

ENROLL

*"My proposed regiment seems to be under very fair headway"*
To James Freeman Clarke[14]
Worcester. Nov. 5. 1861

*Dear Sir*

My proposed regiment seems to be under very fair headway, & I wish to ask whether you could be induced to go with me as Chaplain?

It is one of the posts easiest to fill & hardest to fill well. I believe that you could do much good in the regiment, beginning as it will with a higher tone of character than the average; & I think that the army is becoming a power so formidable that is essential to the safety of the nation that a high tone of character *should* prevail in it. This consideration has almost as much weight as the antislavery one in inducing me to take part in the war.

The election of chaplain is made by the staff officers & captains of companies, so that I shall hv. no power to offer it, as from myself. But I am satisfied that the suggestion would be received with great pleasure, should you consent to accept the appointment.

Very cordially yours
T. W. Higginson

PS. I shall probably be associated in the command with Capt. Saxton US.A. now of the naval expedition, or some similar man, *satisfactory to me.*

*"I confidently expect to go in some way"*
To Louisa Storrow Higginson
Worcester. Nov. 24. 1861

*Dearest Mother*

I have been waiting to know my prospects a little more clearly, but if I wish for that I must wait longer still. I suppose Gov. Andrew returned fr. Washington yesterday or today & I hope to see him tomorrow or Tuesday. What new views may be in his mind, it is impossible to say, or even whether he will return desiring to hurry or postpone the organization of new regiments. I confidently expect to go in some way, but whether in the arrangement I originally planned, or not, I cannot now say. He has staid away

14. Dr. James Freeman Clarke was Mary Channing's minister, and she took TWH to attend his church; TWH credited Rev. Clarke with leading him to think of entering the ministry, and Clarke delivered the "charge" at TWH's ordination in 1847. See James Freeman Clarke, "Charge," in William Henry Channing, *The Gospel of To-day: Discourse Delivered at the Ordination of T. W. Higginson, as Minister of the First Religious Society in Newburyport, Mass., Sept. 15, 1847, Together with the Charge, Right Hand of Fellowship, and Address to the People* (Boston: Wm. Crosby and H. P. Nichols, 1847), 37–44.

longer than was expected & though this has given me time to act to a certain extent, it has been in an unsatisfactory way, as I was not treading on firm ground at all. I have got my ten companies planned out, but whether he will think they promise sufficiently I do not know, for he judges everything for himself, & sometimes impulsively.

Henry Lee[15] says "of course the Governor *ought* to be governed by his aids, but he is not & they have to yield to his decisions. He is not a man of practical judgment, nor does he understand men;—my judgment (with a dull grimace) is a great deal better than his; it ought to be, for I am older than he." Nevertheless the Governor has his own way & his aristocratic aids are very deferential to him.

Certainly he has done better than Banks wd. hv. done—for he works much more straightforwardly & commands confidence far more entirely. Banks though honest himself was always unfortunate like Fremont, in having those about him who were not.

We have been reading Cecil Dreeme[16] with astonishment for it's ability; it is far superior to his army articles in the Atlantic[17] which were too slangy to suit me, though very graphic. This has great vigor & originality & though a series of tragedies is yet predominantly healthy & pure, remarkably so. I really think he might have done great things in literature, wh. had not occurred to me before. The execution is in some places crude, but on the whole it ranks him decidedly above George Curtis.[18]

The New Counterblast[19] in this Atlantic is mine & I hv. a piece on

15. Major Henry Lee Higginson.

16. Theodore Winthrop, *Cecil Dreeme* (Boston: Ticknor and Fields, 1861). The title character in this novel was said by TWH to have been inspired by the figure of William Henry Hurlbut (later Hurlbert), a college classmate and close friend of TWH's, who also inspired TWH's own novel *Malbone: An Oldport Romance* (Boston: Fields, Osgood, & Co., 1869).

17. Theodore Winthrop died on June 10, 1861, in the disastrous defeat suffered by Union forces on an expedition from Fortress Monroe. He had published "New York Seventh Regiment," *Atlantic Monthly* 7 (June 1861), 744–56, and "Washington as a Camp," *Atlantic Monthly* 8 (July 1861), 105–18, both parts of his "Sketches of the Campaign in Virginia." A third unfinished sketch is included in an article commemorating him, "Theodore Winthrop," *Atlantic Monthly* 8 (August 1861), 242–51.

18. George W. Curtis, who wrote a "Biographical Sketch of the Author" for Winthrop's *Cecil Dreeme*, was a noted social reformer and writer who edited *Harper's Weekly* after 1863. In his early career as a journalist he wrote *Nile Notes of a Howadji* (New York: Harper, 1851) and *The Howadji in Syria* (New York: Harper, 1852), helping to popularize a romantic fascination with the East; later he published *The Potiphar Papers* (New York: G. P. Putnam and Company, 1853); *Lotus-eating: A Summer Book* (New York: Dix, Edwards & Co., 1856); and *Trumps: A Novel* (New York: Harper & Brothers, 1861).

19. Thomas Wentworth Higginson, "A New Counterblast," *Atlantic Monthly* 8 (December 1861), 696–705.

"Snow"[20] in January wh. I think you will like. Part of it is founded on a description I wrote at Brattleboro some 15 yrs. ago I should think. Appropriate, that a blast shld. precede Snow—as much so as that military change in Missouri which Mary says nobody but she has noticed the propriety of—that Gen. Frost[21] is to take the place of Gen. Rains.[22]

We have got double windows in for the first time & are planning to make the house comfortable. Margaret is coming back tomorrow. Mary is doing quite well again & sends love.

I will write again when I know anything more definite.

Ever affectionately<br>T. W. H.

*"the uncertainties of human life . . . seem hardly greater in war than in peace"*
To Louisa Storrow Higginson
Worcester. Aug. 15. 1862

*Dearest Mother*

I have something to say which may surprise you, though after what you have said, I think you will not regret it seriously. I have obtained authority to enlist a military company for 9 months, I to go as Captain.

I was deciding on this while you were here, but for some reasons did not wish to mention it. I am glad I didn't, or I should have thought that this was what produced your Cholera Infantum or whatever it was.

I do not think I should ever have made up my mind to go for 3 years—but those recruits were raised slowly here, & I decided that I never could hold up my head again, in Worcester or even elsewhere, if I did not vindicate my past words by actions though tardy. It seemed to me also, which is more important, that beyond a certain point one has no right to concentrate his whole life on one private duty.[23] Mary will make the best of it, as she always does—& will either go to Boston if I can find suitable accomodations—or stay here. In either case I have written to Carrie Andrews[24] to come & stay with her while I am away—as she offered to do

20. Thomas Wentworth Higginson, "Snow," *Atlantic Monthly* 9 (February 1862), 188–201.

21. Brigadier General Daniel Marsh Frost (1823–1900), Confederate.

22. Brigadier General Gabriel James Rains (1803–1881), Confederate.

23. TWH refers to the responsibility of caring for his invalid wife, Mary Channing Higginson.

24. Caroline Andrews (later Mrs. Rufus Leighton), a friend from Newburyport, Massachusetts, who had been one of TWH's helpers in the evening school he organized there.

before. If she is well enough (& I think she is or soon will be) she will come.

I dare say this will seem hard to you, dearest mother, but I remember that you acquiesced before, & I think you will again. Nine months is not a great while after all—& as for the uncertainties of human life they seem hardly greater in war than in peace.

The Lieut. Colonel of the regiment will be Dwight Foster, Attorney General of the state & one of our best men. I suppose I might hv. some reg-imental position by pushing for it but I shall not. My proposed company takes greatly here, & many of our best young men are joining in it[.] It will not be long probably, that is not many weeks, before the regiment is full.

Mr. Verry told me of your being sick & I am glad it was no worse though bad enough. Write soon.

Ever faithfully
T. W. H.

Mary sends love & is sorry you had so bad a journey.

### *"I have now 27 recruits"*
### To Louisa Storrow Higginson
### Worcester. Aug 22. 1862

*Dearest Mother*

It is quite a relief to my mind that you are able to acquiesce in my plans; I felt especially anxious in knowing that you were so poorly.

Mary has decided not to go to Boston & if you knew what a relief it is to her, you would not be sorry. To all the good reasons she has written, she might hv. added this—that in Boston there is no room to be had! There was but one, & that was let next day. I spent hours in exploring the vicinity of Essex St. & could find nothing tolerable. She will feel far less homesick at the Lincoln House,[25] can walk out more freely than fr. those high stepped Boston houses—& can take her own things, &c. Then, if I shld. be delayed weeks in camp, she cd. see me far oftener. The McFarlands will be there through Sept'r—& the LeBarons[26] are talking of going there for the winter. The more we think of it, the more we like the plan. Having Ann with her she can have her work done to suit herself & can even send her home to cook a little, in case of need.

Thank you very much for your bank-note, dear Mother, but I really don't think we can make any use of it, as my pay will be sufficient to cover

---

25. The Lincoln House was a boarding house in Worcester, Massachusetts.
26. Martha Le Baron was a neighbor in Worcester.

this. My first intention was to send it back in this letter—but I shall keep it a little longer, as it may be necessary for me to have some funds in advance, but I shall wish to repay it before I go, because we really shall not need it.

Mary says all women are more or less *cats*, & she is particularly so, & that is why she don't want to go to a strange boarding house.

I have now 27 recruits, very nice fellows, & shld. hv. many more, but that all the other towns are all paying bounties, & it will not be decided whether we pay one, until Monday so they are waiting to see. By the end of next week I hope to be full, & go soon into camp.

I enclose my manifesto,[27]

Ever affectionately

T. W. H.

## "*I have . . . had a street drill of my company*"
### To Louisa Storrow Higginson
### Worcester. Aug. 29. 1862

*Dearest Mother*

I am going to Boston today with my company roll full, to get authority to choose officers; & next week we expect to go into barracks in a large building a little out of town. I hv. filled up much more rapidly than any other company—had 61 in advance of the bounty, wh. was not voted till Wednesday night. Everybody praises the material of my company & their appearance on the street. I have taken them out twice.

I was so relieved that you liked the Lincoln House plan. I feared you might not have a pleasant impression of the house, but I am confident that Mary will be comfortable there, & she is certainly a different person now fr. what she would be with the weight on her mind of so great a prospective change as going to Boston, her theory being that all women are more or less cats & she especially so.

Margaret is coming back on Saturday; her health & spirits are all right again & she is earnestly desirous to go with Mary & do all she can for her.

I will tell you more about my company hereafter.

Ever affectionately

T. W. H.

PS. I have come fr. Boston & have had a street drill of my company, marching them by the house, much to Mary's edification. I hv. authority to

27.  TWH published a large announcement—practically a sermon—calling for volunteers in the Worcester *Spy* (August 16, 1862), saying "Criticism is idle without action . . . If you are going, go now."

elect company officers tomorrow: & we shall go into camp when the barracks are ready—perhaps by the end of next week.

I had a glimpse of the Corcoran procession & of him,[28] a quiet looking man. They say Fremont's reception[29] was magnificent & his speech reads very admirably, though he is said to be no orator. Two bouquets were carried fr. the platform to Jessie[30] who sat in an adjoining gallery; this showed her to the audience & produced great enthusiasm.

Mary sends love.

*"I don't think I ever did anything better than I have done all this"*
To Louisa Storrow Higginson
Lincoln House.
Worcester. Sept 7. 1862

*Dearest Mother*

We have been here just 24 hours & have done very well as to everything but bed, & that will be modified tomorrow. Mary is much pleased with the rooms, as she has reason to be; & she is more entertained than annoyed by the drilling, which is of course far less than when the camp was here. Our camp will be in a diff't direction.

We find the table ample & meats & bread so far good though the butter & the water are not. Last night we had plenty of those blackberries for wh. you sighed. The little Rosebushes still bloom, baby & all; papa McFarland has appeared—the others return on Monday.

Margaret finds it quite entertaining here; we hv. brought many of our own things, & look quite homelike. Mary has parlor on one side (piano & sofa) & bedroom on the other; & Ann's adjacent room is invaluable. Ann looked rather homesick at first, but soon discovered an intimate friend among the girls of the house & was very happy.

Our room is lower than yours & is directly under the beautiful elms.

28. Michael Corcoran (1827–1863), an Irish emigrant, was captured at 1st Bull Run. When Confederate Secretary of War Judah P. Benjamin vowed to inflict on a high-ranking Union prisoner whatever punishment was meted out to the Confederate captain of the *Enchantress* who had been captured by Union naval forces, Corcoran and his fellow prisoners drew lots for the dubious honor of being held hostage, under threat of capital punishment, in this retributive standoff. He was finally exchanged in August 1862 and met with a hero's welcome in the North.

29. Major General John Charles Frémont (1813–1890), the former Republican candidate for President (in 1856), was forced by Lincoln to resign in June 1862; a favorite of abolitionists because of his strong antislavery outlook, he was widely feted upon his departure from the military.

30. Gen. Frémont's wife, the writer Jesse Benton Frémont.

Opposite is Dr. Woodward's[31] where the whole family spend all day & evening on the doorstep or in chaises & are quite amusing. The furniture of the room is really handsome & the paper quite pretty; we brought our own air-tight.[32]

I have my commission & we go into barracks when they are ready—say Wednesday or Thursday. I drill my company every afternoon two hours outdoors & enjoy it much. They learn fast & their marching is much praised. I don't think I ever did anything better than I have done all this, so far. The lieutenants of the company are those I planned to have from the beginning; both of them have been much with me in the Gymnasium[33] & they are excellent fellows. John Goodell (1st lieut)[34] is a remarkably capable, strong, prompt person, reliable as the North Star & able to succeed in anything he attempts. He has a splendid physique, though not tall—a rich brunette complexion with fine eyes. He has never been in the military line, but learns very quickly. Luther Bigelow (2d)[35] is a bookkeeper like the other, & was out for 3 months with the army last year; still he is not well drilled & he is almost too gentle; though sweet & refined; still perhaps it is in him. My 1st sergeant is named Dunlap[36] a teacher, an Amherst College graduate; I have to train him also, but he learns easily. Most of the privates are quite young, but very nice fellows; I hardly know an exception. They are a remarkably goodlooking, well bred set, every body says; & some very handsome men.

At the Quartermaster General's office on Friday I found Charles Higginson[37] helping him & he took me home to dine! I had heard so much of the forlornness of that household that I was very agreeably disappointed; we had quite a gay time, & I found Uncle Jas. & Aunt Martha[38] two very pleasant & bright elderly people. They were very cordial to me, & I wish I had been there a great deal more.

I hv. heard from Stephen about Robert;[39] he is not here, of course,

31. Dr. Rufus Woodward, physician and naturalist, had been TWH's classmate at Harvard and now practiced in Worcester.

32. A kind of heating stove.

33. TWH had been, for some time, a gymnastics enthusiast who cultivated his physique and athletic abilities, and a habitué of a local Worcester gymnasium.

34. First Lieutenant John B. Goodell.

35. Second Lieutenant Luther H. Bigelow.

36. Sergeant George E. Dunlap.

37. Charles James Higginson, TWH's first cousin.

38. James Perkins Higginson, TWH's uncle (his father Stephen's brother) and his wife Martha Hubbard Babcock Higginson. Charles James Higginson was their son.

39. First Lieutenant Robert Minturn Higginson, 5th Massachusetts Colored Cavalry; a son of Stephen Higginson, TWH's older brother.

there being no camp now. I suppose they are very anxious about him, but he is a boy sure to fall on his feet, & the family tie is so strong among that household, that he will be sure to let them know where he is before long; so don't fear for your grandchild.

Ever thine<br>T. W. H.

Charlotte Hawes says I ought to organize a company of 3-years-drummers out of Chatham St.—for that there are certainly drummers enough of that age to fill a company.

### *"Tomorrow I go into barracks"*
To Louisa Storrow Higginson
Worcester. Sept. 14. 1862

*Dearest Mother*
Tomorrow I go into barracks & must write a little first. Mary is as well as can be expected, considering Margaret's not having been very well & a Republican Convention having occurred. Our room is large & comfortable, & Ann takes good care of Mary's domestic arrangements; the meat is almost always good, the bread occasionally & the butter never.—but these defects can be partially remedied from outside. The McFarlands are here & the Dodges, but neither for a long time.

I have been drilling my companies for a week or two, several hours a day & every body is surprised at their rapid progress: they will be far superior to any other of the companies going into camp, so far as I can judge. The Adjutant General, rather to my amazement, announces Regiment No 51, as consisting of Companies raised by T. W. Higginson, Worcester, though in fact I can only be said to have raised two. This seems to imply that I am likely to be elected to a field office, which is very possible; but we are to try & get Lt. Col. Sprague of the 25th, who is now here for Colonel. This would be heaven for us all, as he is a perfect Henri La Rochejaquelin[40] to me, in sweetness & charm, & the greatest possible favorite here, tall, fair, low voiced, graceful, a natural nobleman. He has been a year in the service & can teach us everything. He & I are quite friends & it would seem too good to be true, only that everything has flowed so effortless to me thus far that any imaginable good luck seems credible. He it is of whom Miss Rebecca Kinnients remarked, sitting among a mob of ladies sewing for the

---

40. Henri du Vergier, comte de la Rochejaquelein (1772–1794), young royalist nobleman who joined the counterrevolutionary peasant uprising in the Vendie, an economically backward and fervently Catholic region of France, in 1793.

25th Regiment—Col. Sprague's photograph being passed round to refresh them—"Oh let me look at my darling Augustus." "Miss Kinnients" remarked the lady who sat next, "allow me to introduce you to Mrs. Sprague"—that fortunate lady sitting next her on the other side.

If we fail of him we may have Mr. Scandlin[41] who was Chaplain of the 15th Reg't, & figured in battle of Ball's Bluff: an Englishman & a natural soldier.

I don't expect to remain many weeks in barracks; the place is not as picturesque as the Brattleboro place, over which the McFarlands are enthusiastic.

Mary's chief despair is about her *books* for the winter—she thinks she must take a subject & read about it—only there isn't any subject she cares about. Margaret suggests Geology, as a good solid permanent diet.

I shall write before long from "Camp John E. Wool."

Ever affectionately<br>T. W. H.

Mary sends love.

*"nine hundred men snore in concert in one vast hall"*
To Louisa Storrow Higginson
Camp John E. Wool
Worcester. Sept. 26. 1862

*Dearest Mother*

I am going to write a few words tonight, hoping they will reach you by Sunday. I hope I duly forwarded a letter Mary wrote you some days ago; but I live in such a whirl, I hardly know.

Today I had to go down to Boston to help settle an unfortunate division of feeling here, as to which companies shld. go into the 51st Reg't. It has been quite annoying, as two companies have been much provoked with me, in consequence: & at this moment the matter is being finally settled, whether they are to go with the regiment or not—probably not. I hope not as they are bad companies & poorly officered.

This has given extra solicitude to me; if all the regiments were like my company it wd. be clear enjoyment. I feel just like a father of a family when I go up to the quarters at meal times & see my sage first sergeant[42] taking tea out, in the bunk of the two nice Johnson boys,[43] sitting between them

41. William G. Scandlin.

42. Sergeant George E. Dunlap.

43. Private John F. Johnson, 19 years old, of Northborough, was in TWH's Company C; there were three other Johnsons in the Massachusetts 51st, one of whom, Private

behind a pine board, eating baked apples, illumined by a stearine dip[44] stuck in a potato. Or later when four beautiful voices sing quartettes. My sergeants hold evening prayers, to which many of the company go, sometimes half; & at nine there is a roll-call, after which all go to bed & nine hundred men snore in concert in one vast hall, with scarce a partition between.

At five a.m. comes a rolling of drums, like churning & boiling in one, which is the reveillé, called in military parlance *revalee*, to which all the men bundle up & one commissioned officer at least to each company—then drill fr. 6 to 7 & then breakfast & four hours more drilling through the day. We still hv. radiant weather, & when it is known finally who are to constitute the regiment, we shall settle down nicely.

Today I came fr. a run down to Boston & found Mary in good health & spirits, as you may suppose when I say she had walked up to Mrs. LeBaron's & taken tea—a two year's vision—walking back after the street lamps were lighted, a thing almost unprecedented to her—as was the teaing out without me; I never knew her [to] do that since we were married & it is a superb indication of weaning. I really think Dr. Lewis's flesh brushes[45] are beginning to work. Our faithful Ann went with her & was an excellent attendant.

I hv. had an unread Atlantic for a week & was amused to find, on strolling in at Ticknor's,[46] that a life of studious leisure seemed quite a fascinating thing to me; it being but about a month since I deserted it.

---

Lewis Johnson, 31, in Company A, was also from Northborough. Privates Cornelius W. Johnson, 22 (Company E) and John W. Johnson, 40 (Company E) were from Southborough and Westborough, respectively.

44. Stearin or stearine is a colorless, odorless ester found in animal and vegetable fats and used in the manufacture of candles.

45. Dr. Dio (Dioclesian) Lewis (1823–1886), a prominent health reformer (champion of the "Movement Cure," which prescribed muscular exercise as preventive medicine, along with other therapies), opened his Normal Institute for Physical Education in Boston in 1862; he addressed himself particularly to the chronic invalidism of his women patients. He advocated cold water for bathing, vigorously applied with coarse bathing mittens ("flesh brushes"). In *Weak Lungs, and How to Make Them Strong* (Boston: Ticknor and Fields, 1864)—part of which had been published as "Weak Lungs, and How to Make Them Strong," *Atlantic Monthly* 11 (June 1863), 657–74—he recommended that cold water be applied to the body "with that vigor and earnestness which men display in boxing" and that the bather then "rub the skin dry and red" (p. 184). His gymnastic regimen enjoyed great popularity in reform circles; see "The New Gymnastics," *Atlantic Monthly* 10 (August 1862), 129–48.

46. The *Atlantic Monthly* was published by Ticknor and Fields, the publishing company headed by George Ticknor and James T. Fields.

"Heigho, yawned one day King Francis
Distance all value enhances
When a man's busy, why leisure
Strikes him as wonderful pleasure
Faith! & at leisure once is he
Straightway he wants to be busy."

Ever thine
T. W. H.

## *"Old Higgie is so strict, so strict"*
### To Louisa Storrow Higginson
### Worcester. Oct. 4. 1862

*Dearest Mother*

We are sailing smoothly now at the camp; one of the objectionable companies having been removed to the other camp, & the other going. They cannot yet be said to love me, & I heard yesterday of an inebriated Irish private singing along Main St. "Old Higgie is so strict, so strict," &c while another in a similar condition came to the company quarters yesterday saying that he was drunk & wished to go to the guardhouse, but it is all resulting very well.

I am much pleased with the officers of the 8 remaining companies; none are highly cultivated, but almost all are intelligent & manly & the majority are fine looking—more so than usual.

Yesterday we marched over the hills into Auburn,[47] about three miles, to visit the homestead of one of our company named Rice,[48] a nice rosy boy. As we descended I suddenly became aware of waving handkerchiefs in an orchard & found that there was a small outdoor entertainment for us, men women & children some thirty or forty between two great appletrees with an American flag hung above, a table with bread & butter, doughnuts, cheese & apples; & the parish minister to make a speech. So we partook of these various entertainments & responded with songs which the boys do very well, & some cheers, before we left for camp. On the way we stopped & similarly saluted a lady who had aided in the affair, but had been prevented fr. going by sickness in the family. Then we marched back to camp arriving after dark.

I regularly spend Sunday & the night following with Mary & come in about every other day for several hours. I think we may be here a month.

47. Auburn, Massachusetts, a town south of Worcester.
48. TWH's Company C had Privates George D. Rice, 20, and Henry S. Rice, 23, both of Auburn.

Several of the new 9 months reg'ts are said to be now under orders for Newbern N.C.,[49] but there is no intimation about ours—only Col. Sprague thinks he can get us into Burnside's division.

I hv. been entirely well, so far & have found it a comfortable way of living & Mary is certainly gaining. She will send this note with hers.

Ever thine<br>T. W. H.

### "a divertisement of men alone"
### To Louisa Storrow Higginson
### Camp Wool. Oct 13. 1862

*Dearest Mother*

One of the richest things we have here in the barracks is the dancing. About once a week the men have a regular ball; the bunks at the middle of the building are moved on one side, candles are stuck about the rafters, one or two kerosene lamps suspended, two fiddlers hoisted on a top bunk, with Stuart Brown[50] our Adjutant in a red jockey cap to call the figures; & all take partners to the extent of 30 or 40 couples. The ladies are distinguishable by a handkerchief tied to the arm, & conduct themselves with much propriety, & as the younger & more delicate are naturally selected to act in this capacity, they sometimes acquit themselves with much grace especially in the rare intervals when a waltz or polka is permitted. But these airy side dishes seldom come in—the bulk of the entertainment consisting of country dances of the very solidest description, thorough heel-&-toe work, & no flinching—as you wd. think could you hear them over my head at this moment. I can remember nothing but the remotest of the Brattleboro public balls which can in the least rival the amount of work accomplished; these perhaps being even more concentrated since they not only begin at 7. but close at 9. The men not yet being uniformed exhibit every variety of shirts and jackets, while here & there the shoulderstraps of some lively young Lieutenant flash through the struggling mass. My young Lieutenant Bigelow after looking on for a while was swept away by the charms of the prettiest of the Sergeants, named Fairweather,[51] & I last saw him winding through the "Portland Fancy" with her. Up aloft, on all the cross timbers of the roof along the upper row of bunks, are perched the spectators, all masculine; the dim lights

49. Union forces under General Ambrose Everett Burnside, after capturing Roanoke Island in February, moved on New Berne, North Carolina, occupying it on March 14, 1862, and establishing a foothold on the North Carolina mainland.
50. J. Stewart Brown.
51. Sergeant George F. Fayerweather, 22, of Westborough (Company E).

glimmer on dusky figures & particolored caps, while the floor rocks with the perpetual surge of motion. Without the excitement of love or wine, with simply the pent up physical energy of two days inaction during a storm, they dance like Maenads or Bacchanals,[52] their whole bodies dance, in the pauses between the figures they throb & tremble all over, as they keep time to the music; sometimes solitary uncouth men who are not dancing begin to whirl & frisk alone by themselves in corners, unnoticed & unnoticing. In each set there are mingled grim & war-worn faces, looking old as Waterloo, with merely childish faces from school, & there is such an absorption, such a passionate delight that one would say dancing must be a reminiscence of the felicity of Adam before Eve appeared, never to be seen in its full zest while a woman mingled in it. It is something that seems wholly contrary to all theories of social enjoyment—& then to think that these New Englanders are called grave & unenjoying! In all the really rustic entertainments I have ever seen, from Katahdin to Kansas, there has been a certain stiffness wh. I supposed inherent & inevitable; I remember a ball of lumbermen at *South Moluncus* or *Number Three* in Maine[53] that was as joyless as Beacon St:[54] & yet here in these barracks I have beheld a scene where the wildest revelry absorbed every person, & yet without woman or drink. There is no swearing or vulgarity, they are too much absorbed for that; it is all perfectly real to them; they look forward to it & back upon it as any other young men might look on any other ball & no one could dream to hear them speak of it, that it is all a divertisement of men alone.

*"I have to give all the nervous energy I can spare"*
To Louisa Storrow Higginson
Worcester. Sunday
Oct 26. 1862

*Dearest Mother*
I believe I have not written regularly, but time passes very rapidly & the days are a good deal alike. As yet I have not had a trace of ennui, because I have no leisure. There is none during the day, except when it rains, & four

52. In Greek mythology, maenads are women members of the orgiastic cult of Dionysus; bacchanals are participants in the ancient Roman Bacchanalia, a festival in honor of the god Bacchus (another name for Dionysus).
53. Travelers to remote settlements in Maine, as TWH notes in "Going to Mount Katahdin," *Putnam's Monthly Magazine* 8 (September 1856), 242–56, eventually "got beyond towns with names to them." "No. 3 is a very little settlement . . . supported entirely by the lumber business" (p. 245).
54. Beacon Street in Boston was an exclusive residential location of the upper class; here it connotes rigid social propriety.

evenings in the week are taken up with meetings—that is, two for officers' school which as yet is a failure—two I give to my non-commissioned officers, meeting in my room. These last are equal or superior to the commissioned officers of the regiment in intelligence & refinement, so it is very pleasant & we hv. nice times. My room is quite comfortable, with an airtight stove, wh. burns when the wind blows one way & don't burn when it blows t'other.

The commissioned officers are now growing well acquainted & are a good set on the whole as the various traits come out. The Captains are the best, we hv. no actually bad ones, though several are mediocre or *slack*. As usual the new men are the best & the men of militia or actual service the poorest—make most mistakes & are most negligent; reason, because they rely on their own impressions & limited experience, while the new men anxiously make sure of the "Regulations" or the "Tactics"[55] or the Colonel for everything. The best of them discover with me how annoying it is to be scrupulous & punctilious where others take it easy. Still the stricter officers command most weight in the end.

The two Captains who satisfy me are Wheeler of Grafton[56] & T. D. Kimball of Oxford[57] (we hv. two Capt. Kimball's—the latter a very handsome young medical student the former a noble looking six foot Saxon, sound & simple hearted in his manhood, one of Tom Hughes'[58] type of men: son of a rich machinist here in Worcester, himself a Harvard graduate, who after travelling in Europe settled down as a farmer in Grafton, with a private school like Miles's; he is the man among them all who will "do to tie to" as they say out West. My lieutenants are the best of the lot & all is harmony among us three, then there are some nice attractive boys among the others, with a mixture of older men, respectable county Sheriffs & such, good though not graceful & then another set of precarious morale who will go up or down according to the influences.

Col. Ward who commands the post I heartily like; there is little of him beyond the military but that is excellent—he is always frank & decided & just; always sustains those who wish to do right, but is not so severe on wrong doers as if it were his own regiment; but after all I shall be glad to

---

55. *Regulations for the Army of the United States, 1861* (New York: Harper & Brothers, [1861]); Casey, *Infantry Tactics* (1862).

56. Captain William Fisk Wheeler.

57. Captain Thomas D. Kimball.

58. Thomas Hughes, an English barrister, politician, and writer, best known as the author of *Tom Brown's Schooldays* (London: Macmillan, and Co., 1857), which advocated what became known as "muscular Christianity," a combination of physical courage, moral rigor, patriotism, personal loyalty, self-reliance and Christian piety.

find Col. Sprague so good a disciplinarian—that being, after all, three quarters of a Colonel. The Captains can do the parental, at least I can, to the men; but it is absolutely necessary to have somebody overhead who will establish a uniform standard of discipline.

We now hv. dress parade & battalion drill—of course in so military a place as Brattleboro you know what these mean; the first is an easy form; the last is drilling as a regiment & is very interesting. After what I have learned fr. the books it comes very easy but as I command the right flank company I hv. to give all the nervous energy I can spare, to keep up sharply to orders often new & often inaudible; but the company now marches so well that the result is always satisfactory & we hv. made no bad mistakes.

This week we are to have two more companies; one of the two wh. were ejected, & another more desirable; this gives the ten companies & we shall probably choose field officers this week. The Lt. Colonel will be Harkness,[59] Adjutant of the 25th whom Sprague desires to bring with him—a splendid soldier though with some defects. I may be chosen Major & may not, & don't concern myself at all. We are to have a regimental ball in Mechanics Hall[60] to celebrate the election, & shall probably be off for Newbern before many weeks.

It is doubtful whether my company retains permanently the right of the line; you will be surprised at my speaking of this; but you have no idea of the importance these trifles assume, in the little world of the camp. Wisely said Goethe "thought expands, but lames; action animates, but narrows."

Mary sends love & thanks Anne for her kindness about the shawl.

Ever thine<br>T. W. H.

*"our rather monotonous life"*
To LOUISA STORROW HIGGINSON
WORCESTER. NOV. 2. 1862

*Dearest Mother*

Time glides away very fast in our rather monotonous life & Sunday comes round again before I can imagine it possible. This week has been made tender & thoughtful by hearing of the death of that most gifted & fascinating creature, who has been like a child to us for many years,

59. Elijah A. Harkness, as TWH reports in the following letter, in the end became Major instead of Lieutenant Colonel.

60. A public building in Worcester, erected by the Worcester County Mechanics Association (dedicated in 1857), where classes for workers, labor meetings, lecture series, industrial expositions, musical concerts and social events were held.

Harriet Hale[61] of Newburyport. She died with her newborn baby, last week; having written us a beautiful letter the week before, full of sacred & tremulous hopes & saying "If I die, no one must mourn, for I have had too much bliss." It was her fair child & all her family have suffered peculiarly under such circumstances. Her genius always seemed so affluent & fine that it would seem to impoverish the world to lose such an one, were not such an existence evidently indestructible. When a mere child her resources of (winningness) were Cleopatra-like & inexhaustible, & as she has grown older she has developed all solid qualities of womanhood, together with a sudden genius for painting; & this maternity seemed so to crown her life that it's whole round appeared completed.

We hv. chosen our field officers—Sprague Colonel, Capt. Studley[62] (of the 15th reg't) Lt. Col. & Ad. Harkness (of the 25th) Major. Harkness was to hv. been Lt. Col. of the 54th reg't, which is broken up, & part of it annexed to ours—so it was a sort of joint ticket. Had the original programme been carried out, I shld. probably have been Major, but for that I care nothing. Now we fear Harkness may not accept, in which case Sprague will not—still I think it will all go smooth; in which case we shall have altogether the ablest *field* among the N.E. 9 months reg'ts. I am Senior Captain, at present, with "the right of the line"—that is, marching first in column—& my company & Lts. were very glad not to hv. me promoted—which was pleasant.

On Thursday we had a regimental ball at Mechanics Hall, which went off very pleasantly. Margaret went with me & was saturated with shoulder-straps.

We hv. everything now but guns & may be ordered off at any time. The steamers return this month to Newburn, but I think a Springfield reg't will go instead of ours & we at the next trip of the vessels.

Studley is a plain man of excellent character & a good soldier; was imprisoned at Richmond after Ball's Bluff last year. Harkness is a little fellow, all steel; & Sprague a chevalier. The two latter being favorites in the North Carolina department, our regiment would doubtless stand well there.

Mary is well & is now reading *Senoco*'s Morals as Margaret rather hastily interpreted the ancient Seneca.

Tuesday the whole regiment goes home to vote, & it will seem just like a holiday in college. Thank you very much for the pretty thread case, whose contents will be [ ]ly[63] available for somebody.

Ever thine<br>T. W. H.

61. Harriet Hale, a friend from Newburyport, Massachusetts.
62. Lieutenant Colonel John M. Studley.
63. The manuscript is illegible here.

We shall probably have our dear Dr. Rogers for Surgeon of the regiment isn't that good!

## *"We have orders to leave"*
## To Louisa Storrow Higginson
## Nov. 3 1862

> *By Telegraph from* Worcester,
> *To* Mrs Louisa Higginson
> We have orders to leave this week. Probably Thursday

T. W. H.

## *"I take great pleasure in offering you the position of Colonel"*
## To Thomas Wentworth Higginson
## Beaufort South Carolina
## Nov 5ᵀᴴ 1862.

*My dear Sir.*

I am organizing the 1st Regiment of South Carolina Volunteers with every prospect of success. Your name has been spoken of in connection with the command of this Regiment, by some friends[64] in whose judgment I have confidence. I take great pleasure in offering you the position of Colonel in it, and hope that you may be induced to accept. I shall not fill the place until I hear from you, or sufficient time shall have passed for me to receive your reply. Should you accept I enclose a pass for Port-Royal of which I trust you will feel disposed to avail yourself at once.

I am with sincere regard

Yours Truly
R. Saxton
Brig: Genl:
Mil: Gov:
Mr T. Wentworth Higginson

## *"ours will be a splendid regiment"*
## To Louisa Storrow Higginson
## Worcester. Nov. 9. 1862

*Dearest Mother*

Our field officers hv. received their commissions & take command tomorrow, for which I am very glad. A regiment needs at least 3 persons to

---

64. See the November 10, 1862, letter to TWH from J. H. Fowler below.

take care of the officers. If I like Col. Sprague as well as Col. Ward I am quite satisfied—but Col. Ward is but one man, with a wooden leg & two camps to look after. With three first class officers of experience, ours will be a splendid regiment & I shld. far rather be a Captain in it than Colonel of a raw regiment with no one of more experience than myself to look to; which is the case with most of the nine months troops. We are more sure of an honorable position & at the same time more likely to be carefully kept & judiciously handled. In mere drill, experience is of little value for one man can learn it better in a month than another in a year, & my company is admitted to be the best drilled & disciplined in the regiment; but the main part of the military sphere is beyond this, in the proper care of the men, & here experience is of immense value.

As for our destination or time of leaving, we as yet know nothing, but the latter cannot be very far off. If we go to Newburn we cannot go for a fortnight or more; if we go with Banks we may be ordered to New York at least, any day.

It is snowing hard again & the men take it rather hard—yet they are more goodnatured than one wd. expect, on the whole. All my company have bought new blue overcoats in place of the shoddies[65]—some for cash, some for credit.

On Tuesday the lady friend of the company gave us a dinner at City Hall.

Mary & Margaret are well & send love. We will send a photograph when successful. Mary is reading Beecher's Eyes & Ears,[66] & likes it.

We have had a beautiful letter from Emery Hale,[67] with the most interesting things about dear Harriet & a long tress of her superb hair.

Ever thine, with much thanks for your & Anne's note

*"the demands of the movement"*
To Thomas Wentworth Higginson
Beaufort SC Nov 10 1862

*Rev T W Higginson*
Dear Sir, We have taken the liberty of mentioning your name to Gen Saxton, Gov. of this Depost—for the Colonelcy of 1st Reg SC Vols—Colored. Our deep interest in the cause and knowledge of your devotion to it

65. Overcoats of inferior quality, either because previously worn or because made of poor quality wool.

66. Henry Ward Beecher, *Eyes and Ears* (Boston: Ticknor and Fields, 1862).

67. Husband of Harriet Hale, a friend from Newburyport, Rhode Island.

and capacity to serve it here, is our only excuse. Gen was well pleased with the suggestion and promised to write you at once. We hope you will appreciate the demands of the movement at this time and make the sacrifice whatever it may be. The Pres. has authorized 5 regs to start, this is the first, the Hunter reg having disbanded. We have over 500 men in camp already, some of them already distinguished for immortal deeds. The late achievements of one Co, in Florida are most promising, braver fighting and more successful has not been done, prisoners brought here by thier own slaves, with thier breth[ ][68] from captivity. Some 25 rebels killed & wounded only 2 of ours a little wounded a whole Company of Cavalry routed by a few Negro pickets and important salt works destroyed are some of the incidents you will soon see pub in the Tribune. The field is vast the opportunities are abundant, the soldiers are ready. The opposition is also fierce, but we will succeed. The key is to form no idle camp in which men enter to die and rot. It is to be a school for learning letters, & life, and a field for *work*. Rev. Mr. Billings formerly Unit Minister Concord & Chaplain of NH 7th is Lieut. Col. *True to the Cause* Dr J. M. Hawks thorough & true antislavery of Manchester N.H. is Surgeon. They are anxious that you should come and be our leader. As for myself I should be sadly disappointed should anything keep you away. It seems to me that the success or failure of this reg. is to be a most important fact [ ][69] solution of this whole Negro question hence my deep interest in it.

Yours most truly J. H. Fowler[70] Chaplain

## "We have marching orders"

TO LOUISA STORROW HIGGINSON
CAMP WOOL
WORCESTER. NOV 12. 1862

*Dearrest Mother*

We have marching orders (wh. I hv. seen) to go to Newburn by the return steamers. Only two reg'ts. are to go, & we shall hv. a steamer to ourselves which will be far more comfortable. They finally sailed on the 10th & will be ready to sail again in ten days or a fortnight fr. that time. I suppose you will prefer the Newburn destination, as being so much easier of access; Mary does. Yesterday we had a visit fr. Emery Hale, Harriet's husband, which we greatly enjoyed; he had such interesting things to tell; & brought two beautiful engravings she left us; "Capri" & "The Rest at Eve."

68. The manuscript is torn here; presumably the word is "brethren."
69. The manuscript is torn here.
70. Rev. James H. Fowler.

Caro. Andrews is to be married in Dec'r to Mr. Leighton of Boston now a gov't clerk in Washington, a very superior person; he reported & edited Theo: Parker's progress.[71]

Waldo & Stephen are coming

*"this letter . . . may change all my plans"*
To LOUISA STORROW HIGGINSON
WORCESTER. NOV 16. 1862.

*Dearest Mother*

Directly after Stephen's & Waldo's visit, I found this letter[72] on my table. It may change all my plans. I have telegraphed to Gov. Andrew at Washington for leave to go to Beaufort & see Gen. Saxton, there to decide on accepting the post, which is, of course, in itself very attractive. Nevertheless I have almost decided not to sacrifice a certainty for an uncertainty, & not resign my present post till I am sure of a more important one. It came very unexpectedly. Yesterday I came in & told Mary. Margaret's exclamation was "Will not Uncle Wentworth be in bliss! A thousand men, every one as black as a coal." Then I went to Boston & saw Edward Hooper (Dr H's son) & others who hv. been at Port Royal, & their information leaves me still in doubt, how far it will be a desirable situation. But if I can get a temporary furlough, I shall certainly go in a few days to N.Y. there to await the steamer for Port Royal, as it's going is very irregular. If I cannot get this leave of absence I shall probably forego the Saxton offer rather than resign on an uncertainty.

I saw Stephen & Charles J. H.[73] in Boston, both of whom were much pleased with the proposition.

Our reg't will probably leave in about a week, for Newbern. Col. Sprague's rule is perfectly delightful—a silken glove & a hand of iron.

Ever thine
T. W. H.

71. Rufus Leighton edited a number of Theodore Parker's published sermons. *A Sermon of the Public Function of Woman, Preached at the Music Hall, Boston, March 27, 1853* (Boston: R. F. Wallcut, 1853), contained a note, "The following sermon is part of a long course of sermons on the Spiritual Development of the Human Race . . . ," so perhaps TWH has this series on "development" in mind.

72. The November 5, 1862, letter from Brigadier General Rufus Saxton, above.

73. Either TWH's brother Stephen Higginson or his cousin Stephen Higginson Perkins; Charles James Higginson, a cousin.

*"a man of marked ability and of indomitable perseverance"*
TO RUFUS SAXTON

COPY OF COL. SPRAGUE'S LETTER OF INTRODUCTION

HEAD QUARTERS. 51 MASS. REG.
CAMP WOOL. WORCESTER
BRIG. GEN. SAXTON
NOV 19. 1862

*My Dear Sir*

Capt. T. W. Higginson of my regiment has permission from the War Department to go to Beaufort S.C. & is ordered to report to you. I should very much regret to lose him from the regiment, were I not convinced that he cd. render greater service to our country in the position to wh. you have been pleased to call him.—but I cannot let him go without bearing hence my own testimony as to his fitness for the position.

Capt. Higginson has never been in active service, but he is a man of marked ability & of indomitable perseverance. He commands a company second to none in the regiment in all that pertains to soldierly bearing, discipline & drill, & I doubt not he would be an acquisition as a field officer in a Mass^ts regiment.

Devoted as he is to the cause of the oppressed by long & persistent effort with a good knowledge of human nature & an ability to govern, I regard him as peculiarly fitted for his new field of labor.

I am very respectfully your obedient servant

A B R Sprague
Col 51st Mass

*"if I don't come home jet black you must be very grateful"*
TO LOUISA STORROW HIGGINSON
HEADQUARTERS 1ST S.C. VOLUNTEERS
CAMP SAXTON
NOV. 28. 1862

*Dearest Mother*

I have just heard that there will be a mail tomorrow, so shall send off a second budget of journal for Mary which I suppose she will forward for you. We are expecting a steamer in a day or two, with Gen. Hunter & a mail.

I have been here now 4 days & have settled down so completely into my new life that it does not seem to me that there is any novelty in it. Today in looking at my best company, drilling with the musket it suddenly occurred to me that all soldiers were not black & it seemed as if a white company would look very odd. You must remember that since I left Worcester I have

247

hardly touched foot on any soil but this plantation, scarcely delaying an hour or two in N.Y. or in Beaufort & only having left the Camp once since my arrival. So my whole faculties have been switched off in this new direction with absolutely nothing to distract me & if I don't come home jet black you must be very grateful.

Shall I never meet with anything that *lasts* strange & novel? To wander out on Thanksgiving evening, to follow a bright fire light & come upon a blaze of logs beneath a great live oak tree, with a circle of my soldiers sitting blissfully around it, the glow reflected gorgeously from their red legs & not dimly from their shining cheeks & white teeth & rolling eyes—the innumerable funereal plumes of waving moss on the great branches above them & the high pale moon beaming through;—all this might seem, perhaps, a little variation from the routine of Chatham st. & Lake Quinsigamond;[74] but it seemed to me very natural & reasonable, & I had only to accept my share of sweet potatoes & peanuts from the ashes, & listen with infinite gusto to the unequalled comic display with which ole Cato, the orator of the circle was narrating his escape from "de seceshky."

And this after four days only!

The camp is on a picturesque plantation with superb trees; though the live oaks have but a deathly beauty. I am well & live very comfortably & have nice cooking & most excellent officers who have received me in the most unexceptionable way. There is nothing in the world which Gen Saxton will not do for me & the regiment within the limits of his power—unfortunately he is at some points checked & hindered by Gen. Brannan—still when Hunter arrives he will be more free. It is his darling hobby & my only fear is of his doing too much. It is amusing to me to find myself keeping him back. He is a thoroughly admirable man, such as it is astounding that West Point & the army have left so unspoiled.

Do not regret that I am here. I shld. hv. missed the best fortune of my life had I not come & this I shld. say were I recalled tomorrow. It does not tire me so much as our Camp in Worcester did, & will still less after things are more thoroughly in order. I do not have the tiresome nightwork which I had nearly once a week there, as officer of the day. At present we are not likely to have any more expeditions—as we are to get better drilled first: those were a sort of guerilla affair, though the men did splendidly.

Please write profusely—ever with love.

T. W. H.

We had 518 in Camp by today's morning report.

74. TWH lived on Chatham Street in Worcester, Massachusetts; Lake Quinsigamond, just outside Worcester to the east, was where he often went swimming, boating, bird-watching and flower-gathering.

*"I enjoy it all exceedingly, I assure you"*
To James T. Fields
Headquarters 1st Reg't
South Carolina Volunteers
Camp Saxton
Beaufort. S.C.

*Dear friend*

Does it seem odd to think of me as commanding at Dress Parade in a jet black regiment, standing before a line of countenances so dusky that I can't see whether they stir during Parade Rest, & causing five hundred inky hands to flop down together at the word "Shoulder Arms"?[75] Can you fancy me strolling out at evening & coming upon a great circle of my soldiers sitting blissfully around a campfire, the light blazing on their scarlet trousers & scarcely less on their shiny faces & ivory teeth & rolling eyes, all lighted up with merriment as "ole man Cato" narrated, with infinite mimicry & dramatic fun, his escape from "de seceshkey"?—The flame glimmering up also into a vast patriarchal live oak, with its thousand funereal pendants of gray moss overhanging the group—& the high & silent moon over all. Yet these things seem matters of course to me already, after being here four days.

The regiment now comprises 518 men & they are constantly coming in; well organized in ten companies & well officered. They are very much like white soldiers only more joyous & more docile & learn the drill quite as readily. I enjoy it all exceedingly, I assure you.

What I want to ask of you is to get for me & send by mail the following books, addressing me at Beaufort. S.C.

1. Beard's Life of Toussaint L'Ouverture[76] (there is a cheap English Edition, by some Unitarian publisher)

2. Nells' Colored Patriots of the Revolution[77] (for sale at Antislavery office 221 Wash. St.) & charge them to me.

75. Parade rest is a particular stance adopted during the ceremony of dress parade, with the right foot six inches behind the left heel, left knee slightly bent, body upright upon the right leg, rifle resting upon the right shoulder held by two hands crossed in front with their backs outward, the left hand uppermost; in this position "the soldier will remain silent and motionless," *Regulations*, 41. Upon the order to shoulder arms, the soldier is to "drop the left hand quickly by the side," Casey, *Infantry Tactics*, 1:39, 40.

76. John Reilly Beard, *The Life of Toussaint L'Ouverture, The Negro Patriot of Hayti: Comprising an Account of the Struggle for Liberty in the Island, and a Sketch of Its History to the Present Period* (London: Ingram, Cooke, and Co., 1853).

77. William C. Nell, *The Colored Patriots of the American Revolution with Sketches of Several Distinguished Colored Persons. To Which Is Added a Brief Survey of the Condition and Prospects of Colored Americans* (Boston: R. F. Wallcut, 1855).

I suppose you sent me, at Worcester, the copies of Atlantics containing my Insurrection Papers[78] for wh. I sent, & my wife has probably forwarded them in a package as they arrived too late. If you did not, please mail them to me.

With kind regards to Mrs. Fields

I am sir cordially
T. W. Higginson
Col. Commanding
1st Reg't S.C.V.

I send for Mrs. Field's autograph collection a document from one of my black sergeants.

*"the vexed ghosts of departed slave-lords of the soil"*
To Mary Channing Higginson
Camp Saxton
Dec. 10. 1862

Dearest, Some one is going straight to N.Y. tomorrow, who will take & mail this, so it may reach you before one which I sent to the office yesterday. I then wrote also to Waldo: with which exception I have hardly written to any one but you. Of course I wrote to Ingersoll Bowditch.

There was a report of steamers last night, but they brought no mail only papers to Dec. 3. wh. I hv. not seen. No letters yet fr. thee save the 2 first (Nov 20 & 22) which came together. Very soon a steamer must come & bring me several. I have written twice a week to you. Nov. 25. 28. Dec. 3. 6. 9. Probably our communication may be somewhat diminished by the Banks expedition, taking some vessels wh. used to ply here.

The change of destiny of the Banks expedition affects us somewhat, diminishing the chance of our being used in any grand advance, & leaving us to smaller forays—but as yet we are not well drilled enough for even those. I now drill a different company each day, in order to observe their weak spots. I don't see that they do better than white troops, but they do as well.

My Lieut. Col. & Major are both quite efficient in recruiting, wh. is important. Tomorrow they go down the coast to Fernandina & St. Augustine, for recruits & will probably bring back nearly enough to fill us to the minimum number 830. We are 633 today.

78. Thomas Wentworth Higginson, "The Maroons of Jamaica," *Atlantic Monthly* 5 (February 1860), 213–22; idem, "The Maroons of Surinam," *Atlantic Monthly* 5 (May 1860), 549–57; idem, "Denmark Vesey," *Atlantic Monthly* 7 (June 1861), 728–44; idem, "Nat Turner's Insurrection," *Atlantic Monthly* 8 (August 1861), 173–87; idem, "Gabriel's Defeat," *Atlantic Monthly* 10 (September 1862), 337–45. These essays on slave revolts were later collected, with several other historical essays, in idem, *Travellers and Outlaws: Episodes in American History* (Boston: Lee and Shephard, 1889).

When the steamer comes in I look anxiously for Dr Rogers from whom I hv. heard nothing. James I fear cannot get here so soon. You know he is to be Captain—the only vacancy now left among the officers. Young Kemp, who came on with me in the steamer, has decided not to join us, for which I am sorry, as he is a nice fellow—but he may be Sup't on this very plantation.

This morning we had a white frost, but the day grew mild as usual. My little stove is burning—I call it Fever & ague, from its intermittent heats & chills.

Who should drive out to see me today but Harriet Tubman who is living in Beaufort as a sort of nurse & general care taker; she sent her regards to you. All sorts of unexpected people turn up here.

I live comfortably, darling, & Wm & Hetty give us nice things to eat: oysters twice a day lately & perennial corn bread, sweet potatoes & hominy all cooked to perfection. Pigs run about the camp & exasperate me by marring the dignity of dress parade, till I almost resolve to let the soldiers kill them—I would if they were composed of anything but pork.

I wish you could see how pretty our encampment looks, with it's 250 tents glimmering white in the moonlight, on the level plain which is swept smooth every day:—the dying cook fires glimmering within the picturesque palmetto enclosures. The wild curlews hover & wail all night invisibly around us in the air, like vexed ghosts of departed slave-lords

## *"I seem like Rajah Brooke in Borneo"*
To Louisa Storrow Higginson
Headquarters 1st Reg. S.C.V.
Camp Saxton
Beaufort S.C.
Dec. 10. 1862

*Dearest Mother*

There is a chance of sending by a passenger to N.Y. obtaining a little more speed than usual, & so I will write a word. I am perfectly well & stationary here in camp, as we ought to be for a month to come, to get the men well drilled—or partially drilled, at least. We are now living in our tents wh. is far pleasanter. I have a nice little single bedstead wh. came accidentally into my hands, I sleep very comfortably on & in blankets—have a secretary to write at, two chairs & two pails of water, & everything handsome about me, like Dogberry.[79] A little camp stove which I call *fever & ague*, al-

79. Dogberry, a constable, in William Shakespeare's *Much Ado About Nothing* (1598): "I am a wise fellow, and which is more, an officer, and which is more, a householder, and which is more, as pretty a piece of flesh as any is in Messina, and one that knows the law, go to, and a rich fellow enough, go to, and a fellow that hath had losses, and one that hath

ways hot or cold—no bottom to it, set on sand, a tunnel & a funnel. The adjutant & I board with a nice pair, William & Hetty, just outside the lines & have abundance of milk, oysters, corn bread & hominy. The days are mild & sunny, the nights cold & sometimes a white frost.

My regiment has now 630 & they come in tolerably fast. They are easy to discipline & drill, & do as well as any white reg't of equal date,—as well as the 51st. I enjoy it all very much & hv. never for a moment regretted my promotion: though, without my two months in that regiment, it wd. hv. been almost impossible for me to undertake this. As it is I find no great difficulties to encounter, & the work is not so hard as in the 51st, & quite as interesting.

No tidings yet of Dr. Rogers or his nephew James—indeed I hv. only heard once fr. home & that a few days after arriving—several mails are now due. The Banks expedition having passed here, we probably shall not have a very favorable chance for communication with the North, this winter, so many transports have been taken up by that. I hardly know if I am glad or sorry that Banks has not come here—I mean, I don't know whether this regiment will gain or lose by it.—as likely to gain.

As I sit in my tent door & adjudicate contested cases where the lingo is almost inexplicable, and the dusky faces grow radiant & sometimes majestic with eager expression, I seem like Rajah Brooke in Borneo.[80] Or like Whittier's lost Southern playmate,

"The dusky children of the sun
Before me come & go."[81]

---

two gowns, and everything handsome about him." William Shakespeare, *Much Ado About Nothing*, in *The Complete Works*, ed. Stanley Wells and Gary Taylor (Oxford: Clarendon Press, 1986), IV.ii.77–83.

80. Sir James Brooke, Rajah of Sarawak (1803–1868). Higginson may have known of Rajah Brooke from Sir Henry Keppel, *The Expedition to Borneo of H.M.S. Dido for the Suppression of Piracy: With Extracts from the Journal of James Brooke, esq. of Sarawak*... (New York: Chapman and Hall, 1846), or from one of Brooke's own publications, e.g., Sir James Brooke, *Narrative of Events in Borneo and Celebes, Down to the Occupation of Labuan: From the Journals of James Brooke esq., Rajah of Sarawak, and Governor of Labuan* (London: J. Murray, 1848), or idem, *The Private Letters of Sir James Brooke, Rajah of Sarawak, Narrating the Events of His Life from 1836 to the Present Time*, 3 vols. (London: Bentley, 1853). See also G. Reynolds, "Borneo and Rajah Brooke," *Atlantic Monthly* 18 (December 1866), 667–82.

81. John Greenleaf Whittier (1807–1892), a poet, abolitionist, and editor. His "My Playmate," appeared in *Home Ballads & Poems* (Boston: Ticknor & Fields, 1860). "She lives where all the golden year / Her summer roses blow; / The dusky children of the sun / Before her come and go." *American Poetry: The Nineteenth Century*, vol. 1 (New York: The Library of America, 1993), 470. TWH wrote about him in "John Greenleaf Whittier," *Contemporaries*, The Writings of Thomas Wentworth Higginson, Vol. II (Boston: Houghton, Mifflin, 1900), 60–71.

This level sand, these white tents, these flickering nightly fires, these picturesque palmetto huts, these wild nocturnal orgies, half camp meeting, half fandango[82] make me feel as if I had passed into some remote quarter of the globe. The very listening to these people is like adjusting the ear to some foreign tongue. Imagine one of the camp washerwomen saying to me dramatically today "I took she when she am dat high, & now if him wants to leave we, bet he go," the person thus chaotically portrayed being a little adopted girl who had deserted her.

Gen Saxton has to encounter so many petty obstacles that I sometimes think any of his plans may any day fail, despite his great capacities, & thus we be set adrift. But if I were to be thrown out of the service tomorrow, I never shld. be sorry for having left the 51st Reg't. so interesting & valuable to me has been my whole experience here.

My opportunity proved a failure, but I can send this somehow ere long.

Ever thine

T. W. H.

## "these will yet have to fight to get the promise fulfilled"
To Louisa Storrow Higginson
Camp Saxton. Dec. 22. 1862.

*Dearest Mother*

I cannot write much, but hearing that Lieut. Washburn[83] (brother of John Washburn—he is a cavalry officer) is going straight to Worcester tomorrow, I want to send some letters—the mail goes more slowly.

My birthday has been celebrated chiefly by raising our great garrison flag whose flagstaff is before my tent door. Gen. Saxton was here to see our "battalion drill"; I drew them up before the flag and presented arms to it; then they gave 3 cheers for "the red white & blue", which they know all about. Gen. Saxton was sweet & cordial as he always is & says he never comes without finding some improvement, though he comes every other day, almost.

I enjoy the battalion drill, every afternoon very much—they "formed square" on the third drill, which any masculine observer will tell you (Lizzie doubtless knows too) is getting on wonderfully fast.

For New Years Day, Gen. Saxton plans a great gathering of all the freed people of the department, here, oxen barbecued, speeches &c. Probably it

---

82. A lively Spanish or Spanish-American dance in triple time; also nonsense or tomfoolery.

83. Lieutenant Colonel Francis Washburn, 4th Massachusetts Cavalry.

will take place; & really it is as great a time for them as the 1st August in the West Indies,[84] only that these will yet have to fight to get the promise fulfilled. If the devotion of Gen. Saxton's life can sustain them, they will have it. How you wd. admire him.

I have yr. second letter, mailed Dec. 8. Tell Louisa her lines fr. Luria were thrilling & fascinating; I cannot recall them. I shld. like them written in the beginning of my journal, Anna's copy. I am so glad she is making one, because I am not going to write anything for print, now, & this will be my only memorial of this most interesting experience.

I fare very well, have plenty & variety of food, except meat, for which I have oysters—& am perfectly well. As to cold one finds out by degrees how to avoid it—water has been once skinned over in my tent & my odd little stove "Fever & Ague", keeps me too warm in the evenings, often. We expect the Delaware in every day, with Dr Rogers & James, I hope.

This is all I can write—Mary will send you some Journals.

Ever thine
T. W. H.

## "How happy I was"
To Louisa Storrow Higginson
Camp Saxton
Dec. 26. 1862.

*Dearest Mother*

I shall hv. no time to write more than a note. Just at dinner time on Christmas Day, as we had been taking a preliminary bath in the river, down skimmed a boat & out stepped Dr. Rogers & James. How happy I was. I hadn't known I shld. care half so much & did not till then realize that I had been entirely among strangers—so easily had I made myself at home.

They are pleased with everything & every body likes them. With them came Gen. Seymour whom they like & who was with Maj: Andersen in Fort Sumter. He is not aware that he is to succeed Gen. Saxton, nor do we believe it at all. Also came Gen. Saxton's nice old father fr. Deerfield who is to be his private Sec'y—also, Messrs. Hawks & Wright of Deerfield, who are to hv. charge of this plantation, vice the present occupant. They don't look interesting.

I send Gen Saxton's Proclamation. We are to have a celebration here on Jan. 1, & our flags presented—there is another set *beside* Mr. French's.

My new guests are to board with the Adjutant & me, & they think we

84. West Indian Independence Day, August 1, was often celebrated by abolitionists in the United States.

live in clover, as we do. The regiment gets on very well & numbers now 733. or properly 746. I don't suppose this quiet life will last many weeks longer—we are improving fast in drill.

Mary will probably have a chance to send very soon, by Thomas Earle[85] who is coming out here, a small bundle, but I have what I really need. She will have a small instalment of Journal to send you, but not very much. I am more busy just now, but it may not last.

Ever affectionately<br>
T. W. H.

Being sleepy, I have after all said nothing of yr. letter mailed the 16th wh. arrived the 25th (they had a week's passage, unusually long.) Thank you for it all. Mr. Ingersoll's lines are very ingenious, & Anne's letter was delightful to me: I shall write to her.

## *"The Freedom Jubilee"*
### To Louisa Storrow Higginson
### Camp Saxton. Jan. 2. 1862 (i.e., 1863)

*Dearest Mother*

I have only time to write a word, but have sent Mary a long account of the Freedom Jubilee of yesterday which was a complete success & a very happy scene. Some thousands of people here & all went off well. In the evening we got letters which was very nice—it was the same on Christmas Day & on my birthday. Yours came telling me about the Fire at the Hospital &c & you said Anna was going to write but she didn't. Waldo & Sally Bowditch[86] wrote also, wh. was kind. I get the NY Tribune regularly (Daily) & Boston papers only occasionally & hear about once in 10 days so don't feel far from home.

In the meeting yesterday it was announced that Fremont was Commander in Chief wh. was received with enthusiasm of course. The pickets above shouted it across—a way news often gets to Beaufort days before a mail.[87]

I enjoy having Dr Rogers & James—& want for nothing. They mess with the Adj't & me. Both are very efficient & popular already. The reg't has now 750 & there are 100 waiting for us, to be sent for, at St. Augustine.

Among the Superintendents here yesterday were Mr. & Miss Ware, children of H. Jr.—& H[ ] a young minister their cousin—all adorned

85. Second Lieutenant Thomas Earle, a friend from Worcester who served in the Massachusetts 25th.

86. Waldo Higginson, TWH's brother; Sarah Rhea Higginson Bowditch of Brookline, Massachusetts (TWH's first cousin, who married William Ingersoll Bowditch).

87. Charlotte Forten, more suspiciously, noted in her journal that "as it was picket news, I greatly fear that it is not true." She was right. *The Journals of Charlotte Forten Grimké*, ed. Brenda Stevenson (New York: Oxford University Press, 1988), 431.

in the inevitable goo[ ][88] of wares. The new Sup'ts on this plantation are named Wright & Hawks, both fr. Deerfield, & looking rather nonplussed under the new circumstances of farming. Old Mr. Saxton is here to be his son's secretary, a dear old soul. We hear good accounts of Gen. Seymour.[89] The military men say the army will never obey Fremont.

## *"nothing in the landscape to show aught but beautiful peace"*
## To Louisa Storrow Higginson
## Morris Island[90]
## Jan. 6. 1863

*Dearest Mother*

I am here as witness before a Court Martial & very glad to have this glimpse at the place. I am sitting in Gen. Stevenson's[91] headqrs. where the Ct. is held, close by the beautiful beach with the great roar perpetual of ocean outside, of which cannonading would seem an idle interruption though we heard a little of it outside. Still in coming the length of Folly Island & then looking about here, the accumulation of tents & men & teams among these sandbanks looks so wonderfully aimless—such an antlike activity with no sight or sound of any supposed object—it seems like a deaf man's glance at an orchestra in full blast. If one did not know that Cartridge boxes & cannon meant war, there is nothing in the landscape to show aught but beautiful peace. Folly Island is wooded, much more than I expected; this island is bare, but the interior country is softened by woods & white buildings or villages gleam out here & there with that fascinating interest which all within the rebel lines possesses—"so near & yet so far."[92]

## Thursday. Folly Island

I am as far as Stono Inlet[93] on my way home, waiting here for a steamer. I staid two nights with Col. Halliwell[94] of the Mass 54th, a splendid fellow.

88. The manuscript is illegible here.

89. General Truman Seymour assumed command at Port Royal Island, December 26, 1862.

90. Morris Island is near the entrance to Charleston Harbor, South Carolina.

91. Brigadier General Thomas G. Stevenson.

92. "He seems so near and yet so far": Alfred Lord Tennyson, "In Memoriam," Canto 97, *The Works of Alfred Lord Tennyson*, ed. Hallam Lord Tennyson, 6 vols. (New York: Macmillan, 1908), 2:407.

93. Folly Island at Stono Inlet is just south of Morris Island, at the entrance to Charleston Harbor.

94. Colonel Edward N. Hallowell.

Morris Island is bare, cold, forlorn, crowded, no room for the camps. Folly Island is picturesque & charming a superb hard beach for 7 miles with the sand bluffs wooded or bushy & far more becoming to the shore than our barer ones. The camps are beautifully arranged along this bluff & many had been trimmed for Christmas with arches & wreaths of evergreen, so it seemed a triumphal way along the beach. Gen. Gillmore's quarters are two miles from here.

I had to leave Beaufort before the mail was sorted, so have nothing yet by the Fulton. My health is about the same—no worse. Every thing portends a quiet winter at least for us, as Gen. Gillmore told me he shld. not move us from Beaufort except in some special exigency—and as I find all other regiments are longing to get to Beaufort I suppose this is to be considered good luck.

I had no chance to go to the other end of Morris Island it rained so & was so misty. I could have seen nothing otherwise I should hv. visited Forts Wagner & Gregg.[95]

The New Year's Jubilee wd. have been a great affair but for the unusual cold & went off well as it was. My sword is very handsome. The next day the Tribune correspondent came to camp for my speech & the inscription on the sword. Of course I can't give the former, but gave the latter. "Tiffany & Co New York" wh. he thought brief & appropriate. There was no time for any other. In haste

T. W. H.

We hv. had mercury down to +20° at night, & hardly above freezing all one day

*"lovely weather, rosebuds, moonlight and soft airs"*
To Louisa Storrow Higginson
Camp Saxton
Jan. 7. 1863.

*Dearest Mother*

I hear there is a mail going today, so will write a few words. All well & happy I enjoy myself greatly with Dr. Rogers & James. We are having lovely weather, rosebuds, moonlight & soft airs; but yesterday a furious rain, about the first since I came. It was six weeks yesterday since I took

95. Confederate Batteries Wagner and Gregg, on Morris Island, assaulted and overcome later in the year; Gregg was at the northern tip of the island, while Wagner was about a mile south of there, at a narrow part of the island.

command & for the first time I rode down to Beaufort, visited some camps & dined with Gen. Saxton.

I also saw Gen. Seymour whom I thoroughly liked—manly & true & though somewhat conservative not wholly so. But he is *under* the objectionable Brannan, who however has never troubled *me*.

The pickets shouted news yesterday that an armistice was declared for 6 mos. but nobody believes it.

In haste thine<br>T. W. H.

*"You don't know how pastoral I feel"*
TO MARY CHANNING HIGGINSON
CAMP SAXTON. JAN. 9. 1863.

Dearest I see no way save to be "writing & flinging in blindly" as Charlotte hath it. Vessels are now coming & going all the time, many with troops; but they say there is to be no forward movement here for six weeks, I suppose for fear the Charlestonians shldnt. be ready. We hv. had officers by dozens to see us, for two or three days, if they mean half what they say, they think well of us—at any rate they ought to do so. No tidings of Montgomery[96] yet, but his camp is laid out, close by ours. Tonight Dr. Rogers has ridden over to St. Helena Island, to visit Miss Forten, who sends us little ginger Cakes—which by the way Dr R. basely locks up in his absence. They are nice & it's too bad. Our sick list is larger since the expedition, fr. excitement fatigue &c, & it troubles the Dr. These men are not tough, not so much as the officers. I hv. been uniformly well, nary pellet. Today it is warmer again. James & I bathed in river, frogs sang loud at evening (a recent accomplishment) & the mockingbird is extending his song. You don't know how pastoral I feel, when I contemplate my little flock of sheep straying round to find something to nibble; as soon as they succeed they will grow fat & we shall nibble them. They are proslavery sheep, as Kansas used to say. Adjutant's wife daily expected sailed fr. NY. in a barque Jan. 30.—then comes wedding, 8th Maine band, regiment in a hollow square, bride & bridegroom in middle, pho-

---

96. Colonel James Montgomery, whom TWH had known as a daring scout in Kansas, and had enlisted to lead his abortive 1860 scheme to rescue Albert Hazlett and A. D. Stevens, the associates of John Brown, when they were awaiting trial in Virginia. Montgomery now commanded the 2d South Carolina Volunteers, another black regiment that was being raised.

tographer astride. The good soul is quite bent on this mode of matrimony. The cloud that hangs over it is, all the women per. last boat were sent straight back & he is trying to dodge that result. I think the course &c will run smooth.—Dr Rogers Jas & I hv. unanimously elected Miss Forten fille du regiment; I forget whether this was the cause or consequence of ginger cakes. Do you know at Fernandina I tea'd with 3 schoolmistresses & it was quite bewildering, I had forgotten there were so many women in the world. Then I dined with Mrs Col Hawley[97] of Hartford & her sister Miss Foote, cousins of Emily Hale's & pleasant; I knew them here first. I gave them a sheep. Here I never see a white woman, save 2 Irish Lieutenantesses just going North—& Mrs. Dr. Hawks who stays out here occasionally.

I hv. sent for two more Lieuts. fr. the 51st, Stephen Greene whom Marg. knows & a young man named Stayner. I have sent also for a young man fr. Boston highly recommended by W Phillips & Theoph. Parsons,[98] one of the Cadets named J. W. M. Appleton, but not one of *the* A's[99] probably. I infer fr. what somebody writes that Thos. Earle says he was to hv. been Senior Captain in 2d. Reg't—not at all—*a* Capt. he probably wd. hv. been. What a miserable business all that is. Dr. R. groans over it, I doubt if Jas knows it. James was prevented fr. the most adventurous parts of an expedition, but did splendidly whatever he undertook, as he always does; I am thankful I made him Capt. instead of Lt. He is a great favorite, with officers & men, as is the Dr. The latter is already the universal confidante, of course, if the officers want me to do anything they tell him. His whole heart is in this thing, even more than you cd. hv. supposed.

The paymaster is at Hilton Head & I hope to get *some* money within a fortnight. Goodbye my darling I love your little pencillings by the way. I hv. written to Jas. Fields abt my book[100] & asked him to send me Titan as you don't seem to hv. bought it. Ever thine

97. Wife of Colonel J. R. Hawley.

98. Wendell Phillips (1811–1884), an orator, vehement antislavery crusader (as well as women's rights and labor reformer) with whom TWH had been regularly associated. TWH wrote of him in "Wendell Phillips," *Contemporaries*, The Writings of Thomas Wentworth Higginson, Vol. II (Boston: Houghton, Mifflin, 1900), 257–79. Theophilus Parsons (1797–1882), lawyer and professor of law at Harvard.

99. TWH's maternal grandfather, Thomas Storrow, had married Anne Appleton, so the question here is whether this cadet is perhaps a member of that family.

100. TWH's *Outdoor Papers* (Boston: Ticknor and Fields, 1863).

## "I feel like Hosea Biglow's militia officer"
## TO MARY CHANNING HIGGINSON
## CAMP SAXTON. JAN. 14. 1863.

*Dearest*

Another mail is just in 5 days only from it's predecessor; & I hv. two letters—fr. Abby Hutchinson[101] & from Mrs. Brown[102]—so you see there is
some use in female friends: she gave me news of you two days later than
you did, madam. I have also a newspaper of the 6th, though I hv. never received any from you dear. Today we have a great squad of recruits fr.
Florida, nearly ninety—filling the regiment to about 850, thus making it
the legal size & pleasing Gen. Saxton very much. He is still teased by Brannan, but Gen. Hunter is constantly expected. I sent you 2 sheets of journal
the 5th darling & $2\frac{1}{2}$ on the 13th.

We are constantly improving & shall soon march up to Beaufort & be
reviewed by Gen. Saxton. I hv. been several times to Beaufort, last time in
a boat; the boatmen sang to me all the way; I am taking down many of
these "spirituals"[103]—they are fascinating. I kept the men waiting for my
return & said I was sorry—one of them said cheerily "Wait all day upon
you, Cunnel"—afterwards he said "I told de boys upon de wharf, see
yonder, boys, him dar's our Cunnel, him's de best man in de state," & then
he covered his face like a child, as if he had gone too far. What do you
think I went for, to a tailor's, a black tailor's. I hv. bought Dr. Rogers uniform coat, made by Theo, had it let out in the chest, the back & waist being perfect & it is the most elegant garment I ever had. When any
occasion requires the Doctor to be magnificent, I am to whip off my
shoulderstraps & put on his. So we shall both hv. a dress coat. No longer
will the sentinels in Beaufort shoulder arms remotely to my buttons
(salute for a Captain) & then hastily present arms when my Colonel's
straps come within ken. I feel like Hosea Biglow's militia officer, who had
brass enough outside "let alone what natur had sot in his featers, to make
a 6-pounder out on."[104] Also I wear little white chokers, like what Marg.

101. Abby Hutchinson was a young woman TWH had known from antislavery and
other reform associations, member of a family singing group that performed at antislavery meetings.

102. Possibly the wife of TWH's Worcester friend, Theophilus Brown, the tailor.

103. One of the first serious collectors of African-American vernacular music,
TWH first published many of them in "Negro Spirituals," *Atlantic Monthly* 19 (June
1867), 685–94; this essay later became chapter 9 of *Army Life in a Black Regiment*.

104. James Russell Lowell issued *The Biglow Papers* (Cambridge: George Nichols,
1848), collecting satirical texts he had previously published in the *Boston Courier* 1846–

always yearned for. Shan't I send you a "Daguerre."[105] Dr. Hawks' wife has come to live in camp, a tall, good-natured rather girlish young woman. We have a sort of circus tent, made of old sails, where she & the Chaplain teach, & they have "shouts" in the evening. She brought some lovely English violets just plucked in Beaufort. I often think, now, how this winter climate wd. delight you, for you would not feel the nights in the house & you wd. revel in the days. This morning was May. Yesterday I saw 4 blue birds, & a butterfly. I like the climate ever so much better than at first, though Jas & Dr. both think it debilitating; still the latter is better, than at home, though his work tires him; but now we hv. a second ass't surgeon, whom he likes. There is certainly less coughing in the camp. I laugh at Dr. R. for the delight with which he talked with a Dr. who had been among yellow fever at Key West—had 200 cases of it.

*"one of the most daring expeditions of the war"*
To Louisa Storrow Higginson
Steamer Ben Deford
Feb. 1. 1863. 9 Pm.

*Dearrest Mother*

Tomorrow morning we shall be in Beaufort & I may have a chance to send this, & I will merely say that we hv. made one of the most daring expeditions of the war, forty miles up the St. Mary's river fought a Cavalry Company in open field & defeated it overwhelmingly & many other things wh. you will see in my Report to Gen Saxton. The men have behaved splendidly & I hv. enjoyed it inexpressibly. When the whole is known, it will establish past question the reputation of the regiment. In haste thine

T. W. H.

We hv. iron, lumber, rice, a flock of sheep, 7 prisoners, a cannon & a flag! It has been just *my* luck.

---

1848, in which, in homely New England dialect, the patriotic jingoism of Mexican War fever was ridiculed. Hosea Biglow, a country youth visiting Boston, resists (despite the glamorous appearance of the officer) the importuning of a "cruetin Sarjunt" who tries to enlist him, an officer who "hed as much as 20 Rooster's tales stuck onto his hat and een-amost enuf brass a bobbin up and down on his shoulders and figureed onto his coat and trousis, let alone wut nater hed sot in his featers, to make a 6 pounder out on." *The Biglow Papers [First Series]*, ed. Thomas Wortham (DeKalb: Northern Illinois University Press, 1977), 49.

105. A photograph made according to the process invented by Louis Daguerre, using a light-sensitive silver-coated metallic plate; these were popular with Civil War soldiers as souvenirs for loved ones.

*"the regiment goes on improving"*
To Louisa Storrow Higginson
Camp Saxton, Feb 16, 1863

*Dearest Mother*

I will write a line, having sent Journals to Mary. Since our expedition we
have been quiet, though I don't know how long we may remain so. We
have just had letters & papers up to the 6th, but my report had not been received—it has reached you long ere this, I suppose. Our trip was certainly
a complete success. [ ][106] trouble about Charleston was much greater at
the North than we felt here. Troops are gathering here & are to move ere
long, apparently—but I think it quite as likely that we may be ordered to
some other station: where my action would be more independent. The
regiment goes on improving—now they hv. got dark blue pants which they
like far better than the odious red. They look very neat & assisted at the
nuptials of our adjutant & Miss Hattie A. Somerby, with great decorum. It
is growing springlike here now, flowers opening & mocking birds practic-
ing new solos every morning

Today I am going down to Hilton Head for the first time, to see Gen.
Hunter about several matters. Some of the new-landed regiments have
been behaving very badly towards the negroes the Mass. 24th formerly
Col. Stevenson's, among them—but not in this neighborhood.

Ever thine
T. W. H.[107]

*"the personal experience of these men has been a liberal education to them"*
To Ralph Waldo Emerson
Headquarters 1st Reg. S.C.V.
Camp Saxton. Feb. 20. 1863

*Dear Sir*

I thought it might be pleasant for you to know that your Hymn[108] was
read aloud to this regiment during the services last Sunday, by our good

106. The manuscript is illegible here.
107. A map drawn by Higginson showing the road from Beaufort to Hilton Head,
with Camp Saxton in between, can be seen in the gallery.
108. Ralph Waldo Emerson, "Boston Hymn," *Atlantic Monthly* 11 (February 1863),
227–28. Read at the Boston Music Hall, January 1, 1863, in a celebration of the Emancipation Proclamation, the poem presents the voice of an angry God declaring, "I break
your bonds and masterships, / And I unchain the slave: / Free be his heart and hand
henceforth, / As wind and wandering wave" (p. 228).

Dr. Rogers. It was his own impulse to do it, and I was glad to have it done. For though they might not understand all the verses in detail, yet the spirit of the hymn was evidently comprehended. The personal experience of these men has been a liberal education to them, in respect to the principles of liberty; on that point their minds are very clear, you cannot entangle them nor sophisticate them.

Very respectfully yours<br>
T. W. Higginson, Col. comdg

I send some autographs of my Sergeants, which may interest you.

*"a very good test of the men"*
To Louisa Storrow Higginson
Headquarters &c
1st Reg. S.C.V.
Camp Saxton. Feb. 24. 1863

*Dearest Mother*

Grass is growing green, jasmines twine & blossom in the tree tops & fill my tent with fragrance, peas are two inches high on some of the islands, & it is as raw & chilly a day as one could desire to shiver in.

I have heard fr. Mary since my Report[109] arrived, but not from any others of my kin. The Affair was a very good test of the men, who behaved very well. I think it very probable that we may be ordered away from here to some other point ere long, for they do not mean to give us any prominent share in the advance on Charleston; & will be more likely to send us elsewhere.

The more I can be thrown by myself & left free to act, the better I shall like it. Col. Montgomery arrived last night, with 120 men as the nucleus of his regiment, & he will be sent with us wherever we go, probably. His military experience will be of unspeakable value to me; how far our ideas of discipline will coincide, I don't know; it looks as if they would be less strict.

I am unspeakably grateful that I got into this service, not merely from its opportunities & interests but, because there is so much that is petty and unsatisfactory in these ordinary military arrangements that I am well out of them. I enjoy the method & system of the army, but it by its very nature puts so much power into such poor hands, from McClellan downward.

Our army does not seem to me as vicious as many suppose—but slouchy & slovenly, ill-kept & ill-handled. In this respect the navy is far su-

109. "Report of Col. T. W. Higginson, First South Carolina Infantry (Union)," *The War of the Rebellion: A Compilation of the Official Records of the Union and Confederate Armies*, Series I, Vol. XIV (Washington: Government Printing Office, 1885), 195–98.

perior to it; there is an universal neatness & discipline which forms a re-freshing contrast. Water is a cleaner element to be sure.

I am perfectly well—Mary will send you a sheet of journal. The steamer is whistling which is to stop here for letters. Ever affectionately

T. W. H.

*"I liked the absence of cant"*
To Louisa Storrow Higginson
Headquarters 1st Reg. S.C.V.
Camp Saxton
March 3. 1863

*Dearest Mother*

I am trying to get a chance to write but the men hv. been paid today—alas, not the officers—& they keep coming to consult me about private affairs. We are under marching or rather sailing orders & expect to remove to another camp ere long—where, I cannot properly say—*not* very near Charleston, I assure you.

Opinions differ here about the attack on that city, supposing it to be that, but the general impression is sanguine, though they are keeping the vessels here most unreasonably. But the delay cannot last much longer.

This photograph may puzzle you but it is Higginsony & handsome. It is Lieut H P Higginson,[110] now Sec'y to some General in Tennessee; he is son of Perkins H.[111] who sent this photograph as the best recommenda-tion. Their letters were very cordial & simple, & did not even go so far as to affect the slightest interest in the peculiar characteristics of the regiment—only dwelling on the prospects of promotion involved—not precisely the way to propitiate either Gen. Saxton or myself—though I liked the absence of cant. His chances are not great there being such a competition for these Commissions. Two Captains in the Maine 8th wish to be transferred to the same rank in the 2d Reg't.

I dined with Gen. Saxton today & was interested to find that he was Lieut. under Gen. Phelps[112] as Captain—in Texas.[113] He praised Gen

110. Perhaps Henry Frederick Higginson, TWH's first cousin.
111. Perhaps James Perkins Higginson (TWH's uncle), father of Henry Frederick Higginson.
112. Brigadier General John W. Phelps, a Vermont abolitionist, who in 1862 orga-nized five companies of black soldiers to defend Camp Parapet near New Orleans; when his superior, General Benjamin Butler, ordered him to put these recruits to work as la-borers, he resigned in protest, writing, "I am not willing to become the mere slave-driver you propose, having no qualifications that way," and returned to Vermont.
113. I.e., in the Mexican War.

P's knowledge & sincerity, & told odd stories of him. He was somewhat ill in those days & fancied he was losing his mind, so made Saxton play chess with him at daybreak daily to test it. Gen. S. said they were hard games to play—if Gen Phelps lost, he was convinced his mind was failing—if he won, he accused Gen. S. of not trying to beat him & drew the same inference so it had to be a series of drawn games.

Gen Saxton thinks it wd. be very improper to antedate Gen S's commission & make him outrank men of more service & does not think Gen. P. would favor it.

My eyes are closing. Direct Hilton Head S.C.

Ever affectionately
T. W. H.

*"we sail for Fernandina"*
To———
STEAMER BOSTON
HEADQRS. ATLANTIC OCEAN
—OR RATHER HILTON HEAD
WHERE WE LIE TILL AFTN
MARCH. 6. 1863

then we sail for Fernandina, arriving early in the morning.

Just got yr. letters written after hearing of our expedition—they went via Newbern

My headquarters are on this str. Col. Montgomery is on "Burnside" & Lt. Col. Billings on "John Adams." We move the whole camp—to remain

Direct to Port Royal, S.C. for the present. Letters will arrive about as often, but a few days older.

All well

Ever thine
T. W. H.

*"A little skirmishing at present, but no great danger"*
To LOUISA STORROW HIGGINSON
HEADQUARTERS. JACKSONVILLE.
MARCH 12. 1863.

*Dearest Mother*

We have taken the prettiest town I hv. seen, without a gun: pretty river, trees & houses. My abode is a sort of palace: one of the finest houses I ever saw, with even a billiard room. It is a very healthy place. & once New England-y & prosperous, as was the whole river.

Ever thine, in haste<br>T. W. H.

A little skirmishing at present, but no great danger

*"we have had rather an anxious time"*
To Louisa Storrow Higginson
Headquarters. Jacksonville
March 19. 1863
Midnight

*Dearest Mother*

All well & safe though we have had rather an anxious time, holding with 900 men a post twice before held & evacuated by our troops because it was supposed to require a garrison of 5000. Tonight reinforcements hv. arrived & we are all right; it really is not a hard place in itself as you will see by the map I send,[114] an almost impassable swampy creek surrounding part of it. We have also cleared woods, built forts & got guns mounted. The place & climate are beautiful, roses, heliotropes & orange flowers & butterflies twice as big as any I ever saw—I have acquired from rebel sources a fine sorrel horse Rinaldo by name, formerly the property of a rebel officer & though riding is circumscribed it is pleasant—so I shall enjoy life in proportion as I feel less care. My household arrangements are an amusing mixture of superb & military. Mary will send my journal—or what there is.

Ever thine<br>T. W. H.

*"The colors are better apart, for military service"*
To Louisa Storrow Higginson
Headquarters
Jacksonville
March 22. 1863

*Dearest Mother*

I am well & the garrison just reinforced by the 6th Ct & 8th Maine regts—I command the whole now—but tomorrow may bring Col. Rust who as Senior Col. will command the post; though I expect that either this

114. This map is missing.

will be temporary or we shall go to another post, farther up the river. It is quite safe here now & the troops outside seem to hv. withdrawn beyond skirmishing.

There is a strong impression that Gen. Hunter is coming down here, on a visit at least—if so he probably will be here in a day or two & my plans will be clearer.

Everything so far has turned out so consonant with our expectations from this regiment that I hv. not much fear of my being seriously thwarted, which would be the case if put under the orders of Colonels of white reg'ts. The colors are better apart, for military service—let us take posts & the white troops garrison them.

> In haste ever thine
> T. W. H.

Love to the young mamma & young grandchild.[115]

## "Probably my regiment will go farther up the river"
To Louisa Storrow Higginson
Headqrs. 1st S.C.V.
Jacksonville Fla
Mar. 27. 1863

*Dearest Mother*

I write by various vessels going to diff't places & take the chance of reaching you.

We hv. now 2 white reg'ts here & Col. Rust is in command. We get on perfectly—he is a man about the stamp of Mr. Kingsley of Bratt's—*heavier*. He may be here only temporarily, we are all waiting for Gen. Hunter & nobody knows. Probably my reg't will go farther up the river, which we shall like. The river is broad & safe, no high banks fr. which to fear attack, & there are two points on the right bank Pilatka (75 miles) & Magnolia (35) either of which would be a good point for us. Both are health resorts in winter & have large buildings & wharves. Both give more access to the slave population than this & one farther fr. troops & railroads. There we shall be by ourselves.

> In haste, thine
> T. W. H.

115. This probably refers to Mary Louisa Higginson Cabot (TWH's niece, daughter of his brother Francis John), who gave birth to Elizabeth Higginson Cabot on February 1, 1863; the child survived only till August 21, 1863.

*"shells are not so very dangerous"*
To Louisa Storrow Higginson
Headquarters 1st S.C.V.[116]
Jacksonville, Florida.

*Dearest Mother*

I will send a word by a steamer we are forwarding to Fernandina. I am well, & like life, on the whole, as usual. Col. Rust is now in command—of the 8th Me Reg't but they only brought 10 days rations of which 7 days are gone. As a last resort to drive us out the rebels have one big gun a great way off with which they occasionally throw a shell into town—but we hv. learned that shells are not so very dangerous so many are thrown under or over or fail to explode.

Col. Montgomery with his handful has gone up the river to land & strike in; & we are going ere long to take up some other post—farther I hope fr. a *railroad* wh. is a great bother in an enemy's hands.

I got 32 letters by last mail & get yours always so don't be anxious.

Ever thine T. W. H.

*"We are ordered to evacuate Jacksonville"*
To Louisa Storrow Higginson
Headquarters &c
On board str. J. Adams
Mouth St. John's River
March 30. 1863

*Dearest Mother*

So far hence (to Beaufort)—indeed it seems as if it were going half way to New England. We are ordered to evacuate Jacksonville & a great blow to us it is & *seems* most unnecessary, just as we had got it in condition to hold. I have been sending you a shower of little notes, by various routes, which may never arrive. I am perfectly well, as usual, & though sometimes I hv. been quite anxious & fatigued, it has not hurt me at all. We are ordered back to Camp Saxton—but what to do there we know not. Possibly to do garrison duty for Beaufort—possibly to go thence to Fort Pulaski & relieve the 48th N.Y. for that is one rumor—I hope not true. At any rate I suspect

116. The copy-text has a pencilled notation at the top, "without date." Although it is numbered out of proper sequence in the Houghton Library, it obviously belongs to the period of TWH's service in Jacksonville, and so has been editorially placed in its correct order.

they have corked up our energies for a short time—but if they have much of a fight at Charleston they may need us yet.

What a patriarchess you are becoming my dear mamma, with your accumulating grandchildren, as well as your 77 years. I feel like a wandering young prodigal to be chasing about here while you are having birthdays— but I don't expect to stay forever; nor should I want to do it. I have had greater privileges thus far than I can expect to continue permanently— most Colonels would give a good deal for the opportunity of independent action which I have had.

We may have to stay here several days before crossing the bar, but I shall send this by Mr. Page the Tribune correspondent who goes straight to Hilton Head, whereas I must touch at Fernandina.

Ever thine<br>
With love to all<br>
T. W. H.

MARCH 31
    hope to reach Fernandina tonight

*"we have happened into the most fascinating regions and life"*
To LOUISA STORROW HIGGINSON
HEADQUARTERS 1ST S.C.V.
ADVANCED PICQUET STATION
PORT ROYAL I.
APR. 8. 1863

*Dearest Mother*

Fate & Gen. Hunter's aids tried to put us down, but our luck was too strong for them & we have happened into the most fascinating regions & life, riding all day through lanes overarched with roses & woods dense with young emerald leaves & looking across the streams to the wooded & sunny mainland of South Carolina. A life that is as good as anything we have had, were only the zest of immediate danger added. In case the rebels ever try to cross we are to give notice of their approach, but I have no notion that they will. We see the pickets from every point on the river & at the narrower places they can just shout across & are provoked that our soldiers won't converse. Too far to see their color! Great guns booming at intervals from Charlestonward & on the whole, life goes well. Mary will send a trifle of journal. Life will be more like play while this lasts, than any we have had.

Ever affectionately

   —yr. letters just rec'd after long gaps.

T. W. H.

*"This charming life among Cherokee roses & peach blossoms"*
To Louisa Storrow Higginson
Headquarters
1st S.C.V.
Advanced Picquet Station
Apr. 10. 1863

*Dearest Mother*

Only to say all well up to this time. This charming life among Cherokee roses & peach blossoms will last awhile till the Charleston Expedition comes back wh. may be very soon as I see no prospect of success there. Then we may be sent to Florida again, or anything may happen
 —Gen. Butler sent here
 —Gen Saxton sent away
 —both which are being talked of at Washington.

I don't think we are in much danger of an attack here though the rebels destroyed a small gunboat in sight of our picquets yesterday— through disgraceful carelessness on board the boat. Two Monitors[117] are disabled (one put back here with turret so bent, it can't revolve) & Ft. Sumter not yet reached or breached. How funny some of the rumors were about the capture of our expedition—one Democratic paper writing my obituary! Next time remember how easily such things are got up.

Ever thine
T.W. H.

*"These are queer creatures, these freedmen"*
To Mary Channing Higginson
Apr. 16.[118]

"Good morning, Cunnel, how you find youself this morning, sa"; that is what they say to me, & I to my superior officer the celebrated T.

It makes me happy dear, to think of you: you act so well upon Gail's maxims,[119] & seem so strong & well. Margaret too must be well or she cd. not write such mad epistles, very funny too. I don't get many amateur-

117. Large armored warships, so named after the USS *Monitor*, which proved itself against the Confederate ironclad *Virginia (Merrimack)* on March 9, 1862, off Hampton Roads, Virginia.

118. Copy-text has "1863 prob." in pencil here.

119. Gail Hamilton's advice to female correspondents of soldiers, in "A Call to My Country-Women," *Atlantic Monthly* 11 (March 1863), 345–49.

friendly letters, only my few regular correspondents, & almost all the rest are applications for commissions—these are very tiresome & now I hardly ever answer them. I have lately written to Martha LB.[120] but I only write to you & mother.

The Chas. Follen arrangement has fallen through for a reason you must keep to yourself. The impression is very strong among those who hv. been on picquet in this vicinity before (especially the Mass Cavalry) that he is intemperate. I attribute it partly to the fact that he habitually uses whiskey & defends it—& partly to a peculiar simpering way he has,—but it *may* be true insomuch that I told him of it & declined receiving him unless he wd. entirely give up liquor while in the army, which he at once refused to do, regarding it as almost an insult, though he was perfectly polite & friendly about it. He said he cared nothing for giving up liquor; it was the insulting implication that he was a suspected man, who must be checked of his liberty; & this was really sincere so it ended the matter; a great disappointment to him I think, but not to me, as I have some one much superior in his place, a Malden (Mass) man named Brown,[121] a man whom I hv. known in Boston anti-slavery rows, & a famous Sharpshooter—a splendid powerful six footer whereas Chas. is a trifle soft & sloppy though I shld. hv. liked him too. Brown is now Sup't of a plantation at the Ferry & poor moping disappointed Merriam will probably take his place, as neither Montgomery nor I will hv. him. Montgomery must now hv. 600 in his reg't, having many drafted men. These are queer creatures, these freedmen; they are so used to having their destinies determined for them that they acquiesce at once when drafted, & you wd. not know them fr. the others.

The paymaster writes that he is really making up our payrolls & we shall probably be paid in a week [ ][122] is no hurry & W. D. wrote me the most characteristic epistle, which I can't find, saying he wished he were with me & wd. send more whenever I wished.

So if I am paid in full to March 1, you will have enough to keep you along, dearest & I need very little. The $200 I sent before was what Mr. Bowditch[123] sent me for the horse; I knew that cd. wait.

Do you know about Mrs. General Lander?[124] I was at her house today,

120. Martha Le Baron.
121. Second Lieutenant A. B. Brown.
122. About nine lines of the letter are cut off here.
123. Probably Henry Ingersoll Bowditch (husband of TWH's cousin Sally Bowditch), who had helped post bail for TWH when he was arrested in 1854 in connection with the attempted rescue of the fugitive slave Anthony Burns.
124. Jean M. Lander, volunteer nurse, widow of General F. W. Lander.

though she was out. In the parlor is a striking photograph of her husband, a good deal like Sam Johnson.[125] She would attract[126]

*"heap o' howdy"*
TO LOUISA STORROW HIGGINSON
U.S. FORCES, PORT ROYAL ISLAND,
HEADQUARTERS, BEAUFORT, S.C., APR. 22 1863.

Dearest Mother I happen to find in Beaufort somebody who leaves this P.M. for Boston so I may write a few lines, sending "heap o' howdy" wh. is the favorite African message, howdy meaning how d'ye. Life is pleasant & tropical (all but absence of fruits) on Advanced Picquet. We hv. to ride at night occasionally inspecting picquets & then it is lovely. Days are warm often, 86° & 90° in shade at noon, then cool again; varying as much as in N.E. Quantities of roses & magnolias now: all disturbances far off, at outer stations, where they try sometimes to cut off a picquet, & fail. Now the Expedition has gone to Charleston again & will probably come back as before— meanwhile we shall remain, where we are. It is healthy enough, where we are, I apprehend no trouble though we shld. stay there all summer. The Arago is below with letters & probably Dr. & Mrs. Howe,[127] but *probably* this must go before the mail comes up.

Ever thine with love
T. W. H.

*"people won't write all on one side"*
TO MARY CHANNING HIGGINSON
APR. 23. 1863

Dearest; I have your sweet letters: they grow better & better. I get very few letters except to ask commissions for I can't answer & even under pres-

125. Samuel Johnson (1822–1882), a friend of TWH from Harvard Divinity School days, and a ministerial colleague who shared his liberal inclinations.

126. The obverse of the nine cut lines is here.

127. Dr. Samuel Gridley Howe (1801–1876), a Boston politician and abolitionist, organizer of the Vigilance Committee of Boston, who had been along with TWH one of the so-called "Secret Six," conspirators who supported John Brown's attempted fomenting of slave revolt; he later helped to raise funds for John Brown's legal defense, and was now one of three members of the American Freedmen's Inquiry Commission, created in March 1863 by the War Department to investigate the condition of freedmen within Union lines. TWH wrote about him in "Dr. Howe's Anti-Slavery Career," *Contemporaries*, The Writings of Thomas Wentworth Higginson, Vol. II (Boston: Houghton, Mifflin, 1900), 294–301. Howe's wife was Julia Ward Howe, writer and author of "The Battle Hymn of the Republic." TWH wrote of her in "Julia Ward Howe," *Carlyle's Laugh and Other Surprises* (Boston: Houghton, Mifflin, 1909), 285–312.

sure of Gail Hamilton people won't write all on one side. But I care as much for them as we did in Fayal & it's the best thing anybody can do, if they cd. only believe it. Hadn't I better try *Sarah Balch?*

About Gen. Hunter, darling, I should think you wd. see that there's no use in talking about anything *in advance* with one who has twice evacuated Jacksonville. I hv. no expectation of ever being *unreasonably* treated by either of the Generals, whenever any immediate demand is made, not involving persistency of purpose. What *is reasonable* will depend entirely on the progress of the[128] The Lt. Col.[129] all but cried to go home & show his martyred hands to the Concerd ladies who had previously planned a festival for him in City Hall! Heaven forgive me if I wrong him, but he is an uncommon baby, for his size. Dr Rogers thinks Margt's theory of the briars very probable. They crack some jokes on him, the officers: some say the rebels tried to crucify him; others that he knelt to pray for mercy & so the shots went through the uplifted hands. I don't know what ever to do with him, when he comes back.

Dr. Hawks is at Beaufort, where is our hospital; & Dr Minor has fever & ague, but Dr. Rogers stands it very well. James is in great spirits with 19 recruits & a new tall Lieutenant—a treasure—Brown.

*"I want the Atlantic"*
To James T. Fields
Headquarters 1st S.C.V.[130]
Advanced Picquet
Port Royal Island
May 6. 1863

*Dear friend*

First I want the Atlantic, which one gets here a month or two behind-hand—please regard me in the novel light of a subscriber.

Then I want Mrs. Browning's book about Greek & English poets;[131] & also Frothingham's (O. B.) little book of Hebrew parables "from the lips of the teacher" or some such matter,[132] for our lady teacher to read to our grown up children.

---

128. Half the sheet is missing here.
129. Lieutenant Colonel Liberty Billings.
130. The copy-text has "To J. T. Fields" written in pencil at the top of the page.
131. Elizabeth Barrett Browning, *The Greek Christian Poets and the English Poets* (London: Chapman & Hall, 1863).
132. Octavius Brooks Frothingham, *Stories from the Lips of the Teacher* (Boston: Walker, Wise, 1863).

Now you have got me out of the way you can publish poor stories to yr. heart's content I suppose—Marrying by Proxy![133] How admirable Gail Hamilton née Dodge is growing.[134] With kind regards to Mrs. F. believe me yours most cordially

T. W. Higginson
Col. comdg.
(force of habit)
Direct to *Beaufort S.C.*

*"Intensely human"*
To Louisa Storrow Higginson
Headquarters 1ˢᵀ S.C.V.
Advanced Picquet.
May 6. 1863

*Dearest Mother*

Here we still stay & still find it very pleasant. Only the days are some-times very warm & besides the riding there is so much writing, one grows sleepy at night & letters keep getting postponed. Only think, your last waited several days at Hilton Head because Louisa addressed Port Royal & didn't put on the reg't & as that mail missed Mary's letter, it was bâd, as one of the drummers said he should feel, if killed without having had any defensive weapon but the professional drumsticks. "Cunnel,["] said he, ["]if I was to get killed, & hadn't had something to defend myself with, I should feel *bâd*"—which seemed so just that I at once sent in a requisition for drummers' swords.

Anna's implorings about my fall from bed were delicious. I have never done it since. Now I have actually an old sheet! wh. rouses the indignation of my officers, whom I have sternly cut down to valises. But I tell them: make yourself comfortable wherever you are—only when you move, crawl into a valise again. You have no idea how hard it is to keep *down* the baggage of a regiment. It is just like in family movings—at first you feel like throwing away yr. property—then you can't resist the temptation to stow it in somewhere. If spare-room epics were to chronicle it all, there would be a pretty catalogue.

*May 10th.*

Mary writes splendid letters, about "kittens & sleds" as Gail Hamilton

133. J. P. Quincy, "Betrothal by Proxy: A Romance of Genealogy," *Atlantic Monthly* 11 (April 1863), 420–34.

134. Gail Hamilton (pen name of Mary Abigail Dodge) published "Gala-Days," *Atlantic Monthly* 11 (May 1863), 629–42.

prescribes;[135] but I wish more people wrote to me. If they only would take my note (of hand) to answer them after I got home. Nothing so rare as epistolary disinterestedness; the most self denying saint hints at an answer in the Post-script. Stephen is splendid about sending me papers; in a better world some-body will send him Paradisaic Journals & Saturday Evening Heavenzettes.

Don't Mary send you my Journals (private) not that anybody is content with a secondhand article, but they might supply useful statistics.

Thanks for the maplesugar which we have for dessert—also I offer it to guests instead of whiskey, now that our blessed Florida syrup is getting low. By the way piquante girlish little Mrs. Saxton belabors her husband with appending Champagne & whiskey to her supply of lemonade for Gen. Hunter after the review; & I was glad to be able to testify that he reverted to the lemonade finally—though perhaps this was characteristic. But poor Gen. Saxton seemed to think it hard to require an army officer to develope *all* the virtues! Not that he said this—his head never coins sentences, though his heart often forges them finely—as when he told Cap. Hooper[136] to answer the elaborate inquiries of the Committee about the freed blacks with "*Intensely human*". I suppose every man or woman's climax is found in the shortest sentence he ever achieved. Gen. Hunter's *Give them as good as they send* endorsed on the letter of inquiry about picket shootings, is his maximum of capacity.

I expect to stay here for the present & very likely be ordered to Florida again by & by.

Goodbye with love
T. W. H.

*"sympathy, success, approbation"*
TO MARY CHANNING HIGGINSON
ADVANCED PICQUET.
MAY 9. 1863

Dearest the box came night before last, but I hv. had no time to write. I am sure you & M.[137] could not have wished for a more enthusiastic reception; it

135. Gail Hamilton, "A Call to My Country-Women," *Atlantic Monthly* 11 (March 1863), 345–49. Hamilton urged American women to support the war effort, specifically contending that "the great army of letters that marches Southward with every morning sun is a powerful engine of war," but that women's letters to soldiers must not be filled with "tears and sighs" but with an optimistic picture of the home life they were defend-ing: "Fill your letters with kittens and Canaries, with baby's shoes, and Johnny's sled, and the old cloak you have turned into a handsome gown" (p. 347).
136. Captain Edward Hooper.
137. Very likely Margaret "Greta" Channing.

was Christmas & New Year's in one. The Chaplain & Major enjoyed it as much as James & the Dr. indeed more, because where people have bundles they drop into them & are seen no more, but others rejoice at longer range. Marg't's tracts went the round & were rec'd with enthusiasm.—she is a funny child. All were delighted with the maple sugar & the sugarplums; even the tin box of the latter was precious. The fig paste having just held out to this time, will now be succeeded by the other confectionary. The chocolate was a most happy thought & appeared at tea with the little cakes. The shirts & socks are superior, but the sheets brought down on me the wrath of the household, I being considered the ascetic of the institution. It seems as if we never shld. hv. any but cool nights they grow no warmer & yesterday morning the mercury was only 53°. A fire wd. be pleasant almost every eve'g—yet everything is in full bloom & the immense blackberries are just ripe we have never had any strawberries to speak of—all this is episode. How nice to send those two stories just as I hv. finished Titan & am reading it over again, wh. I rarely do. I got the May Atlantic here, & now hv. sent to Fields for it, to come regularly. I hv. sent also for Frothingham's book & Mrs. Browning's.—The marking on those shirts was very superior: I never dreamed of new ones. Those socks with the flag were pathetic, I have hung them up by Mrs. Howe's poem about the flag[138] wh. everybody must bow to. The Chaplain says if any of us is taken a prisoner, he must send a flag of truce & get those socks to be hanged in. He is as unexpected as you or Marnie. Have I acknowledged all. Oh, the shoes I suppose I shall need in time, but on this sandy soil one never wears out shoes, especially if one never walks. I suppose I hardly walk so far in a day as you do.—As to the Commonwealths[139] we save up AntiSlavery papers to send to the rebels who are hungry for news, across the Ferry. Besides, I like the Commonwealths.

Last night, darling, yr. three ltrs. came—one enclosing Marnie's. This takes you to May 1.—you hear in 5 days, but I never in less than 7, seldom so recent. I always begin with the last, to see if you are well, do you; This time I am leaving one unopened. The dumb waiter is magnificent. If that reservoir for the Bellows' don't cost more than $15 let them have it. Tell me how yr. money holds out & how much you pay a week. About a furlough during the summer, dear, I entertain no doubt at all—that is the only fixed point: even of that I can't tell how early or how late. Your letters are sensible & beautiful dear, always fresh. We laughed over Mr. Pierce's croaking.[140] First he hardly ever saw me before & second he was here just as we

138. Julia Ward Howe, "The Flag," *Atlantic Monthly* 11 (April 1863), 443.
139. *Boston Commonwealth*, an antislavery newspaper.
140. Edward L. Pierce, Treasury agent, had visited Port Royal from late March to early May 1863.

were pitching camp & I probably cut him rather short. Do not doubt that my old sin of good nature still holds out—the Captains complain that their men always threaten an appeal to de Cunnel.

Gen Saxton declares I acquitted Stockdale & O'Niel by smoothing down my testimony & suggesting charities. I can't surely look "stern" for the men are usually on the broad grin when I heave in sight. I don't believe, darling that I am changed at all. You ask if I wd. like to see you: I assure you I'm not changed in that.

You used to wonder if I wd. feel dissatisfied at home after the war is over, or my share of it done: I never feared it; that is not my way. The pleasure I take in it is no such ecstatic thing, that it should abolish everything else. I never for a moment feel that this life is any worthier than my life anywhere else. Of course I enjoy it, but I enjoy all life & then "I like a variety" as I always said at table. I have had my usual good fortune, you know, so far; sympathy, success, approbation. I can't tell how it wd. seem if those were taken away. Then there is a good deal of vexatious writing not that I shld. dislike that if I had time, for you know how much red-tape I hv. in me but it interferes with other matters, & takes vitality needed for other things. That will be the drawback of these Southern colored regts; I spend hours daily in doing what in white regts wd. be done by a secretary detailed fr. the ranks; my Adjutant also wd. hv. a secretary & cd. help me far more; & my Lt. Col. & Major are worthless for writing. As for drilling you needn't be troubled, precious little of that can now be done; almost every day, after dress parade, I drill the four Companies off duty. They keep up the "manual of arms"[141] very well at Dress Parade—the rest is a little rusty, wh. is inevitable on picquet.

I had lots of letters by the Arago, darling—four fr. you, very nice & capital. I read scraps to Dr R. & he laughs & slaps his knees till his trousers will wear out; I read him Margaret's & Charlotte's too. I have a good note from Bab.[142] & always hear fr. Mother—nobody else except for commissions; all female friends are faithless save the above. I find the time of the 51st is up July 13 & Jas. R. confidently expects to go then; I don't think he cares so much, but Dr R. is bent on his going through College. I don't know that he will get away & rather fear the effect on him if he don't, but I shan't borrow trouble. Dr. R. is fresh & bright; how he does enjoy Bell's[143] notes, wh. are

141. The manual of arms is the elementary set of exercises performed by a soldier with his gun; see Casey, *Infantry Tactics*, 1:36–63.

142. Probably Barbara Channing, TWH's sister-in-law (his wife Mary's sister).

143. Bell Rogers was Dr. Seth Rogers' wife; he proudly showed her notes to Charlotte Forten, who found them "full of touching and beautiful affection." *The Journals of Charlotte Forten Grimké*, ed. Brenda Stevenson (New York: Oxford University Press, 1988), 461.

commonly very sweet—do you like her? I never can think of her as attractive.

I am reading over *Titan* at odd moments, my only book & enjoy it much. Though it is more confused than any of his books. I thought Gail Hamilton was coming up among real authors till I read Gala Days,[144] wh. is cheap & miserable.—flashy. Dark Ways[145] is distressing. They say in H. P.'s[146] Harper story[147] she sets the heroine on fire, I believe the only form of torture she has never tried. I am delighted at your sending these novels, I like to read a little bit every day, if I can.

Dearest I think all yr. back letters hv. come now—so don't be anxious. Hetty is here, she washes for us & W^m cooks; we hv. a cooking stove— plenty of milk & eggs & rice & hominy & bread—peas & blackberries beginning—meat scarce.

It is splendid about the dumb waiter; & I think Germantown[148] is of all others the place for you. I didn't mean to insult you dear by thinking you better—but you seemed so.

Goodbye, dearest.

Love to Marg, to whom I shall write.

Thine am.

Stephen is so kind about sending me papers!

*"thus do great events link on to small ones"*
To MARY CHANNING HIGGINSON
ADV. PICQUET STATION
MAY 16. 1863

A second rainy day, though rain of the most summery kind. We are all excited with the rumors arriving in so many ways of successes in V^a. It is said that the NY Herald of the 7th confirms the reports we get fr. Edisto Is-

144. Gail Hamilton, "Gala-Days. I.," *Atlantic Monthly* 11 (May 1863), 629–42; idem, "Gala-Days. II.," *Atlantic Monthly* 12 (July 1863), 17–29. Collected in *Gala-Days* (Boston: Ticknor and Fields, 1863).

145. Harriet E. Prescott, "Dark Ways," *Atlantic Monthly* 11 (May 1863), 545–65.

146. Harriet Elizabeth Prescott (later Spofford) (1835–1921), helped TWH in the evening school for working people he established in Newburyport; she was something of a protegé as a writer, and eventually became widely published and successful.

147. Harriet E. Prescott, "Rosemary. In Three Parts.—Part I: Prophetic of the Rose," *Harper's New Monthly Magazine* 26 (May 1863), 803–8. "Part II: The Rose in Bloom" and "Part III: Rose Leaves When the Rose Is Dead" appeared, respectively, in *Harper's* 27 (June 1863), 41–53, and *Harper's* 27 (July 1863), 195–200.

148. Germantown, Pennsylvania, at this time a health resort, which Mary may have been thinking to visit.

land Picquets of Hooker's being actually in Richmond.[149] This morning the rebel Picquets called across to ask us if we knew where he was? which seemed tantalizing.

Didn't I ask for a thinner vest, darling, the one with bright buttons, I thought I did. I wish too I had asked for some towels, & some gauze to keep out the flies—but those I can perhaps get here. They are the greatest trouble, mosquitos annoy me but little, nor do sandflies—hardly ever at Dress Parade. Nights always cool so far; sometimes uncomfortably hot at noon. We enjoy the nightly chocolate, the maple sugar & Mrs. May's little cookies—the confectionary melted a good deal but the tin box is admirable.

We have now a profusion of blackberries, wh. make it seem more than ever, like sea-shore without any sea (as Marg. said) because they recall Pigeon Cove.[150] But I haven't seen a woman in this department so big as Isa—or Miss Susanna!

I hv. read Sylvia's Lover[151] once & can't read it again—so different fr. Titan which I read over & over. It seems to me poor & very joyless though the delineation of character is good & Sylvia sometimes recalled Harriet.[152] Mistress & Maid[153] *opens* far better. I hv. sent for Mrs. Barrett's book & Frothingham's.

Perhaps Hooker's victories will give that cheerfulness to the public mind wh. J. T. F.[154] thinks favorable to book publishing; & thus do great events link on to small ones & affect Literary Colonels. I never feel the smallest desire to write anything for print here & have not written a word with that intention since I left home; it seems a sort of profaning this experience & mixing incompatible lives. Hereafter in some Germantown quiet, I may grind it into paint.

Gen. Saxton groans over all these troops doing nothing, though he says *he* has less desire for active service than before his marriage. I don't think anything will be done, but I am satisfied that many thousand troops might be kept fr. leaving Charleston for Virginia by simply making a *feint* here with a few regiments, & then withdrawing. But Gen. Hunter is not

149. Major General Joseph Hooker (1814–1879), commanding the Army of the Potomac, was in fact defeated at Chancellorsville, Virginia, May 1–4, 1863, by General Robert E. Lee.

150. Pigeon Cove, Massachusetts, a fishing village on Cape Ann, was a favorite seaside retreat of TWH.

151. Elizabeth Gaskell, *Sylvia's Lovers* (London: Smith, Elder & Co., 1863).

152. Probably Harriet E. Prescott.

153. Dinah Maria Mulock Craik, *Mistress and Maid* (London: Hurst and Blackett, 1863).

154. James T. Fields.

at all disposed to any such thing & we shall stay here without disturbance except what we make ourselves, I expect; unless we are ordered back to Florida. If we are, I don't suppose it will be to Jacksonville, but to some other point, such as we shall like better. Jacksonville is not now the point where we can be most useful: for it can be just as well held by white troops.

I believe I told you that a squad of picked men have been sent off by Gen. Hunter under the general plans of that eminently sane individual Mr. Merriam! I mention this so that you shall not be afraid if you see any reports about their being captured or killed which they certainly will be if the plans are carried out. Capt. Randolph & Dr Hawks, who are with Merriam were pronounced by Gen. Saxton "three lunatics together["]— on which Mrs. Saxton with her usual saucy frankness suggested that the Major General commanding the Department (Hunter) ought to be with them for a fourth! She is a fair haired, fresh, piquante, girlish little thing idolizing her General & fearing nothing in the universe. I quite enjoy her. Though she seems more "Dora"-ish[155] than she is.

> Goodbye
> Love to Margaret

*"All quiet along the Coosaw"*
To LOUISA STORROW HIGGINSON
HEADQUARTERS 1ST Reg. S.C.V.
ADV. PICQUET STATION
MAY 18. 1863

*Dearest Mother*

All quiet along the Coosaw[156]—one result of which is that they can send as many troops as they please from Charleston to Richmond whereas a very little alarm here would keep them safe at home. Gen. Saxton chafes very much under the inaction—not so much for himself because his civil & military functions fill his time,—as for the waste of so many men & so much material. But I don't think it troubles Gen. Hunter at all he is dreamy by habit & efficient in spasms; a singular compound; I suppose there may

155. Dora Spenlow, the gay and charming fairy-like child who enchants David Copperfield but proves, after their marriage and despite her girlish charms, to be dim-witted and sadly bereft of the "character and purpose" that would have enabled her to be a satisfying companion to her husband. Charles Dickens, *David Copperfield*, ed. Nina Burgis (1850; Oxford: Clarendon Press, 1981), 552.

156. See Journal, above, April 17, 1863.

be an hour or two in each month when he is roused into seeming like a soldier.

Waldo has just written me a letter, & Stephen is faithful in sending me papers. I have had an ocean of writing but am now getting on comparatively dry land & it will not be so bad again, as Colonels are no longer to have the responsibility of ordnance, which they have had. Don't trust the Tribune correspondent, he has a loose notion of facts, though well disposed towards us. I see he talks of the Negro brigade being sent on a secret expedition, under Montgomery—all nonsense, but M. will probably be sent somwhere to fill up his regiment, as he has done here all that drafting can do & has only 560 men, so many are rejected by the surgeons.

It is a great satisfaction to me to feel, now that Colored regiments are so multiplying that the *peculiar* responsibility which at first attached to this diminishes, & that any disaster or failure on our part would now do little harm, whereas at first it might have defeated the whole thing. It is not likely that any more regiments will be organized in this dep't, for want of material, but elsewhere there must be many.

There is no oppressive weather as yet, only sometimes at noon—nights always cool. We now get quantities of immense blackberries, like the Northern cultivated kinds. We miss grass, but in other respects the country is beautiful. Grass and female society I might say; but Mrs. Dewhurst is always fresh & enjoyable and Charlotte Forten, that quadroon rose, is coming to make her another visit. The only women I ever go to see in Beaufort are Mrs. Saxton, always the same gay, saucy, schoolgirly little thing—one wd. know her original name to have been Tillie Thompson: —and General Lander's widow who came out hoping it was war & she was to be head-nurse. She was Miss Davenport, an actress, & quite an intelligent & earnest person; English, dignified & rather fine looking. Little touches of the stage are entertaining—rising & stepping to the door to see if Maj. Bannister, her lodger, had come in—"Ha! it is the Major?" then half turning her head, with a waving of the hand to me from the doorway—"'Tis he!"

I have an impression that there are people at the North who occasionally ask what they can do for such as me. No matter who they are—tell them to *write letters, without expecting answers*. To that rarest & loftiest test of human virtue, how few respond! Love to all—Ever affectionately

T. W. H.

A squad of my men are off on a wild goose chase in Georgia & Florida, none of my doing. If anything happens to them don't think it is I.

I have sent for Miss Barrett's / Mrs. Browning's little book.

*"still here and likely to stay"*
To Louisa Storrow Higginson
Adv. Picquet. Port Roy. I.
May 26.

*Dearest Mother,*

I have no time to write, I fear, except that I am well & we still here & likely to stay. Montgomery goes South tomorrow on a recruiting expedition with his reg't, probably to stay; & we hear no more yet of the reoccupation of Florida. If we stay here all summer I can at least have a furlough by July. My large Lt. Col.[157] is due tomorrow; how I wish some parish or heiress wd. fall in love with his mild beauties, & induce him to resign. Wouldn't I endorse it?

What Bangs is Laura Pell to marry? I shld. like to know for I always liked her. I wish some of my officers wd. be married, & bring their wives here. Mrs. Dewhurst is as fresh as her first syllable.

Ever affectionately T. W. H.

*"I wash my hands in de mornin' glory"*
To Louisa Storrow Higginson
Advanced Picquet
June 5. 1863

*Dearest Mother*

I got your kind budget of letters, but have no time to answer. It was kind in Francis[158] to write & I hope he will do it again. All in this department are wondering if Gen. Hunter's order of removal is coming in the next boat. *Most people hope it is.* I am suffering keenly through him—he having sent a party of my regiment under an insane young man named Merriam (of the John Brown affair)[159] who shot one & has got 3 others imprisoned & to be court-martialed, Robert Sutton among them. I have suffered keenly about it & if there is justice or reason left in Gen. Hunter shall save them fr. a punishment wh. belongs rather to the incompetent officers.

Montgomery's raid was a most brilliant success, though I don't believe in burning private houses, as he does. Nearly 800 contraband!

157. Lieutenant Colonel Liberty Billings.
158. Probably Francis John Higginson, TWH's eldest brother, a physician living in Brattleboro, Vermont.
159. Francis Merriam, a one-eyed enthusiast who had offered his money and personal services to Frank Sanborn in 1859 and then was sent to aid John Brown; TWH had judged him at the time to be mentally unbalanced or retarded, and protested against Sanborn's use of such an unreliable envoy.

Dr. Rogers met one old Uncle Tiff, pockets, hands & mouth full of *bread*. ["]You're happy aren't you,["] quoth Dr. ["]Bress you, Massa,["] said the poor old soul—["]I ain't had so much to eat in *nine years*"!

I went to see the Mass 54th the night they came (last night) & was delighted with the officers—the best style of Boston. I saw Frank Higginson, a nice fellow. The only evil in bringing black regiments here is the prospective intriguing who shall be Brigadier General. The report is that Gov. Andrews means to push *me*, wh. I hardly believe—& that he sends the 54th here for that reason. "I wash my hands in de mornin' glory" as my soldiers sing.—wash them of the whole affair.

Thank you for sending Martha's[160] letter, I haven't read it, but shall like to. Fancy poor dear Martha, trying to decide at which precise moment to cross Broadway!

Please tell Stephen I enjoy his bundles of newspapers. I am perfectly well—ever thine

T. W. H.

I feel no anxiety abt. yr. sharing my journal I don't care who sees it—but only as to whether Mary sent it promptly

*"Cabals and intrigues"*
TO MARY CHANNING HIGGINSON
CHIEF QUARTERMASTER'S OFFICE,
10TH ARMY CORPS & DEPT. OF THE SOUTH,
HILTON HEAD, PORT ROYAL, S.C., JUNE 10TH 1863.

Dearest The Arago is in, with a lot of letters for me—how you must have stirred the people up—Emeline Everett, Mary Curson,[161] Barbara,[162] Ade' May, Emily Dickinson[163] & Charlotte[164] as usual, all fe-

160. Possibly Martha Le Baron; perhaps Martha Hubbard Babcock Higginson (Aunt Martha, wife of TWH's Uncle James Jackson Higginson); or this could be TWH's half-sister, Martha Salisbury Higginson Nichols.
161. Mary Curson (or Curzon), a cousin of TWH, at whose home, called Curzon's Mills or Artichoke Mills, 3 or 4 miles outside of Newburyport, he and Mary stayed for a time following his dismissal from his pulpit in 1849.
162. Presumably Barbara Channing, Mary's sister.
163. Emily Dickinson (1830–1886), the reclusive Amherst, Massachusetts, poet who approached him following publication of his "Letter to a Young Contributor," *Atlantic Monthly* 9 (April 1862), 401–411, sending him her poems and initiating a correspondence. TWH co-edited her poems after her death. He wrote of her in "Emily Dickinson," *Carlyle's Laugh and Other Surprises* (Boston: Houghton, Mifflin, 1909), 247–83.
164. Charlotte Hawes.

male, so much the better, they write so much more entertainingly. Gen. Saxton is back, but with no very definite news, it seems to me—nobody knows yet if Gen. Hunter is to be removed or not—there is a report of a Brig. Gen. Gilmore, but whether he is coming to be under or over him, nobody knows. *I* wd. rather have almost anybody, it seems to me, but don't repeat this. The trouble is, nobody can [ ]<sup>165</sup> or predict anything here. I think it clear that Gen. Hunter's staff are resolved to push Montgomery for Brigadier General, & that was why the 54th Mass. was sent to report to him at St. Simons', instead of being left at Beaufort. I so thoroughly hate all *competition* with any one, that I wish they would send us Edw. Wild or *import* a Brig. Gen. somehow. I see also a disposition to annoy me in certain small ways—all which complicates the problem of my going home. My *expectation* is to get a furlough in August, but not to apply for a discharge from the army this season, unless sick or wounded, or subjected to some great injustice—so that all these Calamities will play into your hands, if they occur. Beyond this I know nothing. If promoted I should not refuse it, though I will not raise my finger to procure it; & I rather expect it will come, because even if they force Montgomery in first, there will be room for more than one, if they go on collecting colored troops here. I hate to think about these things; it is so much easier to command one isolated regiment than to be swept into Cabals & intrigues.

I am glad, darling, that you have had Anna & Barbara, for you must enjoy it; Margt's letter is bright as usual; I never thought of having a Mrs. Clapp in the family, but there's no telling. When I was a boy, I couldn't see why Mr. Cushing didn't marry Anna, but he never did. I expect to attend her wedding, in a higher sphere, to some very superior angel. Do tell me if Lucy Chase wrote those admirable letters from a Potomac hospital, in the Commonwealth?<sup>166</sup> by far the best I have seen?

As for Florida, nothing seems to come to a head—still a general impression that it is to be re-occupied, though I doubt it, at present. Now that it is found colored troops can operate in this region just as well, I think it is quite as likely that we may stay here, & perhaps make Expedi-

---

165. The copy-text is illegible here.

166. Louisa May Alcott's "Hospital Sketches," recounting her experiences as a hospital nurse in Washington, D.C., appeared in the *Boston Commonwealth* May 22– June 26, 1863, before appearing in book form, *Hospital Sketches* (Boston: James Redpath, 1863).

tions hereabouts; unless we make a regular advance, which I hardly expect.

I don't think I shall stay out on picquet much longer, for though it is a very pleasant life, & very healthy for the troops, it interferes with drill & they lose on that; & if other colored regiments come here, I want mine to be in good condition.

We had several very warm days & they weakened Dr Rogers a good deal, so that I don't feel so sure of his standing the heat. The rest of us bear it pretty well—& so does he when it grows a little cool. I want a surgeon very much, for Dr. Minor 2d asst Surg is sick also—not from climate—& Dr. Hawks will probably be promoted out of the regiment.—I hope so—I never want to see him again, after this last tragedy. That crazy Merriam is to be *Captain* in the 3d S.C. reg't, which is forming down here at H.H. under Gen. Hunter's immediate supervision—with this pleasant result.

Our book looks very nice & I wish for some copies to give away. Goosey, these are the Out Door Papers[167]—the Indoor Papers (historical &c) are for a separate volume some time or other. I hv. hardly had a peep at this.—Mademoiselle,[168] Rupert,[169] Letter to Young Contributor,[170] Women & Alphabet,[171]—Maroons,[172] Nat Turner &c[173] are for by & by, the more practical papers in this vol. *ought* to come last,

167. Thomas Wentworth Higginson, *Out-Door Papers* (Boston: Ticknor and Fields, 1863).

168. Thomas Wentworth Higginson, "Mademoiselle's Campaigns," *Atlantic Monthly* 2 (July 1858), 193–206.

169. Thomas Wentworth Higginson, "A Charge With Prince Rupert," *Atlantic Monthly* 3 (June 1859), 725–37.

170. Thomas Wentworth Higginson, "Letter to a Young Contributor," *Atlantic Monthly* 9 (April, 1862), 401–11. This was the essay that inspired Emily Dickinson to write to TWH and seek his advice on her poetry.

171. Thomas Wentworth Higginson, "Ought Women to Learn the Alphabet?," *Atlantic Monthly* 3 (February 1859), 137–50.

172. Thomas Wentworth Higginson, "The Maroons of Jamaica," *Atlantic Monthly* 5 (February 1860), 213–22; idem, "The Maroons of Surinam," *Atlantic Monthly* 5 (May 1860), 549–57.

173. Thomas Wentworth Higginson, "Nat Turner's Insurrection," *Atlantic Monthly* 8 (August 1861), 173–87. TWH wrote two other accounts of slave revolts, "Denmark Vesey," *Atlantic Monthly* 7 (June 1861), 728–44, and "Gabriel's Defeat," *Atlantic Monthly* 10 (September 1862), 337–45. All five of his articles on slave rebellions were eventually collected, along with other essays, in *Travellers and Outlaws: Episodes in American History* (Boston: Lee and Shepherd, 1889).

so as to culminate gradually; rising at last to (Isaac Davis)—see last page!

I shall write again by this mail. Now I am going to see Gen. Hunter.

Goodbye darling dearest
T. W. H.

*"show soldiers & real soldiers"*
To Louisa Storrow Higginson
Hilton Head. June 10. 1863

*Dearest Mother*

I have some spare time in the Paymaster's office & can answer yr. last. I am sorry you don't like Cambridge; I find my heart inclining towards it with kindly affection here at a distance, especially since Charles Norton[174] wrote me which was very kind of him. But my indignant plaints have stirred up multitudes to write me; don't mention it for I want them to keep on. Not till this mail have I had letters enough. I am down here for the day on a Court Martial & other business & we are still on Picquet, likely to stay unless I ask to be relieved which I hate to do, it is so pleasant & the men like it so, though it is bad for their drill. Still I may do it, now that Gen. S. is back; if colored reg'ts are to be multiplied, I must get back to our old condition of drill, which picquet & Jacksonville hv. impaired. It is hard to be show soldiers & real soldiers at the same time.

Gen. Phelps probably understands Gen. Hunter very well; yet I don't think that the latter's mind is ever troubled by a doubt of his being a soldier. I don't believe he will be removed, his policy represents the President's, & his inaction is normal, & no more than other departments. The *business* of the dep't is well done, only there is nothing to show for it, all carving & no meat.

Mr. E L Pierce is back here again, in some Treasury function; so is Col. McRae[175] of the National Contraband Commission, he is coming out to

174. Charles Eliot Norton (1827–1908), editor, author, educator. A noted Harvard teacher of art history, he was also a regular *Atlantic* contributor. TWH wrote of him in "Charles Eliot Norton," *Carlyle's Laugh and Other Surprises* (Boston: Houghton, Mifflin, 1909), 119–36.

175. Possibly TWH means James McKaye, one of three members of the American Freedmen's Inquiry Commission, who reported to the Secretary of War on June 30, 1863. Their report, citing TWH extensively, is in *The War of the Rebellion: A Compilation of the Official Records of the Union and Confederate Armies*, Series III, Vol. III (Washington, D.C.: Government Printing Office), 430–54.

see me tomorrow. He travels with a phonographer, think how dangerous; more alarming than Miss Martineau's[176] trumpet, into which Mary says it was impossible to bawl anything but "Fine morning". No other fact seemed sufficiently unquestionable. Every word I say to the McRae must be carefully taken down. I shld. think it would tempt one to gigantic inventions, as the aforesaid trumpet did W^m Story.[177]

Certainly the whole condition of the ex-slaves on the plantations seems remarkably good. They are self supporting & industrous & have impressed me very favorably—far more so than I dared to hope. Every morning the roads are full of women & old men walking early into Beaufort with great baskets of fruit & vegetables on their head & at night the procession comes out. Nor do they ever seem idle except at noon; & the crops look well.

Montgomery's raid was a great success freeing 800 people in a day—now he has gone down the shore. Encamping at St. Simon's island. He is an unequalled guerilla, but he has no system. After all one must consume his share of red tape as of dirt, nor hv. I ever tried to cut it without having to tie it together again in the end. It takes a great deal of machinery to keep 900 men in good condition, let alone a larger number.

I hope you will like the looks of my book, it appears well to me, but I almost forget how books ought to look, though I hv. got Mrs. Browning's Essays[178]—& Titan which I read over & over. Mary Curson writes that when she reproached her mother with juvenility, that dear soul plaintively responded "How *can* I grow old while you let me read Titan & have such beautiful weather"! Which perhaps accounts for my mamma.

How nice it was, Wendell Phillips speech doing you so much good. It was one of the best things he has done. This war seems to me glorious, however slow, when I think of these freed men & women here. These are days of the Lord, each a thousand years.

We have had a few days of suffering from the heat, no more. Worse may be coming, but as yet the summer weather has been lovely, & has not hurt any of us.

Ever affectionately
T. W. H.

176. Harriet Martineau (1802–1876), prominent English writer and reformer, supporter of abolition; she used an ear trumpet to compensate for her deafness.
177. William Wetmore Story (1819–1895), a lawyer turned writer (author of *Roba di Roma* [New York: C. Scribner, 1862]) and sculptor, a Cambridge acquaintance of TWH.
178. Elizabeth Barrett Browning, *Essays on the Greek Christian Poets and the English Poets* (New York: J. Miller, 1863).

*"I will have none but civilized warfare in my reg't"*
To Louisa Storrow Higginson
Beaufort S.C.
June 19. 1863

*Dearest Mother*

I can write but little; an unexpected mail goes tomorrow. We are encamped here on the parade ground—a fine place—several more regiments hv. moved away & it really seems as if Ethiopia were coming uppermost, for though Gen. Saxton has given up the military command of the post in dudgeon, yet Col. Davis who is in command is very kind & obliging to us though Editor of a Copperhead newspaper. Gen. Gillmore I hv. not yet seen; he is very busy going from post to post day & night. He was classmate of Gen. Saxton at West Point, who thought poorly of him, tho' he says he is now a good officer.

Montgomery's raids are dashing but his brigand practices I detest & condemn—they will injure these people & make a reaction at the North. I never allowed such things save according to strictly military principles & it is *perfectly* easy to restrain the negroes; they are capable of heroic abstinence. I will have none but civilized warfare in *my* reg't, but the public may not discriminate.

Only think of the Savannah ladies coming down in steamboats to see the triumphs of the Fingal, which their jewelry built[179]—they hastened back.

Two different persons, who hv. been on board, today tell me the Fingal is terribly *dirty*, whereas our gunboats are so intensely clean. It enables Admiral Dupont the handsome & stately old gentleman, to retire in glory & it really does him credit.

Much love to all; a sudden tide of letters has set in towards me—may it last.

Ever affectionately with much love to all
T. W. H.

*"burning & pillaging I utterly detest"*
To Mary Channing Higginson
Beaufort. S.C.
June 19. 1863

Well dearest there is another mail going tomorrow & it gives me a chance for a little note. Isn't the capture of the Fingal splendid, you know the ladies of

179. On June 17, 1863, at the mouth of the Wilmington River in Wassaw Sound, Georgia, the Confederate ironclad ram *Atlanta*, converted in 1862 from the steamer *Fingal*, was attacked by the Union's monitors *Weehawken* and *Nahant*, finally surrendering to the captain of the *Weehawken*. Confederate women often formed gunboat societies and raised funds for building ironclads by means of fairs, raffles, or the sale of their possessions.

Savannah bought it with their jewelry & two steamboat loads of them came down to see the triumphs of their pet, but they had to trot back. She is at Hilton Head & I hope to see her. I like being here, dear, very well, I have not yet seen Gen. Gillmore & have no impressions of him. He & Gen Saxton were classmates at West Point & were not on speaking terms,—Gen. S. despised his character. But he thinks him a good officer & he is immensely active so far, dashing round day & night. Dr. Minor, our 2d ass't surgeon, is going home to Hartford for health & may go & see you, he is one of the salt of the earth though only 20 yrs. old. I want you to see his good honest face, true as the sun, & I wd. rather have his opinion on anything than that of $\frac{3}{4}$ of my officers. Dr. Rogers is so-so, & will I hope get through somehow—even shld. he break down I think he wd. only go home & return in the autumn.

Montgomery's career is brilliant but I fear he will do great harm; his burning & pillaging I utterly detest & never allowed it except under strict military laws. It is perfectly unnecessary too with these troops. I hear Col. Shaw does not like it.

How very pretty & successful Margaret's leaves are,—thank her for them, wh. I forgot to do in writing to you.

Goodbye dearest, I am getting my last Ordnance Returns into shape & after this shall never hv. so much writing as by a new Order the Captains hv. all the ordnance in charge. Ever thine am—

*"no one dares to treat us otherwise than well"*
To Louisa Storrow Higginson
Headquarters 1st S.C.V.
Beaufort Parade Ground.
June 22. 1863

*My dearest Mother*

I have a few minutes & an unexpected mail, so will write & say that I am well & things go well. We are in camp & hoping for an opportunity of action, but there is never any telling what may happen in this Department; we may be sent to the north or kept here to the end of time. Gen. Gillmore is an immensely busy man, flies round day & night; is hardly ever at his headquarters: my impression is that he will be succeeded in the permanent command by Gen. Saxton, & will himself hv. charge of the force wh. is nibbling at Charleston. But nobody can tell. Meanwhile my reg't is in the best condition, & if we are of no use to any one it is not my fault. In truth we are of as much use as any of the white reg'ts, very few of whom now remain on the island. Somebody must stay here, & though I don't care to be the somebody, it might be worse.

Dear old Mr. Saxton is going home to Deerfield in the next steamer, & has promised to go up to Brattleboro & see you. Do make much of him a more simple & honest soul does not live & he is antislavery through & through, & will tell you all about our matters here. Much of the General's lifelong antislavery principle he gained from his father.

It is not yet oppressively hot here, save for a few hours at noon; the nights are perfectly comfortable & I hv. known weather just as hot at the North. We hv. an excellent camping ground & find tent life very agreeable.

I do not know how we shall like Gen. Gillmore, but it is a comfort to be relieved from the spasmodic uncertainty which marked all proceedings under Gen. Hunter. As respects general policy toward colored troops, the policy of the government now sweeps away all opposition & no one dares to treat us otherwise than well.

My health is as usual better than any one's around me, though none of my officers are yet much impaired by the climate; & everybody admits that our troops in Beaufort last yr. stood it very well.

I am reading Count Gurowski's Diary[180] at odd times & find it very entertaining, though one does not feel sure but some of the prophecies may hv. been retouched after the events.

There is a large mail in by the "Union," but not yet distributed.

Ever affly
T. W. H.

*"Any artist would prefer to have his soldiers black"*
To Louisa Storrow Higginson
Hilton Head. June 26 1863

*Dearest Mother*

I am not stationed here but spent last night here to see Gen. Gilmore who is rather attractive, seeming to be dashing frank & cordial—apparently full of ambition to do all he can here, & willing to use all the means he has. Having made some discoveries on picquet I think the chance is of my being allowed some independent operations from Beaufort which may bear on the great nibble at Charleston wh. he is attempting. Gen. G. is a

180. Count (Adam) Gurowski (1805–186?), a colorful and eccentric character from a noble Polish family, migrated from France to America in 1849, socialized with the literary and intellectual elite, and eventually took up residence about the beginning of the Civil War in Washington, D.C., where he frequented the political salons. His *Diary from March 4 1861 to November 12 1862* (Boston: Lee and Shepard, 1862) contains a record of the political and military gossip of the time. See Robert Carter, "Gurowski," *Atlantic Monthly* 18 (November 1866), 625–33.

tremendous worker, comes & goes day & night & is the greatest contrast to Gen. Hunter's easy after dinner style.

Montgomery & the 54th Mass. are recalled fr. St. Simon's Island & put here for a time—or just across fr. here on St. Helena Island, where I shall hardly see them. The officers of the 54th have never had a glimpse of my regiment; this I mention because Stephen seemed to confound their criticisms on Montgomery's guerilas with "Cunnel Higginson's reg'lars" as mine call themselves.

Last night on Dress Parade a white soldier said audibly behind me "By—to think of my living to see a nigger regiment drill better than the 104th Pennsylvania. But they do." The 104th is the best white regiment here.

My claims of *superiority* to the white reg'ts here in soldierly appearance may seem extravagant, but you must remember that there are no *good* white reg'ts anywhere except regulars & a few others—chiefly from Mass^tts—& then that my men hv. some great advantages. All white soldiers *look* dirty, whether they are or not, from the sunburn & the beard, whereas my men's complexions are the best possible to hide it, a shiny black skin always looks clean. Then the light blue pantaloons of our army hv. the same disadvantage over the dark blue of my regiment. I observe this difference in the 54th Mass. Then the artistic effect of the line of white officers against this sombre & steady background is very good. Any artist would prefer to hv. his soldiers black.

People are in a spasm of kindness about writing to me. I can't expect it to last, but it is very nice while it does. I look forward to a time when ordnance writing will be got under, as people do to the last weed in their gardens—and then I can answer them.

Stephen's letters make me feel how gifts & opportunities go together. Think of his having ten children of whom to write the latest statistics in his letters—soon he will hv. an own domestic correspondent in each of the more prominent nations of the globe—& all out of his own homestead.

Love to all
T. W. H.


*"It was very boarding schooly, the box"*
TO LOUISA STORROW HIGGINSON
HEADQRS. 1^ST S.C.V.
BEAUFORT S.C.
JULY 2. 1863

*Dearest Mother*

Last night the box appeared, having come by this "Arago"[.] No catastrophe inside save the collapse of one jelly bottle in a box, distributing

carmel sweetness in unexpected places, even to the outside of "Elizabeth." I hope the inside doesn't need it. But no great harm was done,
thanks in part to the beneficent towels of which I was very specially in
need. It was very boarding schooly, the box—& I shall struggle to be generous & share it with the boys. Biscuit ginger cakes, maple sugar, prunes,
sweetmeats, little bottle of jelly &c all came triumphant, but towels
& chocolate were the best. Down here I can't get milk Coffee I drink at
morning, but never at night, so this supplies. A box is good even with
"noffin in it," as Carrie Channing[181] in infancy reproached Mrs.
Tracy's[182] basket. Much more one like this.

Frank Higginson & Cabot Russell[183] dined here today, never having
visited my camp before—nice manly boys—the latter square & short with
great square head & hair oiled. I gave them of the box. The 54th chafe under the burning of Darien[184] & their reproachful letters from home—& it
didn't console them to hear that one of my lieutenants & 25 men took it last
autumn & didn't burn it.

Frank was manly & quiet about his brothers, though no want of feeling
evidently.[185]

The pens we now get are the only steel pen made in this country & I
hope the manufacturers will either cease or improve.

I am happy, dearest mother, in thinking that you enjoy my book indeed
I think your pleasure in "Water Lilies"[186] was what chiefly led me farther
into that channel. I have hardly seen any notices of the book, but knew it
would be praised as all new books are. I have heard nothing about the sale,
& cannot arouse any very great interest.

The 52 Pa. are to celebrate July 4th & hv. asked me for an oration!! I may
make a speech with others.

Gen. Saxton is a good deal depressed, I think & does not seem well,
shows more sensitiveness than he should on Gillmore's being put over

181. Carrie Channing (later Cabot), TWH's niece (daughter of his wife's sister
Ellen), came to live with him in 1853 along with her mother and her brothers Walter and
Eugene (her sister Margaret was already a member of TWH's household).

182. A friend from Newburyport.

183. Captain Francis L. Higginson, 54th Massachusetts; Captain Cabot Russell,
54th Massachusetts, killed at Fort Wagner, South Carolina, July 18, 1863.

184. Darien, Georgia was attacked on June 11, 1863.

185. Two of his older brothers, Major Henry Lee Higginson and Captain James
Jackson Higginson, served with distinction in the 1st Massachusetts Cavalry.

186. Thomas Wentworth Higginson, "Water-Lilies," *Atlantic Monthly* 2 (September
1858), 465–73. This essay was now included in TWH's newly-published *Out-Door Papers*,
along with other *Atlantic Monthly* essays, published between 1858 and 1862, on such topics
as health, physical fitness, masculine vigor, wildlife, floriculture, and seasonal weather.

him. I have no doubt that he had been led to expect the command of the Department & now I think he wishes to get out of it. He scarcely ever comes to the camp now, my dealings being almost wholly with Gen. Gillmore, & with Col. Davis of Pa (who commands this post) & both are as kind as possible. Gillmore is like a driving railroad man.

Cousin Eliza Guild has written me a very kind note—how [ ][187] she seems. Chas. Norton wrote one also—it is funny to have these unexpected epistles crop out. Next I expect to hear from Dr. Dewey[188] or Miss Dix[189] or Alexandra the Dane.

Nice old Mr. Saxton goes by the Arago—as imperturbably cheerful as Mr. Gordon though less peculiarly elegant.

Ever affectionately
(even before the box)
T. W. H.

*"We are peacefully here & likely to remain"*
To Louisa Storrow Higginson
Hdqrs. Beaufort S.C.
July 8, 1863

*Dearest Mother*

We are peacefully here & likely to remain; while most of the troops are ordered to Folly Island, Gen. Gillmore's scene of operations. One small job has been allotted to us, incidental to the main operation, & that is all. To this I do not object, because I think if there is much done in that region, we shall ultimately have a hand in it; & if not, there will be a good deal of hard fatigue duty to be done. Gen. Gillmore is a man of superior energies & will take Fort Sumter if it can be done with his force, & I think it can: at all events have far more hope of it than before. He & Gen. Saxton are on very good terms, though I think there is some old West Point rivalry between them, perhaps, wh. makes it harder for Gen. Saxton. Then the latter was undoubtedly promised command of the Dep't shld. Gen. Hunter go away.

I am well so far, though not so strong as at home—therm° fr. 80° to 90° in shade at noon, but comfortable at morning & night. It's a very good climate for sleep, I find, & for appetite. Dr. Rogers has yielded for a time & Mrs. Lander has taken him to her house, she is a noble, generous creature, thoroughly highminded & full of brains; we all like her more & more.

187. The copy-text is illegible here.

188. Possibly Orville Dewey (1794–1882), Unitarian clergyman and author.

189. Perhaps Dorothea Lynde Dix (1802–1887), National Superintendent of Women Nurses.

It was too bad the mails by the Arago were stopped but it was a military measure.

Love to all. Ever thine
T. W. Higginson

*"I had a knock on the side"*
To Louisa Storrow Higginson
Hdqrs. 1st S.C.V.
Beaufort S.C.
July 12. 1863

*Dearest Mother*
Only time to say that we have had another expedition up the S. Edisto River past Wiltown nearly to Jacksonboro RR. Crossing.—30 miles & brought away 200 contrabands—such a scene—"like notin' but de Judgment Day" they said. I had a knock on the side, not breaking the skin, I don't know from what, which still lames me somewhat but it doesn't amount to the dignity of a wound, though the papers may spread it. I submit to be quiet for a few days & be taken care of, but I am in camp & hv. a nice time. You need not fear any bad results. Ever thine

T. W. H.

*"It only felt like a smart slap"*
To Mary Channing Higginson
Hdqrs. 1st S.C.V.
Beaufort S.C.
July 12. 1863

Dearest I have no time to write more than a word, but a mail may go. We have had another expedition up the South Edisto River 30 miles, nearly to the RR Crossing at Jacksonboro got 200 contrabands—such a scene "like notin' but de Judgment Day" the poor things said. I had a knock in the side from a piece of wood or perhaps of spent shell—it did not break the skin but jarred me somewhat & *might have been* bad Dr R. says, had it been worse—that seems the amount of it. It lames me a little, & I shall keep still a day or two, or as long as necessary so don't be disturbed if you see some marvellous tale in the papers. I will write a full account presently. We were gone 36 hours. Perhaps Dr. Rogers will go on this "Fulton" but I don't think he can get ready in time. I tell you the thing precisely as it is dear, & you have no reason to be anxious. It only felt like a smart slap & was no more. I have no pain, only a little lingering stiffness & bruise, no fever, sleep sound, can walk about, but try to keep still, sitting or lying. I am in camp but can go to Mrs. Lander's whenever I wish. You can see that Dr. R. would not think of going home if he had any cause for anxiety about me—and if he don't go, it will be because he can't get his leave of absence in time. Goodbye darling, glad you liked Mrs. Dewhurst[190]—don't know what you tell me abt Mr. Cowing for nor about Sally's preserves.[191]

Love to M. Thine own l. d.

*"why it is Arcadia, Syrian peace"*
To Louisa Storrow Higginson
Beaufort S.C.
July 14 1863

*Dearest Mother*

Of all the humbugs of war, command me to being "wounded." Sound sleep, steady pulse, appetite moderate but reliable, good digestion, no pain, no dressings or doses, a pleasant languor, nothing to do & no wish to do anything, a beautifully kept house & nobody but Dr R. & myself in it, the hostess herself absent,—chocolate, toast, beefsteak, ice, water-melons,—to lie all day on a breezy balcony with green leaves & floating clouds,—why it is Arcadia, Syrian peace[192] immortal leisure. I blush to have bought it so cheaply as by a mere black & blue spot on the side, to show where a bombshell did *not* touch me. The Dr says (Francis being one of the "profession") "Say that all the danger to be apprehended was of inflammation of the abdominal wall, but that danger is now entirely past, & nothing is needed but quiet." You see, because of temperate habits, the abdominal wall entirely refused to be inflamed & that settled the matter. It is simply as if I had had a fall at the gymnasium & had to keep still a few days. When I sit or stand up I feel weak & am somewhat lame, as if with a rheumatism or stitch in the side, but I need no help in dressing or bathing.

Mrs. Lander is at Folly Island, seeing about the wounded there. Her house is as large & capacious as her heart & she treats Dr. R. & me as if we were exiled Stuarts.[193] She reminds me of Anne with a shade less of health & more of self confidence,—with a stage vivacity yet lingering in her

190. Hattie A. (Somerby) Dewhurst, wife of First Lieutenant George W. Dewhurst (Adjutant).

191. Sarah Bowditch.

192. TWH may be alluding here to George W. Curtis's portrait of Syrian (and, more generally, romantic Oriental) bliss in *Nile Notes of a Howadji* and *The Howadji in Syria*.

193. James II (ruled 1685–1688), a zealous Catholic convert, fled to France in the face of the invasion by the Protestant William of Orange.

manner, & a purity of voice & articulation that would put Louisa in bliss to hear. Strong, shrewd, & conquering, stainless & fearless, a thoroughly rich & noble woman.

Before you get this I shall be up & about again by all appearance—so don't be hoping it will be anything to run home on.

Love to all—ever thine
—T. W. H.

I am about writing to Stephen.


*"a black & blue spot, as big as my two hands"*
To Mary Channing Higginson
Beaufort S.C.
July 14, 1863

Well dearest I am having a nice lazy time for a week, in a contentment that makes a so called wound appear a great humbug. I feel just as if I had had some mishap at the Gymnasium, lamed my hip a little & weakened me by the shock. There is absolutely nothing to get up anxiety about, not enough for a decent excuse for going home. We are now satisfied that nothing touched me, but the shell passed within about six inches of my side, just above the hip making by the concussion a black & blue spot, as big as my two hands. In that region I am somewhat lame, like rheumatism, but all organs are perfectly right, sleep sound, pulse undisturbed, appetite moderate but steady; require no help in dressing or walking, have no treatment save an occasional wet cloth & lie all day on my camp bedstead upon a lovely balcony with boughs & birds & breezes around me. Mrs. Lander is away at Folly Island, the seat of war, & all the nice clean housekeeping goes on for Dr. Rogers & me. Dr. R. says I am in the condition of a person nearly struck by lightning & all that is necessary is quiet. In a more stimulated system he says there wd. be danger of inflammation, but this is the 4th day, without any, & there is no fear. This is all there is to tell, dear, I keep back nothing.

If, as is probable, my quiet is to be a matter of days only, all right—if it had been of weeks & months I shld. probably have gone home. Now, there seems no need of that, though no doubt this increases, rather than diminishes, the prospect of a furlough this summer.

Dr. Rogers is doing well, lives an easy life, like me, & will probably go very soon home.

Boat loads of wounded are coming in from Folly Island & every hour brings some new rumor. We are gradually & surely advancing there.

There is always a breeze here & no suffering from heat. I had chocolate, toast & beefsteak for breakfast, & we have ice & great watermelons—isn't it living in clover. I am almost ashamed to think how pleasant I find it. Now goodbye, dearest, don't despise me.

Thine am, own.

Dr. R. says "Say that all wh. was to be apprehended was inflammation of the abdominal wall & that danger is now entirely past." You see, owing to temperate habits, the abdominal wall entirely refused to be inflamed, & there's an end of it.

*"a twenty days furlough"*
TO LOUISA STORROW HIGGINSON
HEADQ (FORCE OF HABIT)
WATERCURE. WORCESTER
JULY 27. 1863

*Dearest Mother*

I telegraphed to you this morning. Left Beaufort on Thursday & got to NY Sunday P.M. just in time for the night train here. Astonished Mary about 7 a.m. Ann was dressing her hair as I entered the door & Mary had her back to me—Ann exclaimed "Why Mrs Higginson only look here" & Mary thought I was a present of fruit.

There is hardly an external trace of my wound left & I don't think it did me any internal injury whatever. But I have not fully recovered my strength & as Beaufort air has not much tonic in it—though healthy & not so warm as here if I may judge fr. last night & today—Dr. Rogers thought I had better take this chance for a twenty days' furlough.

I have good appetite & digestion & sleep & all that, so I am all right, you must perceive. I can't tell when I shall come to Brattleboro. Probably next week: but shall not have much spare time.

The 54th was badly cut up & Shaw certainly killed.[194] The other officers not dangerously wounded—Frank Higginson was not in the fight; having been sent on other service. After the battle, he was left in command—his seniors being killed wounded or missing. Cabot Russell (Capt.) was probably killed.

With love to all, till I see you.

T. W. H.

I spent 10 days at Mrs. Lander's with Dr. Rogers—she was very kind, tho' mostly away—we voted playing sick very good fun, in other people's houses.

My reg't was not in the fights at James or Morris Islands.

194. Colonel Robert Gould Shaw (1837–1863) was killed by a ball in the chest, July 18, 1863, during the assault on Battery Wagner by the Massachusetts 54th.

## *"I am well enough"*
To Louisa Storrow Higginson
Worcester
July 31. 1863

*Dearest Mother*

I am going up on Monday to stay with you till Wednesday. I am well enough, but don't gain strength very fast which may prove an excuse for getting my furlough extended a little, at which Mary exults.

In haste<br>T. W. H.

## *"myself 'me one' as my men say"*
To Louisa Storrow Higginson
Worcester. Aug 7. 1863

*Dearest Mother*

It was certainly wicked in me not to write you before, but I had so much to do I let it slip. I find we cannot go to Pigeon Cove, there being no room, & I am so much better that I only expect to stay a week over my time, but shall go in the Arago, Sunday week (16th) I may run down to Pigeon Cove for a day, myself "me one" as my men say.

I have had a very kind letter from Uncle James,[195] inviting me to come & stay there, & sending a check for $50 "for war purposes & for the Colonel in particular." Charles H.[196] writes that he shall not go as my quartermaster unless the "ought to" compels him, as if there were a chance it might, but I don't expect it, though I wish he would go.

Dr. Rogers has come & gone to Newport—bringing fair accounts of the regiment in my absence. All seems peaceful at Beaufort—as it certainly is here. I found Margaret here & have enjoyed her—Barbara came the same day: we begin moving today from the house in Chatham St.[197]

It is cooler here now & we are doing very well—Mary is about the same; has not ventured on the elevator again yet.

195. James Perkins Higginson, TWH's paternal uncle.
196. Charles J. Higginson, TWH's first cousin (son of James Perkins Higginson).
197. Apparently while TWH was home on furlough he helped move his wife out of their house and, perhaps, into a boarding house; within a few months she moved to Newport, Rhode Island.

I rode down with W^m Hunt[198] who is painting Mr. Dana.
I hope you are nicely again.

With love to all<br>T. W. H.

*"my piece in the next Atlantic"*
To Louisa Storrow Higginson
Worcester. Mass.
Aug. 12. 1863

*Dearest Mother*

Yours & Louisa's notes came last night; I am so sorry you have been sick.

I am getting on well, despite the heat. You know we had to give up Pigeon Cove, no room there; I thought of going down there for a night, but finding Fields was not there, & being delayed in getting off fr. Boston thither, substituted a drive out of town with Chas. Higginson which I enjoyed much, through beautiful Brookline, visiting Sarah Bowditch, Fanny Head & lastly Louisa Cabot,[199] where we arrived after dark, too late to see babes or Louisa or indeed do anything but hear Louisa's voice, which is worth a long journey in the dark to hear; I had forgotten how delicious her articulation was & perhaps shld. hv. thought less of it by daylight. She & Frank held the babe by turns as it was ailing; & had it not been the warmest & mosquitoest of nights I shld. hv. begged to see the other bairns by candlelight.

I slept at Uncle James's where I was most hospitably entertained: Charles found me a Quartermaster who is to go out with me to Beaufort next Sunday. I did my chores, had some photographs taken, not yet ready, dined with Waldo & Stephen came back.

I saw Frank Cabot[200] again yesterday morning & he said the baby was no worse; had diarrhoea aggravated by heat & sleepless nights & needed chiefly change of weather which has now partially arrived.

Thanks to Louisa for the farther contributions to the Personal Recol-

198. William Morris Hunt (1824–1879), a painter who lived in Brattleboro, Vermont.
199. The first two are TWH's cousins: Sarah Rhea Higginson Bowditch and Frances Saltonstall Higginson Head (both daughters of TWH's uncle, James Perkins Higginson). Mary Louisa Higginson Cabot was his niece (daughter of his brother Francis).
200. Francis Cabot, husband of TWH's niece Mary Louisa Higginson Cabot.

lections of the late Rev. George Dogood which I expect one day to publish, when he ascends like a prophet from some high mountain. You will think this quite in my line after reading my piece in the next Atlantic "The Puritan Parsonage"[201] written long since & delayed ever since I went away.

I expect to go to N.Y. Sat'y night, but may have to go in the morn'g.

Ever affectionately<br>T. S. Higginson

Mary wants me to say that the moths eat up the pretty edge of this pink thing, & she wants to know if Anna can knit her an other one. She sends her love

I want to have by return mail, the address of Mr. W. G. [ ][202] who sent me the Shakspeare—look on the title page—his college &c. I am to have for a lieutenant Mirant Saxton[203] the Gen'l's youngest brother & friend of Storrow's & Frank's

*"I feel very well & quite fit to go"*
To LOUISA STORROW HIGGINSON
ASTOR HOUSE
STETSON & CO
NEW YORK.
SUNDAY. AUG 16. 1863
8 AM

*Dearest Mother*

Here I am, on my way Southward. Steamer sails about 10 probably. I feel very well & quite fit to go.

I notice in the papers the impression given that my reg't is now at Morris Island, but I think this proceeds simply fr. the fact that it was enumerated with the other forces under *the command* of Gen. Gillmore, which of course we are[.] You will hear from me about Aug 28 by the return Arago. Hope you like the Photographs

With love to all, ever thine<br>T. W. H.

Mrs. Stephen Higginson
Brattleboro
Vermont.

201. "The Puritan Minister," *Atlantic Monthly* 12 (September 1863), 265–80.
202. The copy-text is illegible here.
203. Second Lieutenant Merand (or Mirand) W. Saxton.

*"I want to see my black babies"*
To Mary Channing Higginson
On board str. Arago
Aug. 19. 1863.

We expect dearest to get as far as Hilton Head tonight—perhaps to go up to Beaufort. We have had a swift trip, somewhat uncomfortable because of a strong fair wind, which makes the steamer roll. But still it is wonderfully unlike the "Azor"[204] of chaotic memory—what is called here motion wd. there have been called rest.

There are two very pleasant navy officers on board, Capt. Steedman who was at Jacksonville with me & whom I like greatly & Capt. Stevens[205] who preceded me up the St. Mary's, the only other person who has made that perilous trip. We hv. enjoyed comparing notes. Capt. Steedman now commands the "Powhatan"[206] & has Frank Higginson on board, of whom he speaks very highly, & I am glad Frank shld. be in so good a school. Capt. S. is a native Charlestonian & yet thoroughly loyal & manly.

On the wharf in N.Y. I saw Mr. Elisha Rogers, whom I always like, you know. He hinted at the possibility of his coming down here with his wife, to take a plantation. He don't speak of the E. E.[207] family with overflowing affection, & does not see why all the pride shld. be on their side, inasmuch as "Annie ran after James a great deal more than James after her—& owns that she did."

Dr. Dibble of Beaufort a meek little mouse of a man who is on board here—says that Mrs. Lander has left the Dep't., not to return, by desire of the surgeons—that she was indiscreet & imperious in her dealings with the Drs & they cd. not get along with her, &c. I hope she will come back, but I can easily conceive that she would not work well in harness.

I had a very happy vacation, dear & am glad you did not send me word that you were engaged, like Mrs. Angier, when I first arrived. Please take all the rides you can, darling, for my sake: I know it must be so important to you: & you do not get air enough, I am almost sure of it.

I do not see that I am not perfectly well, & feel no anxiety about myself. It seems very natural to be going this way & I want to see my black babies:

204. In "Fayal and the Portuguese," *Atlantic Monthly* 6 (1860), 526–44, TWH's account of a voyage he and his wife made to the island of Fayal in the Azores in Autumn 1855 (returning June 1856), he mentions "three weeks of rough sailing in the good bark Azor" (p. 544) on the return trip.
205. Captain Stevens, in the gunboat *Ottawa*, had previously ascended the St. Mary's and came under intense fire from the bluffs along the river.
206. Captain Charles Steedman.
207. Edward Earle.

& it seemed equally natural the other way, and I equally wanted to see the girl I left behind me.

The naval officers think it will be many weeks before we get control of the forts at the mouth of Charleston harbor, which ought to be done, they say, before going up to the city.

There is not a single lady passenger which is quite remarkable. Young Saxton did not appear.

You wd. hv. liked to see pretty little Nelly Horton, her hair taken up into a waterfall behind, but blowing about in little curly tendrils all over her head; except in this respect she did not seem a day older, nor did the other. Perhaps they appeared a shade more "second rate" than formerly,—but I don't know. Nelly says "some better." They are tired of Jamaica Plain[208] & going to move into Boston.

There are several officers on board from the new colored reg'ts at Philadelphia.[209] I find the examination they pass at Washington is so good that they will secure a better-informed class of officers than in any of the white volunteer regiments.

They have new boats on the Norwich line which are really luxurious, & they stop only three piers from the Arago so that the transfer is very easy. The gangway up to the Arago is a broad sloping plank, wide & with solid sides to it, which you could ascend without great difficulty.[210]

I wrote in NY. to Mr. Black 173 Wash. St. sending $8 for the large photograph & $3 for the dozen small ones ordered.

## *"The Mark Tapley element in me"*
To Louisa Storrow Higginson
Hdqrs. 1st S.C.V.
Aug 23. 1863

*Dearest Mother*

Arrived the 20th & have been very inexplicably well & in high spirits ever since—partly because of the Mark Tapley[211] element in me—every-

208. A suburb of Boston.

209. A committee of civic leaders in Philadelphia secured authorization to recruit black soldiers in the summer of 1863, and rapidly raised ten full regiments; one of them, the 3d U.S. Colored Troops, was present at the surrender of Battery Wagner, September 6, 1863.

210. Apparently during TWH's furlough the idea of Mary joining him at Port Royal, as other officers' wives had done, was discussed. In his October 1 and 9, 1863, letters to his mother, and his October 10 letter to his wife, TWH mentions his decision that Mary should not come to be with him.

211. Mark Tapley is a young man in Dickens' *Martin Chuzzlewit* who characteristically seeks to test his good-naturedness by placing himself in circumstances not conducive to it,

body looked so forlorn in the regiment & yet it was so easy to put every-thing right, or get all started at least in the right way. There is much sickness among officers—my new Lt Col Strong & Major Trowbridge both go North to get well, but the worst is over, for that period of intense heat was the same here, & I rejoice to hv. escaped it.

We shall either stay here for the present or go out on picquet again—probably the former.

Mary will send my sheet of journal. Your box was safe here & I hv. chocolate eno' for a lifetime & drink it daily. Many thanks

I came out with my friend Capt. Steedman, now of the Powhatan who spoke highly of Lieut Frank, & that youth himself came on board for his Captain. I had not seen him since he entered the navy—he was not so *very* handsome as the photos I thought—but goodlooking enough & *very* pleas-ing[.] The P. comes here to coal soon & I shall see him.

Lt. Col. Billings was dismissed for incompetency by a Board of Exam-iners. It is humiliating & you mustn't worry if some of his tears take the form of ink, though he can hardly be so foolish. I pity him a good deal.

In haste
Ever thine
T. W. H.

I hv. read all yr. nice letters wh. I found here—as good as fresh ones. Serg't Sutton has just returned to camp.[212]

Capt. Steedman is superior to any naval officer I hv. met & I am glad F. shld. be under him. He commanded the naval forces at Jacksonville & I knew him well. A Charleston man, but thoroughly true.

*"our camp is at a very beautiful place"*
To Louisa Storrow Higginson
Hdqrs. 1st S.C.V.
Beaufort S.C.
Aug. 28. 1863.

*Dearest Mother*

I am perfectly well & enjoy myself. Things go well in the reg't, for though I am short in respect to officers, still I am rid of some who were a

---

since, as he says, "with my good health and spirits it would be more creditable in me to be jolly where there's things a going on, to make one dismal." Charles Dickens, *Martin Chuz-zlewit*, ed. Margaret Cardwell (1843–1844; Oxford: Clarendon Press, 1982). 115.

212. Sergeant Robert Sutton was court-martialed for mutiny following the raid, led by Francis Merriam, mentioned above, letter to Louisa Storrow Higginson, June 5, 1863. Sutton received a full pardon and returned with honor to his regiment.

great incumbrance as Lt. Col. Billings & Capt Tonking, & promotions hv. taken place which are a great improvement. Then our camp is at a very beautiful place, the most so we hv. had—it was changed in my absence. The lines extend almost to the brink of a bluff above the river, where it curves just outside Beaufort, so we look along the town, one way, & along Beaufort the other: the ships & steamers & a great reach of the river lie directly before us, seen beneath a few pine trees. It is quite comfortable now & there is no increase of sickness, though some of the officers are still very sick in Beaufort. I think I am better than at any time this summer & my duties not as great as at some times. For aught I see, we are likely to stay here some time though we may go on picquet; this is more likely than to Morris I. where troops abound. They say there are 45,000.

What I miss most is my messmates Drs. Rogers & Minor, the Adj't & wife & Qrmaster. Dr. Minor will return soon, but the Adj't is seriously ill in Beaufort with jaundice—he looks like *thin* gold—gold leaf perhaps. I wish his wife were here & shall perhaps write to her.

I was so glad you liked the photographs—the one I liked far the best was the small profile—the attitude is better than the large one, or rather the chair was better. The front face I do not like so well.

The Powhatan has been at Hilton Head, but it was not Frank's turn for leave. His companion & friend McNair came up, a pleasing well bred youth, like most of the naval officers.

All agree that Ft. Sumter is reduced, but that we cannot safely take possession till other forts are. Gen. Gillmore has one gun wh. can throw shell into Charleston—some 5 miles. & has coolly notified them to withdraw the women & children, the first time probably that such a request ever came from 5 miles off. All now depends on removing the obstructions (piles) east of Ft. Sumter between that & Moultrie[213]—because the Monitors cannot go to the west side of Ft. S. drawing too much water.

You ask why Lt Col. Billings left—he was examined at my request by a military board & dismissed for incompetency. Mrs. Lander went North for change of air but the surgeons don't mean she shall come back if they can help it. There is something to be said on both sides; she being doubtless imperious & unmanageable.

Ever thine<br>T. W. Higginson<br>Col. cmg.

213. Fort Moultrie, on Sullivan's Island, across from Fort Sumter at the entrance to Charleston Harbor.

*"My trip home was a dear little oasis"*
To MARY CHANNING HIGGINSON
HDQRS &C. BEAUFORT S.C.
AUG. 30. 1863

My darling I got yr. two letters by the Fulton & one fr. Bratt. How they like the picture, I'm so glad. You know I haven't the sitting one, but think the other vignette admirable. I have given Mrs. Saxton one: & the officers all like them.

I am very happy, dear, because I see it was right to come back. My trip home was a dear little oasis & you may tell Mrs. Clapp I shall always love the watercure as much as any of her lone women can. It was a great relief dear to hear that you were happy because you thought I was: it's a great deal better than behaving like a goose. Perhaps it did me good mind & body, the change; I feel in a quieter mood, though mine is always pretty quiet, than since I first came out here. I have no restless ambition, never have had; & am content to let things take their course; have no tremendous desire to go to Morris Island even, but will take it when it comes, though I don't think it will. I expect that we shall stay as we are for the present. Capt. Dutch[214] (Navy) says the highest ambition of most Naval officers is to lie at anchor & keep their ships & crew *clean*, & for the present that seems to be what I am doing. The severity of heat is plainly past, & it is now cool & rainy every night—all say it is much healthier than last year, & I suppose the only autumnal danger will be of chills & fever, to which I fancy I hv. no great aptitude.

I enjoyed the many letters I found here & read them all carefully. I am going to write to Charlotte P. H.[215] Mr. Jillson may have everything left in the house & welcome, only the pictures Charlotte kept. I want you to pay Charlotte the $5 for Marg't's room for this quarter ending Oct. 1.—She may resist but ought to take it. I suppose as to money she will be better off, now, & hardly more lonely

You know, dearest, the Bellows' are authorized to spend $30 for a cistern, & send the bill to you. Waldo is all right about the dividend.

Isn't it too bad for the Beaufort ladies of color. I made a General Order that they should only come here on Sunday & here the first Sunday is a hard rain.

Why weren't you interested in Lady Audley;[216] I am very much though I divine it all; I think Mrs. Brad. quite remarkable. The Atlantic is poor & I

214. Captain J. C. Dutch, commander of U.S. blockading vessel *Kingfisher*.
215. To Charlotte Hawes, post haste.
216. Mary Elizabeth Braddon, *Lady Audley's Secret* (London: Tinsley, 1862).

hv. tried to guess which of those very poor stories is Rose Terry & which Gail Hamilton.[217]

Dr. Minor has given me a silver plated "collapsion" cup (shuts up in rings)—& a little fork & spoon with knife. He is detached for duty at Hilton Head now, but I hope not for long.

I send you some cotton, which is getting ripe.

Aug 31 Goodbye, [ ], steamer going a day too soon.[218]


*"it looked pleasant morally if uncomfortable bodily"*
To Louisa Storrow Higginson
Hdqrs. 1st S.C.V.
Beaufort S.C. Sept 8. 1863

*My dearest Mother*

Still at anchor here & until I get more officers, I hope to remain so. While we are so I can do very well as my good health still continues, & the worst of the work of getting to rights is over. Besides, almost every day is cool & pleasant now & much like a New England September. We have the pleasantest camp we ever had & have thoroughly learned the only safe camp rule, namely if you are put anywhere for a day to go to work as if you were to spend the rest of the war on that precise ground.

All day & night we hear the heavy remote boom of the great guns on Morris Island & Charleston harbor, & it wd. seem hard to stay away but for the heavy fatigue duty which I know is thrown upon the Colored regiments there. Not from ill will but because they endure the work in summer better.

*Afternoon*—The guns boomed in good earnest & the report now is of the evacuation of Forts Wagner & Gregg (no doubt of it)[219]—& an attack on Sullivan's Island[220] commencing—This does indeed look promising.

I have no added light yet respecting Mary's coming here this winter, nor shall I before the end of the month, I suppose. Dr. Rogers expects to come down about Oct. 20, & hopes to bring Annie Earle, James' intended with him. Though her parents try to hold out stoutly.

217. The August issue does contain a contribution by Gail Hamilton, but none by Rose Terry. Gail Hamilton, "Side-Glances at Harvard Class-Day," *Atlantic Monthly* 12 (August 1863), 242–50. At this time contributions to the magazine were printed unsigned, so perhaps Higginson mistook Louisa May Alcott's contribution, "Debby's Début," *Atlantic Monthly* 12 (August 1863), 160–82, for a Rose Terry story.

218. This line is added in pencil; several words are smudged or erased.

219. Batteries Wagner and Gregg, on Morris Island, were found on September 7, 1863, to have been evacuated.

220. Union monitors fired on Fort Moultrie, on Sullivan's Island, September 7, 1863, but it did not fall.

Thirty sick & wounded arrived fr. Morris I. today, including a rebel Major & Surgeon. I saw a black soldier borne along on a stretcher by four white ones & it looked pleasant morally if uncomfortable bodily. They are certainly quite as well off in hospital here as whites; indeed better for they have a larger constituency in the town & receive more attention. No one can realize what a different position in all other things this military respectability implies.

Storrow will hv. had interesting experiences at Morris Island no doubt, though I don't see what he is there for, unless Maj. Stearns is there too. I dare say he will come here first or last.

Nothing heard of Mirand Saxton the General's youngest brother, who desired a commission in this reg't but I dare say he will come. He is a friend of Storrow's & Frank's.

Give my love to all, Lizzie especially who is I hope better. I have not yet spoken of the dear little baby, the first of that new generation to pass away.[221] It must have seemed strange & touching to you, dear mother. With true love to all

Ever thine<br>T. W. H.

Mary will send a sheet of journal

*"rheumatiz is a citizen of the world"*
To Mary Channing Higginson
Hdqrs. 1ˢᵗ S.C.V. Sept 8. 1863[222]

Well darling your little pet Minor will be made happy; I have an order fr. Gen. S. at my request, recalling him fr. H. H. & sending down Dr. Schofield to relieve him. Dr. Hawks doesn't like it a bit; nothing but Dr. Rogers can ever make him & M. work smoothly together; but he & S. did splendidly being both quacks, whom you know dear we well regulated homoeopaths don't approve. I say we, having just cured Lt. West[223] of a sore throat, by the most fearfully random shots of Belladonna & Hepar.[224] This same Lt. W. a fine agreeable Protestant Irish *gentleman* (as FLB. wd. say) looked with delight at the address of yr. letter & declared it was by an

---

221. Elizabeth Higginson Cabot, born February 1, 1863, died August 21, 1863; this child was the daughter of TWH's niece Mary Louisa Higginson Cabot (daughter of TWH's brother Francis John); thus the baby was Louisa Storrow Higginson's great-granddaughter.

222. "1863" is added in pencil.

223. Either First Lieutenant James B. West or Second Lieutenant Harry C. West.

224. Plant extracts used in homeopathic tinctures.

English lady—no American lady ever wrote that. You poor child, I fear rheumatiz is a citizen of the world.

You don't know what an improved set of officers I've got. Captain Dolly I shall have courtmartialed & dismissed the service as soon as he comes from the North—& Capt. Randolph I have a plan to dispose of, & then I shall feel as happy as Tom Beecher[225] when two out of his three church committee were in the State Prison.

As for Lt. Col. Strong I hear very poor accounts & doubt if he gets well; he has only lost since leaving here, & hadn't much to lose. The Adj't will be saved by going home this boat—he has his leave.

One of Gen. Gillmore's staff was here today & says Storrow is at Morris Island—he doesn't know for what. I am surprised, as Maj. Stearns is said to be in another direction. Probably S. will come here.

My NY Times comes daily & I enjoy it as you do yr. Journal—it comes up to the very day of sailing.

There my darling this is all I now have time for. I have written Mrs. Earle (Edward) polite but distinct—you know she wishes me still to pursue poor Gen. Gillmore—but as a man has just been put in arrest for urging a rejected application it is a pretty plain hint.

Goodbye dear [ ][226]

*"They do drill so pretty"*
To Louisa Storrow Higginson
Hdqrs. 1st S.C.V. Camp Shaw
Beaufort S.C. Sept. 15. 1863

*Dearest Mother*

We still live, in a peaceful condition, picking up the loose ends & getting gradually into shape. No signs of our being ordered away, nor do I care to be because the colored reg'ts have to do so much fatigue duty at Morris Island; we have enough of it here, though only our just share—still the Quartermasters & Engineers always prefer our men, I often wish for them that power of making themselves disagreeable which the elder Mr. Weller vainly invoked for himself "it's a horrid sitiwation to be so much sought after."[227] If they were white soldiers I wouldn't object, but they do drill so pretty, I hate to see 'em do anything else.

225. Perhaps Thomas Beecher (1824–1900), an unconventional Congregational clergyman known as "Father Tom."

226. The copy-text is illegible here.

227. In chapter 52 of *The Pickwick Papers*, Tony Weller, widower for the second time, complains to his son Samuel that he is beset by widows proferring consolation and

Hot sun but cool airs most of the day & I smell nothing like yellow fever anywhere & don't see why this year there shld. be any trouble. I am well & having just conquered a supply of milk daily, have no fears for the future. I find that even my sleepfulness which I always supposed a self existent thing, sufficient unto itself, is partly dependent upon the cow—nothing takes the place of her. She puts instantly that solid bar of sleep between day & day, of which Emerson speaks in case of Englishmen.[228] Probably from the opacity of the fluid though nature here waters her milk by leaving her vegetation unwatered.

I hear nothing of Storrow & don't know if he has gone back or is coming here. There is not very few communication between here & there & travelling, not official, is a good deal checked.

I don't wonder at Lizzy's being puzzled by the picture of Walter, but I remembered her wishing for me as she showed me her book, so I thought I would send her this, which I had; accidentally I sealed & sent it without writing in it, & it went by private hand to N.Y.

I have had one or two good notes from Sarah Draper née Atkins whom I remembered as a child; she is interested in circulated petitions for complete emancipation. She speaks as if her life had known great sorrow, unkindness &c—tell me something about her.

We are very anxious about the Chaplain who went with a few men on an excessively daring expedition on the main land. There is reason to fear his capture in which case he would probably be hanged, having no uniform to screen him from the fate of a spy. But he has a wonderful faculty for getting into scrapes & out of them, & I hope for something better.

Our mails are very irregular just now in going as the "Fulton" will be delayed & other steamers probably go first—so I will send this to take it's chance.

With love to all
Ever affectly
T. W. Higginson
Col. comg.

---

other favors. "'Wot a thing it is to be so sought arter!' observed Sam, smiling." Charles Dickens, *The Pickwick Papers*, ed. James Kinsley (1837; Oxford: Clarendon Press, 1987), 808.

228. "They eat, and drink, and live jolly in the open air, putting a bar of solid sleep between day and day." Ralph Waldo Emerson, *English Traits* (1856), in *Essays and Lectures* (New York: The Library of America, 1983), 804.

*" 'Scroby' the indomitable"*
To Louisa Storrow Higginson
Camp Shaw
Sept. 24. 1863

*Dearest Mother*
I can't write much this mail for want of time on the last day, but I send some Journal through Mary. I am still well & now consider my epoch of fatigue over, my major, "Scroby" the indomitable, having returned in tip top condition & able to relieve me very greatly. We have had splendid October weather, almost Princeton[229] like, so that one cd. do anything; & now I shall take some holidays. Beaufort is quiet, females stealing slowly back. In the reg't all goes well; my crack company (G) is just back fr. a very hazardous expedition on the main land, got up by Capt. Bryant a very daring scout here, who asked for them. Sergt Sutton & Corporal Long (who went to burn the bridge at Jacksonville) were in it. One corporal lived 7 days without food, if you can believe it. They cut the wires & read despatches for 5 hours & finally had to retreat. My Chaplain, the operator & a Lieut of the 4th S.C.V. (just started) were captured & one soldier—probably of this reg't. So we hear by the NY Herald of 19th. All the rest are back safe. These are the first prisoners we hv. ever lost.
Thanks for yr. letters & for sending Waldo's which are always characteristic & entertaining.

Ever thine
T. W. H.

*"I am in rather a state of collapse"*
To Louisa Storrow Higginson
Beaufort. Oct. 1. 1863[230]

*Dearest Mother*
I hv. decided that for various reasons Mary ought not to come here.—as I cannot go for her especially,—can't get leave
Just at present too I am in rather a state of collapse, having succumbed after a few days prostration in camp, from mere debility, nothing worse & having come in here to Mrs Hale's Officer's Hospital[231] to rest & be away fr the nursery. I hv. a slight diarrhoea not severe, some appetite & can now

229. Princeton, Massachusetts, where TWH summered in 1853 and 1862.
230. "1863" is added in pencil.
231. Mrs. Elizabeth B. Hale, the "queer Mrs Hale" TWH had encountered on the steamer when he first came to Port Royal (see above, Journal, November 22, 1862).

digest[.] With milk eggs soup & Scotch ale I shall come up readily especially as the malarious season is almost over. I have a large room & a balcony & William & fare nicely Pulse 72°–75°.

Nobody sees any signs of positive trouble it is merely negative—I thought very likely I should hv. such a fit after the Major came. So you needn't be anxious. Perhaps I can write again

Ever thine<br>T. W. H.

Mrs Hale is a busy little Bostonian—*Mrs Sykes* softened by North End & the Music Hall.[232] She is *very* kind.

## "Doing well only 'powerful weak'"
To Louisa Storrow Higginson
Beaufort Oct. 2. 1863[233]
24 HRS. LATER

*Dearest Mother*

Doing well only "powerful weak." fair appetite & digestion improving steadily, but can't sit or stand much, head too blurry & weak—I sleep a good deal after my fashion, don't read much & keep quiet. I need nothing but some ale for wh. I hv. sent. Nobody can find anything but "General Debility" & nobody dreams of sending me North, I am happy to say. I am being taken very good care of & quite satisfied with my condition.

Ever thine<br>T. W. H.

## "a sort of good natured Hurly Burly Hall"
To Louisa Storrow Higginson
Officers Hospital
Oct. 9. 1863

*My dearest Mother*

I remain in this peaceful abode, more peaceful outside than inside perhaps, though my special career exhibits no want of that attribute. We have

232. The allusion may be to the Mrs. Sykes in Charlotte Brontë's *Shirley* (1849; Oxford: Oxford University Press, 1981), a "tall, bilious gentlewoman" who "had had a cough for the last twenty years" (pp. 109, 110), a proficient gossip and devotée of the local clergy; in short, a rather dull and smug country lady. TWH suggests that social and cultural improvement (i.e., through attendance at the Boston Music Hall) has made Mrs. Hale somewhat less provincial and ordinary than Mrs. Sykes.
233. "1863" is added in pencil.

days lovely as those of a Northern October, & more unvaried, & why they don't give strength more rapidly I can't conceive; they go through all the motions of it, but without a result. Here am I a legitimate subject of it, sound mind & limb, no specific ailment, eat well & sleep well & do all but get well. That is I am still very weak; sit up now some 4 hours a day or more & walk out once or twice to the river at the end of the garden which is rather larger than yours. My theory is that in about a fortnight when frosts & Dr. Rogers arrive I shall take a faster start. At any rate it is evident that it is merely a question of time, & at this season all is in my favor—if it were spring I probably shld. not dare to risk staying here.

There are but few officers here & one poor fellow Capt Badger U.S.N.[234] so infinitely worse off than I that I feel like a culprit of health beside him, leg broken by a ball & now lying 33 days in one position & the wound doing very badly at that. It must require great faith in the value of a limb to hold on to it under such circumstances, especially since Palmer's advent.[235]

This house is a sort of good natured Hurly Burly Hall,[236] where W[m] and I pursue our sequestered housekeeping. Mrs. H. I never see; occasionally a hurried step in the entry & a quick dash at the door announces Miss Sentinel a short damsel with round shoulders auburn curls & good natured waxen face & tongue like a locomotive; she flits in without visible errand, eagerly turns over everything in the room as if looking for something which never yet has been announced or found, talking miscellaneous information all the time, & then suddenly out again, murmuring that she must get some water, or some such dim proposition,—and is seen no more.

234. Perhaps Captain Oscar C. Badger, Lt.-Commander of the U.S. Ironclad *Montauk*, which bombarded Fort Sumter.

235. B. Frank. Palmer, whose leg had been amputated at the age of ten in consequence of an accident, invented an orthopedic limb for himself which he later manufactured for others. Oliver Wendell Holmes, TWH's old friend, wrote about the "Palmer Leg" in "The Human Wheel, Its Spokes and Felloes," *Atlantic Monthly* 11 (May 1863), 567–80, where he acknowledged that because "the limbs of our friends and countrymen are a part of the melancholy Harvest which War is sweeping down" the artificial limb was newly beneficial.

236. In Louisa May Alcott's "Hospital Sketches," first published in the *Boston Commonwealth* in May-June 1863, then collected as *Hospital Sketches* (Boston: James Redpath, 1863), Nurse Tribulation Periwinkle is assigned to the "Hurly-burly House" or "Hurly-burly Hotel," which has been converted into a military hospital in which "disorder, discomfort, bad management, and no visible head" were the usual state of affairs. See *Hospital Sketches*, in *Alternative Alcott*, ed. Elaine Showalter (New Brunswick: Rutgers University Press, 1988), 3–73 (quotation, p. 51).

I hv. quite as much company as is desirable, what with officers & civilians & sympathetic females who suggest corn starch and look aggrieved that I am not [in] bed, which I haven't been for a day

Mary's letters go to my heart, poor thing, with her buoyant hopes of coming out here which I have had to destroy, & yet it seemed impossible to do anything else.

Thanks for my letters I am glad you enjoyed Cousin May Ann's & Cousin Louisa's[237] visit so much.

Ever affectionately
T. W. H.

*"every patient . . . wants to be pulsed & thumped & auscultated a little"*
To Mary Channing Higginson
Officers Hospital
Oct. 10. 1863

Well my darling today I think I really feel somewhat stronger, for almost a week I have seemed so stationary—no reason why I should not gain, except that I did not. No new symptoms develope, only the same "General Debility"; at night I shld. have "sweats" but for the beneficent sulphuric acid: fifteen drops make a sort of lemonade & save me. This is the *weakest* thing I do, I suppose, & while this lasts, I have no strength to count upon. If it were a hot season coming on, of course it wd. not be safe for me to stay here otherwise I shall stay unless I shld. find myself growing positively worse or some latent disease developing of wh. there is now no sign.

Of course I am eager to have Dr. Rogers come, because I have much faith in his diagnosis of disease & none at all in that of Drs. Hayden & Minor, whom I see. Theirs consists of "How are you today? Can I do anything for you?" more friendly than searching. Of course every patient, of well regulated mind, wants to be pulsed & thumped & auscultated a little, & to think that somebody else knows what's what.

I think as little as I can about your plans which I murdered, it makes me feel so guilty; yet I believe I was right. I need to get your next letters darling.

The only thing that comforts me is the thought that if you are better than you hv. been for years, another autumn may find you equally so.

Even now you must see, apart fr. all else, if there is a chance of my being compelled to go North after all;—& when one is as weak as I, there is no telling what may happen—it would be a mistake for you to come here.

237. Possibly Louisa Gore Higginson, TWH's first cousin (unmarried daughter of his uncle, James Perkins Higginson).

This house is queer—there is a speechless sister whom I never see—the mother & other sister never cease talking an instant. Little Miss Sentinel is a miniature Sarah Chase, at any hour she bursts the door in with a great stamp & enters smiling—never a sign of an errand, but always begins looking on all the tables & under newspapers for something never yet explained or found—talking & smiling all the time, about "the bees are out" or something equally ["]foreign"; then suddenly jerks out again murmuring something about "must go for water," or "oranges" & comes no more. She has round shoulders, a waxen face & tangled brown curls; is overwhelmed with ennui at having only 6 invalids in the house (& no domestics at present) & wants to go to Morris Island for occupation.

The pleasantest person in the house is a young Dr. Willard[238] of the Navy, who is taking care of a wounded Captain—him I find to be yr. cousin, Robert by name, Sidney's *brother*. He is very kind & companionable. After I had cross-questioned him & fitted him with a cousinry I told him that people fr. Boston & that region didn't bore each worse than any other people *after* they had got the genealogical arrangement fairly settled & found out who was who. Up to that time they were of course intolerable,—until all the cross questioning was ended.

Do you remember young Albert Browne then of Salem & the Burns affair who went to see me at Pigeon Cove that summer? By a singular coincidence he has just been to see me here—he is now Military Secretary to Gov. Andrew & long since spoiled by that & corpulence. His father a kind pleasant man is to take E. L. Pierce's place here.

Goodbye my dearest darling [ ][239]

*"I lead a rather agreeable single-gentleman life"*
TO LOUISA STORROW HIGGINSON
BEAUFORT S.C.
OCT. 17. 1863[240]

*Dearest mother*

I gain slowly & not lose & have no idea of coming home—no occasion for it—Dr. R. began vehemently on that point, but as he has found more of my condition has subsided. He sees that nothing is the matter, chest all thumped & found right, & virtually admits that I shall do well enough here. I now ride over to camp on horseback every day or two, for entertainment

238. Dr. Robert Willard.
239. The copy-text is illegible here.
240. "1863" is added in pencil.

& shall perhaps go to a plantation & spend a few days, & there is nothing pending to *hurry* me to duty before I am ready. The nightsweats wh. were the worst symptom at first, though I kept them away by taking nightly 15 drops of sulphuric acid, a blessed thing for that, (does Francis[241] use it?) have been outgrown I think, though I still take 8 drops, lessening a drop nightly. Appetite & digestion all right. I lead a rather agreeable single-gentleman life (Margaret's ideal of bliss)—William brings my meals & makes a fire morning & evening of blazing pine; I hv. visitors & books enough & strength comes—but slowly.—Mrs. Hale the impulsive offers me the room all winter to sleep in, gratis—but I shan't accept, though till the end of the month I shall probably sleep in doors.

Gen. Gillmore's letter abt Frank is worth having. He is cordial, & not slow to praise, but this was going a little out of the way. Everybody ridicules Dahlgren,[242] army & navy both—but they say now he has positive orders to move, I hv. a belief that the destinations are not so formidable.

You speak of a *box*, therefore I will offer some hints. My supply of chocolate is very ample, also of preserved milk or whatever it is. Little ginger cakes soften & spoil. Those little drops & sweetmeats in the long cylindrical box were very consoling, & fig-paste is always welcome. A well devised plum cake in a pasteboard box wd. come well & wd. be very agreeable as cake of any kind rarely appears in these parts. This is quite enough to say, as the great charm is in the surprises & not knowing what is coming.

Mail goes suddenly. This may go

T. W. H.

*"I continue to gain strength, though slowly"*
To Louisa Storrow Higginson
Beaufort S.C.
Oct. 19. 1863[243]

*Dearest Mother,*

I sent you a letter, cut off suddenly, because the steamer was a day too early—after all I believe it did not go. This is only to say that I continue to gain strength, though slowly, & that I am going to ride out tomorrow with Dr. Rogers to "Seaside" where there is a nice Quaker family with whom I shall stay a few days & recruit, before going to Camp again. Dr. R. has

241. Francis John Higginson, TWH's brother, a physician.
242. Admiral John Adolph Bernard Dahlgren (1809–1870), commander of the South Atlantic Blockading Squadron.
243. "1863" is added in pencil.

written fully to Mary, explaining why he don't send me home. Pray send Maria Champe's[244] letter. I have just written to Stephen & to Chas. Higginson

*"thrust through & through by malaria without knowing anything about it"*
TO MARY CHANNING HIGGINSON

TWO $20 BILLS ENCLOSED

AT MISS LAURA TOWNE'S
"THE OAKS" PLANTATION
ST. HELENA I.
OCT. 24. 1863.

Dearest, this is the second place of my sojourn. Tuesday Dr R. drove me over to Friend Hunn's, where Lottie Forten lives—a place called Sea Side, chiefly because you cannot get within sight of the sea, though you sometimes hear it at night—that is 8 miles fr. Beaufort & yesterday good little Lottie drove me back here, which is a sort of headquarters for the island, though only 2 miles fr. Beaufort—for here dwells Mr. Tomlinson, the General Superintendent[245] and also Miss Towne,[246] *the* homoeopathic physician of the department, chief teacher and probably the most energetic person this side of civilization: a person of splendid health & astonishing capacity, sister of Mrs. Danagh the artist, brought up in Phil[a] & taught medicine by the Female College & homoepathy by Heaven. I think she has done more for me than any one else by prescribing homoeopathic *arsenic*[247] as a tonic, one powder every day on rising & it has already I think (3 doses) affected me. In other respects I don't think it's any better here than in Beaufort, only of course more entertaining. Mr. Hunn keeps a store to which the colored people for miles round perpetually throng—

244. Maria Champe Storrow, TWH's cousin (daughter of his mother Louisa's brother Samuel Mary Appleton Storrow, who had married a Virginia heiress with a plantation near Alexandria, Virginia).

245. Reuben Tomlinson, a former Pennsylvania bank clerk, who came as a superintendent in the summer of 1862 and later became General Superintendent of St. Helena and Ladies Islands.

246. Laura Towne was a teacher and physician among the freedmen on St. Helena Island. See *Letters and Diary of Laura M. Towne,* ed. Rupert S. Holland (1912; New York: Negro Universities Press, 1969).

247. A poisonous substance used, in highly diluted form, as a homeopathic remedy.

this of course was amusing, then the family are pleasant & there was a good deal to interest me. I continue well except as to strength, with an abundant appetite & plenty of good food—eggs, milk &c, but I cannot ride (on horseback) or walk far without fatigue, & lie down a good deal. It seems foolish to keep saying I am improving & yet do it so slowly—yet it is true. Dr Rogers says I hv. been thrust through & through by malaria without knowing anything about it, because of temperament while James Rogers for instance has fever & ague & all sorts of things & it sticks in all his secretions & he is vividly conscious of it, & yet after all is no more affected by it than I—This is what he says; *I* don't know anything, save that I am weak & want to be stronger.

Miss Murray[248] who assists Miss Towne is English & is expecting her mother & sister fr. Newport where they live. She shivered at the idea of anybody's going to Newport to be warm: says the winds are so cold.

I'm expecting W^m fr. Beaufort whither I hv. sent him for my letters by Arago, wh. arrived yesterday. I expect to hear fr. my darling.

An old Aunt Phillis was in this morning, sighing over a little boy she has the care of—"mus' take um to de wood for whip um". Why? I asked. "No use for whip um in de house, Miss Laury (Towne) hear de first slap, come flying, say 'Stop, stop No for whip'! So ebrybody take um child to de wood, far place, for whip um! Massa! *can't fetch up boy widout whip*"!—This picture of the whole maternal population of the place, scudding for the woods with malcontent children under their arms, to whip them in peace beyond interference of Miss Laury, was too much for me.

This is just opposite the Eustis' plantation,[249] across a creek, we can see the houses. They say everything goes better when he is away, the people can't get over their distrust of him as representing the "secesh" masters. Moreover the personal dislike remains ever since his first attempts to manage them, when he would not pay his house servants any wages, & treated them in all respects as slaves. They say on the plantation that Mrs. Eustis promised them they never should be under Massa Frederick,[250] as he was the *hardest* of all her sons.

Johnny Hunn[251] (a good natured boy about 13, sitting by Lottie Forten in the Evening) "Lottie what was that you were reading that day in the po-

248. Ellen Murray.
249. Frederick A. Eustis's plantation, on Ladies Island.
250. Frederick A. Eustis.
251. Member of the family of John Hunn.

etry book about *a witch*" (cross examined); "About a witch & a girl & she made her promise something and she kept a-sleeping"? (I've at last discovered it was the Lay of the Brown Rosary![252])

Miss Alcott[253] wants to come down here—& the Whittiers.[254]

*"the pet and belle of the island"*
To Mary Channing Higginson
The Oaks Sunday Oct. 25. 1863.

My dearest Your one letter came yesterday. By this time I hope you understand, dearest, that I am not coming home. Indeed I cd. not as Gen. G. has just issued an order sending invalid officers to St. Augustine, Florida instead of North. Jas. Rogers will probably go there instead of home, quite a disappointment—[ ][255] I am gaining much dear—more here than anywhere else: for instance I go up & down stairs whenever I want to & think nothing about it, whereas at Mrs. Hale's I never did it more than twice a day & with effort, & I lie down very little now. Miss Towne who has been here fr. the very beginning & is very wise, says that I shall regain my strength & feel perfectly well this winter & then next summer it will go away again. Should that prove so, *then* wd. be the time for decided & final action; until then there wd. be no sort of propriety in my resigning or applying for furlough so that is all entirely settled dear. Next spring we will see [ ][256] down seriously I shld. not hesitate to resign then.

The weather is growing cold—today it is quite raw & uncomfortable. The family hv. partly gone to the Church where it is Communion Sunday—they hv. it once in 3 months & they say the elders pull away at the

252. Elizabeth Barrett Browning, "The Lay of the Brown Rosary," *The Poetical Works of Elizabeth Barrett Browning*, ed. Ruth M. Adams (Boston: Houghton Mifflin Company, 1974), 108–116.
253. Louisa May Alcott wrote to TWH November 12, 1863, in reply to a letter from him containing commendation and frank criticism on her story "The Brothers," which he read in the *Atlantic Monthly*. "Don't you want a cook, [or] nurse . . . I am willing to enlist in any capacity . . . to be busied in some more loyal labor than sitting quietly at home spinning fictions when such fine facts are waiting for all of us to profit by & celebrate." *The Selected Letters of Louisa May Alcott*, ed. Joel Myerson, Daniel Shealy, and Madeleine B. Stern (Athens: University of Georgia Press, 1995), 96–97.
254. John Greenleaf Whittier and his sister, Elizabeth Whittier.
255. Two lines of the letter are cut off here.
256. The obverse of the two cut lines is here.

wine in a style wh. is quite vivacious—they use a dozen bottles for several hundred people, & then take up a collection to pay for it.

Isn't it queer, Mrs. Murray, who lives here, is an Englishwoman who has been living in Newport & has described to me the Dame house[257] &c & thinks it pleasant. Miss Towne knows it too. They say she (Mrs. D.) has an excellent reputation for kindness &c. They were surprised at her taking you in winter. They say her price in summer is $8 or $10: but still perhaps it will be better for you to stay there. Then if you like it; or if I am obliged to come on we might go to Pigeon Cove.—I have not seen the Dewhursts yet; Lt. Col. Strong is better & will come in 20 days more, he thinks.

I send you $40, dear two $20 bills & I sent one a week ago, when I sent Geo. Curtis' letter; in a week or two I hope to get a check, for $200.

I am better off here than at the Hunn's; there it was crowded & I had my camp bed in the parlor, & I had to talk too much; here I hv. a nice room & a tin hat. I have given up my medicine agst. night sweats, & don't need it.

Isn't it odd, there was a decided prejudice among the freedpeople against Lottie Forten even now old Aunt Phillis[258] calls her "dat brown gal" & says "She's notin but a nigger any way"; & at first the domestics didn't want to make her bed &c—said she might do it herself. But when they heard her *play on the piano* it quite put them down, & soon all grew fond of her. Miss Towne says "she is *the* pet and belle of the island."

Tomorrow I expect to go back to Beaufort though I may not so soon, they are so kind & hospitable here. I only meant to stay one night, & go home yesterday.

Goodbye my dearest darling

257. A boarding house in Newport, Rhode Island, kept by Mrs. Hannah Dame, a Quaker, to which Mary removed in November 1863, and where TWH and his wife lived upon his return from the war.

258. Although TWH may be referring to an actual woman named Phillis, more likely he alludes to a literary stereotype familiar from Mary H. Eastman, *Aunt Phillis's Cabin; or, Southern Life As It Is* (Philadelphia: Lippincott, Grambo & Co., 1852). One of the many so-called "anti-Tom" novels written to counteract the antislavery influence of Harriet Beecher Stowe's *Uncle Tom's Cabin*, this novel features an Aunt Phillis, "a tall, dignified, bright mulatto woman" (p. 102), who scorns Abolitionists to the point of refusing freedom unless it is freely given her by the master she loves, and who exhibits such "noble qualities" as contempt for slaves blacker and less well-bred than herself (p. 104).

*"staying about as ladies do"*
To Louisa Storrow Higginson
At Miss Laura Towne's
"The Oaks" plantation[259]
St. Helena Island
2 miles from Beaufort
Oct. 26. 1863

*Dearest Mother*

I am on a sort of tour of visiting, staying about as ladies do, without any particular object. I have spent three days at Friend Hunn's[260] the kindest of Quaker's—the place is called Sea Side, because sometimes you can hear that potentate roar at night, when he sleeps badly—nothing nearer. He has a nice family, the sweetest Quaker wife, and Charlotte Forten lives & teaches there, our pretty little Quadroon "daughter of the regiment." It was very pleasant there & entertaining—Friend Hunn keeps a store which is thronged all day by the Ethiopian oddities for miles round.

One thing pleased me, the ladies all declared that the colored women had excellent taste in dress, the prettiest patterns of calicos always went off first & they disliked gaudy things especially red—I have noticed the same with my men who always disliked the red trousers.

This is a beautiful island more so I think than Port Royal, & the teachers & Superintendents, as I hv. always heard, much superior. Miss Towne with whom I am now staying is a remarkable person, probably the most energetic in the department, not excepting Gen. Gillmore. She is fr. Philadelphia, of a good family there, sister of Mrs. Danagh the artist,—has educated herself as a homoeopathic physician, prescribes for half the island & teaches the other half, besides keeping house beautifully & partly carrying on the plantation. I expect to stay here in two days.

As for health I am in just the state you would like to have me if I went to Brattleboro invalided, able to sit & lie about & talk, & with an enormous appetite. It isn't the most uncomfortable form of illness, especially where one gets such nice fare—nevertheless I would like a little strength, were there any to be had. By degrees it is certainly coming though, only such ridiculously slow degrees

259. The Oaks, on St. Helena Island (directly across the creek from the Eustis plantation on Ladies Island), by the ferry across which ran the road from St. Helena Island to Beaufort and Port Royal Island; formerly Daniel Pope's plantation.
260. John Hunn, a Quaker who, with the help of his daughter Elizabeth, opened a store for freedmen on St. Helena Island, near the Oaks plantation.

William has gone to Beaufort for my letters per Arago, so I can't answer them yet. It was very nice in Lizzy to write me—I thank her, with my love.

An old Aunt Phillis, the plantation patriarch was here this morning, sighing over an impracticable little boy she has the care of. "Mus take um to de wood for whip um," she averred. Why so? I asked. "No use for whip um in de house, Massa, Miss Laury (Towne) hear de very first slap, come flying, say 'Stop Stop! No for whip'! So ebrybody take he child to de wood, far place, for whip um! *Can't fotch up boy widout whip*"!

This picture of the whole maternal population of the place, scudding for the woods, with children under their arms, to enjoy a season of undisturbed chastisement, beyond reach of Miss Laury, was too much for me.

The Eustis plantation is just opposite, across a creek, we can see the houses. They say all goes better when he is away, as the people cannot get over their distrust of him as representing the old "secesh" Masters. The total absence of any trace of feudal affection among these people is certainly one of their most surprising features, to me. I have never been able to catch a glimpse of any such thing.[261] Besides, F A E was very much disliked personally on his first experiment here; he treated them all as slaves, & gave his house servants no wages, which they knew he had no right to do. At his last visit he was much more judicious. They say on the plantation that old Mrs. Eustis always said they never shld be put under Massa Frederick, as he was the hardest of her sons.

I am gaining every day now, & Miss Towne, who has been here longer than almost any one, & seen the climate thoroughly, says that I shall be perfectly well & strong this winter, but that very likely next summer will take my strength all away again. But it will be time enough to attend to that when it comes.

No letter from you by Arago (sailed 19th) still we do not always get all the letters the same day, & one may turn up.

*"We are going out on picquet"*
To Louisa Storrow Higginson
Hdqr. Camp Shaw
Nov. 2. 1863

*Dearest Mother*
The steamer again goes prematurely. I am doing nicely, getting quite strong, have been in camp for a week, but sleep at Mrs. Hale's. No letter fr.

261. Two manuscripts, not consecutively numbered, have been joined here; the latter has a pencilled notation at the top, "1863?," and its content makes it continuous with the former.

you by two last strs.—last Sept. 30 by [ ][262] Sturgis, who seems a nice youth, a little *conscious* I thought, but most eager for a fight. We are going out on picquet (for 20 days only) this week & I hv. invited him to go, offering him a front seat opposite the rebels. All goes well, Lt. Col. coming soon, Scrobie in full force, Dr. Rogers well.

In haste thine<br>T. W. H.

*"The men are singing tremendously tonight"*
To Mary Channing Higginson
Camp Shaw. Nov 6 1863

My dearest, a short letter has come just before yr. grand rush for Newport; I am so glad you have a good woman; day after tomorrow I shall hear of yr. arrival there probably. I am getting well & have been returned to duty for ten days & in camp altogether for three & no harm done. In 3 days the Reg't goes out on picquet; I am not going for a week at least & shall stay here with Dr. Rogers who will stick by the Hospital. I hv. writing to do & then shall go over to St. Helena for a few days, probably, to pick up a deserter or two & see those friendly people again.

We are having very mild weather rather unfavorable for strength—still I gain.

Nov. 8. Sunday

Tomorrow the regt goes on Picquet. The Arago is in at Hilton Head today, but we shall not get the mail tonight. Now we hv. mails about twice a week but they do not go as often. I shall put this in without waiting for the mail.

O *wasn't* Sally's[263] jelly delicious! It requires great self control to appropriate it really to the Hospital. Unfortunately I am too well to have a real claim on it. I am just writing to thank her—it came safe only two bottles were broken—there were two boxes of it. Dr Rogers was delighted with it, he thinks most of the delicacies sent under the form of hospital supplies (not to us though) only hurtful but this jelly will be good for drinks.

I had the pleasure of carrying one bottle to Frank Higginson (George's son) who is here sick, inheriting my room at Mrs. Hale's. He is not very ill, but it has been going on long & he is quite run down, & needs rest & better

262. The copy-text is illegible here.
263. Sarah Rhea Higginson Bowditch.

food than he is likely to get there. Probably he will go over on St Helena, like me. I like him, he is a very intelligent manly fellow & is an admirable officer, but that he is quick tempered, they say. He says Storrow spent most of his time *sketching* at Morris Island, though nominally on very important business for the colored regiments.

The men are singing tremendously tonight, nothing ever stirs them up like any project of a move on the morrow.

We are beginning to get oranges, not very sweet—like those we first had at Fayal, no,—they are better than those.

Tell me dear if you arranged with John Barker or any one to get Miss Bellows' rent. I suppose you did not pay for my uniform coat, the paymaster is expected back on this boat & then I can send you a check—I have sent $80 in $20 bills in 3 d'fft letters—have they arrived?

Lieut. Henry Stone, (Eliza's brother)[264] has got Anne Earle's pass transferred to *his* young lady, a Miss Stacy of Maine who is to come here & marry him—not to live in camp though. He is an excellent fellow.

I thought you might like Dr. Minor's picture, poor as it is. Now my dearest goodbye—tomorrow I shall know about you in Newport.
Love to Margaret.


*"a d——d saucy Yankee as they ever met"*
To Louisa Storrow Higginson
Camp Shaw
Nov. 10. 1863

*Dearest Mother*

I am quite nicely now & can do all I wish, though I judiciously moderate my wishes. For instance I hv. let the reg't go out on picquet without me, but unhappily there has come a cold snap which with the white tents & the few lingering cripples who move slowly about, gives us quite a sensation of being left snowed up in the Arctic with Kane or Franklin.[265]

Sarah Bowditch sent down two boxes of currant jelly for Hospital Supplies—it was nice as herself & I greeted Frank L. Higginson George's son with a jar on his arrival—he is here sick, taking my very room at Mrs. Hale's the day after I moved out. I like him, he is very manly & simple, & is highly praised as an officer, except that he is hasty tempered—he is simply "run down" & needs rest & change of air, which last he cannot get, unless

---

264. First Lieutenant Henry A. Stone.

265. Elisha Kent Kane, *Arctic Explorations: The Second Grinnell Expedition in Search of Sir John Franklin, 1853, '54, '55* (Chicago: S. C. Griggs & Co., 1856); Sir John Franklin.

to St. Augustine where they now send sick officers. He will probably go over to St. Helena Island & stay.

It was amusing to hear him describe his efforts to pin Storrow down to a practical plan of life, suited to the Lee mind. Storrow thought on the whole he should prefer to go to Germany & learn to play the organ. This was when S. was at Morris Island.

Frank's manners are very courteous, quite unlike Henry's.[266]

His family affection & Bostonism are very strong—but those things grow, out here, I assure you.

Wasn't it queer about your letters—*none* dated in October have come, this last is of Nov. 2d, by the Arago, telling of the Billings arrival; we have heard nothing of his Hunter appointment, but some profane person in Beaufort today pronounced them well matched. As an inspector of *arms* he would be useful, being an excellent mechanic & understanding fire arms very well.

Stroby continues a jewel, & Lt. Col. Strong has just returned, nearly well. No news of the Chaplain except sometimes through fugitive slaves who report that the rebels pronounce him "a d——d saucy Yankee as they ever met", which I can easily credit. Under the new agreement about Chaplains he would be released did he not belong to a colored reg't—& may be as it is. Somehow it is impossible for any of us to speak seriously of the Chaplain's being a prisoner, we always laugh because we all have a feeling that the rebels must have the worst of it.

James Rogers resignation wh. was refused last fall is now accepted *at Washington*—thanks to an indomitable Quaker mother-in-law-in-prospective who got Gov. Andrew into her harness. He will go back to Harvard, instead of bringing his bride out here: but we have a much more attractive little lady here in Mrs. Chamberlin.


*"building castles in the air for the future"*
To Mary Channing Higginson
Headqrs. 1st S.C.V.
Camp Shaw. Nov. 18. 1863.

Dearest I am very rich this mail—had 9 letters of which 3 were fr. you & four fr. mother—two having been missent to N.C. Yours were nice & long darling—thank you very much; Marnie's came too & gave just the account of yr. transit for which my last letter asked. I can now see you at Newport, Cat & two kittens. I felt sure you wd. hv. more personal society to

266. Captain Francis Lee Higginson; his brother, Major Henry Lee Higginson.

enjoy there, but thought you might feel some want of electricity in the moral atmosphere. If you enjoy, dear, building yr. little plans, & writing them to me do so. I agree with you that at the end of my military pilgrimage, we might try Cambridge[267]—indeed as people grow older they gravitate toward their birthplace. I found when I was sick that my dreams were more of Cambridge than anywhere else—I mean day dreams building castles in the air for the future. Ties of blood strengthen as we grow older & it seems as if my brothers & sisters were collecting near there. Once separated from Worcester I do not care particularly about returning there—at least I hold places at arms' length & feel that I can choose. You speak of boarding dear but you know that for four people it costs a good deal more than keeping house.

Then again, I have taken so strong a hold of this whole movement for the blacks that if I shld. leave employment among them some other kindred employment might seek me & I might not be able to keep out of it & this might affect the question of where we shld. live, even were I out of the army. To solve this great problem of emancipation many hands & brains will be needed, & though I feel *now* no call to connect myself with it, how can I tell how I might feel by & by? If I were offered a post like General Saxton's for instance, I do not think I should *now* accept it—but how differently it might look when the time came, I can't say.

Something wd. depend on my health this winter—if the climate & labor are too much for me, of course I shld. not return to it even for the most interesting duty & if I could have you with me. And as I am not likely to leave the army *except* on the ground of health, it is likely that after leaving it, I should continue to live at the North only. Yet how nice it wd. seem if Fate would select that ideal place where I could have an honorable duty & you the milder climate you need. Well who knows what may turn up & meanwhile we will locate our chateaux in Cambridge.

I am well now & expect to be—stay down here from inclination & business not health. Last Sunday I went out to the picquet stations & back Monday, riding perhaps 13 miles each day, besides walking a good deal & was not badly tired. Besides,[268] I slept at night on the floor in Dr. Minor's little room; he dropped asleep like a baby while I waked & meditated of possible incursions of the enemy,—soon I heard sounds which indicated them; I raised my head; then they came nearer, then there came something like the explosion of a small shell & a thump in the corner of the

267. Cambridge, Massachusetts, TWH's childhood home.
268. Two separate autograph manuscripts, not numbered consecutively, nevertheless appear to be fragments of the same letter, and are joined here editorially.

*325*

room. The fire still glowed & presently I saw the largest rat I ever looked upon, trot placidly forth into the centre of the floor, just between Minor & me, & look round to see what he might devour. Luckily it was neither of us & I waked in the morning with all my features complete; but should not again select that floor to spread my blankets on. M. said with his usual innocence that he didn't believe any rat would—this one had run over him the first night, but had not tried him since.

It seemed very pleasant at the Picquet Stations though not so lovely as last spring. The 20 days are half gone & I don't expect to go there to stay.

I shall mail this tonight darling & write again tomorrow.

Thine am.

Love to Margaret.

The rebels have made several attempts to land in small parties & surprise our picquets & the men hv. enjoyed it very much.

## "5 Colonels, 3 very fat, standing in a row"
To Louisa Storrow Higginson
Camp Shaw. Nov. 19. 1863

*Dearest Mother*

4 letters from you by this steamer—two had gone to N.C.—suppose you try simply S.C., no more, & that may stop it. The two last came safe. As I happened to hv. 3 letters fr. Mary & 1 fr. Marg't, I was well off indeed—they were none too many. The Virginia letters I hv. not yet time to read.

The reg't is out on picquet; I hv. been out there once & now it is fr. no want of strength, but because Scroby is all sufficient there & I have some business & writing wh. are best to be done here. Gen. Saxton is bent on reviews & brigade drills this autumn, & had a review yesterday. One reg't looked as nice as ours, but none marched comparably to it.

Tomorrow night he has a sort of lesson in Brigade Drill (3d vol. Casey)[269] for the Cols. & Lt. Cols. Fancy 5 Colonels, 3 very fat, standing in a row to recite! but he calls it a "conversation". I don't know what he'll make of it for he has no *ease* of manner, but moves in straight lines.

The General's brother Myrand is here to be Lieutenant with me, a handsome boy, friend of Storrow's & Frank's, I think I shall like him.

I am well now, for all I can see, & wish Dr. Rogers were; he was taken with vertigo & has been laid up for 2 days. I fear he will have to resign, but try to stave it off while I can. I don't mean that this attack is dangerous, but

269. Casey, *Infantry Tactics*, 3:1–155.

he is very weak & delicate, so much so that I sometimes think it wd. be a relief to have him away & yet we shall miss him so much.

James is here, his resignation having been accepted through his determined mother in law—& it is now too late for him to go back to college & he is far from grateful at the interference. It seems a great pity.

The reason of the delay of Gen. Gillmore is now said to have some connexion with movements in the Southwest—perhaps to keep the rebel army here which wd. be thrown against Grant if we took Charleston.

My dear Anne how could the transcriber of my Journal ask me if I had been at St. Simons Island. We were two days there on my first expedition; it was there we got the Railroad Iron; I was often at Thos. Butler King's[270] beautiful place, but not at Pierce Butler's[271] which is some miles away. But Scroby, the indomitable, garrisoned the island all last summer with a colored company after the Hunter regiment was disbanded, & *he* knew some of the very slaves she describes & can tell you their stories by the hour together, with the most perfect imitation of their dialect I ever heard—how he would entertain & thrill you. He was intensely interested in Mrs. Butler's book.[272] He had a skirmish there in which the first black soldier fell for the U.S.—& his name was *John Brown*. Wasn't it strange. Per contra I had a John Brown who has deserted.

*"comfortable in my tent"*
To Mary Channing Higginson

CHECK ENCLOSED.

Nov. 19. 1863

Dearest I am very anxious about Dr. Rogers, he had an attack of vertigo & has been in bed two days, hardly able to sit up at all; he has had such attacks before, at home, & knows what to do & James is here. Nothing alarming, but it increases his feeling that he must resign—indeed he has done so, but I don't quite give up the hope of his staying & Dr. Marsh, principal Sanitary Commissioner, who is here today & a great friend of his, says he ought to stay, even if he is not able to do *full* duty. If he is to be

270. Thomas Butler King (1800–1864), born in Massachusetts, married Anna Matilda Page and inherited a cotton plantation on St. Simon's Island, Georgia.

271. Pierce Butler was the absentee owner of a plantation on St. Simon's Island who married the actress Fanny Kemble.

272. Frances Anne Kemble, *Journal of a Residence on a Georgian Plantation in 1838–1839.*

killed by it I don't want him to stay, but if he can be as well here as at home I shld. like it, even if he can't do all he wishes. We hv. a nice room for him in town & he goes there tomorrow to stay at night at any rate, as long as he wants.

I hv. written to a Dr. Tremaine Asst. Surg. 24th Mass.[273] with whom I came down on the Arago, asking him to be Dr. R's successor. He is fr. Nova Scotia, highly educated in medicine, & I liked him much. Dr. Hawks is promoted into the 3d S.C.V. Lt. Sampson our best soldier takes Capt. Dolly's place, & Lt. Thompson James'. Poor old Capt. Randolph has also resigned at my request. These are improvements except James'—he felt *dreadfully* at first I think,—as if he had been treated like such a child to hv. his resignation accepted through begging, by Mrs. Earle, when it had been declined in the regular military way. Now it is too late for him to go back to college, & he will just be sat upon by his mother in law the rest of his life. We can't console him, the Dr. & I, for we feel as bad. Now he talks of going into business in N.Y. (!) but Mrs. E. will never allow that. I think the whole connexion is a curse to him.

Why didn't you tell me that dear little Emily Brown was married. I saw it by accident.

Lt. Col. Strong is here, but not at all strong—I should not wonder if he were to resign; he has talked of it a little to the Dr. that universal confidant. Scroby's immense success is a great drawback to him.

Tomorrow night the Colonels of regiments here (5) meet at Gen. Saxton's for a lesson (he calls it a "conversation") on Brigade Drill. Fancy us standing in a line to be questioned? I think Gen. S. will be more uncomfortable than any of us, he has not much ease of manner, but moves in straight lines.

Young Myrand Saxton came down to be a Lieutenant, a handsome young fellow, rather elegant in air & a friend of Storrow's & Frank's at Deerfield.

James R. was going by this steamer, but his uncle's illness detains him, as he likes to hv. James with him.

I am very comfortable in my tent, far more so than last winter's, I have a good stove and floor, & very picturesque vestibule of gray moss-work to keep the wind away—then the buffalo-skin is sublime.

I shan't send more money unless you want it.

273. Dr. William S. Tremaine, assistant surgeon of the 24th Massachusetts; he was promoted to surgeon of the 31st U.S. Colored Troops and, as TWH notes below (letter to Louisa Storrow Higginson, February 7, 1864), did not join his company after all.

## *"the negroes are the true owners of the soil"*
TO LOUISA STORROW HIGGINSON
CAMP SHAW. NOV. 26. 1863

Dearest Mother—Today is Thanksgiving & I have been invited to dine, very kindly, by a Mr. Conant on the plantation of which he is Superintendent—They are very nice people & I thought of going but could not—it is some way off. I am on a Court Martial which bids fair to be exciting as it is a matter of life & death, a conspiracy of some conscripts here to desert to the enemy. They were betrayed by the colored man whom they bribed to take them over, & the scene in the court when the witness identified the accused in the midst of half a dozen others whom we had brought in was very dramatic, inasmuch as he also identified another man who had not been suspected & would not have been but for this accident, but who is now in custody.

It was such a thing as happens in novels & the scene was worthy of Miss Braddon. Nearly a thousand conscripts & substitutes hv. been sent here to different regiments & the men appear very well.

I get your letters regularly now, there were only a few weeks when North Carolina opened & swallowed them. The Virginia letters all arrived, & I shld. hv. been very sorry to lose them. They seemed like a scene from Peveril of the Peak.[274] Maria's[275] are sweet & noble I think, & for the tone of Sam's,[276] you must remember how peculiarly hard was the ordeal he had to go through; he had no resource except to harden himself a little in presence of such domestic antagonism. It seems Aunt Eliza has succumbed; I thought she clung to the Union.

James Rogers goes home tomorrow, his resignation accepted. Dr. R. is sick with vertigo, but growing better. We shall lose him too fr. the reg't.

There has just been an exciting fight on the main land between two of my companies & a company of Cavalry led by dogs, five bloodhounds were killed & we have the body of one which James R. has skinned & takes to NY for stuffing that we may keep it as a trophy. A sergeant & 10 of our men went beyond the rest 6 miles, nearly to Pocataligo & brought away 26 contrabands. My men took 2 prisoners & lost two by drowning.

O the box came about a week ago—a perfect success, nothing injured; the cake was pronounced delicious by the few who are here & I am keeping it along till the rest of the mess return, three days hence. Also the guava

274. Sir Walter Scott, *Peveril of the Peak* (Edinburgh: Archibald Constable, 1822).
275. Maria Champe Storrow.
276. Samuel Mary Appleton Storrow, TWH's maternal uncle (father of Maria Champe Storrow).

& confectionery were very nice, figs, towels, Mrs. Kemble all arrived safe. William was much pleased with the gift which I think Hetty will enjoy even more than he, for she smokes the most, though neither very much. The box really got here very promptly & made a sort of Thanksgiving present: I am greatly obliged.

Frank L. Higginson is over on St. Helena Island, gaining a little & with some faint hopes of going North. Cousin George writes that he may come here next steamer.

I have read Maria's letters; how intensely interesting they are; I can appreciate them so well, having seen so many such ruined homes; but here the luxuriance of nature & the recent prosperity is such that nothing else is ruined & generally there was nothing but association to make the houses beautiful. Then one has the feeling of course that the negroes are the true owners of the soil, & so long as they are here, it seems as it should be.

There are reports of Gen. Saxton's resigning but I don't think he shows any symptoms of it; he was talking to me yesterday of various plans—one of getting this changed to a Cavalry Regiment, as there is great need of cavalry here. Nothing will come of it, horses are too scarce. These men wd. make capital cavalry, & to be mounted would be their dream of bliss. But it isn't likely to be realized.

Ever affectionately<br>T. W. H.

Give my love to Maria Bell if you write again.

I send you a notice I wrote of our Quartermaster—it was for a little book his father was to print, but he puts it in the paper.

Love to all<br>Ever affly<br>T. W. H.

If Rev. Liberty should abide with you, it would be what Aggie used to call a singular cuzzidence.

*"Coming soon enough for you"*
To Mary Channing Higginson
Camp Shaw. Nov. 26.

Dearest I shall write a little & send by James Rogers. I don't know about his going to Newport, he may go back to Cambridge. Dr. Tremaine Asst. Surg. of the 24th Mass has consented to be Dr. Rogers' successor, wh. is a great relief to both of us. He is thought very highly of & I took quite a liking to him, coming out in the "Arago." He is rather young, very pleasant & manly, an English Canadian, schooled in Boston & England—has been a surgeon in the Eng. army a little while I believe. Dr. Rogers will stay here for the present.

We hv. had quite an excitement in a fight of some of our men on the main land where they brought away 27 colored people & 2 rebel pickets & beat off a cavalry company headed by *five bloodhounds,* all of whom were killed. We hv. the body of one wh. Jas. Rogers has skinned & takes to NY to be stuffed & shown. Two of my men were drowned & six wounded.—One edifying result is that there was a flag of truce a few days after & the rebel officers readily held official communication with our officers wh. last summer they wdnt do.

One amusing thing was, just before the fight began, the pickets across the river farther down were taunting our pickets—Why don't you come over, to which our men answered—*Coming soon enough for you* & even as they spoke the firing up the river began & the rebels forthwith mounted their horses & went off in a hurry.

Isn't Miss Alcott's writing[277] square & queer & like Mrs. Childs'.[278] Distinct but not inspired. Think of yr. not dwelling more on Eugene Thayer's glories. Fancy Lizzy in Cambridge, calling on Mrs. Sparks.[279] I think Eugene's is really a very fine career; I shld be much pleased if Storrow could do as well.

I was too late for my dinner, but have been too busy to be lonely & even if you speak of dinner we had some fresh beef. This morning at Court Martial we had a scene worthy of Miss Braddon.[280] The chief witness was a colored man whom these deserters had bribed to take

277. TWH is very likely thinking here of Louisa May Alcott's story "The Brothers," *Atlantic Monthly* 12 (November 1863), 584–95. Later reprinted under the title "My Contraband," the story has to do with a Union nurse, Miss Dane, and her servant, Bob, who is an escaped slave (or "contraband"); they are given the task of caring for a captured Rebel sick with typhoid who turns out to be Ned, the white half-brother of Bob, who had sexually violated Bob's wife Lucy. Nurse Dane persuades Bob not to take revenge on his now defenseless half-brother; instead he enlists in the Massachusetts 54th under Col. Robert Gould Shaw and is mortally wounded by Ned, whom he meets in hand-to-hand combat during the assault on Fort Wagner.

278. Lydia Maria Child (1802–1880), a prominent writer, editor, abolitionist and reformer, whose *The Frugal Housewife: Dedicated to Those Who Are Not Ashamed of Economy* (Boston: Marsh & Capen, and Carter & Hendee, 1829) was among TWH's favorite childhood reading. TWH wrote about her in *Eminent Women of the Age: Being Narratives of the Lives and Deeds of the Most Prominent Women of the Present Generation* (Hartford: S. M. Betts, 1868).

279. Possibly the wife of Jared Sparks, eminent historian and biographer, a friend of the Higginson family during TWH's childhood and later, a lecturer he heard at Harvard.

280. That is, worthy of the type of sensational melodrama for which the popular English novelist Elizabeth Braddon was known.

them to the main land. To see if he cd. recognize the prisoner, we sent out for half a dozen soldiers fr. the streets & put in among them: & after a long examination faced the witness round & made him pick out the right one. He did it almost instantaneously & then pointing to the next man said impressively "*Dis de odder man*" meaning the accomplice, who was supposed to be in prison awaiting trial; & yet in this stray soldier from the street he found the real man! We arrested the man at once & now there is reason to believe that he really was an accomplice who wd. probably never have been detected had he not been brought into court in this random way.

Goodbye dearest darling I shall tell James to mail this a day & a half after he gets to N.Y. so as to surprise my dear little girl.

Thine own.

*"Every colonel has to struggle . . . to keep his chickens together"*
To Mary Channing Higginson
Camp Shaw. Nov. 27 1863

Well my dearest I remember Theo Brown[281] proposing in the boat among the lilies—"Suppose for once we have lilies *enough*" & I am sure you have letters enough this time. I am going to send you this one notelet more with Miss Alcott's note. James Rogers went this morning, but the boat goes early tmorrow. This is Friday, on Monday the reg't comes in, & I hope to keep them together a little, though I suppose they will be detailed about again, like all other regiments. Every colonel has to struggle all the time to keep his chickens together.

Mrs. Fields has written me another very pleasant note. It so happened Mrs. Dodge's letter went over by Flag of Truce within a few hours after arriving here though it might have waited months.

Dr. Marsh of the Sanitary Commission wants our *bloodhound* exhibited at the Sanitary Commission's great Fair in Boston, after it is stuffed. It is a splendid dog.

Do you know I am *sure* Geo. Curtis wrote the Gospel of Peace.[282] It is so

281. Theophilus Brown, a tailor, TWH's Worcester friend.
282. Richard Grant White, *The New Gospel of Peace According to St. Benjamin* (New York: The American News Company, 1866). From July 27, 1863, to May 19, 1866, White published anonymously in the New York *Evening Post* this series of mock-biblical political satires against Copperheads, styled in imitation of an Elizabethan English translation of an ancient Eastern manuscript written in the nonexistent "Iangkie" language. For a time there was considerable public speculation about the real identity of the author; others mistakenly guessed as TWH did that the author might have been George W. Curtis.

like the Zay-nees of Yang-ki[283] which he wrote in Putnam's—though that was a failure. I got your 2d part.

Goodbye now darling
Thine am.

In the skirmish the other day one sergeant was refused permission to go with the party because he had a bad cough, & might give the alarm. He explained to his Capt. that when he had to cough, he would scrape a little hole in the ground, put his head down, cover it with the cape of his cloak & *cough into the hole*; on these terms he was allowed to go & did good service.

Goodbye you dear little girl.

## *"doing tolerably well"*
## To Louisa Storrow Higginson
## Headqrs. 1st S.C.V.
## Camp Shaw. Dec. 5. 1863

*Dearest Mother*

Just time to say—doing tolerably well & likely to do so, though not so well as at home. Very busy with reviews & brigade drills. Reg't back fr. picquet & all going well. Mary had a *very* small installment of journal, but you had lots last time.

Ever thine
T. W. H.

## *"Lieutenant White in place of a Lt. Brown"*
## To Mary Channing Higginson
## Headqrs. &c Dec. 5. 1863

Dearest I am in despair for fear I shall fail altogether to write to you, the time is being so devoured: we hv. had a hard week of official Inspections, Brigade Drills & Reviews. I enjoy the Brigade Drills much, Gen. S. conducts them & four regiments take part; I think mine does best, but perhaps each little Col. thinks the same. Thursday Gen. Gillmore reviewed us & seemed listless & out of spirits. Today a Capt. [ ][284] has been here sent expressly fr. Washington to examine the condition of colored troops in this dep't; he is very cordial & complimentary.

283. George W. Curtis, "The Zay-nis of Yan-Ky," *Putnam's Monthly Magazine* 3 (May 1854), 523–35. Purporting to be "Translated from the Chinese of Tay-Kin," this rather labored parody of an Oriental tale satirizes the conventions of travel writing, American social customs and political affairs of the time, and other matters.

284. The copy-text is illegible here.

I am doing pretty well, though not so well as at home. I hv. a sort of mild chronic diarrhoea such as is quite common here & hard to cure; it does not trouble by night at all, only I have 3 discharges a day instead of 1—it does not weaken me, though, I have had it several weeks, still I want to cure it & think colder weather will[.] We hv. frosty nights now, therm. 30° or lower Nov 29 & 30 at night,—water froze in tent, but my buffalo is delightful. Colocynth & aloes[285] are useless, but Miss Towne prescribes Phosph. Acid which I am trying. She prescribes for Frank H. too, who has the same thing but worse & complicated. Dr. Rogers has gone to "Sea side" (Hunn's) for a week, he is weak but not dangerously ill.

I get yr. letters, love, & am glad you are better & enjoying Newport. If you don't take me to any worse place to live than *that* I can stand it & per-haps shld. like it as well as Cambridge. How grand the news is about Grant[286]—Gen. Saxton knew him when Quartermaster, years ago, & had to leave the army for hopeless intemperance. Now Gen. S. thinks he does not drink.

Gen. S. wants to hv. a grand festival at New Years under auspices of our reg't & Wendell Phillips to come here & speak to the freedmen. I am to write, but don't think he will come. I wish he would & he deserves to do it!

Dr. Minor has now the entire medical care of the reg't & the sick list was hardly ever so small; which delights him. Also he reads Chas. Auchester[287] loud, o' evenings, to pretty little Mrs. Chamberlin & the baby—3 infants in a mist.

How capital Edward Hale's Man without a Country[288] in the Atlantic,

285. A colocynth is lemon-sized, yellowish-green fruit, growing on a vine, the pulp of which is a strong laxative; aloes is also a laxative drug, derived from the juice of a partic-ular species of aloe.

286. Major General Ulysses Simpson Grant (1822–1885), commander of the Divi-sion of the Mississippi, broke the siege of Chattanooga, Tennessee, and secured dra-matic victories at Lookout Mountain and Missionary Ridge, Tennessee, November 23–25, 1863. TWH wrote about Grant in "Ulysses Simpson Grant," *Contemporaries*, The Writings of Thomas Wentworth Higginson, Vol. II (Boston: Houghton, Mifflin, 1900), 302-28.

287. Elizabeth Sara Sheppard, *Charles Auchester: A Memorial* (London: Hurst and Blackett . . . , 1853).

288. Edward Everett Hale (1822–1909), a college friend of TWH and Unitarian minister with whom he sometimes exchanged pulpits, was also active in the New En-gland Emigrant Aid Society, sending antislavery settlers to Kansas. He published this fa-mous short story about Philip Nolan, who is punished for his part in the Burr Conspiracy (and for his impetuous declaration at his trial, "D—n the United States! I wish I may never hear of the United States again!"), by being sentenced to live out his days aboard U.S. naval vessels, completely divorced from all contact with his native land. "The Man Without a Country," *Atlantic Monthly* 12 (December 1863), 665–79. TWH wrote about

but I guessed it before I got through, though the profound Journal said "Frederic Ingham, US.N."

We are to have a Lieutenant *White*[289] in place of a Lt. *Brown*,[290] which seems going backward for this regiment. Hereafter officers are to be appointed directly from Washington, on Gen. Gillmore's recommendation.

Goodbye, love, this will be my only letter by this mail so you see you have ups & downs. Love to Marg't

Thine am.

I am amused at your enjoyment of bells & belles.

Last mail I sent a letter by James Rogers & told him to keep it 24 hrs. so as to come in after the others.


*"not sick & not quite well"*
To Mary Channing Higginson
Hurlbut — Crane. — On Wednesday, Dec. 2, at
St. George's Church, Stuyvesant square, by Rev Stephen
H. Tyng D.D., William H. Hurlbut[291] and Maggie Havins,
daughter of Theodore Crane.[292]
Camp Shaw
Dec. 12. 1863

Only think of my coming on this, almost the only time I ever read the marriages in the N.Y. Times. Who the unfortunate Maggie is, I don't know, probably somebody rich, indeed I hv. a vague notion that T. C. is a rich

---

Hale in "Edward Everett Hale," *Carlyle's Laugh and Other Surprises* (Boston: Houghton, Mifflin, 1909), 157–72.

289. Second Lieutenant Nelson S. White.

290. Second Lieutenant A. B. Brown.

291. William Henry Hurlbut (later Hurlbert) (1827–1895), a Charlestonian who was TWH's fellow divinity student at Harvard, about whom he rhapsodized in *Cheerful Yesterdays* (Boston: Houghton, Mifflin and Company, 1898): "a young man so handsome in his dark beauty that he seemed like a picturesque Oriental; slender, keen-eyed, raven-haired, he arrested the eye and heart like some fascinating girl" (p. 107). "I never loved but one male friend with passion and for him my love had no bounds—all that my natural fastidiousness and cautious reserve kept from others I poured on him; to say that I would have died for him was nothing" (Qtd. in Mary Thacher Higginson, *Thomas Wentworth Higginson: The Story of His Life* [Boston: Houghton Mifflin, 1914], 126). Hurlbut was briefly a minister, then a journalist and playwright; personal scandal followed him, though TWH remained loyal even when others dropped Hurlbut, and even when Hurlbut stopped answering his letters.

292. This wedding announcement is clipped from a newspaper and pasted onto the letter.

merchant. I wish our Cousin S. H. T.[293] wd. come out here to visit his teachers & I wd. ask him about the wedding.

Today has been a real Virginia rain such as we have rarely had here; but the men have been tolerably comfortable in their tents, having made immense progress in taking care of themselves since last winter. So have the officers indeed; my tent is far more comfortable & the buffalo skin is delightful & a perfect soporific. I shall probably wish to sleep under one all the rest of my life.

I have been reading Rumor[294] by author of Chas. Auchester; it is mild enough I assure you. Louis Napoleon figures in it under the name of Porphyro—also apparently Beethoven & Turner or characters modelled on them. She certainly draws lovely women, real as can be, though her inspired men are peculiarly unpleasant. It is a book you would hate.

So Mrs. Fields wrote the Organ Ode;[295] I always had a fancy that she did; & they are belaboring Mrs. Howe for her critique on it & the organ in the Commonwealth, wh. seemed to me reasonable enough. I hv. always thought the organ must look out of place in the Music Hall, though only Mrs. Howe has dared say so. I thought Curtis' critique on Longfellow[296] rather feeble—also The Birds of Killingworth.[297] If the people of Newport don't read, goosey, how can they have good bookstores. Probably your relations don't & there are others who do. One thing will please me much, dear, that you should see Hazard, & people who call on you, & it will *trouble me very much* if you shut yourself up & shrink from seeing people. Remember this, and that I don't have many things to ask of you, love.

I see a letter fr. Jas. Rogers to the Dr. mailed at Worcester, he meant to stay a week or two in NY. first. I pity him for I think he has fettered his whole life.

Thanks for the Old Mill, & I am glad to have seen it; indeed I shall always be delighted that I had one glimpse at Newport, so can imagine you so much better.

I see that Hurlbut is also to publish a History of McClellan's Campaigns.[298] Rather a slow subject.

293. Rev. Stephen Higginson Tyng, who performed this marriage.

294. Elizabeth Sara Sheppard, *Rumor* (Boston: T. O. H. P. Burnham, 1864).

295. Annie Fields, *Ode Recited by Miss Charlotte Cushman, at the Inauguration of the Great Organ in Boston, November 2, 1863* (Boston: Welch, Bigelow, 1863).

296. George W. Curtis, "Longfellow," *Atlantic Monthly* 12 (December 1863), 769–75.

297. Henry Wadsworth Longfellow, "The Birds of Killingworth," *Atlantic Monthly* 12 (December 1863), 680–85.

298. William Henry Hurlbert, *General McClellan and the Conduct of the War* (New York: Sheldon and Company, 1864).

Eustis is here again & called at my tent in my absence—also that Mr. Willson of Grafton the LeBarons used to admire. Dr. Rogers is still on St. Helena awaiting his papers for departure—so is Frank L. Higginson who hopes for leave of absence to go North. He said Ida Aggasiz[299] had written him a note but he didn't show it.

I keep on about so so—not sick & not quite well.

Farewell darling<br>for a few days

It's nice to have the steamer so regular—we are always expecting one to come or go.

## "a rather formidable gathering of Ethiopia"
To Louisa Storrow Higginson
Hdqrs. 1st S.C.V.
Camp Shaw. Dec. 13 1863

*Dearest Mother*

James Rogers bequeathed me a gold pen, so if you see any rare elegance in my handwriting, you will understand. I am so so, on duty & yet obliged to economize myself. The fevers of this climate I seem entirely proof against, but there is a tendency here to low chronic diarrhoea, rather complicated & hard to throw off, which I share; so that I have to be careful.

So far as comfort is concerned, I am much better off than last year, as is the whole regiment; we have all learned much in the way of comfort. Almost all the tents have little fireplaces though they have almost nothing of which to make funnels except the omnipresent preserve-cans, set one upon another & you see a little row of these sticking up funnily, behind the tents, out of the ground for the fireplace is dug *down instead* of built *up*, except where some happy man gets a haul of bricks.

My greatest treasure is my buffalo skin which gives comfortable & sleepy nights. I don't see how I ever did without it.

Today Frank Hagens a handsome mulatto who always impresses me from his name as a sort of relative, came to ask my consent to his marriage. "He's a girl as dark as my hair, Cunnel, but I lub he; somehow or other I always have lub de dark girls best" as if he spoke from a limitless experience. It coincided so precisely with that young fop's opinion in

299. Ida Agassiz, eldest daughter of Jean Louis Rodolphe Agassiz, the eminent Harvard naturalist. She married Major Henry Lee Higginson (Francis Lee Higginson's brother) on December 5, 1863.

"St. Olave's"[300] that I think it worth recording, as you perused that work.

Waldo's letter was entertaining & carried me back to the days & land of public meetings. Forward also to a rather formidable gathering of Ethiopia here on New Year's Day when swords are to be presented to the General & me, by Ethiopia in person; and there are visions of a sable dance or ball in the evening. We hv. invited Wendell Phillips to come, but I don't much expect him. Still it seems as if he *ought* to see these people in liberty. It was Gen. S's notion, to write him.

Mrs. Lander is here again, but I doubt if she spends the winter, as house room is very scarce & she meets nothing but hostility from the Doctors.

Dr. Rogers has resigned, from ill health & we expect a Dr. Tremaine from the Mass 24th, whom I like. Hereafter our officers are to be appointed direct from the War Dep't & I don't know what bearing that will have.

It is wonderful, the absurdity of newspaper correspondents. The Tribune describing the bloodhound affair on the main, represented the men as returning into Beaufort in triumph bearing on their bayonets the gory bodies of the five dogs. The only actual entry was by four wounded men in an ambulance—& one dog's carcass was sent in a cart next day. But we *did* send it to N.Y. for stuffing.

One of Frank Leslie's correspondents once offered Stroby to insert his picture full length for a trifle in money which that sturdy bricklayer declined.

*"What do we have to eat?"*
To Louisa Storrow Higginson
Hdqrs. 1st S.C.V.
Dec. 19. 1863.

*My dearest Mother*
What do we have to eat?

Corned Beef   Tongue
Lamb's Tongue (in vinegar, which I don't use)
Fresh Beef   Chickens (rarely)
Wild Ducks, even a solitary Canvass Back

300. Rev. Cuthbert Scrymgeour, a fortune-hunting cleric who is "*au fait* on the subject of fancy ties" and otherwise exemplifies "shallowness and frivolity, garbed in a silken cassock and white cravat," is known to have "frequently informed his college friends, he 'rather liked a dark girl.'" Eliza Tabor Stephenson, *St. Olave's: A Novel* (New York: Harper, 1863), 69, 72, 81.

Marsh Hens    Opossums
Rabbit (These last occasionally)
Eggs 50 to 75 cts. per dozen
White Potatoes    Sweet Potatoes
RiceHominy
Oysters without limit
Baker's Bread, the best I ever knew.
Apple Pies    Mince Pies.

I do not know why you think we do not live well, for we certainly do; & we have now a very comfortable cabin for cookhouse & eating house. We hv. also *napkins*.

I remain about the same, neither sick nor well; it is not very uncomfortable & I am able to do my duties after a fashion, yet I should be sorry to think I never am to be any better, even in this climate, and I certainly shall not stay at the risk of any permanent disability. At present the season is in my favor & I can afford to reason very differently from what I could if it were June: when the influences would be different.

We are busy with preparing for New Year's Day, when I shall again order my 10 oxen for dinner & a great concourse is expected. Wendell Phillips cannot come, but I did not expect him. My $75 sword has come, selected by Frank Shaw,[301] but I hv. not seen it. Gen. Gillmore is to be here at the celebration though I don't much care to have him—his interest in all this being rather of the galvanized description. Nothing can be more certain than that he allowed the colored troops to be most unreasonably used, as to fatigue duty, not from any hostility but from inattention; & the correspondents may in vain try to cover it up. The fact of a second order being issued by him on the subject instead of vindicating condemns him, for in military usage the remedy for a neglected order is not a second order but a Court Martial.

Dr. Rogers sails for home tonight of course we shall miss him greatly, yet I shall be glad not to have the responsibility of so delicate & valuable a life. I think we shall like Dr. Tremaine who is to be his successor, now asst. Surg. 24th Mass, at St. Augustine. I came down with him last trip & liked him enough to select him.

I have sent Mary two sheets of Journal wh. she will forward. Our attractive little Quadroon, Charlotte Forten, has written an account of her experiences here which is to appear in the March Atlantic.[302] I read it &

301. Possibly Francis George Shaw, father of Robert Gould Shaw.

302. Charlotte Forten, "Life on the Sea Islands. Part I," *Atlantic Monthly* 13 (May 1864), 587–97; idem, "Life on the Sea Islands. Part II," *Atlantic Monthly* 13 (June 1864), 666–76.

passed calmly over all the puffs of myself assuring her that Fields would discreetly pare them all down, as he did E. L. Pierce's.[303]

I am infinitely obliged to Louisa for the children which are sweet; that is a new device to keep babies still under the guise of photographing their dolls—just as one gets the best pictures of mothers by inducing them to bend over their babies.

Did you read Edward Hale's Man without a Country in "Atlantic"? I thought it admirably done.

Love to all
Ever affectionately
T. W. H.

*"every Colonel is court martialed first or last"*
To Louisa Storrow Higginson
Hdqrs. 1st S.C.V.
Dec. 21. 1863

*Dearest Mother*

Here we still are though 2 regiments are ordered away, perhaps to Savannah; as they are the two poorest I infer that Gen. S's wishes were consulted—this brings down his garrison to a minimum size again; it has been larger. Everybody talks Savannah but nobody knows.

Gen. Gillmore is to have a reception at his quarters at Hilton Head on Wednesday, at any rate & a party of us are going down with the General in a steamer at 6 to return at 12.

Christmas Day the colored people hv. a great Fair in Beaufort & on New Year's we hv. a barbecue here & were to hv. a dance in the eve'g but there is to be one at the principal restaurant, kept by colored people, with the tables cleared away, so ours is given up. This saloon was to hv. been called Higginson Hall but the painter objected telling the proprietors that the other Colonels might take offence so that immortal honor was lost. Instead, the proprietor is one of six (all black) who hv. made up $60 to buy a sword to be presented me on New Year's Day. Frank Shaw is to choose it. Gen. Saxton is to have one also.

At this ball the people hv. to go before the countersign is out (9. P.m.) & return after it is taken off (5 am or so) Thus they have to "dance all night."

We are given to festivities, these Christmas times. Yesterday it was a wedding. Lt. Stone (of Newb'port) imported a bride pr. steamer, Miss

303. Edward L. Pierce, "The Freedmen of Port Royal," *Atlantic Monthly* 12 (September 1863), 291–315.

Stacy from "No. 3" in Maine,[304] sister of our delightful guide John Stacey of Katahdin memory.[305] She arrived at 7 am. & was Mrs. S. by 5 P.m. having been hospitably taken in by good little Mr. Harris, Post Chaplain. Lts. Dewhurst & Chamberlin & *their* wives, with myself, were the only guests. The bride wore high necked white muslin, trimmed with red white & blue—quite a handsome, dark eyed, hale looking girl—she is not to live in camp but on "sweet St. Helen's isle."

Another frivolity is Court Martials. I find that every Colonel is court martialed first or last as every child has measles. Of five Cols. here one Col. White was c.m.'d before I came here another (Col. Rust) afterwards. I hv. sat upon Col. Sammons the 3d. & now am sitting on Col. Van Wyck the 4th. When this is over I shall be the only one left. This Col. Van Wyck is the famous Investigating Committee man & now is being investigated. The charges against him are serious & it seems funny to be trying one who has been so noted in trying others. He is a very pleasant man enough—but as one of his soldiers remarked "he ain't much of a *military* man", as if that were a contingent grace of Colonels which they might or might not possess.

I hv. enjoyed our Brigade Drills very much & Gen Saxton handles them very well. The 1st S.C.V. has held it's own very well, of course leading as to *marching*.

Dr. Rogers has been very ill with remittent fever, dangerously, but is now better & will go home in about a fortnight. Frank Higginson cannot manage to get home but is growing better in spite. I am about the same as before—able for duty but not in prime condition.

What doth Liberty[306] with a gold banded cap, that is navy not army; perhaps it alludes to the combined maritime character of his capture of Pilatka "by himself entirely"—how our men did enjoy that story of Louisa's. I let them laugh at him now he is out of the army.

I have very kind letters, fr. Messrs Sumner & Whiting[307] about the pay

304. "No. 3" was the name of a very small settlement in the remote mountainous interior of Maine.

305. TWH took a trip to Mt. Katahdin in Maine in the summer of 1855, and published an anonymous account of it, "Going to Mount Katahdin," *Putnam's* 8 (September 1856), 242–56, in which he adopts the narrative persona of a female leader of a group of hikers. John Stacy is therein described as "the fine looking youth in a red shirt" (p. 246) at whose farmhouse their wagon stopped one night and who then agreed to serve as their guide.

306. Lieutenant Colonel Liberty Billings, discharged July 9, 1863.

307. Massachusetts Senator Charles Sumner; TWH wrote of Sumner in "Charles Sumner," *Contemporaries*, The Writings of Thomas Wentworth Higginson, Vol. II (Boston: Houghton, Mifflin, 1900), 280–93. William Whiting was solicitor of the War

of our men, which take a load off my mind—they say our claim is unquestionable & there is no doubt of the action of Congress. Since then I observe Henry Wilson's bill putting pay up to $16 "Too much good" as the men say for very good—as if they had had so little good that enough was too much.

Speaking of enough, we had today 3 wild ducks for dinner & a chicken—the former delicious, one was canvas back. But this pays for many banyans as to meat, though all else abounds including *oysters*. Don't send me crackers or biscuit, they soften so, & we get good cheese here. The last remnants of *the* cake are disappearing *very* good it was though none too plain.

In rattling haste for the mail is premature

T. W. H.

*"to be the officers of law in the scene of their old bondage"*
To Mary Channing Higginson
Hdqrs. 1ˢᵀ S.C.V.
Dec. 21. 1863

Dearest darling I have got three letters & can hardly send one, the steamer returns so immediately. I am about the same & do not think I am overworking or losing ground. I shall try not to do either. It is cold now, freezing in the tent at night & that must be good for me. There are various movements going on from Hilton Head & two regiments going from here, also the Mass. Cavalry, but we seem to be fixtures, & are presently to be part, that is a portion, on Provost Guard duty in Beaufort,—that is the police. Hitherto my men have never taken part in this—it is the only military duty they have not done here & it will be quite an experience for them, to be the officers of law in the scene of their old bondage. They do guard duty, too, so well & thoroughly that it is very appropriate. Of course I had rather have them all together in camp, but as there are to be so few troops here, that will not be practicable. One of my Captains will be Provost Marshal of the town, & if Jas. Rogers were here, I shld. take him. It will seem odd to be the main garrison of a town where a year ago we seemed a sort of outcasts or at best an experiment, outside all regular organizations.

Next Wednesday Gen Gillmore gives a grand reception at his quarters in Hilton Head, the night *before* Xmas Eve. A party of us are to go down at 6 P.m. in a steamer with Gen. Saxton & come back at 12. Christmas Day,

Department, whose letter of December 4, 1863 (attesting that "the faith of the Government was pledged to every officer and soldier enlisted under" the instructions given to Gen. Saxton authorizing him to enlist black soldiers), TWH refers to in his Appendix D to *Army Life*, "The Struggle for Pay."

the colored people have a Fair which enlists all hands & at New Year's a great dinner. Did I tell you that swords were to be presented to Gen. Saxton & me? Mine is to cost $60; the money was given by six men in Beaufort, men quite well to do, who have made money by keeping saloons &c. It was put in Gen. S's hands who sent it to Frank Shaw to buy the sword. I believe FS. is coming out here then.

Among late arrivals are Mrs. Severance,[308] who is to live at Hilton Head & a Miss Lee of Templeton a friend of Sarah Butman's & who reminds me of her; she has come down to teach & will be one of the most attractive persons here if within reach. A Miss Iveson of Lynn came with her, rather superior. Just now Col. Beecher[309] called to see me of the 1st N.C.V. He is sunburnt & long bearded with the brusque decided air of the tribe.

Yesterday we had Henry Stone's wedding; Miss Stacey appearing per steamer in the morning, to be married in the afternoon; a fine, hale, intelligent looking girl, admirably fitted for her new life here. She is a sister of that John Stacy our Katahdin guide whom we liked so much. Good little Mr. Harris the Post Chaplain, had invited her to his house, where his good little wife was matron. The bride wore white muslin high in the neck & with fuller sleeves than anything but a bishop ever wore; trimmed as bishops are not wont, with red white & blue ribbons, & natural flowers in her hair—fantastic rather, but effective. We liked her very much—Mr & Mrs Chamberlin & Dewhurst & I being all the guests. We had wedding cake & bride cake emanating from Maine & past their earliest freshness, but it seemed stylish. She is not to live in camp but on St. Helena I. some six miles away.

Dr. Rogers has been really very ill with remittent fever—now he is better decidedly though still weak & confined to his bed entirely. By the next steamer we expect a document fr. Washington which will enable him to go home—we shld. hv. felt so badly if he had not lived to that! He has a very comfortable room in Beaufort & plenty of care & a nice old Dr. Marsh of Vt. (Sanitary Commission) prescribes for him in a way that delights him.

Frank Higginson, too is a great deal better though he has given up all hope of getting North I believe.

I hv. very good letters fr. Messrs Sumner & Whiting about the pay of the men, which take a weight off my mind; & now I see there is a bill proposing even $16 per month.

Just off a Court Martial I am put on another for trying Col. Van Wyck,

308. Caroline Severance, an advocate of medical education for women.
309. Colonel James C. Beecher, 1st North Carolina Volunteers (later 35th U.S. Colored Troops).

but it will only last a few days, probably. My Lt. Col. Strong is to be court martialled also for alleged misbehavior on the Edisto expedition. I don't think they can prove it—it is one of our younger Captains who brings the charge. It may lead ultimately to his leaving the regiment, of which we shall all be glad, for of course his defects can less be pardoned in a Lt. Col. than in a Major.

One of the men has just brought me in a cocoanut which his mother sent him from Key West among others—it is in the [ ]³¹⁰ this cold day.

Did you get my last letter with the check in it? This photog. is the regimental baby who lives under the bed; unless you care to keep it, send it to mother.

How kind people are to Marg't & oh! isn't Charlotte wonderful—I shld. judge from her letters that she was queen of two kingdoms, Washington & Worcester, & suspect she was too grand for [ ].³¹¹ She certainly has a wonderful gift at falling on her feet & having other people fall at them. If she had not written to you I wd. send you her letter.

I have sent for "Gen. Butler at New Orleans",³¹² shall I send it to you afterward? [ ]³¹³ Love to Marg't to whom I shall write a word only. Tomorrow is my birthday, forty & not fat. Merry Christmas dear & Happy New Year

*"as if made of better clay"*
To MARY CHANNING HIGGINSON
HILTON HEAD
JAN. 8. 1864

So far on the way back my darling. The Fulton was ordered back when we met her & I may be able to get my letters & answer them by her, but it is not likely. I feel as if I had been a thousand miles, it takes so many changes of conveyance fr. Morris I. here—first horseback—then a rowboat—walked 3 miles—4 in an ambulance—a great steamer,—a little steamer & now I am waiting for one more steamer to take me to Beaufort.

Col. Montgomery I found on board the Ben De Ford & as we were at first the only passengers we coalesced very pleasantly of which I was glad,

310. Several lines of the letter are cut off here.
311. The copy-text is illegible here.
312. James Parton, *General Butler in New Orleans: History of the Administration of the Department of the Gulf in the Year 1862: With an Account of the Capture of New Orleans, and a Sketch of the Previous Career of the General, Civil and Military* (New York: Mason Brothers, 1864).
313. Several lines of the letter are cut off here.

as he once told Dr. Rogers he shld. never hold any but official intercourse with me & I *must* be on easy & pleasant time with everybody even if I don't respect them. M. is a terrible hater, but no one wd. hv. imagined fr. our manner that we were anything but loving friends which is the style I prefer, though I find most people like a straight-out quarrel. If M. were wise he wd. see that while he & Col. Littlefield are both straining every nerve to command brigades, I, with claims senior to theirs, am not raising a finger for it—& he would therefore count me out of the fight, but I don't think he does. Littlefield has always seen this & has always been very friendly to me for that reason, while hating Montgomery.

It was very pleasant to find so high a tone among the young fellows in the Mass 54th Chief Quartermaster a thoroughly a manly, English sort of style Col. Halliwell,[314] Lt. Col. Hooper[315] of Boston & Maj: Appleton.[316] I did not think the look of the reg't superior to mine but it rained, so I cd. hardly judge. The officers are *too* young. The latest arrival went down with me, a son of Rev Mr Newell[317] of Cambridge. I knew him by the resemblance of his handwriting to his father's on the card upon his trunk, & then he introduced himself.[318]

Nothing gives a Democrat a better glimpse of aristocratic privileges than to travel in a military dep't—when men see you are a Colonel, all difficulties are smoothed & all privileges accorded, unless a General heaves in sight & then you are nothing & it is astonishing how soon one learns to claim for one's self these special privileges as if made of better clay. It must be far more so with noblemen born, since they have nothing else fr. childhood; & no doubt they easily convince themselves that it is in the fitness of things. It is rather despicable in this military case, but sometimes very convenient.

On passing through Hilton Head the other way I spent a pleasant evening with Mrs. Severance & borrowed a French book, think of such a thing here! It is a volume of Miscellanies by George Sand with her criticisms on her own work, Consuelo &c—very frank & wise. I saw there also Jean Ingelows Poems[319] & can't imagine why they are so admired. I am reading Charles Auchester with new delight, but [ ][320]

314. Colonel Edward N. Hallowell.
315. Lieutenant Colonel H. N. Hooper.
316. Major J. W. M. Appleton
317. Captain Robert R. Newell.
318. The copy-text reads "hiself."
319. Jean Ingelow, *Poems* (Boston: Roberts Brothers, 1863).
320. The rest of the letter is missing.

*"the results now gained for the colored people & the nation"*
To Louisa Storrow Higginson
Hdqrs. 1st S.C.V. Jan 10. 1864

*Dearest Mother*

I am having a delightful time with letters & boxes! perfectly splendid; Friday morning I returned fr. Morris Island & found a mail & that very eve'g brought, most unexpectedly, another mail: before I had fairly mastered these came last night yr. box & now I hear at the Express of another box, & altogether it is perfectly Christmas; the boxes were so unexpected. I at once "toted" a supply of crackers cheese chocolate & ginger cakes into the Qmaster's tent where Dr. Minor was reading Charles Auchester to Mrs. C. & the baby; & we agreed that never was anything so good; the cheese especially is infinitely beyond anything we get here, a sort of more substantial cream. Then the[321] ginger cakes were thin & crisp & flaky, like the dreams of youth. "Just like mother's, George" murmured little Mrs Chamberlin with her angelic face, rolling up her blue eyes with her mouth full—George nodded decisively, while Dr. M. with face scarcely less angelic, murmured "Splendid". Afterwards I went to the Adj'ts tent with similar results & on the whole Field & Staff the effect has been conclusive. The little chocolates are piquant & do not harden as the creams do. The envelopes came like manna & I only wished for a little notepaper, which is low here in one sense & high in another. I meant also to ask for a piece of old carpet to put beside my bed & two good flannel shirt, of which the purchaseable article is too thin & short. The pressed leaves were very pretty & the books mild & unpretending. I am well off for books, Stephen (I suppose) sent me his Deerfield pastor's book,[322] wh. looks simple & good, & I have others.

What the other box may be at which you hint, I can't imagine—nor who "the family below" may be, nor how far below. It sounds like an Infernal Machine, but that makes it only the more exciting.

I was none the worse for the trip to Morris Island & enjoyed it. On the whole, I gain rather than lose; I am able to be on duty though sparing myself somewhat, & do not lose strength any more.

You are mistaken my dear sympathetic Anna, as to my not enjoying this winter as much as last. I think I do, quite as much. My cares are lighter & the many anxieties which then oppressed me have vanished before the assurance of success beyond all dreams. Who could have foreseen a year ago

321. The copy-text reads "the the."
322. James K. Hosmer, *The Color-Guard: Being a Corporal's Notes of Military Service in the Nineteenth Army Corps* (Boston: Walker, Wise, and Company, 1864).

the results now gained for the colored people & the nation—& due so largely, as I believe, to the success of that one experiment. Then the whole social position of the regiment is so different that officers as well as men feel it all the time. "The first S.C.V. *runs* Beaufort", is now a common remark here; since we have a recognized & leading place everywhere. Then my domestic arrangements are far more homelike & pleasant; I am far more comfortable in my tent, far better served, we have built a cosy wooden mess-house and have a bright & congenial mess. I do not really miss Dr. Rogers, because the relief is even greater than the loss. Feeling less *positive* vigor I am less eager for action & can lead contentedly a less adventurous life, so you see my usual sunshine accompanies me & I assure you I would not exchange the certainties of this year for the hopes of last.

In haste for a special mail thine

*"my blameless Ethiopians"*
To Louisa Storrow Higginson
Hdqrs. 1st S.C.V. Beaufort S.C.
Jan. 14. 1864.

*Dearest Mother*

The second box was even more astonishing than the first—a wilder diversity of crackers & bolder combinations of corn starch & olives with literature & blackberry brandy. It was very entertaining & I had in the ladies to superintend the opening & avert danger in case it were an infernal machine after all. All the eatables will find a market somehow, you may be sure: my greatest exigency is how to dispose of Extract of Ginger: but my blameless Ethiopians hv. tough palates & perhaps I can pass it off for their favorite beverage Castor Oil. I had a nice supply of books—Henry Michels[323] & Stephen sent the warlike experiences of their respective pastors; Jas. Fields sent the Wayside Inn[324] & his wife's Organ Ode in snow white array; Dr. Channing sent Levana[325] which I prized most of all, a wonderfully wise & suggestive book. I have written to Martha[326] to thank

323. Henry Michels sent George H. Hepworth, *The Whip, Hoe, and Sword; or, The Gulf-Department in '63* (Boston: Walker, Wise, and Company, 1864).

324. Henry Wadsworth Longfellow, *Tales of a Wayside Inn* (Boston: Ticknor and Fields, 1863).

325. *Levana; or, The Doctrine of Education*, trans. from the German of Jean Paul Friedrich Richter (Boston: Ticknor and Fields, 1863).

326. This could be Martha Le Baron, Martha Hubbard Babcock Higginson (TWH's aunt, wife of his uncle James Perkins Higginson), or his half-sister, Martha Salisbury Higginson Nichols.

her. All stray books wh. I don't care for I turn in to our Officers Library, which is as yet small, but rather popular.

The winter glides by fast much more cold & wet than last yr.—perhaps Feby will be softer. It is our sickly season next month & we await it with much interest; it looks so far as if we were to be more healthy than last year. Dr. Tremaine is here on a visit, (who is to be Dr. Rogers' successor) & I think we shall like him. He is a handsome, soldierly looking man born in Nova Scotia, & has been Ass't Surg. in the English army. He prefers colored troops because he thinks they will be more like regulars & their officers have ultimately a higher position than volunteer officers. Besides, he likes the men.

An admirable new order has just arrived, obtained by Gen. Saxton through Chas. Sumner, whereby these lands will be "pre-empted" by the colored people in 20 acre lots, instead of being sold at auction. This is a great boon, as otherwise speculators wd. bid over them, as happened in a late sale at Hilton Head, where the former slaves subscribed & bid $2000 for the plantation where they were bred, & a speculator bid $2500 & got it. All soldiers white or black have a chance to purchase & I have serious thoughts of investing a trifle, so as to be a landholder in South Carolina.

My Lt. Col. is being tried by Court Martial on charges preferred by a Captain, of misbehavior on our Edisto Expedition—but they are not just & I think nothing will come of it. He is as amiable as ever through it all—a great contrast to Col. Billings who was apt to be touchy—Col. Strong rather errs on the other side. His health is not good & I think he will resign before spring. Scrobie thrives, growing bigger every day & has just sent for his wife. I am growing better in health, I rather think—certainly not losing & have a notion I can get well yet, without going North, which I am loth to do till summer. Col. Littlefield, just fr. Washington, says that colored troops are to be sent down here fr. the North, glad to hear it.

Ever affectionately
T. W. H.

Your letter on my birthday was charming, my mamma. I sent it to Mary.

*"Baby flourishes & so do we all"*
TO LOUISA STORROW HIGGINSON
HDQRS. 1ST S.C.V. BEAUFORT S.C.
JAN. 22. 1864

*Dearest Mother*

I wish you could see how comfortable I am in my new tent, built like a house in one large room; it is delightful. A large & handsome cat shares it with me, having squatted upon me, sometimes literally; she is very [ ]³²⁷ & very intelligent, likes to sit up & gaze into my face. She never has anything to eat & is very fat. The other night I left her gazing half awake into the open stove (she having slept one laborious nap on my couch fr. my rising to my retiring) when I packed myself in & found my feet imperfectly covered. I said to myself O that Pussy knew it; whereon she instantaneously sprang up & couched immoveably till morning, thus assimilating to *toast* the feet aforesaid.

One of her kittens, wishing to suit ages, sleeps on baby's feet in like manner.

Baby flourishes & so do we all; I am growing decidedly better; first I tried Agnes'³²⁸ blackberry & that did me good, then I stopped it for certain reasons & that was still more beneficial; then I consulted dear old Dr. Marsh of the Sanitary & got some medicines which I haven't opened, & that has done me still more good; so I really am on the gain, wh. is all I can expect at present.

I send some copies of "the Young Quartermaster["]³²⁹ with a remarkable engraving of a certain Colonel which you may recognize. The book is affectionate though formidably evangelical & has some good things about the regiment, though the good Q.M. did me great injustice in thinking me opposed to his Sunday School at Jacksonville—so says Dr. Minor who is equally Orthodox. I always respected his sincere belief & tried to save him fr. any raillery on the part of others.³³⁰

Sarah Bowditch has sent me Jean Ingelow's Poems wh. she admires. I didn't at first care for them, but they improve & there is a good deal of thought & sweetness in them.

327. The copy-text is illegible here.
328. Probably Agnes Higginson, TWH's niece (his brother Stephen's daughter).
329. Luther Goodyear Bingham, *The Young Quartermaster: The Life and Death of Lieut. L. M. Bingham, of the First South Carolina Volunteers* (New York: Board of Publication of the Reformed Protestant Dutch Church, 1863). This is an inspirational account of a young "Christian soldier" by his father, a minister. Lieut. Bingham joined the regiment on October 20, 1862, and died July 20, 1863, from effects of exhaustion suffered on the military expedition up the Edisto River; in terrible heat he supervised the loading of 200 refugees and their belongings onto a steamboat, and may have suffered sun-stroke (p. 116).
330. In one of Lieutenant Bingham's letters home, quoted in the text, he wrote, "The Colonel and others make a great deal of sport of me for being orthodox . . . Most of the field and staff being Unitarians, you can imagine that I have to breast quite a current, to stand up for my side of the question. The Colonel does not give slight cuts, by any means, and especially when I take any prominent part, like starting a Sunday-school in Jacksonville" (pp. 86–87). TWH's letter commending Lieutenant Bingham is printed herein (pp. 161–67), and the "remarkable engraving" of TWH charging Prince Rivers as color bearer never to give up the flag appears as well (opp. p. 184). See the gallery.

Just now a steamer went past with 500 of the 55ᵗʰ Pa. who hv. gone home to re-enlist with my scapegrace friend, Col. White, at their head—it looked very pleasant, though our men wouldn't care to follow.

After the weeks of cold & rain we are now having exquisite days—frogs at night & mocking birds in the morning. Spring will be here before many months. In a week fr. Monday we go out on picquet for 20 days again, & this time I expect to go. It is such a comfort to have the camp so much healthier than last winter—but that charming person, Lottie Forten, is severely ill with small pox over on St. Helena I. wh. makes us feel badly. Still it is a trifling disease here, compared to its Northern types.—though we are all being vaccinated.

Goodbye—thank Lizzy especially for her note. Mary has a sheet of journal to send.

Ever affectionately
T. W. H.

*"I have done my duty entirely"*
To Mary Channing Higginson
Camp Shaw. Jan 28. 1864

It is impossible to dream of any weather more delicious than we have had steadily day & night for one week; it is like the very choicest of our days in latter May; if you had arrived during this weather, you wd. have never wished to live anywhere else on earth; while I, being experienced, draw no such inference. This unspeakable weather does me no harm & perhaps some good; I am certainly better than I was, tho' with no reserve of strength, I find, for any extra work. An evening party for instance after the day's duty, tires me.

I do not find the [ ][331] indulgence & apologies of a semi-invalid condition nearly so disagreeable as I had supposed, which for one who has been thought to pride himself on his physical condition, is a good deal to say. I can understand a gradual sliding into slippers & dressing gown, far better than formerly—or Wasson's[332] condition. Everything has its compensations, though not to the extent of equalizing human conditions, of course. Then I feel so sure of being well again whenever I go North, that I always feel I hold my health in my hand, whenever I choose to regain it.

331. The copy-text is illegible here.
332. David Atwood Wasson, a radical young preacher in a neighboring town when TWH was at Newburyport, and later TWH's assistant in the Free Church, Worcester; Wasson was also a frequent *Atlantic* contributor.

I want you to understand, dear, that as to the *war* I feel that I hv. done my duty entirely & have no more compunctions. As to these people, I feel much more clinging yet, & it will be hard to leave them & the work I feel I am doing for them—hard to leave South Carolina & feel that I desert them—*that* is why I require some ample season of health to sustain me in going away. Sometimes I sympathize with those of my officers who wish to stay here forever, but this is not often. The current land sales bring this thing to a test, & enable one to judge of one's own feelings.

Then there is so much that is disagreeable in the dependence of an army officer on the orders & interests of his superiors, that I often long to be my own master. Not that I ever feel this for a moment about anybody at *this* post where all goes smooth, only in connexion with Dept. Hdqrs.

Letters have come, a dozen! partly official. But oh dearest, was yr. letter fr. that wonderful Charlotte be like mine? How cd. you take it so coolly if so. Her mingling of passion & glory, sentiment, upholstery & the grand tour, is too good for a novel. "To nevermore be called anything colder than cherub" "In the summer we plan to travel wherever I shall decide (Rand)—Europe not excepted. But I wish to see America first." "My superb parlor." "He has influence enough to obtain almost anything he wants, when we shall find out what that is."

And above all "You will laugh, as I do, at the name of Storm Vanderzee Boyd—but now he is never anything but 'Van'—my Van."

This carries out the upholstery so completely, so irresistibly suggestive of di-van; & recalls so the Harrison songs of, ["]Little Van, Van, is a used-up man"![333]

Poor, little, brown, velvet-eyed, wary, gracious, figurante Charlotte with her false curls & her spread eagles & her Sodom & Gomorrah generally—that she should come to glories like this—

*"a great flurry & hurry & for nothing at all"*
To Louisa Storrow Higginson
Headqrs. 1st S.C.V.
Camp Shaw. Feb. 7. 1864.

*Dearest Mother*
We hv. been called in fr. picquet with great flurry & hurry & for nothing at all, so far as we can yet see—Gen. Gillmore evidently intended to send

---

333. William Henry Harrison (1773–1841), ninth President of the United States, defeated Martin Van Buren (1782–1862), eighth President, in the election of 1840; TWH is presumably remembering a campaign ditty of Harrison's.

us off on the expedition which has just left for parts unknown, under Gen. Seymour. It may hv. been because Gen. Saxton remonstrated, but at any rate the Expedition has gone & we have not. The order was to be in readiness to move at a moment's notice & so we are, but we don't expect to go. If I were better & stronger in health, & liked the prospective leader, I shld, be disappointed, as the men generally are—as it is I am rather divided in inclination. Not so Mrs. Chamberlin who remarked at dinner while we were discussing who wd. get the laurels of the Expedition, "I don't care who gets the laurels", her color mounting up in it's usual pretty girlish way—*so long as we don't*,—which all agreed was dealing handsomely with Fate & putting no fine pretence upon it.

Louisa hints something dim about flannel shirts, & last night appeared a small box, neat as possible, but which I hardly thought cd. contain them; opening it, I found a handsome field glass in a case, beautifully done up & engraved inside *not* with my name, but with Robert Small's, who to be sure deserves it well. It was from a Miss E. C. Greene of Norwich, Ct. one of the most devoted workers for soldiers in the country, said to be rich too, but perhaps only fr. the liberality of her private gifts. She sent us a box of hospital supplies last winter, which was a perfect work of art, the surgeons said. You remember who Robert Small is, Captain of the "Hunter."

We hv. not yet a surgeon in place of Dr. Rogers—Dr. Tremaine has failed us & we are trying after a Dr. Harrison who is highly praised & said not to drink whiskey. Surgeons are by far the worst class of officers in the army, in this respect, partly perhaps because they hv. more opportunity, as they always hv. liquor among their supplies. There are however marked exceptions & some of the most agreeable officers whom I hv. met are Surgeons & of the highest character—but these are exceptions.

It gives a strange feeling of relief fr. responsibility to think that we are *not* going away—I feel that I hv. nothing to do & yet the ordinary duties of every day are certainly sufficient; the weeks go fast & I hv. no leisure. I remain about equally well gaining rather than losing, but hardly either. I find myself stronger since it grew colder again, these few days. We had a [ ][334] of almost June weather.

Chas. Norton has kindly sent me some newspapers & pamphlets—I hv. not seen the North American.[335] I shall send for Count Gurowski's second

334. The copy-text is illegible here.

335. TWH's mother may have drawn his attention to any of a number of articles recently published in the *North American Review*. One possibility is the review of William A. Hammond, *A Treatise on Hygiene, with Special Reference to the Military Service* (Philadelphia: J. B. Lippincott & Co., 1863), which appeared in *North American Review* 97 (October 1863), 483–507. Hammond was Surgeon General of the U.S. Army, and the review quotes with

volume,[336] his first entertained me so much. The author of "Miles O'Reilly" is Col. Halpine,[337] Gen. Hunter's[338] chief of staff, an Irishman & of much talent, but unprincipled. "Pet Marjorie May["] sent me & I enjoy—

*"I certainly do not intend to be an invalid for life"*
To Louisa Storrow Higginson
Camp Shaw. Feb. 9. 1864

*Dearest Mother*

We are to go after all; this morning Gen. Saxton had an order to send us, as soon as the 4th N.H. reports here fr. Morris Island to relieve us. That may be tomorow or may be some days hence, as transportation is just now scarce. We are ordered to Jacksonville to report to Gen. Seymour. It seems odd to go there again & report to the very man who got us ordered away last Spring. What will be done after that (the main expedition having arrived already) we cannot say; whether we shall remain at some point on the river, or march inland no one knows. The force already gone seems immense for the purpose 3 brigades of Infantry, 8 batteries 1 cavalry battalion, 1 reg't mounted infantry in all some 10,000 men. I went last year with less than 1000, so I think Gen. Seymour is quite as safe. The 54th & 55th Mass. are gone or going & the 2d. S.C.V. with several other colored regiments. If we are brigaded with them, I suppose I shall command a brigade which I shall like—but how far Gen. Seymour is likely to favor Gen. Saxton's pet regiment remains to be seen.

---

satisfaction a paragraph of Hammond's disparaging comments on the aptitude of the negro for military service (and, more generally, for civilization) concluding, "The experiment of making a soldier of him must be considered as not yet completely decided" (p. 487).

336. Count [Adam] Gurowski, *Diary from November 18 1862 to October 18 1863* (New York: Carleton, 1864).

337. Charles Graham Halpine, *The Life and Adventures, Songs, Services, and Speeches of Private Miles O'Reilly (47th Regiment, New York Volunteers)*(New York: Carleton, Publisher, 1864). Originally these humorous squibs appeared pseudonymously in the New York *Herald.* On the staff of General Hunter, Colonel Halpine (1829–1868) prepared Hunter's first order for the enlistment of a black regiment. He claimed for his doggerel poem, "Sambo's Right to Be Kilt," a decisive influence in persuading white soldiers to accept the creation of the 1st South Carolina Volunteers: "Though Sambo's black as the ace of spades, / His finger a thrigger can pull, / And his eye runs sthraight on the barrel-sights / From undher its thatch of wool. / So hear me all, boys darlin', / Don't think I'm tippin' you chaff, / The right to be kilt we'll divide wid him, / And give him the largest half!" (p. 56).

338. Major General David Hunter (1802–1866).

Of course my great anxiety is about my health, but if I am to break down & give up the Southern Department I may as well do it there as here. Florida is healthier than here, though *not* for my special complaint. Still, on the whole I grow better & may continue to do so. I hv. now been ailing too long to retain the old *conceit* of health, and shall hv. no false shame to surmount. I certainly do not intend to be an invalid for life, if timely discretion can prevent it & Frank H's experience was a good warning for me, though he was far more ill than I. If two months or so hence I find myself for any long time unfitted for duty, I shall either ask a furlough or resign, however flattering a prospect may open.

Now that it is all settled I do enjoy the thought of seeing Florida once more, though under such different auspices. It is a fascinating region & I think many Northern people will go there to live.

The secret was well kept & it was only a surmise that the expedition went to Florida, till it was heard from. My guess was Savannah, with a *diversion* in the direction of Florida. It seemed too large a force for Florida alone.

I will send this today & write again before we leave.

Love to all
Thine own
T. W. H.

*"waiting day by day"*
To Louisa Storrow Higginson
Camp Shaw still.
Feb. 12. 1864.

*Dearest Mother*

We are waiting day by day for the 4th N.H. to come fr. Morris Island & now it seems as if it never were coming & the men begin to think we shall not go after all but I suppose it is only that all the steamers are busy; it is now 4 days we hv. been waiting & we are quite ready. Stirring news came from Florida & that seems so like our own ground, we want to be in the affair. The others are doing all that we planned out to do. One squad of our men is there, detailed on board the John Adams, working the guns; but all the rest are here. With so large a force as Gen. Seymour has, Florida is likely to be an easy victory.

The box has come—two days ago & one of the checked shirts at present adorns & consoles me, it is a comfort to hv. something with length to it, they sell such wee little things here. I may come even to Anna's prescription, but haven't yet. The Carpet is admirable, why did I never ask for it before; I can't take it to Florida, but shall leave it with Hetty. The paper was just what I wanted; stationery costs immoderately here & it's far cheaper to have one's friends provide it; note paper I mean especially.

We are getting nicely through Feby which is our sickly season, last year with 3 surgeons the sick list averaged 96 & now, with only one, 30. This was partly the fatigue & excitement of our first expedition last year; but I think it is chiefly the chimneys to the tents wh. make such a gain; it seems to ban-ish that tendency to pneumonia & pleurisy which then beset them. Last year everybody noticed the continual coughing at Dress Parade, all along the line, & now one rarely hears a cough. All our trouble now is Small Pox which rages fearfully in some of the plantations & had carried off some of our men who were absent on duty, while it affects those in camp but lightly; we are never without a little outlying settlement of tents, devoted to this complaint.

We are ordered to report to Gen Seymour at Jacksonville, but they say very few troops are left at Morris Island & that may be what delays the 4th N.H.

*Sat. 13th.* The 4th N.H. has come & still we are not gone—no trans-portation & we must wait until there come steamboats for us & as Gen. S. does not want us to go, he will not hurry them. Still I think something must surely be sent for us in a day or two. They will surely hv. all the fun over, whatever it may be, before we get there, if we linger at this rate. It is possi-ble that I may have a larger command in Florida, but that is secondary. If I can see the men where they will see service & still be well treated that is the main thing. The latest rumor is of a separate department for Florida & Gen. Hunter in command there.

The Atlantic is in with the mail—it is delightful to hear such good accts of Mary's condition this winter & you don't know what nice notes I get fr. Margaret; the girl steadily improves, though in her own unexpected ways. Think of her blossoming out into a talent for painting when music always seemed her one gift.

I haven't spoken of health yet, but I am *really* growing better, not on brandy or blackberry cordial, but on rice & hominy. I shall keep this open till the mail goes, unless we go first.

Goodbye with love to all. I send you some Worcester conundrums.

Ever thine TWH.

Feb. 15. Today the Delaware has come for us & we embark tomorrow, for Jacksonville. You can direct there, though it will make no great differ-ence. All are in high spirits & glad to go.

*"Peace evidently has its defeats no less than war"*
To Louisa Storrow Higginson
Camp Shaw. Beaufort S.C.
Feb. 23. 1864.

To think of our being still here & all prospect of our departure vanished—& that a few cases of varioloid alone stood between us & the miserable defeat in Florida.[339] I can hardly regret it now, for the whole thing was ill-managed as it seems to me. But I hv. not time to write much & Mary will send you some sheets of journal. At any rate here we are & going out on our tour of picquet again tomorrow, & shall have a peaceful time probably, unless Gen. Gillmore is moved to make some stir here in order to call the rebel troops back fr. Florida, where they hv. completely outgeneralled him thus far. I fear you hv. been anxious about us, after hearing through Southern channels of this defeat & that black troops were in it. There was a Col—of the 8th US. Col'd[340] & this reported, you may have been anxious, unless his name was given.

There is much feeling about it all here & Gen Gillmore is freely censured. He threw it all, last night, on Gen Seymour who, he said, had disobeyed orders. But the whole plan of the Expedition of course is Gen. G's responsibility & he knows that if he sends half his troops to Florida, Beauregard can equally well spare half of his who can get there in half the time.

I am about the same in health & pleased at going out on picquet the lovely weather having reappeared. My gain in health[341*] has not quite held it's own since the fatigues of our really arduous trip to the steamer Delaware & back, but I shall get it back again. I can handle my special complaint if I do not succumb under General Debility when warm weather fairly sets in.

I feel as if I had been from home ten years when persons come in so changed I don't know them since we parted in Mass^tts—for instance Un-

339. At Olustee, Florida, Union forces under Brigadier General Seymour advanced against Confederate troops under Brigadier General Joseph Finegan; two Union regiments, the 7th New Hampshire and the 8th U.S. Colored, gave way at the opening of the battle; the Confederates continued to attack, and Union troops finally retreated to Jacksonville, having suffered 203 killed, 1152 wounded, and 506 missing.

340. Colonel Charles W. Fribley, 8th U.S. Colored Troops, killed in action at Olustee, Florida, February 20, 1864.

341. *"The same *as when*"? Dr. Jennison. 1840. [TWH's footnote.] Dr. Timothy Lindall Jennison was a Cambridge physician; TWH as a child attended the Dame School kept by his daughter.

derwood,[342] ex-Atlantic editor, a few years ago a very handsome young man with a blond beard & now a handsome old one with ditto white as the proverbial driven. He asked me privately how I managed to keep that development in correct tint—I thought of recommending Ma'am Allen.[343] Peace evidently has its defeats, no less than war.

Thanks for yr. letters, but I really think the Rev Liberty is not as black as you paint him, he has very good traits, though shallow vain & lonely. Of course a man who is dismissed fr. service for incompetency by an Examining Board wishes to make the best of it & you must pardon even some stretching of truth.

I was so glad to hear something from Maria Bell & mean to write to her myself by Flag of Truce if I can pick up 10 cts for Confederate postage.

I was surpised to see Frank & Robert Higginson's appointments. The 4th Mass Cavalry is coming here with Col. Rand (who was Capt. on Gen Saxton's staff) & a fine officer—& Lt. Col. Washburn[344] brother of John of Lancaster who staid with the Mead's.

Ever thine
T. W. H.

*"we think of . . . demanding 35 days furlough to Africa"*
To Louisa Storrow Higginson
Advanced Picquet.
Port Royal I.S.C.
March 2. 1864.

*Dearest Mother*

I wish you cd. see our pleasant parlor of an evening with it's bright fire in the great fireplace, & pleasant circle. We are really a very harmonious family, when one thinks that there are three pair of husbands & wives, and three besides. The ladies never quarrel & are the best of friends—& never call each other by their first names—strange thing for womankind. The baby helps cement us of course & passes through many arms during the day. We have a hammock of very open network, on the piazza & you can conceive of nothing prettier than baby in that, covered entirely with the meshes, she in her little scarlet cloak & hood, & with her fat little wrists emerging through the net. She looks like the French pictures of Cupids shut up in baskets. Dr. Minor is

342. Francis Henry Underwood (1825–1894), who devised the idea for the *Atlantic Monthly* and then served as assistant editor under James Russell Lowell.
343. Possibly the trade name of a hair dye.
344. Lieutenant Francis Washburn.

her especial favorite & flirts with her a great deal but the father is not anxious, *considering their youth*—he regards it as an affair of school children only, Dr. Minor being just 20 & having to endure many slurs by reason of his youth.

All the regiments here are going home to re-enlist & we think of re-enlisting also & demanding 35 days furlough *to Africa.*

I have a very kind letter from W. H. C.[345] about the pay of our soldiers & at his suggestion I send a memorial to Congress by this mail. Also he writes about Storrow's ordination as Chaplain, which is certainly sufficiently unexpected. I dare say he will be more useful than half the Chaplains. George Higginson must still be very anxious about Jem,[346] but I think he will get through; there seem to be so many helpers.

By this mail I got no letter from you; probably I asked you to direct to Jacksonville—or possibly to Port Royal wh. means Hilton Head; in that case I shall get it today. Mary's letters come as usual.

I keep on about the same in health with slight fluctuations; on the whole gaining. So far as my special trouble is concerned, it is not at all severe, especially if I am very careful about diet. If I could devote myself entirely to health, I could get well here. I have found by experience (& it is since confirmed by Dr. Marsh, the best sanitary authority here) that the *astringent* treatment prevalent here for chronic Diarrhoea—brandy, blackberry cordial, lemons &c, is not nearly so curative as a careful farinaceous diet— what may be called the *natural* diet of the country, milk, hominy & rice, especially the latter. If this is true in general, it must be especially true of me, with my simple habits. But it is true generally that the very few cases which I have known to be *cured* in this climate have been treated in this last way.

I still think that my strength will give out when the really warm weather sets in & in that case I must come Northward. I have no *reserve* of strength whatever: though I feel well, usually, & always have a good appetite.

That battle in Florida was a miserable failure, except for the courage of the men. We should have been in it, but for a few cases of small pox. Now there is nothing said about our going & the garrison here is so small, that it is hardly likely.

Mary will send you some journal.

Ever affectionately<br>T. W. H.

I feel anxious about *your* health, my dearest mother; let us both be careful & feed on air, if necessary.

Direct to Beaufort. S.C.

345. Probably William Henry Channing, TWH's first cousin (son of his paternal aunt, Susan Cleveland Higginson Channing).

346. James Jackson Higginson, son of TWH's first cousin George Higginson.

*"the fascination of perfectly naive broken-English"*
To Sarah———
Headqrs. Advanced Picquet.
Port Royal I. SC.
March 4. 1864.

*Dear Sarah*

Thank you, ever so much for your nice letter & for Pet Marjorie, that most fascinating child; I suppose we have all known those who were like her in real life, but never in books. It is wonderful the fascination of perfectly naive broken-English, as in her letters—or Zagonyi in Mrs. Fremont's book,[347] or the talk of my men. Sometimes I fear they are learning to speak plain & feel a sort of void, like any other father whose children are going through that undesirable initiation but they never do, after all & I think they will hold out my time at least. They hold on to things—Uncle York, Dr. Rogers pet, who leans about against the wall with his arms folded looking like a retired saint in easy circumstances as Dickens would say— Uncle York Brown still thinks that his son John Brown, (the first black man ever killed in battle in U.S. uniform) was the subject of the song which all the army sing. I hope he will never unlearn it.

I send the report received today from our splendid color-sergeant who is left in command of the camp while the regiment is here on picquet. He bears his office statelily I assure you—occupying the Major's tent & having a sentinel before his door.

It is very pleasant out here on picquet, we come to it as a sort of country seat with our 3 ladies & baby. A great dilapidated parlor with hardly a whole pane; & a vast blazing fireplace o' evenings, with arms & accoutrements hung all about, & people reading working or playing perennial Euchre, with which Dr Rogers, bless him, demoralized the regiment forever.

By day or night there are interminable rides through woodpaths over the whole island to the different picquet stations—the Cherokee rose not yet in bloom to wave above our heads, but your favorite yellow jasmine high & nodding & fragrant & abundant everywhere.

Do you know how near we came to being in that infinitely disastrous &

---

347. Major Charles Zagonyi is a central figure in Jessie Benton Frémont, *The Story of the Guard: A Chronicle of the War* (Boston: Ticknor and Fields, 1863). Mrs. Frémont chooses to depict Zagonyi by reproducing "his own quaint Hungarian English, which gives it more emphasis and character, and makes a brief, soldierly effect which is not natural to pens feminine" (pp. 30–31). He says things like "Young men was the guard—but remarkable and extraordinary it was they gone so nice through" (pp. 139–40).

useless defeat of Seymour's in Florida? We were on the wharf to go on board the transport for Jacksonville & all our luggage already on, with hours of labor, when an order came countermanding it & sending us back to camp, because of a dozen cases of small pox in the regiment. The officers & men were horribly disappointed & are so still, though we know now that as senior colored reg't we shld. hv. had a prominent place in the fight & suffered as badly as any. That makes a difference in *my* feelings, but I don't see that the men feel it much. It is *awful* to go on a hospital transport & see wounded men, in that terrible *stillness* they have—& think they might have been yr. own regiment.[348]

The night the first load of wounded came we were having a ball for Washington's birthday—really a fine affair & the description in Childe Harold[349] is not finer than the chill & hush which came over all as in the middle of the dances, General Saxton came in, pale & stern, & with a word stopped every foot & every chord—& said that it was wicked to be dancing amidst such suffering & disaster—Lt. Col. Reed,[350] actually dying, had just been carried past the house. There had been a shadow over us all the evening from the mere rumors; & almost all readily came away, even without waiting for the fine supper—except some few officers & ladies the former chiefly *surgeons*, of course, who staid & had a comfortable meal.

Speaking of health, I am better as regards any specific disease; & have learned how to take care of myself & many of those beauties & mysteries of invalidism of which much is preached & something even practiced. As to strength I have a grave suspicion that I possess next to none, yet so far I do, after a fashion, the work of every day. How it will be a month or two hence I don't know—but when I find out shall act accordingly, for I discover that one invalided beyond a certain point makes a poor commander.

Give my love to the pleasant Worcester circle you describe so willingly; to yr. father & mother especially, & believe me

Ever affectionately yours
T. W. Higginson

348. Two manuscripts, not consecutively numbered, have been joined here editorially. The latter has a pencilled note at the top, "Feb. 1864," but its content makes it continuous with the March 4, 1864, letter to Sarah———, with which it has been here united.

349. George Gordon, Lord Byron, *Childe Harold's Pilgrimage* (1812–1818).

350. Lieutenant Colonel William N. Reed, 1st North Carolina Volunteers (later 35th U.S. Colored Troops), died of wounds received in action at Olustee, Florida, February 23, 1864.

*"trying to throw the blame of his own folly on the colored troops"*
To Louisa Storrow Higginson
Advanced Picquet. P.R.I.
March. 6. 1864

*Dearest Mother*

Two mails in two days & another expected tomorrow—yours & Louisa's of the 17ᵗʰ, missent to N.C.—& yrs. & Anna's later. I send a note to Anna too.

So you got full acc'ts of the defeat at Olusta after all & had not perhaps [ ]³⁵¹ Americans. One or two papers speak of the 1ˢᵗ S.C.V. instead of NC.V. (wh. was there) but not many. I hear Gen. Seymour, as was expected, is now trying to throw the blame of his own folly on the colored troops.

We are here & likely to stay a double 20 days, the regiments having gone fr. Beaufort a good deal to re-enlist & there being none whom Gen. S. trusts enough to relieve us by them. Col. Rust is gone with his reg't the 8ᵗʰ Maine with wh. we hv. had more to do than any other reg't—½ of my line officers are from it, even now.

Being here does not affect my health, either way; sometimes I hv. to ride too much, though the night riding I leave to Scroby. Scroby is growing immensely big & heavy, weighs 200 & rides an immensely heavy horse with a gait like an elephant's & a snort almost as loud as his master's mighty voice. Nothing else would carry Scroby—he lamed the Chaplain's horse in a week by sheer weight. He is immeasurably happy with his quick little English-born wife, rather his superior in cultivation & very admiring. She fits in very well with us, being unobtrusive & sensible, but all three of our ladies are now in great fear of being ordered out of the Dep't—a circular has been sent to diff't reg'ts asking the names of officers' wives, & report says that they are to be all sent away, because the wives of two regular officers made a great scene at Jacksonville. I hope not, for beside the pleasure it has been a very refining influence among the officers.

Do not be anxious about my health; there is no need. I shld. hv. been very sorry to be seriously ill in winter here, as I cd. not hv. gone home to advantage—but if warm weather means debility it must mean *home*, that is all.

I cannot send back the piece by Dickens, for it didn't come, but I have seen it. I hv. told you often my dear, how delighted I was with the shirts & carpet—which arrived Feb. 10—the former was just what I wanted & the

351. The copy-text is illegible here.

only thing I can't get here. The carpet adorned my tent in our [ ]³⁵² before the fire on our bare floor, here on picquet: & I draw my bathing tub to the edge of it every morning.

Louisa asks abt the Bingham family the cousin Amorette or Amorie is still teaching in Beaufort, an ordinary girl, & the dear old tiresome father³⁵³ bores us with letters. "Minnie" is in Brooklyn & Dr. Minor saw & liked her.

Goodbye, ever with love<br>T. W. H.

*"my theory of the greater dangers of peace & Main St."*
TO MARY CHANNING HIGGINSON
ADVANCED PICQUET
MARCH 11. 1864.

My dearest; life constantly illustrates my theory of the greater dangers of peace & Main St.

It rained furiously night before last & when I sat down at my desk after breakfast, Dr Minor pointed out a crack in the plaster of the ceiling, where it was wet, and said Colonel that will come down. Oh said I, my head is hard, I was fitted by nature to command a colored regiment & in about five minutes there came a crash as if the sky was falling & I the lark which was caught. It partially knocked me over, but did not stun me nor make me faint afterwards, but bled somewhat & I had to keep still that day, feeling rather as if I had been in a cavalry fight, which had turned out better than I cd. hv. expected.

MARCH 13.

The cut on my head has healed so as to give the happiest auguries in case I ever get a rap there;—I felt a little shaky next day but at that locality on the head no pain at all.

I enjoy life very well out here & we are really a very happy family. I am not at all severely taxed, indeed I can indulge myself in great laziness if I so desire—& I sometimes do desire. All our mess seem to agree that I shall need a furlough, or need it now—not that they see any want of appetite at meal times either, but that they see me do a good deal of lying down—and I shld. not dare to hint at anything farther than a furlough, to them. But it

---

352. The copy-text is illegible here.

353. Rev. Luther Goodyear Bingham, who compiled the memoir of his son, Luther M. Bingham, cited in note 329 above.

wd. not be for them to decide. Mrs. Chamberlin & Mrs. Trowbridge are going home at any rate for the summer, a month or two hence. Goodbye darling I expect to hear, day after tomorrow.

Thine own.

## "not a soul but was entirely deceived"
To——
ADV. PICQUET. MAR. 20/64
SUNDAY MORNING

Our life here seems like a pleasant country seat with everything very free & easy. Part of the household are just setting off for a little church in the woods about 4 miles off—some on horseback—others in a 4 wheeled farm wagon called by the people on the plantation reverentially "the buggy"—shutters are taken down & laid across for seats, then restored to their legitimate office on returning. Harness chiefly rope of various dates.

We miss the pleasantest people who used to ride out here last year: Mrs. Lander & her household of two paymasters & a Tribune reporter: but there are a good many who ride out here: rather ordinary mostly but ordinary people look pleasantly on horseback.

Last night as we were sitting in parlor, Adj't came in with a handsome young officer in new uniform—really very handsome—who turned out after a while to be Mrs. Dewhurst—far more successful than Abby May. Almost all were entirely deceived & I shld. certainly hv. been, but for a hint I overheard. Then she went over to camp with her husband & Mrs. Chamberlin who introduced her as her brother, Lt. Chandler & not a soul but was entirely deceived. She was easy beyond description, & was infinitely
[ ]354

## "I expect to wilt"
TO LOUISA STORROW HIGGINSON
HEADQRS. 33d U.S. COL'D TROOPS
FORMERLY 1ST S.C.V.
CAMP SHAW. APR. 2. 1864

*Dearest Mother*

I am not a little anxious about you, I assure you, but can only hope from week to week to hear good tidings. Jaundice is a very common feature of ill

354. A page is missing from the copy-text here.

health in this climate & always looks more alarming than it really is, but I have learned not to associate it with fatal disease.

I am doing well enough—gaining with the cool spring, for cool it is & late this year. But we shall soon have days relaxing enough. & I expect to *wilt*—especially with the aid of our new Gen. Birney who is a martinet & a worker, & will leave small opportunity for repose.

Storrow has gone out to our picquet station, but his beaming face looks in occasionally—he is a charming fellow & an universal favorite.

Gens. Gillmore & Seymour have both gone North—the latter I fancy will not return: possibly nor the former. I suspect they mean to leave this dep't in statu quo & concentrate on Richmond. Gen. Saxton is still on Ct. Martial at Hilton Head. The Provost Marshal Capt. Metcalf says drolly "Birney has altered everything Saxton has ever done, except his marriage & he would amend that in General orders if he could." Happily Gen. B. is even more an abolitionist than the other, so the colored people lose nothing, but I fear he is overdoing the thing—governing too busily—especially for a merely temporary commadr. But it is his nature—if he commanded a post for an hour he wd. set every wheel spinning. I shld. hv. commanded the Post during Gen. S's absence if B. had not appeared just in time—& I am sure I shldn't. hv. felt free to start one half the reforms he has originated—if reforms they are to prove. I think Gen. S. tolerates it rather as Butler did Phelps—in order to show people that there's somebody worse than himself.

Louisa's final Billings & Miles tableau was very edifying—so passes St. Liberty from the scene & I'm glad of it—when I visit you in May or June I want no such scare-crows about the fields.

If you could see our baby play with kittens, it is the prettiest thing, she just discovered that there can be anything alive smaller than herself, holding her hands in that pretty timid recoil which Julia Channing[355] caught so beautifully in her sketch of the two children & Kitten—saying to them her sole articulate word—"'*le babee*" & bobbing down her face at them in certain heterogeneous & untrained gulps, meant for kisses & followed by a slight grimace after the fur in her mouth; it makes us shout with laughter as she sits in a bliss upon the bed amid a tent full of adorers. The kittens crawl about in their aimless & blundering way, their eyes still blue almost as hers, & neither young thing quite knowing which is the more formidable, & Mrs. C. & the baby are going North in May also, as most ladies now do in the summer.

Goodbye, dearest Mother—do be better.

T. W. H.

Mary has some journal.

355. Julia Maria Allen Channing, wife of TWH's first cousin William Henry Channing.

*"The literary trade is probably good like all others now"*
To Mary Channing Higginson
HQ. 33ᵈ US. C.T.
Camp Shaw. Apr. 4. 1864

Dearest I hv. just had a visit fr. that sweetest of women, Mrs. Chamberlin "a sweeter woman never drew breath" who comes to beg to beat up an egg in wine, or something, for me at breakfast, & cried a little at the thought of my having to leave the reg't. I suppose you think I ought not to be moved by the tears of other men's wives. But she & all of them feel strongly that our Scroby is an admirable Major but wd. not do for a Colonel & so they all depend very much on me. She is so sweet & innocent, I felt very much as if the baby had come in & cried a few small tears.

As it so happened that yesterday being the first day of summer warmth had keeled me over completely, I had no consolation to offer. I dare say we shall go home at the same time. Yesterday was a very good experience for me, showing me precisely how I shall feel, on many days, this Spring, before I go. Yet it was not very disagreeable, only a kind of languor that incapacitated fr. work & happily came on the easiest day. It was very pleasant doing nothing, out on picquet, but here I don't like to be off duty.

Yesterday I saw a Mr. Cross of Worcester, brother of Mrs. Dr. Harris, & he reports that she is about to be confined, which is a startling occurrence. I wish I cd. tell you how remote & dreamy Worcester seems—farther than Newburyport, & I do not think it is harder to leave, perhaps not so hard. I never shall forget how I missed the *tarry smell* of the seaside wharves at Newb.port & if Newport without the *bury* has the same, I shall revel in it. There are great charms about a seaside place, even if it be as remote from the ocean as Newport—& it's being old & tumble down only helps it. I think the beautiful Main St. in Worcester is what I shall miss the most, after all, for I know the bay & river at Newport will more than replace the Lake, to me, besides that I would live in Labrador for the sake of my poor little girl's being so much better off.

What I enjoyed in Worcester was the radical popular party which prevailed when we went there—a phase now past & not essential to me now—though nothing else could have taken the dust & ashes of Newburyport[356] out of my mouth. [ ][357] for twenty years I cannot be very anxious now. The literary trade is probably good like all others now & I hv.

356. TWH had been effectively dismissed from his pulpit in Newburyport for the political radicalism of his preaching and his social activism.

357. Part of the copy-text is missing here.

no doubt we can make both ends meet somehow & keep Marnie as well as Mrs. Cat, whom I am glad you rely on as an ally through the journey of life.

It is a showery April day & I have before me a glass of wild white lilies which grow just outside the camp & blue violets. I will send this note, dear without waiting for any [] knows but some []³⁵⁸

## "We are leading our usual picnic life"
To Louisa Storrow Higginson
Hd. Quarters Adv. Picquet
Port Royal Island
Apr. 20. 1864.

*Dearest Mother*

I fear I have not been so regular as usual, of late, in my letters: but it is hard to count time here except by the mails, & these are irregular of late, because the steamers go to Fortress Monroe & back with troops, instead of to N.Y. The 10ᵗʰ Army Corps is being removed, with Maj. Gen. Gillmore to command it & the dep't will be chiefly garrisoned by colored troops. Two very raw colored reg'ts, the 26ᵗʰ US & 29ᵗʰ Conn. are the only ones left, in Beaufort except a portion of the 56ᵗʰ N.Y. a white reg't of poor quality & the rest of that is coming back in a month. Until then we are likely to be kept on picquet. Storrow's reg't is at Hilton Head.

We are leading our usual picnic life, with open house, six unexpected visitors at dinner yesterday; somehow or other Uncle John is always equal to the emergency with incidental aid from the ladies. The baby has a new blue sack & is perfectly sweet; she is plump as the proverbial partridge, perfectly healthy, & boils over with excitement to go to any body who will jump her. But our pleasant family will be broken up soon, as Lt. Chamberlin is detailed as Post Quartermaster & goes to live in Beaufort with wife & baby till she goes North in June.

I am doing very tolerably thanks to it's being so far cooler much than last year. Kind elderly ladies like Miss Abbott persist in sending me whatever prescriptions for chronic diarrhoea their friends' nephews found useful on the Potomac—but I have found rice & hominy worth the whole of them & have no longer any solicitude on that subject. I can, no doubt, get a furlough at any time I think best, but shall wait till after May 1—probably about May 10. In June I expect to go with Mary to Pigeon Cove, if we

358. Sections are missing from the copy-text here.

can get in there—& return in autumn to Newport, which is evidently the winter place for Mary.

I think I like quite as well to return to a new place, there is a freshness about it which gives quite a charm. I hate change of abode, but this eighteen months of absence has unsettled all local ties, & so many of the people I cared for have left Worcester that I am entirely reconciled to the change—besides that Mary is so much healthier & happier in Newport & finds such nice people there. Some time or other of course I expect to get back to Massachusetts.

It is only a few days since I suggested resignation to Gen. Saxton & he of course deprecated it very much, saying he would rather have me absent six months & then return. Still he will acquiesce if I insist, but I can do nothing about it till after my going North, for resignations cannot now be sent in, till one's ordnance accounts are audited, which takes several months; but as one's pay goes on too, it is not so bad.

We have had asparagus & strawberries—about a dozen of each. Magnolias just coming out, plenty of roses & azalias & colycanthus & not much else, perhaps you think that's enough.

It is said that three mails came in today, but we only had one & no letter from you in that—but it was only a three days mail & tomorrow may bring me one, as they say three mails came in today!

Ever thine<br>T. W. Higginson

*"I have sent in my surgeon's certificate"*
To Louisa Storrow Higginson
Adv. Picquet. Apr. 27 1864[359]

*My dearest mother*

I hv. only time to say that I hv. sent in my surgeon's certificate & expect to leave in about 10 days: It is growing much warmer, but I am still on duty & feel very tolerably & find plenty of work in soothing the anxious & disaffected who think (of course) that all the reg't is going to pieces when I turn my back.

I shall get off in very good season & without risking anything. It is impossible to fix any date with accuracy, as steamers leave irregularly.

Ever affectionately<br>T. W. H.

Roses in abundance.

359. "1864" is added in pencil to the MS.

*"the event of coming home fr. the wars"*
TO LOUISA STORROW HIGGINSON
NEWPORT, R.I.
MAY 18. 1864.

*Dearest Mother*

I suppose you got my telegram. I am quite tired today, chiefly with the fatigue of transhipment in NY. yesterday, wh. was attended with some bothers, & then the night was interrupted; but on voyage I was nicely & think I shall be again. Cool days make me as well as anybody; & perhaps *Northern* warm ones will. Mary behaved herself creditably & has just remarked over her news papers that if she gets me & Richmond in the same week, she will be doing very well.

My present plan is to go to Brattleboro May 30 & spend three nights & then probably go up again in the autumn. Margaret is coming here for a few days first & it would be very pleasant for me to take her up with me, if you are willing; I may never have the event of coming home fr. the wars again & would like to make it as much of an occurrence as possible & take a large cortége, but if it isn't convenient, say so. You know I never took her anywhere.

Mary longs to have you see my old hat—& thinks that if you or Waldo once saw it, you would never smile again—which seems friendly. She seems quite improved, I think, & is certainly very pleasantly placed here.

The beard I brought home suffered scissors to some extent before breakfast & will be seen no more.

Mary sends her love & says I seem better in health than she expected, & am heavy enough to have nearly broken down one chair already, which encourages her.

Ever thine
T. W. H.

# Chronology

**1823**  Born December 22, in Cambridge, Massachusetts, to Stephen Higginson, steward (bursar) of Harvard College, and Louisa Storrow Higginson. Stephen Higginson, formerly a prosperous merchant, had lost his fortune during President Thomas Jefferson's embargo (1807–1808) and now lived in reduced circumstances. He had two surviving children (out of five) from a previous marriage to Martha Salisbury—Elizabeth Sewall Higginson (later Keith) and Martha Salisbury Higginson (later Nichols)—when, a widower, he married Louisa Storrow, an orphan who had entered his household to help care for his invalid wife and two young daughters. She was 19 years old at the time of their marriage (he was 34) and bore ten children, of whom Thomas Wentworth Storrow Higginson was the youngest. Of TWH's nine siblings, one brother (Edward Cabot) had died in 1814 just short of the age of two, and another (also named Edward Cabot) died at two years of age soon after Wentworth—as TWH was known in his family—was born. A sister, Mary Lee, died at the age of six in 1826. The surviving six siblings were (in order of birth) Francis John (17 years older than Thomas), Stephen, Ann Storrow, Waldo, Susan Louisa, and Samuel Thacher (five years older). Ann Storrow was usually called Anna, and Susan Louisa and Samuel Thacher were generally referred to by their middle names.

**1834**  As older brothers leave home, and unmarried sisters remain, Thomas is increasingly in a predominantly female household, which he later credits with forming his lifelong feminist commitments. Anne Storrow, mother's sister (called Aunt Nancy), takes large role in children's upbringing, especially Thomas's. Stephen Higginson, father, dies at age 63 when Thomas is ten, and Thomas, along with mother, Aunt Nancy, and two full sisters, moves in with oldest brother Francis and his family.

**1837–41**  Enrolled at Harvard College. Lives and boards at home; unpopular with fellow students. Studies Greek with religious poet Jones Very; mathematics with Benjamin Peirce; French literature and language with poet Henry Wadsworth Longfellow; rhetoric with Edward Tyrell Channing. Competes assiduously for grades and class rank. During last year, visits an uncle, Maj. Samuel Mary Appleton Storrow, who had married a Carter heiress and now headed a plantation near Alexandria, Virginia. Does not directly observe "anything undesirable" in the slave system, but overhears the overseer speaking of the slaves' "domestic relations . . . precisely as if they had been animals." Receives Harvard degree in August 1841; brother Thacher, who had gone to sea, fails to return as expected, and as he and his ship are never heard from again, they are presumed lost.

**1841–42**   Teaches for six months in a boarding school in Jamaica Plain, a suburb of Boston; then goes as tutor to the three sons of a widowed cousin, Stephen Higginson Perkins, in Brookline, another suburb. While there, socializes widely with numerous cousins and friends (they play at charades, mesmerism, and clairvoyance) and becomes familiar with various social reform movements; meets young people from the utopian community Brook Farm, which he visits twice. The writings of Ralph Waldo Emerson at this time "took possession of me," he later writes; reads Emerson "over and over" and the Transcendentalist philosopher becomes "a lifelong source of influence." Also deeply moved by writings of German Jean Paul Richter. 1842, brother Francis transfers medical practice to Brattleboro, Vermont, where medicinal springs attract many invalids; mother, Aunt Nancy, and sisters move there too.

**1843**   September, returns to Harvard for postgraduate study, in no particular field; reads widely, goes to lectures, attends reform meetings, chiefly antislavery (hearing William Lloyd Garrison and Wendell Phillips), and liberal churches (hearing Theodore Parker and James Freeman Clarke). Betrothed to Mary Elizabeth Channing (daughter of his first cousin Barbara Higginson Perkins Channing and her husband, Dr. Walter Channing), a member of Clarke's church, and under Clarke's influence gravitates toward the liberal ministry.

**1844–46**   Enters divinity school at Harvard; continues wide-ranging education. Tries opium; meets William Henry Hurlbut (later Hurlbert), a fellow divinity student from Charleston, South Carolina, whose intellectual and conversational gifts ("unequalled . . . for natural brilliancy"), personal charm ("the most variously gifted and accomplished man I have ever known"), and great physical attractiveness ("so handsome in his dark beauty that he seemed like a picturesque Oriental; slender, keen-eyed, raven-haired, he arrested the eye like some fascinating girl") enchant him deeply. Leaves divinity school for a year, 1845–46, uncertain of vocation and preferring solitary study; seeks readmission for fall 1846, having reconciled himself to a career in the ministry.

**1846–48**   Mexican War. Texas is annexed to United States; in peace treaty Mexico cedes vast territories comprising present-day California, Arizona, Nevada, Utah, parts of Colorado, New Mexico, and Wyoming. Free Soil Party forms to oppose spread of slavery into newly acquired territories.

**1847–52**   Graduates from divinity school; invited to the First Religious Society at Newburyport, Massachusetts, a manufacturing town on the coast north of

Boston. Ordained September 15, 1847, by the society itself, according to his request (no ordaining council). During two and a half years in this pulpit, becomes more deeply involved in a variety of reform movements—temperance, women's rights, public education, labor reform and abolition. Preaching becomes increasingly radical and secular, to the dismay of influential members of his congregation. Marries Mary Channing, September 22, 1847. Nominated in 1848 as a Free Soil candidate for Congress, but loses the race. September 1849, resigns pulpit under pressure of increasing dissatisfaction from prominent church members. With Mary, moves to Artichoke Mills (or Curzon's Mills), several miles outside of Newburyport, where they remain two more years.

Writes for newspapers, lectures, teaches private classes, serves on public committees, organizes evening schools for working people, and engages more strenuously in antislavery activities. 1850, Compromise measures passed by Congress admit California to Union as free state, allow New Mexico and Utah to choose for themselves whether to admit slavery or not. Fugitive Slave Law reinforced, requiring non-slave states to return slave property to South; this requirement hardens antislavery resolve among Northern abolitionists, and TWH vociferously condemns it. 1851, participates in planning an abortive attempt to rescue Thomas Sims, a 17-year-old fugitive slave, from the Boston Courthouse.

**1852–56** Called in September 1852 to a new congregation in Worcester, Massachusetts (west of Boston), a Free Church (modeled after Theodore Parker's church in Boston), nondenominational and highly secularized, intensely imbued with radical political sympathies. Visits spiritualist in Boston; during seance fails to contact lost brother Thacher, but does communicate with deceased father. Accepts Worcester pulpit; services are held in Horticultural Hall. Assists operations of underground railroad. 1853, travels and lectures widely, achieving modest renown; wife Mary commences chronic invalidism (symptoms include crippling rheumatism) that will characterize the remainder of her life, with few periods of relative health. Mary experiments with various therapies: homeopathy, electromagnetism, hydrotherapy, and other then-fashionable medical practices.

May 1854, buys a dozen axes and leads a group of men who try to tear down the door of the Boston Courthouse and rescue a fugitive slave, Anthony Burns; a guard defending the door is killed by the mob, and the attempt melts away in disarray. Indicted for his part in the affair, lives under threat of prosecution for a year, but is never brought to trial. Kansas-Nebraska Act repeals Missouri Compromise of 1820, permits all new states to choose whether to admit slavery or not. Republican Party formed in reaction. Summer 1855, climbs Mount Katahdin in Maine with a party of men and women; September 1856, publishes account of the trip in *Putnam's Monthly Magazine*, adopting a female narrative persona. Sails October 19, 1855, for Fayal, island in central Atlantic; spends winter 1855–56 there, but Mary's health does not substantially improve as hoped.

**1856–58**  May 1856, Higginsons return to Worcester from Fayal. Violent contest in territory of Kansas between proslavery and antislavery settlers engages his interest immediately; helps recruit and outfit (with provisions and munitions) parties of emigrants to swell the antislavery population; September 1856, goes to escort a party into Kansas via the overland Iowa route in order to circumvent a blockade of the Missouri River. Writes letters for the *New York Tribune* about the troubles in Kansas. 1857, Dred Scott decision by Supreme Court holds that slave's residence in free state does not make him free; Missouri Compromise declared unconstitutional, and Congressional prohibitions on slavery in territories disallowed. March 1858, publishes first article in *The Atlantic Monthly*, on the weakness and poor health of civilized men and the value of vigorous physical life. Thereafter, regularly publishes historical, political, and literary essays in the *Atlantic*, chiefly on masculine physical well-being, natural history, and slave insurrections. Abraham Lincoln, Republican, challenges Senator Stephen Douglas for Illinois seat; debates are widely noted, but Lincoln loses.

**1858–59**  With five other men (Theodore Parker, Samuel Gridley Howe, Frank Sanborn, Eli Thayer, and George Luther Stearns) Higginson meets periodically with John Brown, the antislavery guerrilla; he raises money for him and plots with him to foment slave insurrection by providing means for slaves to achieve their freedom through violence. October 1859, Brown's seizure of federal arsenal at Harper's Ferry, Virginia, is foiled; Brown is caught and hanged. Among the so-called "Secret Six" conspirators, only Higginson doesn't disavow the attempted Brown revolt (three others flee to Canada, one to an insane asylum; Parker is dying in Italy).

**1860**  Originates a scheme to rescue from Virginia prison two members of Brown's guerrilla band; recruits a Kansas scout, James Montgomery, to lead the raid, but its impracticality puts an end to the plan. Lincoln (Republican) and Douglas (Democrat) run for President, and Lincoln wins on purely sectional vote. December 20, South Carolina secedes from Union. Census counts 4,441,830 African-American slaves in United States.

**1861**  Mississippi, Florida, Alabama, Georgia, Louisiana, Texas, Virginia, Arkansas, North Carolina and Tennessee secede from Union, forming Confederacy of eleven slave states. April 12, Confederacy fires on Fort Sumter, Charleston Harbor, South Carolina, starting Civil War. November 5, Union vessels fight Confederate flotilla in Port Royal Sound, forcing Rebel vessels up inland streams. November 7, a combined land-sea expedition under Flag Officer Samuel F. Du Pont and Brig.-Gen. Thomas West Sherman seizes and occupies the Sea Islands of South Carolina (the Hilton Head-Port Royal area), pounding fortifications and causing Confederate defenders to flee inland and establish lines of defense on the mainland. An important base of operations is thus established on the South Atlantic coast for Union military forces. Plantation owners have fled, leaving large numbers of slaves behind on abandoned plantations, along with the richest cotton crop in recent memory, all of which fall under Union control.

Slaves are understood to be "contraband of war," and a large experiment in converting these laborers to the status of wage earners is undertaken (with the collateral purpose of securing the crops to the benefit of the United States Treasury). Commonly called the Port Royal Experiment, effort is largely conducted by Northern educational, philanthropic and missionary societies which send hundreds of plantation superintendents, schoolteachers, and ministers to the area. Port Royal becomes enclave for black refugees, and a laboratory for the refashioning of the Southern economy according to free labor principles; experiment continues over coming years as the similar U.S. Army experiment in militarization of ex-slaves is undertaken in the same vicinity.

**1862** April 12, Maj.-Gen. David Hunter successfully assaults Fort Pulaski, guarding Savannah Harbor, and declares slaves free in immediate vicinity. May 9, Hunter declares all slaves in Georgia, Florida, and South Carolina to be free; begins in May to enlist black men from among the contrabands as Union soldiers. Congress inquires of the War Department whether Hunter is authorized to organize "fugitive slaves" into a regiment, and War Department asks Hunter to explain his actions; Hunter replies sardonically that there is "no regiment of 'fugitive slaves'" being organized, but rather "a fine regiment of persons whose late masters are 'fugitive rebels.'" When he asks in August for this regiment to be mustered in and paid, and fails to receive such authority, he disbands the troops, keeping a small company together unofficially. These form the nucleus of a new regiment when Brig.-Gen. Rufus Saxton, sent to Port Royal to occupy, cultivate, and guard the abandoned plantations, is officially authorized to raise a black regiment in October. Recruitment proceeds slowly, the mistreatment of the Hunter regiment having inculcated suspicion of the government's good faith among the black population.

TWH publishes "Letter to a Young Contributor" in April *Atlantic*, giving advice to aspiring writers; among those who write to him as a result is an unknown Amherst poet, Emily Dickinson, who encloses four poems that conveyed to him the "impression of a wholly new and original poetic genius." They correspond over coming year, she seeking his criticism and approval. September, having long desired military action, but inhibited by duty of caring for wife Mary in her illness, TWH finally determines that "I never could hold up my head again . . . if I did not vindicate my past words by actions though tardy," and that "beyond a certain point one has no right to concentrate his whole life on one private duty." Enlists in the volunteer army, helping to recruit a 9-month regiment in Worcester and becoming Capt. in the 51st Massachusetts Infantry. Resides at Camp Wool outside Worcester, and strives for discipline and polish in his company. President Lincoln issues Preliminary Emancipation Proclamation, September 22, giving seceded states 100 days to adopt voluntary schemes of emancipation and return to the Union, or have their slaves declared free.

November 5, Gen. Saxton writes to TWH offering him colonelcy of the 1st South Carolina Volunteers, the black regiment then being formed. Under temporary

command of Col. Oliver T. Beard (48th New York Volunteers) and Capt. Charles
T. Trowbridge, Company A of the black regiment undertakes expedition along
Georgia and Florida coasts, November 3–10, destroying rebel salt-works, harassing
Confederate pickets, and bringing away slaves. Another expedition, November 18–
22, raids lumber mills on Doboy River, Georgia, securing large supply of boards and
saws. Col. Beard pronounces this test of black soldiers an unqualified success. On
the eve of his Massachusetts regiment's departure for North Carolina, TWH receives surprise invitation to transfer to the 1st South Carolina; accepts appointment
as Col. of this regiment, arriving in Beaufort by steamer November 24. En route, begins journal in which, over the next year and a half, he keeps a record of his experiences in camp and on military expeditions.

**1863**  Final Emancipation Proclamation issued, January 1; read at celebratory
convocation organized by TWH in Port Royal.

January 23–February 1, leads expedition (three steamers—*John Adams, Planter,* and
*Ben De Ford*) up St. Mary's River, on border between Georgia and Florida. Carry
Emancipation Proclamation to slaves, forage for supplies, and seek recruits. Detachment of men, on a midnight incursion at Township, Florida, come under attack
in woods by Rebel cavalry and beat them off; one soldier killed, seven wounded. The
*John Adams*, carrying 250 men, penetrates 40 miles up a narrow, winding stream into
enemy territory, coming under fire from Confederate forces on shore; collects supply of 40,000 bricks, 250 bars of railroad iron, supplies of lumber, rice and other
provisions including a flock of 25 sheep. Another detachment destroys a salt-works
up Crooked River. Higginson credits Cpl. Robert Sutton, formerly a slave upon the
St. Mary's, as "the real conductor of the whole expedition."

March 6–31, leads expedition (aboard *Burnside, Boston,* and *John Adams*) to occupy
Jacksonville, Florida. March 7, reach Fernandina; March 9, drop anchor at mouth
of St. John's River; reach Jacksonville March 10, occupying it together with part of
the 2nd South Carolina Volunteers (black regiment) under Col. Montgomery, in the
face of little Rebel resistance. Engage in periodic skirmishing with Confederates encamped nearby. White regiments—6th Connecticut and 8th Maine—leave Beaufort March 13 to reinforce Jacksonville; arrive March 23, delayed by rough weather.
Col. Montgomery and 120 men, aboard *Paul Jones*, penetrate upriver 75 miles to
Palatka, taking prisoners and supplies. Suddenly ordered to evacuate, with much regret they abandon Jacksonville March 31.

July 9–11, leads expedition (three boats—steamer *John Adams*, transport *Enoch Dean*,
tug *Governor Milton*—250 men of the 1st South Carolina, and a section of the 1st
Connecticut battery under Lieut. Clinton) up South Edisto River, South Carolina;
July 10, come under fire at Wiltown, 21 miles upriver, where spiles (obstructive posts)
across the river block their passage. Remove the spiles, but frequently are grounded
in the shallow and narrow river, and come under attack from shore repeatedly; 30

miles upriver, give up ascent, within 2 miles of the railroad bridge they hoped to destroy. Back at Wiltown, *Milton* catches on spiles as tide is falling, and is of necessity abandoned and burnt; remaining vessels come under fire again, and TWH is wounded by the concussion of a ball close by his side. Having destroyed rice fields, return to Beaufort with 200 contrabands, 2 prisoners, 6 bales cotton. Two soldiers killed, plus the engineer of the *Milton* and one contraband slave taken aboard.

Failing to recover quickly from injury, takes 20-day furlough, arriving home in Worcester July 27, seeking treatment at the water cure. Visits mother in Brattleboro, and extends furlough slightly when recovery lags, but arrives back in Beaufort on August 20, resuming regimental duties. October, enters hospital, suffering from continuing debility; diagnosed by Dr. Rogers with malaria, seeks respite at various homes in the vicinity. November 9, regiment goes out on picket duty, but colonel stays more comfortably in camp, visiting troops at picket stations occasionally. 1st South Carolina Volunteers hereafter intermittently serve on picket duty and police duty in Beaufort. TWH's time is increasingly taken up with service as judge in court-martials around the Sea Islands. Wife Mary moves to Newport, Rhode Island.

**1864**  Writes to New York *Tribune* protesting failure of government to pay black soldiers in keeping with promises made to them. Addresses New York *Times* similarly in February. Gen. Seymour conducts large expedition to Florida in February, and 1st South Carolina anticipate joining it, but are exempted because of smallpox in the ranks. February 20–22, army advances from occupied Jacksonville toward Olustee, where they suffer serious casualties in prolonged battle; retreat to Jacksonville, sending hundreds of wounded to Beaufort, where they arrive via steamer while TWH and other officers enjoy a ball. As summer approaches, feels progressively weaker: "It is the warmest day we have yet had . . . & a thousand soft arrows shoot through me & take all my strength away." Resolves to come North again on furlough, but with no real expectation of returning to military service. Leaves Beaufort May 14, arriving at Newport later that week; resides there for next thirteen years. Continues campaign for equal pay for black soldiers, writing to *Evening Post* in July and *Tribune* in August and December. Resigns from army October 27. Resuming literary career, publishes first articles about his military experience in the *Atlantic* (October, November, December issues). Mother Louisa Storrow Higginson dies, November 15, at Brattleboro, Vermont. Lincoln reelected, defeating Gen. George B. McClellan. December 9, TWH petitions Congress for repeal of legislation that secured lower pay to black soldiers than to whites.

**1865**  Publishes translation of *Works* of Epictetus, along with numerous essays, book reviews, and editorials. Gen. Robert E. Lee surrenders to Gen. Ulysses S. Grant at Appomattox Court House, Virginia. Lincoln assassinated, April 14. 13th Amendment to Constitution abolishes slavery.

**1866–68**  1866, 14th Amendment grants civil rights equally to all men; debars former Rebels from public office. 15th Amendment guarantees voting rights equally to all men regardless of race. TWH continues periodically to publish essays on military experience in *Atlantic*, later to be collected in *Army Life in a Black Regiment*. Literary criticism, lectures, book reviews, and journalism occupy his time. Proposed for presidency of Harvard, but Charles Eliot is appointed.

**1869**   Novel *Malbone: An Oldport Romance* published, serially in *Atlantic* and then in book form; meets generally with poor reviews. Thereafter mostly avoids fiction writing. *Ought Women to Vote?*, pamphlet, continues commitment to women's rights and announces support of female suffrage, a reform cause to which he will hereafter be continually devoted.

**1870**   *Army Life in a Black Regiment*, memoir of experience with 1st South Carolina Volunteers, published, contents of which had largely appeared in *Atlantic* over preceding years. Becomes an editor of *Woman's Journal*, weekly newspaper of Massachusetts Woman's Suffrage Association (through 1884). Brother Stephen dies at summer home in Deerfield, Massachusetts; TWH while there goes to see Emily Dickinson in nearby Amherst. Writes to wife, "I never was with anyone who drained my nerve power so much."

**1871**   Collects and publishes *Atlantic Essays*.

**1872**   March, oldest brother, Dr. Francis John Higginson, dies. Sister Anna comes to stay with Mary so that TWH can travel to Europe for three months, where he meets Froude, Carlyle, Darwin, Robert Browning, Trollope, the Rossettis, Gosse, Du Maurier, and Tennyson, among other literary and intellectual figures. December, visits Emily Dickinson a second time while in Amherst to deliver a lecture. Resenting the overzealous editing practiced by *Atlantic* under William Dean Howells, switches to *Scribner's Monthly*, which becomes his regular outlet.

**1875**   Publishes *Young Folks' History of the United States*, which sells well (becomes most popular of all his works) and provides steady income. Sister Louisa dies, August 27.

**1877**   September 2, Mary Channing Higginson dies after long illness, at Newport, Rhode Island. TWH goes south during winter, visiting Virginia relatives and a making sentimental trip to scenes of wartime experience in South Carolina and Florida.

**1878**   Account of return to South appears in "Some War Scenes Revisited," publication of which in *Atlantic* (July) marks return to that publishing venue. Leaves Newport and travels abroad in the spring; in Europe from April to October, visiting Scotland, Germany, France and England. Meets many of the same literary friends seen on last trip in 1872, and also Matthew Arnold, Victor Hugo, and Turgenev. Returns to take up residence in Cambridge, where he will reside permanently for remainder of life.

**1879**  February, marries 34-year-old Mary ("Minnie") Potter Thacher (21 years his junior), whom he had known as a literary friend in Newport. Honeymoon in Harper's Ferry, West Virginia, visiting sites associated with John Brown's revolt, including place of his execution. Elected to Massachusetts legislature as Republican representative from Cambridge (serves two terms, until 1883). Pushes women's rights, labor reform, religious freedom; proposal to limit rate of interest charged on bank loans fails in committee. Defends Catholic parochial schools against attack from nativist and anti-Catholic critics, and opposes similar attacks on Irish, Jewish, and Italian immigrants.

**1880**  January, daughter Louisa Wentworth is born, realizing TWH's long-deferred desire for fatherhood, but she dies after seven weeks from cerebral meningitis. December, moves into attractive Queen Anne-style "cottage" on Buckingham Street, Cambridge, specially built for him.

**1881**  July 25, second daughter, Margaret Waldo is born. Revises *Young Folks' History* for second edition to meet steady demand. December, reviews Walt Whitman unfavorably in *The Nation* (December 15), judging him "malodorous."

**1882**  Denounces Oscar Wilde in "Unmanly Manhood," *Woman's Journal* (February 4), also condemning American women who allow him (or his writings) into their homes; incidentally condemns Whitman again too.

**1884**  Bolts Republican party to support Democratic Presidential candidate Grover Cleveland, who is elected. *Margaret Fuller Ossoli*, biography, published in "American Men of Letters" series.

**1885–87**  *A Larger History of the United States* published, 1885. Following year, Emily Dickinson dies, May 15; TWH reads at her funeral in Amherst. 1887, opposes grant of a Federal pension to Whitman, on the grounds that he evaded military service during Civil War.

**1888–89**  Democratic nominee for United States Congress from Cambridge; loses to Gen. Nathaniel P. Banks, Republican, as President Cleveland fails of reelection. *Travellers and Outlaws*, collecting earlier articles for *Atlantic* on slave insurrections along with other historical essays, is published, 1889.

**1890–91**  1890, edits (with Mabel Loomis Todd) *Poems* by Emily Dickinson. Goes to Dublin, New Hampshire in summer, and likes it well enough to build permanent summer house there next year, on Moosehead Lake. *Life of Francis Higginson*, on early ministerial ancestor, published 1891.

**1892–94**  1892, upon Whitman's death, reviews the "nauseating" poet critically in "Recent Poetry," *The Nation* (April 7). Sister Anna dies, November 17, 1892. May 4,

1894, brother Waldo dies, leaving TWH the only surviving member of his immediate family.

**1897–98**  Visits Europe again, with wife and daughter, 1897; entertained by Henry James, meets Thomas Hardy. Annual income now reaches $6,000. Autobiographical memoirs, *Cheerful Yesterdays*, published 1898; contents had appeared in *Atlantic* sporadically 1896–1897. Joins Anti-Imperialist League, seeking to curb American imperial expansionism in Philippines and other Pacific locales. Receives honorary LL.D. from Harvard, long wished for.

**1899–1901**  Publishes *Contemporaries*, containing essay portraits of Ralph Waldo Emerson, Amos Bronson Alcott, Theodore Parker, Lydia Maria Child, William Lloyd Garrison, Wendell Phillips, Charles Sumner and other literary and political associates. Also *Old Cambridge*, history of local literary culture, with chapters on Oliver Wendell Holmes, Henry Wadsworth Longfellow, and James Russell Lowell. 1900, definitive edition of *Writings*, in seven volumes, appears. Supports William Jennings Bryan for President because of his anti-imperialism. Travels to Europe again in 1901, visiting Italy, Austria, Germany and England.

**1905–1907**  *Part of a Man's Life*, further autobiographical memoirs, published 1905. Daughter Margaret marries Boston physician, James Dellinger Barney, in Dublin, New Hampshire. 1906, daughter Margaret has a child, named Wentworth Higginson Barney, first grandchild for TWH; second grandchild, named Margaret Dellinger, will appear in 1908. *Life and Times of Stephen Higginson*, biography of grandfather, published 1907.

**1909–11**  *Carlyle's Laugh, and Other Surprises*, collecting various articles and sketches, issued 1909. Unable to attend National Negro Conference in June, forwards statement reiterating his opposition to universal Negro suffrage, urging educational efforts, industrial development, and racial conciliation instead. Edits last published work in 1910, *Descendants of the Reverend Francis Higginson*, genealogy. Dies May 9, 1911; casket is borne by young black soldiers up the aisle of First Parish Church, Cambridge. Ashes deposited in Cambridge Cemetery.

# Index

Suwarrow, 141
Swift, Jonathan, 10, 182n. 276
Sykes, Mrs., 311, 311n. 232
*Sylvia's Lovers* (Gaskell), 279

*Tactics*, 138, 162, 162n. 247
*Tales of a Wayside Inn* (Longfellow), 347
Tallahassee, Florida, 197
Tanselle, G. Thomas, 33, 33n. 1
Tapley, Mark, 8, 302, 302n. 211
Taylor, Susie King, 58, 58n. 54, 219, 219n. 330
Tennessee, 372
Tennyson, Alfred Lord, 8, 64n. 72, 211n. 319, 256, 256n. 92, 376
10th Army Corps, 216
Terry, Rose (later Cooke), 10, 306, 306n. 217
Texas, 264, 370, 372
Thackeray, William Makepeace, 10, 190, 190n. 290
Thanksgiving Day, 46, 50, 52, 73, 248, 329–30
Thayer, Eli, 372
Thayer, Eugene, 331
Thibadeau, Capt. J. H., 150, 163
3d South Carolina, 285
13th Massachusetts, 224
Thomas, Brig. Gen. Lorenzo, 145, 145n. 205
Thompson, James, 99n. 142
Thoreau, Henry David, 6, 175, 175n. 267
Ticknor and Fields, 236
*Titan* (Richter), 10, 108, 128, 131, 259, 276, 278, 287
Todd, Mabel Loomis, 377
Tomlinson, Reuben, 316, 316n. 245
Tonking, Capt. James H., 149–50, 304
Topsy (Stowe character), 213–14, 213n. 324
Toussaint L'Ouverture, François Dominique, 88, 88n. 121
Towne, Laura, 316–21, 316n. 24, 334
Township Landing, 96, 96n. 138, 102, 111, 374
Tracy, Mrs., 292
Transcendentalism, 10, 13, 370
tree toad, 98
Tremaine, Dr. William S., 328, 328n. 273, 330, 338–39, 348, 352
Trollope, Anthony, 376
Trowbridge, Capt. (later Maj.) Charles T. (Quartermaster), 51–52, 55n. 49, 72, 74, 101, 105, 107, 111–12, 114, 138–39, 143, 147–48, 156, 160, 162–63, 169, 171, 173, 178–79, 186, 188, 195–96, 201–4, 206, 270, 303, 310, 322, 324, 326–28, 330, 338, 348, 357, 359, 361, 365, 374

Trowbridge, Mrs., 201–2, 206, 348, 357, 359, 361, 363
Trudeau, Noah Andre, 31n. 39
Tubman, Harriet, 29–30, 49, 49n. 38, 251
Turgenev, Ivan Sergeevich, 376
turkey buzzard, 121
Turner, James, 336
turtle, 108
24th Massachusetts, 262, 330, 338–39
29th Connecticut (Colored), 216, 366
26th United States (Colored), 216, 366
Tyng, Rev. Stephen Higginson, 334–35

Uhland, Ludwig, 198
Ulysses, 30, 108
Uncle John (cook), 214–15
Uncle Tiff (character from Stowe's *Dred*), 64, 64n. 74, 77, 77n. 98, 160, 283
*Uncle Tom's Cabin* (Stowe novel), 30, 49, 49n. 39, 64n. 74, 101, 156, 160, 160n. 240, 213n. 324, 319n. 258
Underwood, Francis Henry, 356–57, 357n. 342
Utah, 370–71

Van Buren, Pres. Martin, 351, 351n. 333
Van Wyck, Col., 160, 165, 172, 182, 341, 343
vegetation, 44, 46, 98, 111, 215, 256, 269; acorns, 168; aloes, 46; blackberries, 279, 281; clover, 210; cypress, 124, 140; evergreen, 201; feather-grasses, 168; ferns, 19, 200, 215; grass, 46, 104, 210, 263, 281; hay, 215; holly, 201; live oak, 19–20, 46–47, 50, 54, 76, 83, 127, 164, 168, 179, 215, 219, 248–49; mistletoe, 104, 191; moss, 46, 50, 54, 76, 161, 164, 168, 179, 182, 191, 201, 219, 248–49, 328; myrtle, 200; orange, 72, 168; palmetto, 46; peach, 108; peas, 104, 263; petisporum, 46, 200; pine, 19–20, 124, 130, 161–62, 191, 210, 215, 304; plum, 19, 108, 215, 219; pomegranate, 168; sycamore, 132; wild cherry, 108; yucca spicata, 19, 154–55, 215. *See also* flowers
Very, Jones, 13
Vicksburg, Mississippi, 84, 84n. 116
Villard, Henry, 105, 105n. 152
Virginia, 44, 216, 278, 279, 326, 329, 372, 376

Walker, Brig. Gen. W. S., 133, 133nn. 187, 188, 139, 206, 206n. 307
Ward, Col., 106, 240, 244
Ware, Charles P., 76, 76n. 94, 255
Ware, Harriet, 76, 76n. 94, 255
Warner, Charles Dudley, 13n. 18
Washburn, Lieut. Col. Francis, 253, 357